BJÖRN KENNETH HOLMSTRÖM

The Integration Crisis

Yellow Solutions to Orange Problems: A Systemic Guide to the Age of Burnout, Meaninglessness, and Civilizational Compulsion

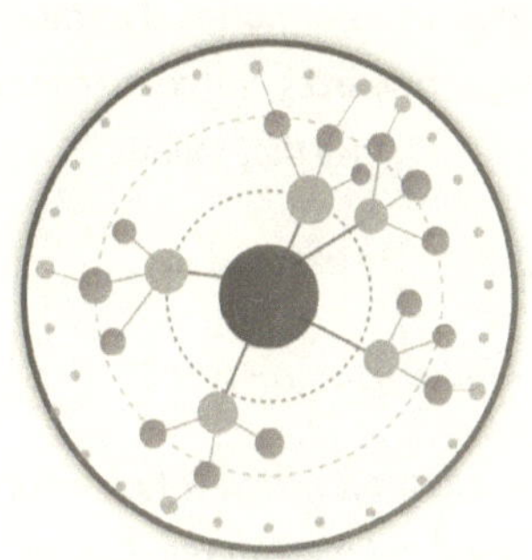

Contents

Dedication

For everyone who has achieved everything they were supposed to want,

and still felt empty.

For those who work harder than ever,

yet feel further from rest.

For the successful who are secretly suffering,

the productive who are profoundly tired,

and the high-achievers who have lost the ability to simply be.

This book is for you—not because you're broken,

but because the systems we built are.

From Patient Zero to Planetary Project

From Patient Zero to Planetary Project

A Personal Preface

I used to be able to sit in simple joy at existence.

Not doing anything. Not producing anything. Not even thinking about anything particularly profound. Just... being.

I could sit on a rock by the river in the Basque Country for an hour and feel the sun move across my skin like it was enough. Nothing missing. Nothing needed. The world felt full, and I felt part of it, and that was everything.

It wasn't just the scenery. I've been in beautiful places since then and felt nothing but anxiety. It was the **capacity**—the internal architecture that allowed me to receive the moment. That is what broke.

I don't remember exactly when I lost that ability, but I know I did.

These days—or rather, these *were* the days before I began this inquiry— my mornings started with coffee and compulsive scrolling through Google Chrome, hunting for interesting articles. I told myself I was looking for writing topics, that I was being productive. But if I'm honest? I was just feeding a need for stimulation that felt bottomless.

The question that began haunting me: *How much of human activity is actually addiction?*

From Personal Symptom to Pattern Recognition

I'm not a systems theorist by training, though I studied engineering physics and worked with systems control. What I am is a synthesizer—someone who sees patterns across domains, connects ideas that don't usually talk to each other, and asks uncomfortable questions about why things that should work don't.

When I noticed my own compulsive behavior, I didn't initially think "systems failure." I thought what most people think: *I need more discipline. Better habits. Stronger willpower.*

But then I started paying attention—not through formal research or surveys, but through observation. The exhausted faces on the morning commute. The way people compulsively check phones between every sentence. The burnout epidemic among the most successful people I knew. The rising rates of anxiety, depression, and "deaths of despair" in the wealthiest societies in human history.

The polycrisis we're living through—climate breakdown, meaning collapse, democratic erosion, mental health emergency, AI disruption—started looking less like separate problems and more like symptoms of something deeper.

This isn't a collection of individual pathologies. This is civilizational design failure.

The widespread inability to simply be present—to rest without anxiety, to attend without distraction, to exist without constant justification through productivity—isn't happening because billions of people suddenly became weak or undisciplined. It's happening because we built systems that make human flourishing structurally impossible.

The Urgency of the Window

I haven't tested these ideas with years of academic surveys. The blog series exploring these themes is just being published. The white paper "Addiction as Integration Failure" hasn't been peer-reviewed.

Some might say: "Wait. Test your ideas. Build consensus."

But we don't have time to wait.

The mental health crisis is accelerating. Burnout rates are climbing. Climate tipping points are approaching. AI is about to disrupt labor markets in ways we can barely imagine. Beneath all of it is the same fundamental problem: we've created a civilization that systematically prevents human beings from functioning as we were designed to.

The urgency isn't about getting credit. It's about getting solutions into circulation while there's still time to implement them. The window is closing but remains open. We have, perhaps, a decade to get this right. This book is written with the humility of someone who knows his analysis might be incomplete, combined with the urgency of someone who sees the window closing.

How This Book Was Built

My approach has been unconventional. Rather than working in isolation, I have collaborated extensively with large language models—Claude, DeepSeek, Gemini, Grok—to develop and stress-test these frameworks.

This isn't just a method; it is a **demonstration of the book's thesis**.

Throughout these pages, I argue that humans need **cognitive scaffolding** to function in complex systems—infrastructure that supports us in processing what our individual minds cannot grasp alone. The AI systems were that scaffolding for me. They allowed me to hold a level of systemic complexity that my biological mind could not sustain on its own.

This book is a product of the very integration it proposes. It is a living example of the principle I am advocating: we do not need to be superhuman. We just need appropriate support structures.

The Structure of This Book

Part I establishes the problem: why success is killing us, how we got here, and why individual solutions systematically fail. It also addresses what I call "the Green Gap"—why progressive critique, while necessary, isn't sufficient.

Part II introduces the principles of what I call "Yellow thinking"—a way of approaching complex problems that transcends both traditional conservatism and progressive paralysis.

Part III presents the solutions: four specific, actionable, evidence-based interventions that together restore integration across all six domains of human experience. This is the heart of the book—not theory but practice, not aspiration but implementation.

Part IV addresses the question everyone asks: "Okay, but how do we actually *do* this?" It's about transition strategy, coalition building, and the specific challenge facing those with wealth, power, or influence who want to be part of the solution.

Part V offers a glimpse of what becomes possible when we succeed—not utopia, but something better: a civilization that enables rather than prevents human flourishing.

* * *

A Quick Note on the Title

You might be wondering: "Yellow Solutions to Orange Problems"—what does that mean?

This book uses a "Color Code" from developmental psychology to map our crisis. **Orange** is the mindset of achievement and material progress that built the modern world. **Yellow** is the systemic mindset needed to fix it.

Don't worry if this feels abstract—the very next section, **"User Manual:**

The Color Code," will give you the full legend for the map we are about to explore.

* * *

An Invitation

If you've made it this far, you're probably someone who:

- Has achieved some measure of success by conventional standards, yet feels something fundamental is missing
- Recognizes that individual fixes aren't enough but doesn't know what systemic change looks like
- Wants to be part of building what comes next, not just critiquing what exists
- Can hold complexity without collapsing into simplistic either/or thinking

In other words, you're exactly who this book is for.

I'm not asking you to believe everything in these pages. I'm asking you to consider the possibility that the exhaustion you feel, the restlessness, the sense that something's fundamentally broken—these aren't personal failures but appropriate responses to a civilization that has, through its very success, made human flourishing structurally impossible.

And then I'm asking you to imagine with me what it would take to fix that.

Not someday. Not in some distant future. But starting now, with the resources we have, in the cities and institutions and communities where we already live.

The quiet revolution begins with the recognition that presence is possible, integration is achievable, and flourishing is our birthright.

It requires only that we stop designing systems that prevent it, and start

x

building civilizations worthy of the human spirit.
Let's begin.

Björn Kenneth Holmström
Stockholm, November 2025

User Manual: The Color Code

Why You Need This

Before you go far in the book, you will encounter phrases like "Orange consciousness," "Green trap," and "Yellow solutions" dozens of times.

You might intuit what they mean from context. But to fully understand the architecture we're building—and why it matters so urgently—you need the legend for the map.

This is that legend.

* * *

Civilization as Software Stack

Here's the essential insight: **Civilization isn't just a pile of stuff. It's a stack of operating systems.**

Every few generations, humanity develops a new way of organizing reality—new values, new structures, new answers to the question "how should we live together?" Each new operating system solves the core crisis of the previous one while introducing new capabilities and new problems.

We call these operating systems by colors (Blue, Orange, Green, Yellow) not because colors have inherent meaning, but because it's cleaner than saying "the achievement-oriented, rational-materialist, merit-based worldview" every time.

The critical point: **We are currently crashing because we're trying to**

run a global civilization on OS Orange.

Orange is brilliant software. It built the modern world. But it was never designed to handle planetary-scale complexity, existential risk, or the question "what happens after we've achieved everything and it still isn't enough?"

We need an upgrade. Not because Orange is bad, but because every operating system has limits.

* * *

The Four Operating Systems You Need to Know

OS BLUE: The Order (≈ Traditional/Mythic)

Core Logic: Truth is absolute. Order is sacred. Duty transcends desire.
What It Built:

- Stable institutions that last centuries
- Moral codes that create social cohesion
- Sacrifice for something larger than self
- The foundation that keeps civilization from dissolving into chaos

The Crisis It Solved: Red's impulsive violence and tribal warfare. "Might makes right" is no way to build a sustainable society.

The Crisis It Created: Rigid hierarchies. Suppression of individual autonomy. Inability to adapt to changing conditions. "Because the rules say so" becomes a trap when the rules are wrong.

Its Motto: *"Do your duty. Honor the code. Sacrifice for the greater good."*

The Tell: Rigid adherence to rules even when they cause harm. Black-and-white thinking. Fear of questioning authority.

Why We Still Need It: Blue provides the stability, discipline, and shared moral framework that prevents societies from fragmenting. Yellow doesn't eliminate Blue—it gives Blue contexts where its strengths shine without letting it run the whole system.

* * *

OS ORANGE: The Machine (≈ Modern/Rational)

Core Logic: Progress through science. Success through merit. Optimization beats tradition.

What It Built:

- The scientific revolution
- Market economies and material abundance
- Individual liberty and social mobility
- The technological power that makes this conversation possible

The Crisis It Solved: Blue's stagnation and authoritarianism. "We've always done it this way" is no answer to genuine injustice or new possibilities.

The Crisis It Created: Endless growth on a finite planet. Meaning reduced to consumption. Community atomized into competition. Burnout as the price of success. **This is the crisis we're living in right now.**

Its Motto: *"Win the game. Maximize efficiency. Achieve more."*

The Tell: Chronic busyness. Measuring self-worth by productivity. Treating rest as wasteful. Optimizing everything including your own humanity.

Why We Still Need It: Orange's scientific rigor, achievement drive, and innovation capacity are essential. Yellow doesn't reject Orange—it prevents Orange from optimizing us into existential crisis.

* * *

OS GREEN: The Circle (≈ Postmodern/Pluralistic)

Core Logic: Multiple truths coexist. Empathy over hierarchy. Inclusion is justice.

What It Built:

- Civil rights movements and social justice
- Environmental consciousness
- Recognition of systemic oppression
- Sensitivity to harm and power dynamics

The Crisis It Solved: Orange's exploitation, inequality, and reduction of humans to resources. "Maximize profit" cannot be the only value when it destroys lives and ecosystems.

The Crisis It Created: Paralysis through relativism. Deconstruction without reconstruction. Sensitivity without structure. The inability to make hard choices because every choice might harm someone.

Its Motto: *"Include all voices. Question all power. Feel all the pain."*

The Tell: Endless dialogue without decision. Fear of being "problematic." Critique without alternative. Compassion that extends to everything except effective action.

Why We Still Need It: Green's empathy, systemic awareness, and commitment to justice are vital. Yellow doesn't abandon Green—it gives Green the structural capacity to build what it envisions.

* * *

OS YELLOW: The Network (≈ Integral/Systemic)

Core Logic: Integration over fragmentation. Systems over single perspectives. Flow over force.

What It Builds:

- Solutions that work across domains simultaneously
- Structures that handle complexity without collapse
- Development that serves the whole, not just parts
- Wisdom that includes and transcends previous stages

The Crisis It Solves: Green's paralysis and Orange's extraction. Both the inability to act and the inability to stop acting destructively.

The Crisis It Creates: We don't fully know yet. Yellow is still emerging. But likely challenges include: abstraction that loses grounding, complexity that overwhelms, or integration that smooths over necessary conflict.

Its Motto: *"See the whole system. Honor each part. Build what actually works."*

The Tell: Ability to hold multiple perspectives without losing your center. Seeing conflicts as integration opportunities. Valuing what works over what feels ideologically pure.

Why This Is The Upgrade We Need: Yellow can run all previous operating systems as subsystems—using Blue's stability, Orange's innovation, and Green's sensitivity—without any single one hijacking the whole machine.

* * *

The Visual Cheat Sheet

* * *

How This Maps to the Book

Part I (The Fractured Human): Diagnosing how OS Orange created success that feels like failure—achievement without satisfaction, productivity without purpose.

Part II (Principles of Yellow Thinking): Understanding the upgrade—how Yellow consciousness operates differently than Orange or Green.

Part III (The Solutions): The Yellow Stack—four interlocking interventions (Cognitive Sovereignty, Sovereign Floor, Sanctuaries, Contemplative Infrastructure) that create the conditions for integration.

Part IV (The Alchemist's Path): How to build Yellow structures while operating within Orange/Green institutions. The transition strategies.

Part V (What Becomes Possible): What the world looks like when we successfully install the upgrade.

* * *

The Prime Directive

We are not here to delete OS Orange.

Science is magnificent. Achievement is valuable. Innovation drives progress. We need Orange's gifts.

We are here to install OS Yellow as the host operating system.

So we can run Orange's powerful applications—its scientific rigor, its achievement drive, its optimization capacity—without letting them hijack the whole machine and optimize us into burnout, ecological collapse, and existential emptiness.

You can't debug OS Orange with the feelings of OS Green. You need the architecture of OS Yellow.

* * *

Important Clarifications

This isn't a hierarchy of better/worse. Each operating system is perfect for certain conditions and problems. Blue consciousness is exactly what you want running your immune system's "us vs. them" detection. Orange consciousness is exactly what you want running your startup's growth engine. Green consciousness is exactly what you want running your conflict mediation process.

The problem comes when any single OS tries to run *everything*.

This isn't about labeling people. Everyone runs multiple operating systems depending on context. You might be Yellow at work, Orange at the gym, Green in relationships, and Blue about certain traditions. The question isn't "what color are you?" but "which OS is running your default settings?"

Development isn't automatic. Moving from Orange to Yellow doesn't just happen because you read the right books or practice enough meditation. It requires genuine developmental work—expanding your capacity to hold complexity, tolerate paradox, and integrate competing values. This book provides frameworks, but you have to do the upgrading.

Yellow isn't the end. There are further stages (Turquoise and beyond) that transcend even systemic thinking. But Yellow is the critical upgrade we need *right now*—the minimum viable consciousness for handling the challenges we face.

* * *

Using This Manual

Throughout the book, when you see "Orange thinking" or "Green trap" or "Yellow solution," you now have the decoder ring.

When we say the crisis is that we're running a planetary civilization on OS Orange, you understand: we built amazing things with achievement consciousness, but it's now creating exactly the problems it can't solve.

When we say we need Yellow solutions, you understand: we need interventions that work across all domains simultaneously, that integrate rather than fragment, that honor complexity without being paralyzed by it.

The color code isn't jargon. It's diagnostic precision.

Use it as the legend for the map we're about to explore together.

* * *

Now you're ready for Chapter 1.

Let's begin.

PART I: THE FRACTURED HUMAN

***

Chapter 1: When Winning Feels Like Losing

Sarah sits in her corner office on the 42nd floor, looking out over the city she conquered. She's 38, the youngest VP in her company's history. Six-figure salary. Stock options. The kind of career trajectory that makes her parents beam with pride when they tell their friends.

She should feel victorious. Instead, she feels hollow.

This morning, she woke at 5:30 AM to the gentle chime of her meditation app—the one she paid $200 a year for but rarely uses. Before her feet hit the floor, her Oura ring had already delivered the verdict: 14 minutes of deep sleep. Her body flooded with cortisol before she'd even brushed her teeth.

She scrolled through her phone in bed. Checked email. Scanned Slack. LinkedIn notifications. Twitter discourse. Instagram lives she's not living.

By 6:15, she was sitting with coffee and her laptop, "catching up" before the official workday began. By 7:00, she'd been in three time zones worth of Zoom calls. By 9:00, she'd already felt behind.

She is winning the career game by losing the biological game.

The victory she worked so hard to achieve now feels like a prison she maintains through constant vigilance.

"I should be grateful," she tells her therapist. "I *know* I should be grateful. I have everything I wanted."

And somewhere in the back of her mind, beneath the quarterly targets and performance reviews, she worries about the climate report she saw on

Twitter this morning. She worries that her "winning" might actually be making the world worse. But she has no idea what to do with that thought, so it joins the background hum of anxiety that never quite goes away.

Her therapist nods with the practiced empathy of someone who's heard this exact sentence seventeen times this week.

* * *

The Epidemic of Successful Misery

Sarah is not unique. She's not even unusual.

Burnout diagnoses increased 42% between 2019 and 2024 in WHO member states. But here's what the statistics miss: the majority of those experiencing burnout are not struggling workers in exploitative conditions (though they exist and matter). They're the *successful ones.* The ones who "made it."

72% of knowledge workers report difficulty sustaining attention on single tasks for more than 20 minutes. These aren't people who failed to achieve—they're people who achieved everything they were supposed to want and discovered it wasn't enough.

The average smartphone screen time increased from 3.7 hours in 2019 to 5.4 hours in 2024. This happened despite:

- Widespread awareness of the problem
- Thousands of articles about digital wellness
- Dozens of apps designed to reduce app usage
- Growing cultural consensus that we're all too distracted

We *know* what the problem is. We *want* to change. And yet, collectively, we're getting worse.

Why?

* * *

The Pattern Beneath the Stories

Meet David, a software engineer at a prestigious tech company. He makes $400,000 a year and hasn't taken a real vacation in three years. Not because his boss forbids it—his company has "unlimited vacation" (which, paradoxically, means people take less). He doesn't take time off because the anxiety of falling behind is worse than the exhaustion of pushing through.

"I'm optimizing myself to death," he jokes, but his eyes don't laugh.

Meet Maria, a social impact entrepreneur who spent ten years building an organization that provides clean water to underserved communities. By every metric, she's succeeding: funding secured, communities served, lives tangibly improved. But she wakes up most mornings with her heart racing, mind already spinning through everything that could go wrong.

"I'm doing meaningful work," she says. "Why do I feel so empty?"

Meet James, who recently sold his startup for eight figures. Financial security achieved. No more hustling required. He should feel relieved. Instead, he feels lost. Without the constant drive to build and scale, he doesn't know who he is anymore. The identity that carried him through years of 80-hour weeks dissolved the moment the pressure released.

"I thought reaching the destination would feel different," he says quietly.

These stories share a pattern:

- **Achievement without satisfaction**
- **Success without rest**
- **Productivity without purpose**
- **Connection without presence**

They worked hard. They did everything right. They played by the rules and won the game.

So why does winning feel like losing?

* * *

The Paradox of Modern Success

Here's what makes this crisis so confusing: *these feelings are not irrational.*

Sarah is objectively successful. Her career anxiety isn't a cognitive distortion—it's an accurate assessment of her environment. One quarter of underperformance, one reorganization, one economic downturn, and her position becomes precarious. The hyper-vigilance isn't paranoia; it's realism.

David's compulsive productivity isn't weakness. In a field where you're competing with people who work 60-hour weeks, taking it easy means falling behind. The optimization isn't pathological; it's adaptive to a pathological system.

Maria's guilt about not doing enough isn't impostor syndrome. There genuinely are more communities that need clean water, more problems to solve, more suffering to address. Her restlessness isn't ingratitude; it's an accurate perception of scale.

James's identity crisis isn't neurosis. When your entire sense of self has been organized around achievement, the absence of clear goals genuinely leaves a void. His emptiness isn't a character flaw; it's an integration failure.

This is what makes the crisis so insidious: **the feelings are appropriate responses to inappropriate conditions.**

The problem isn't that successful people are ungrateful, weak, or broken. The problem is that we've built a civilization that makes human flourishing structurally impossible—even for those who "win."

Especially for those who win.

* * *

When the Medicine Becomes the Poison

Orange thinking—the worldview of achievement, innovation, progress, and material success—solved enormous problems. It lifted billions out of poverty. It created unprecedented technological progress. It gave us antibiotics, airplanes, and the internet. It replaced inherited status with merit, superstition with science, stagnation with dynamism.

These are real achievements. They matter. We should not romanticize pre-modern life or pretend that traditional societies didn't have their own devastating failures.

But here's the thing about evolutionary solutions: they're optimized for the conditions that produced them. And when those conditions change, yesterday's solution becomes today's problem.

Orange thinking emerged as the solution to Blue's rigidity (traditional authority, fixed roles, unchanging hierarchies) and Purple's tribalism (us vs. them, superstition, limited perspective). It succeeded brilliantly at that task.

But now, Orange's very success has created conditions it's not equipped to handle:

Achievement culture created unprecedented prosperity—and chronic anxiety about never having achieved enough.

Efficiency optimization made incredible technological progress—and eliminated any buffer for rest or error.

Meritocracy replaced inherited privilege—and created constant competition where your worth must be continuously proven through performance.

Rational materialism freed us from superstition—and left us with nothing to root meaning in beyond consumption and status.

Individual autonomy liberated us from oppressive community norms—and atomized us into lonely actors competing for scarce resources.

The poison isn't in Orange's gifts. The poison is in the dose. In the inability to stop. In the expansion of achievement logic into every domain of human experience until nothing is exempt from optimization, nothing is allowed to simply *be*.

Success didn't fail. Success succeeded so well it consumed everything else.

* * *

The Treadmill Speeds Up

Here's the truly devastating part: the more we achieve, the faster the treadmill goes.

Every productivity gain makes productivity the baseline. The person who answered emails within 24 hours in 2010 was responsive. Today, not answering within 2 hours feels like neglect. Instant messaging created the expectation of instant response.

Every technological advance that should have freed our time instead filled it with more demands. Email was supposed to eliminate wasteful meetings. Instead, we have more meetings *and* constant email. Remote work was supposed to give us flexibility. Instead, work followed us home and dissolved all boundaries between work and life.

Every optimization that should have created slack instead raised the bar for what counts as acceptable performance.

And here's the economic tragedy beneath it all: In 1990, this level of focus and dedication bought you a house, a pension, and reasonable certainty. In 2025, it barely buys you stability. You're running twice as fast to stay in the same place. This isn't a mindset problem. This is **inflation of effort**—the devaluation of human labor even as its intensity increases.

This isn't natural evolution. This is a system optimizing for extraction, not integration. For productivity, not presence. For achievement, not flourishing.

And the people who feel this most acutely? The ones who succeeded. The ones who won the game.

Because they're the ones who internalized the rules most completely.

* * *

The Question We're Afraid to Ask

Sarah, David, Maria, and James have all asked themselves variations of the same question:

"What's wrong with me?"

They look at their lives on paper and see success. They compare themselves to previous generations who had less and struggled more. They know intellectually that they're privileged. That they should be grateful. That there are people with real problems.

But the hollowness persists. The anxiety continues. The compulsions don't stop.

So they blame themselves. Not enough discipline. Not enough gratitude. Not enough mindfulness. Not enough boundaries. Not enough therapy. Not enough self-care.

They try harder. They optimize more. They add practices designed to create peace while maintaining the pace that prevents peace from ever taking root.

And the cycle continues.

But what if the question isn't "What's wrong with me?"

What if the question is: **"What's wrong with a system that makes successful people miserable?"**

What if Sarah's anxiety, David's compulsion, Maria's emptiness, and James's identity crisis aren't personal failures but accurate readings of civilizational design failure?

What if winning feels like losing because we're playing a game that was never designed for humans to win?

* * *

The View from the Top

There's a particular cruelty to achieving success and discovering it isn't what you thought.

When you're climbing, you can tell yourself: "It will be different when I get there. When I have the corner office. When I make six figures. When I finally prove myself. When I achieve financial security. When I earn respect. When I make it."

"When I make it, I'll finally be able to rest."

But then you make it.

And you discover that the summit isn't a place of rest but another staging ground for the next climb. That financial security doesn't end economic anxiety—it just raises the threshold. That proving yourself once means you have to keep proving yourself. That respect is given and withdrawn based on continuous performance.

This is the secret no one tells you about success: reaching the summit doesn't end the climb. It just reveals there are no summits—only base camps for higher mountains.

You discover that success isn't a destination but a treadmill that speeds up the moment you start to keep pace.

This realization—that achievement doesn't deliver what it promised— is uniquely destabilizing. Because if success isn't the answer, what is?

For many people, this is where the real crisis begins. Not the struggle to succeed, but the aftermath of succeeding.

Not the climb, but the view from the top.

Yet something strange is happening. Quietly, without fanfare, some people are stepping off the treadmill—not into poverty or irrelevance, but into a different kind of success. One that includes achievement but transcends its limitations. They've discovered that the problem isn't ambition itself, but the operating system running it.

In the chapters ahead, we'll meet them. But first, we need to understand how we got here.

* * *

What This Book Isn't About

Before we go further, let me be clear about what this analysis is *not* saying:

This is not arguing that achievement is bad. That ambition is toxic. That we should abandon progress and return to some romanticized past.

This is not claiming that people in poverty, facing discrimination, or struggling for basic survival have it easier. They don't. Material security matters. The freedom that comes with financial stability is real and valuable.

This is not suggesting that successful people's unhappiness is equivalent to or more important than the struggles of those with less privilege.

What this *is* saying is:

Even people who win by the system's rules are being destroyed by the system.

If the winners are miserable, that's not a problem of individual psychology. That's a problem of systemic design.

And if we can understand *why* success produces suffering in those who achieve it, we can understand something crucial about the civilization we've built—and how to redesign it so that human flourishing becomes structurally possible rather than structurally prevented.

* * *

The Rest of This Book

In the chapters that follow, we'll explore:

- **How we got here** (Chapter 2: The Architecture of Orange)
- **Why progressive critique isn't enough** (Chapter 3: The Green Trap)
- **Why the costs are accelerating** (Chapter 4: The Cost Curve Has Gone Vertical)
- **What integration failure actually means** (Chapter 5: The Integration Threshold)

Then we'll move into solutions—not individual band-aids but structural redesign.

But for now, sit with this question:

If winning feels like losing, what game are we actually playing?

And more importantly: **What would a game designed for humans to actually flourish look like?**

Sarah is still in her corner office. David is still optimizing. Maria is still striving. James is still lost.

But somewhere—in pilot cities, in research institutes, in quiet experiments running beneath the noise—people are building the answer.

The question is whether we'll build it fast enough.

And whether enough of us will recognize it when we see it.

Chapter 2: The Architecture of Orange

In 1347, a ship arrived in Sicily carrying rats infected with plague-bearing fleas. Within five years, the Black Death had killed between 75 and 200 million people—roughly 30-60% of Europe's population.

The survivors didn't have antibiotics. They didn't have germ theory. They didn't have the scientific method. What they had were prayers, bloodletting, and the belief that God was punishing them for their sins.

By 1950, a child with a bacterial infection could be cured with a pill.

That transformation—from helplessness to mastery, from superstition to science, from inherited status to earned achievement—is what Orange thinking accomplished. And it was nothing short of miraculous.

Before we diagnose Orange's shadows, we need to honor its light. Because without understanding what Orange solved, we'll never understand why it succeeded so completely—or why its very success now threatens to consume us.

* * *

What Orange Solved

To understand Orange, you have to understand what came before it.

The Blue World: Order and Its Costs

Pre-modern societies organized around what developmental psychology calls "Blue" thinking—traditional authority, fixed hierarchies, unchanging roles, and absolute truth claims.

In Blue worlds:

- Your birth determined your destiny (peasant, noble, priest)
- Authority was unquestionable (king, church, father)
- Truth was revealed, not discovered (scripture, tradition, decree)
- Change was suspect, tradition sacred
- The group's needs absolutely superseded individual desires

This created stability. It created meaning. It created social cohesion. It also created:

- Rigid stratification with no mobility
- Crushing conformity and brutal suppression of difference
- Stagnant economies trapped in zero-sum thinking
- Endemic violence against "heretics" and outsiders
- Deep suffering for anyone who didn't fit the prescribed roles

Women had no legal rights. LGBTQ+ people faced death. Religious minorities were persecuted. Entire classes of people were trapped in hereditary servitude. Innovation was dangerous. Questions were heretical.

The security came at an enormous price.

The Purple Shadow: Tribalism and Its Limits

Beneath Blue's order lay even earlier "Purple" thinking—tribal, animistic, superstitious. Purple saw spirits in every tree, meaning in every coincidence, and clear divisions between "us" and "them."

Purple created belonging. It created enchantment. It created tight-knit communities.

It also created:

- Endless cycles of tribal warfare
- Magical thinking that prevented practical problem-solving
- Xenophobia and violent exclusion of outsiders
- Vulnerability to natural disasters with no understanding of causation

When your child died of infection, Purple thinking told you to appease angry spirits. When crops failed, you sacrificed to rain gods. When another tribe had more, you went to war.

This is the world Orange inherited and transformed.

* * *

Orange's Revolutionary Gifts

Orange thinking emerged during the Renaissance and Enlightenment, exploded with the Industrial Revolution, and reached its apex in the 20th century. Its core insight was radical:

The world runs on discoverable natural laws, not divine decree. Humans can understand these laws through reason and evidence. Achievement matters more than birth. Progress is possible.

This seems obvious now. It wasn't then. It was revolutionary. And it unlocked capabilities that transformed human existence.

Gift 1: Science and Technology

Orange replaced "what does scripture say?" with "what does the evidence show?"

The result:

- Medicine that actually works (antibiotics, vaccines, surgery)
- Technology that expands human capability (electricity, engines, computers)
- Understanding of natural processes (physics, chemistry, biology)
- Ability to predict and control aspects of environment (weather, agriculture, infrastructure)

Life expectancy doubled. Infant mortality plummeted. Diseases that killed millions became preventable. We went from candlelight to electric grids, from horse-drawn carts to space stations, from handwritten letters to instant global communication.

This matters. Every additional year of life, every child who survives infancy, every person freed from preventable suffering—these are real achievements with profound moral weight.

Gift 2: Meritocracy Over Aristocracy

Orange replaced "who is your father?" with "what can you do?"

Instead of inherited status determining your possibilities, achievement became the path to advancement. This was profoundly liberating for everyone born outside aristocracy—which was most people.

Yes, Orange's meritocracy was always incomplete and imperfect. It maintained racial, gender, and class barriers. But the *principle*—that ability and effort should matter more than birth—was genuinely progressive compared to what came before.

This created:

- Economic mobility (the possibility, at least, of rising through skill)
- Innovation and entrepreneurship (anyone with a good idea could try)
- Educational expansion (knowledge became democratized)
- Competition driving improvement (best ideas and products win)

Gift 3: Individual Rights and Autonomy

Orange said: **Individuals have inherent rights that authorities cannot violate.**

This led to:

- The end of slavery (eventually, imperfectly)
- Women's suffrage and rights
- Freedom of speech and religion
- Protection from arbitrary authority
- Recognition of individual conscience

Before Orange, you were property of your lord, subject to king, answerable to church. Orange said: you are a sovereign individual with rights no one can justly violate.

This liberation is real and precious. The ability to choose your path, express your views, practice your religion (or not), marry whom you love—these freedoms were won through Orange thinking, often against fierce Blue resistance.

Gift 4: Material Abundance

Orange's rational organization of production created unprecedented prosperity.

Through:

- Scientific agriculture (feeding billions)
- Industrial manufacturing (making goods affordable)
- Global trade (specialization and efficiency)
- Market coordination (distributing resources dynamically)

Absolute poverty decreased dramatically. Goods once available only to aristocracy became widely accessible. The average person in a developed country in 2025 has access to comfort, variety, and opportunity unimaginable to their ancestors.

This is worth celebrating. Warm homes, abundant food, medical care, education—these aren't trivial luxuries. They're the foundation for any higher pursuits.

* * *

How Orange Actually Works

To understand why Orange succeeded so completely—and why its shadows are so hard to escape—we need to understand its core operating principles.

Principle 1: Optimization

Orange asks constantly: **How can this be done better, faster, cheaper, more efficiently?**

This drive for optimization:

- Increases productivity (doing more with less)
- Reduces waste (efficiency as virtue)
- Enables scaling (from craft to industrial production)
- Compounds progress (each improvement enables the next)

The problem: **When you optimize everything, you eliminate all slack, all buffer, all space for anything that can't be measured and improved.**

Rest becomes wasteful. Contemplation becomes unproductive. Relationships become transactions. Beauty becomes decorative unless it increases property value.

Principle 2: Measurement and Quantification

Orange believes: **If you can't measure it, you can't manage it.**
This creates:

- Accountability (showing results, not just claims)
- Comparability (knowing what works better)
- Feedback loops (data enabling improvement)
- Objectivity (facts over feelings)

The problem: **The measurable drives out the meaningful.** What gets measured gets managed—and what doesn't get measured gets ignored, regardless of its actual importance.

You can measure GDP but not wellbeing. You can measure screen time but not presence. You can measure productivity but not wisdom. So we optimize for the metrics while the unmeasurable dimensions of human experience atrophy.

Because Orange creates value by measuring it, anything that resists measurement—like the patience of a parent, the health of a watershed, or the quality of attention given to a friend—becomes economically invisible. In an Orange world, if it doesn't have a price, it doesn't exist.

This is what I call **the Invisibility of Care**: all the labor that maintains life, nurtures relationships, and sustains ecosystems becomes structurally unrecognized because it can't be efficiently quantified. We end up in a civilization that measures everything and values nothing that matters most.

Principle 3: Competition as Driver

Orange harnesses competition to drive improvement: **The best wins, everyone else adapts or loses.**
This creates:

- Innovation pressure (adapt or die)
- Quality improvement (winners must be better)
- Efficiency selection (waste gets eliminated)
- Dynamic adaptation (constant evolution)

The problem: **Unending competition with no finish line creates chronic anxiety and prevents any genuine rest.**

You can never stop competing. Every achievement raises the bar. Every success creates new competitors. The race never ends because there is no destination—only relative positioning that must be continuously maintained.

Principle 4: Rational Self-Interest

Orange assumes: **Individuals pursuing their rational self-interest will create collective benefit through market mechanisms.**

This creates:

- Entrepreneurship (pursuing opportunity)
- Investment (risking resources for return)
- Innovation (creating value captures reward)
- Efficiency (waste costs you)

The problem: **When everything becomes a market, nothing is sacred. Community becomes networking, relationships become transactions, and every moment demands justification through productivity.**

The assumption that self-interest benefits all only works with functional markets, aligned incentives, and proper accounting of externalities. When these conditions aren't met—and they increasingly aren't—rational self-interest produces collective harm while remaining individually rational.

* * *

A crucial point: These principles aren't inherently destructive. They're what created modern medicine, democratic institutions, and unprecedented prosperity. The problem emerges when they expand beyond their proper domains—when optimization colonizes rest, when measurement displaces meaning, when competition corrodes cooperation, when self-interest dissolves community.

Orange's gift becomes Orange's curse through excess, not through essence.

* * *

The Peak of Orange: Post-War Prosperity

Orange reached its apex in the post–World War II period, roughly 1945–1975 in developed nations.

This was when Orange's promises seemed most achievable:

- Strong economic growth (rising tide lifting boats)
- Expanding middle class (prosperity spreading)
- Technological optimism (nuclear power! Space travel! Computers!)
- Increasing social mobility (education as ladder)
- Stable employment (career with one company)
- Reasonable work–life balance (40-hour week, weekends, vacations)

A single factory worker could support a family, own a home, have job security, and retire with a pension. A college degree virtually guaranteed employment. Hard work reliably led to advancement.

This is the Orange world our institutions and expectations were built for.

This is the Orange world that no longer exists.

* * *

When the Medicine Becomes the Poison

Here's the crucial insight: **Orange didn't fail by its own metrics—it succeeded so spectacularly that it's now consuming the very conditions that made its success possible.**

Every gift became excessive:

Science and Technology → Technological acceleration beyond human adaptation

- We can manipulate attention through algorithms
- We can track and measure everything
- We can be productive 24/7 through devices
- We can optimize human behavior like factory processes

Meritocracy → Winner-take-all credentialism

- Achievement becomes arms race (SAT scores, resume building, credentials stacking)
- "Merit" becomes expensive to signal (elite education, unpaid internships, networking)
- Competition intensifies without expanding opportunity
- Those who "fail" face moral judgment (if system is fair, losers deserve loss)

Individual Rights → Hyper-individualism and atomization

- From "free from oppression" to "free from obligation"
- Community becomes optional, relationships contractual
- No safety net beyond what you personally secure
- Loneliness epidemic as social fabric dissolves

Material Abundance → Consumerism and environmental extraction

- From "meeting needs" to "endless wants"
- Identity through consumption (you are what you buy)
- Planned obsolescence and perpetual dissatisfaction
- Ecological systems pushed beyond regeneration capacity

Optimization → Elimination of all slack

- Just-in-time everything (inventory, staffing, personal schedules)
- No buffer for error, illness, rest, or spontaneity
- Brittleness masquerading as efficiency
- System-wide fragility from over-optimization

Measurement → Metrics gaming and Goodhart's Law

- "When a measure becomes a target, it ceases to be a good measure"
- Teaching to tests, clicks over quality, KPIs over purpose
- What can't be measured (wisdom, presence, care) becomes invisible
- The measurable colonizes the meaningful

Competition → Chronic anxiety and erosion of cooperation

- From driver of improvement to driver of exhaustion
- Competing for scarce positions in winner-take-all markets
- Cooperation becomes strategic, vulnerable to defection
- Trust erodes when everyone is rival

Rational Self-Interest → Tragedy of the commons at civilizational scale

- Individually rational choices (maximize income, minimize cost) produce collective catastrophe (climate breakdown, ecosystem collapse, social atomization)
- Externalities (pollution, inequality, mental health) don't appear in individual profit calculations

- Racing to the bottom becomes rational for each actor while destroying the system for all

And beneath all of this lies a fundamental category error: Orange assumes the human operator is a machine that can be upgraded indefinitely—more efficient, more productive, more optimized. But we are biological organisms with fixed limits. The body needs rest. The nervous system needs recovery. Attention is a finite resource.

The crisis of burnout isn't a personal failing or even a social problem. **It's the Biological Layer screaming "Stop" to a Cognitive Layer that believes it is infinite.** It's a physics violation dressed up as a motivation problem.

You can't debug biology with better time management. You can't optimize your way past the need for sleep. You can't hack your way around the reality that human beings are embodied creatures with needs that can't be eliminated through better systems.

Orange's blindness to biological limits is creating a civilization-wide integration failure. We're running software designed for machines on hardware that's fundamentally biological—and the hardware is breaking down.

* * *

The Acceleration Trap

But Orange didn't just overshoot its targets. Something more insidious happened: **the system began optimizing for its own continuation rather than human flourishing.**

Consider:

Technology was supposed to free us. Instead, algorithms are designed to maximize "engagement"—which means capturing and holding attention through psychological exploitation. Think of social media algorithms:

they don't optimize for human connection or wellbeing; they optimize for "engagement" metrics that serve advertising revenue. The system's goals have decoupled from human flourishing while using human psychology as raw material.

Eventually, Orange logic runs out of external resources to optimize and turns its gaze inward. **It begins optimizing us.** It tracks our attention, predicts our dopamine responses, and mines our nervous systems for engagement data. We stop being the users of the tool and become the raw material being processed.

Markets were supposed to distribute resources efficiently. Instead, they concentrate wealth through feedback loops where capital begets capital, while those without start further behind each generation. Efficiency serves extraction, not distribution.

Meritocracy was supposed to reward ability. Instead, it legitimizes inequality by blaming victims ("if you worked harder, you'd succeed") while the actual determinants of success (inherited wealth, connections, luck) become invisible.

Productivity was supposed to create abundance so we could work less. Instead, each productivity gain raised expectations, eliminated jobs, and intensified competition for what remains. The "productivity paradox"—we're more productive than ever yet working longer hours for less security—isn't an anomaly. It's the logical endpoint of optimization divorced from human purpose.

Orange created a system so successful at optimization that it began optimizing humans as resources to be extracted, rather than beings to be nurtured.

* * *

The View from Inside Orange

Here's why this is so hard to see: **Orange's logic is deeply internalized.** It doesn't feel like an ideology. It feels like reality.

Consider how natural these thoughts feel:

- "Time is money"
- "You're only as good as your last performance"
- "If you can't measure it, it doesn't count"
- "Work smarter, not harder"
- "Optimize everything"
- "There's an app for that"
- "If you're not growing, you're dying"
- "Compete or lose"

These aren't philosophical positions we consciously chose. They're the water we swim in. The operating system running in the background.

This is why individual solutions fail. You can't debug your personal psychology when the bug is in the cultural operating system. You can set better boundaries, but you're still in a system that punishes boundaries. You can practice mindfulness, but you're still in an environment designed to fracture attention.

You can win the game, but the game itself is extracting more than it returns.

* * *

Orange's Tragic Blindness

The deepest tragedy is that Orange can't see its own shadows.

Orange thinking assumes:

- Problems are technical, requiring better optimization
- Suffering indicates insufficient achievement or effort
- Meaning emerges from productivity and success
- Rest is wasteful unless it improves future performance
- Relationships are built through transaction and mutual benefit
- The good life is achieved through individual striving

When these assumptions fail—when achievement doesn't bring satisfaction, when optimization produces brittleness, when relationships-as-transactions leave us lonely—Orange doesn't question the assumptions. It assumes inadequate execution.

The response to Orange's failures is always "more Orange."

Burnout? Optimize your self-care routine.

Loneliness? Network more strategically.

Anxiety? Improve your productivity system.

Meaninglessness? Set more ambitious goals.

Orange cannot recognize that some problems are created by its own logic and cannot be solved within that logic. **This is the definition of a paradigm trap: when the only tools available are the ones that created the problem.**

It's like trying to cure an alcohol problem by drinking more efficiently.

This is why we need something else. Not a rejection of Orange—we need its gifts. But a transcendence of its limitations.

We need Yellow.

* * *

The Transition Zone We're Living In

Right now, in 2025, we're living in a particular historical moment: **Orange is breaking down faster than anything coherent is emerging to replace it.**

The signs are everywhere:

Economic: Work harder, earn less, less security, more competition for shrinking middle-class positions

Social: Atomization, loneliness epidemic, collapse of civic institutions, erosion of trust

Psychological: Burnout, anxiety, depression, addiction at unprecedented levels

Environmental: Overshoot, resource depletion, climate instability, ecosystem collapse

Political: Polarization, democratic erosion, authoritarian appeal, loss of shared reality

Existential: Meaning crisis, purpose vacuum, spiritual hunger with no legitimate outlets

Orange's answers to these crises? Work harder. Innovate faster. Compete better. Optimize more.

This is a system in its death throes, demanding ever more from humans while delivering ever less.

And yet most of us can't imagine an alternative. We're like Sarah in Chapter 1—we know something is fundamentally wrong, but our only tools are Orange tools, which are the source of the problem.

* * *

Why This Matters for What Comes Next

Understanding Orange—really understanding it—is essential for three reasons:

First: We need Orange's gifts. Science, technology, rational analysis, individual rights, material abundance—these are real achievements we must preserve. Yellow doesn't reject Orange; it transcends and includes it.

Second: We have to recognize Orange's limitations. Not because Orange is "bad" but because its core assumptions are incomplete. Some problems require logic Orange cannot provide.

Third: We need compassion for ourselves and others trapped in Orange logic. Sarah, David, Maria, James—they're not weak or ungrateful. They're running Orange's program flawlessly while the program itself has become pathological.

The tragedy isn't that people are running the program wrong, but that the program itself has become pathological while demanding ever more perfect execution.

The system needs debugging. Not the people running it.

* * *

The Question Orange Can't Ask

Orange can optimize anything. It can measure everything. It can compete indefinitely. It can achieve ceaselessly.

But there's one question Orange cannot ask without undermining its own foundation:

"What if optimization itself is the problem?"

"What if some things are more valuable precisely because they can't be measured?"

"What if rest isn't wasteful but essential?"

"What if success without flourishing is actually failure?"

These questions don't just challenge specific Orange practices. They challenge Orange's core logic. And that logic has no framework for addressing them.

This is where Green thinking tried to intervene. And it's both why Green is necessary and why Green alone isn't sufficient.

That's what we'll explore in the next chapter.

Chapter 3: The Green Trap — Why Deconstruction Is Not Construction

Sarah sits in the corner office we met in Chapter 1, but now she's in a different kind of meeting. Not quarterly reviews or strategy sessions. This is the company's Diversity, Equity, and Inclusion committee.

She's learned the language. She knows to acknowledge her privilege before speaking. She's read the books—*White Fragility*, *How to Be an Antiracist*, *The Body Keeps the Score*. She understands intersectionality, systemic oppression, and microaggressions.

And she genuinely cares. The awareness that her success came partly through advantages others didn't have is real. The desire to make the workplace more equitable is sincere.

But here's what's also real: she's exhausted.

The meeting goes around the circle, everyone sharing their perspectives on the latest initiative. There's careful attention to whose voice gets centered, whose experience gets validated. Someone suggests an idea. Someone else notes how that idea might perpetuate harm. A third person acknowledges both perspectives and suggests we hold space for the tension.

Two hours later, they've had a rich conversation about power dynamics, emotional labor, and the violence of urgency culture.

They have not decided anything.

And Sarah realizes: **She's learned everything about what's wrong. She knows nothing about what to build.**

* * *

What Green Solved

Before we explore Green's limitations, we must honor what it accomplished. Because Green thinking emerged to address real failures in Orange logic—and it succeeded in making those failures visible.

Orange's Moral Blindness

Orange thought it had solved the problem of fairness through meritocracy: if everyone competes on a level playing field, the best rise to the top. Achievement measures worth. Markets distribute resources efficiently. Individual effort determines outcomes.

This was always incomplete. But it took Green thinking to show *how* incomplete:

The playing field was never level.

- Women faced systematic exclusion and discrimination
- People of color encountered barriers at every stage
- LGBTQ+ individuals had to hide fundamental aspects of themselves
- Working-class people lacked the networks and cultural capital assumed by "merit"
- Disabled people found systems designed without considering their needs

"Merit" was never neutral.

- Standardized tests measured cultural familiarity as much as ability
- "Leadership qualities" were defined by dominant group norms
- "Professional behavior" meant conforming to white, male, able-bodied standards

- Success required resources (time, money, connections) unequally distributed

Markets didn't distribute fairly.

- Wealth concentrates rather than distributes
- Externalities (environmental destruction, social cost) weren't priced
- Power imbalances meant "voluntary" transactions weren't truly free
- "Rational self-interest" meant those with power pursued their interests at others' expense

Individual responsibility was a myth.

- Your outcomes weren't just about your effort
- Systemic advantages and disadvantages shaped possibilities
- Blaming individuals for structural failures added insult to injury
- "Personal responsibility" became excuse to ignore injustice

Green made all of this visible. And that matters enormously.

Green's Revolutionary Insights

Green thinking brought several crucial capabilities Orange lacked:

1. Systems Awareness

Green sees that problems aren't just individual but structural. Racism isn't just personal prejudice—it's embedded in institutions, policies, and cultural norms. Poverty isn't personal failure—it's systemic resource distribution. Mental health struggles aren't individual weakness—they're responses to collective conditions.

This is a genuine cognitive advance. Seeing systems is more sophisticated than seeing only individuals.

2. Perspective-Taking

Green insists: **Listen to those with lived experience.** Center marginalized voices. Recognize that dominant narratives exclude important truths. Understand that your position shapes what you can see.

This humility is essential. Orange's confidence that rational analysis from any position could access universal truth was naive.

3. Compassion and Care

Green values empathy, emotional intelligence, and attending to harm. It recognizes that "rational efficiency" often means ignoring human suffering. It insists on caring for those most vulnerable.

This moral sensitivity corrects Orange's callousness. Efficiency at the cost of human dignity is not progress.

4. Deconstruction of Power

Green asks: **Who benefits? Who is harmed? Whose voices are centered? Whose are erased?**

This critical analysis reveals how systems that claim neutrality actually serve particular interests. It shows how language, norms, and institutions encode power relations.

5. Pluralism and Inclusion

Green recognizes: **There are multiple valid ways of knowing, being, and organizing society.** Western, rational, individual approaches aren't universal but cultural. Other perspectives aren't deficient but different.

This cultural humility is necessary for a genuinely global civilization.

* * *

These are real achievements. They represent developmental progress. We cannot go back to Orange's obliviousness—nor should we want to.

But something went wrong in how Green thinking evolved. Or perhaps more accurately: Green is necessary but insufficient. And when it tries to be sufficient, it becomes pathological in its own ways.

* * *

The Green Shadow: When Awareness Becomes Paralysis

Green's gifts are genuine. But like Orange before it, Green's strengths become problems when pushed to extremes or applied beyond their proper domains.

Problem 1: Critique Without Construction

Green excels at identifying what's wrong. It can deconstruct any system, reveal hidden power dynamics, and articulate harm with sophisticated nuance.

What Green struggles with is: **What do we build instead?**

Ask Green what's wrong with capitalism, and you'll get detailed analysis of exploitation, extraction, and alienation.

Ask Green what economic system should replace capitalism, and you'll hear: "We need to imagine alternatives beyond the binary of capitalism and communism... We should center the voices of those most impacted... We must address the intersections of class, race, and gender... We need to hold space for multiple perspectives..."

What you won't get is: **A specific, implementable economic model with clear mechanisms and accountability structures.**

This isn't because Green thinkers are lazy or uncommitted. It's because deconstruction is not the same skill as construction. Taking apart is easier than building. Critique requires different capabilities than creation.

And Green has developed extraordinary sophistication in critique while often resisting the practical constraints that construction requires.

Problem 2: Purity Spirals and Callout Culture

Green's moral sensitivity—its attention to harm and insistence on justice—can become a weapon that devours its own.

The logic goes: 1. Harm must be named and addressed 2. Causing harm (even unintentionally) demonstrates moral failing 3. Those who fail to recognize harm are complicit 4. Therefore: constant vigilance for any trace of problematic thinking

This creates:

Purity spirals - Each round of critique raises the bar for what counts as acceptable. Yesterday's progressive position becomes today's problematic view. There's no stable ground, only constant anxiety about being on the "wrong side."

Performative activism - Virtue is demonstrated through expressing the right opinions, using the right language, and calling out the insufficiently pure. Actual impact matters less than signaling correct alignment.

Fear of engaging complexity - If nuance can be weaponized ("you're making excuses for oppression"), people retreat to slogans. Genuine exploration becomes too risky.

Exhaustion and burnout - The emotional labor of constant awareness, the anxiety of potential mistakes, and the energy of performing wokeness drains the very people trying to do good.

And the exhaustion is qualitatively different from Orange burnout. Orange burnout comes from running too fast—the treadmill that never stops. Green burnout comes from **carrying too much**. Green demands that the individual nervous system metabolize the pain of the entire world without the container of structural power to distribute that weight.

It's an empathy overdose. You're supposed to be aware of every form of oppression, attuned to every kind of harm, responsive to every marginalized voice—all at once, all the time, with your individual consciousness. This leads to what psychologists are now calling "compassion collapse"—the point where the system becomes so overloaded that it shuts down entirely.

The biological reality is simple: **human nervous systems cannot carry civilizational suffering without structure to hold it.** Green asks empaths to do alone what requires collective infrastructure.

Alienation of potential allies - People who genuinely want to help but don't have the vocabulary or political sophistication get attacked rather than educated. This drives them away—or worse, toward reactionary positions.

Problem 3: Relativism That Can't Ground Action

Green's cultural humility—its recognition that all perspectives are situated and partial—creates a philosophical problem when it comes time to act.

If all perspectives are equally valid, on what basis do you choose?

If all value systems are cultural constructs, why prefer justice to injustice?

If all claims to truth are power moves, what grounds moral demands?

Green often answers: "We center the most marginalized voices." But this creates new problems:

Which marginalized voices? They often disagree with each other.

What if marginalized communities have conservative values? Do we respect cultural difference or insist on universal rights?

Who decides who counts as marginalized? Isn't that itself a power move?

The result is often paralysis disguised as "holding space for complexity." Decisions get endlessly deferred in favor of more process, more dialogue, more centering of unheard voices.

Meanwhile, Orange keeps building—often badly—because it has no such hesitation about action.

Problem 4: Emotional Reasoning Over Systemic Analysis

Green prioritized emotional intelligence as corrective to Orange's cold rationality. But this created new blindness:

"It makes me feel unsafe" becomes reason enough to shut down discussion.

"I'm speaking from my lived experience" becomes claim that can't be questioned.

"That causes harm" becomes sufficient grounds for censorship.

The problem isn't that feelings don't matter—they do. The problem is when emotional response becomes the *only* criterion for evaluation.

Sometimes people feel unsafe encountering ideas that challenge their worldview—that's not the same as actual danger.

Sometimes lived experience is limited or misleading—individual experience doesn't automatically generate systemic understanding.

Sometimes preventing all discomfort means preventing growth—challenge and conflict are necessary for development.

Green's elevation of emotional safety can create echo chambers where no one is ever uncomfortable—and therefore no one ever changes.

Problem 5: The Activist's Trap

Green often frames the world in terms of oppressors and oppressed, with moral obligation falling on "allies" to defer to and amplify marginalized voices.

This creates strange dynamics:

Savior complexes - Privileged people performing rescue of those they simultaneously claim are more wise and moral. The helper becomes the hero of their own story.

Learned helplessness - If you're oppressed, your agency is denied. You're victim, not actor. This robs people of power while claiming to empower them.

Zero-sum thinking - If some groups are up, others must be down. Progress for one means loss for another. This makes coalition-building nearly impossible.

Identity as destiny - Who you are matters more than what you do. Your race, gender, sexuality determine your moral standing. This is essentialism with a progressive face.

Problem 6: Mistaking Recognition for Justice

Green fought hard for representation, visibility, and recognition of historically excluded groups. These battles were necessary and valuable.

But somewhere along the way, **representation became confused with transformation.**

Having a diverse boardroom doesn't change the logic of extraction.

Black faces in high places don't alter wealth concentration.

More women CEOs doesn't question the premise that corporations should maximize shareholder value above all else.

LGBTQ+ inclusion in the military doesn't challenge militarism.

Green won many battles for representation within existing structures. What it often failed to do was transform the structures themselves.

And Orange was perfectly happy to accommodate diversity demands—as long as the fundamental logic of optimization, measurement, competition, and extraction remained intact.

* * *

The Green-Orange Alliance That Changes Nothing

Here's the insidious part: Orange and Green made peace.

Corporate Green emerged: companies with diversity officers, land acknowledgments, and rainbow logos during Pride month—while maintaining the same extractive practices, just with better optics.

Woke Capitalism appeared: brands performing progressive values to capture the progressive market—while offshoring manufacturing, union-busting, and tax-avoiding.

Neoliberal Diversity triumphed: celebrate identity while ignoring economics, perform inclusion while intensifying competition, acknowledge privilege while maintaining structures of wealth concentration.

The result is what Adolph Reed Jr. calls "identitarianism"—reducing all politics to identity-based claims while leaving economic and power structures untouched.

Green became Orange's conscience without becoming its competitor. It made extraction more articulate without making it less extractive.

Sarah can attend all the DEI trainings, learn all the right language, genuinely care about justice—and still be trapped in an extractive system that makes her miserable while harming the world.

Green made Orange more sophisticated. It didn't make it less destructive.

* * *

Why Green Alone Can't Build What We Need

Green's limitations aren't personal failings of Green thinkers. They're structural to Green consciousness itself.

Green Can't Prioritize

When everything is important and all perspectives must be centered, you can't make choices. Building requires ranking priorities, making tradeoffs, and accepting that some goods must be pursued before others.

Green's radical inclusion makes decisive action nearly impossible.

Green Can't Scale

Green thinking works beautifully in small, intentional communities where everyone shares values and can process everything collectively.

It breaks down at city scale, fails completely at national scale, and can't even conceive of planetary scale governance.

Building systems for millions requires mechanisms Green lacks.

Green Can't Integrate Orange's Gifts

Green rightly critiques Orange's shadows. But it often throws out Orange's genuine capabilities:

- Rational analysis and evidence-based thinking
- Efficient organization and scaling
- Clear accountability structures
- Meritocratic selection (when actually fair)
- Individual achievement and agency

You can't build complex systems without these capacities. Green's rejection of them means it can't build what it envisions.

Green Can't Handle Complexity

Green excels at revealing complexity—showing how everything affects everything else, how all oppressions intersect, how simple solutions miss nuance.

But **revealing complexity is not the same as navigating complexity.**

You can't govern a city by endlessly noting how everything is connected. You need models that track key variables, feedback loops that enable adjustment, and structures that can act despite incomplete information.

Green has no such models.

Green Can't Tolerate Hierarchy

Green sees all hierarchy as domination, all structure as oppression, all authority as violence.

But some problems require coordination at scale. Some decisions need clear responsibility. Some systems need someone empowered to act quickly.

Flat consensus works for small groups making low-stakes decisions. It fails for organizations needing to act with urgency and clarity.

And here's the deeper problem: When you remove formal structure because structure is "oppressive," you don't get equality. You get what feminist organizer Jo Freeman called **"The Tyranny of Structureless-ness."**

Power still exists—it always does. But now it moves through social capital, charisma, unspoken norms, and "who knows who" rather than clear roles and explicit authority. The informal hierarchy becomes more rigid than any formal one because it's invisible, unacknowledged, and therefore unaccountable.

By making power invisible, Green makes it unaccountable. The person who speaks most confidently dominates the meeting, but no one can challenge their authority because officially there is no authority. The tight-knit group makes decisions, but outsiders can't access the process because officially there is no process.

This is often worse than explicit hierarchy—at least with visible struc-ture, you know what you're dealing with and can hold people accountable.

Green Can't Escape Its Own Privilege

The ultimate irony: Green consciousness itself is a luxury good.

The ability to endlessly process power dynamics, center marginalized voices, and hold space for complexity requires:

- Economic security (not grinding for survival)
- Education (access to sophisticated concepts)
- Time (for endless meetings and processing)
- Safety (room to be vulnerable and emotional)

The people Green claims to serve often can't afford Green's methods.

The farmworker organizing for bathroom breaks doesn't have time for four-hour consensus processes. The single mother working three jobs can't attend the emotional processing circle. Green's methods

often exclude the very people they claim to center.

Green Confuses Inclusivity with Flatness

Green often appeals to Indigenous wisdom, traditional cultures, and non-Western ways of knowing. This is valuable and necessary.

But here's what Green misses: **Actual regenerative cultures aren't flat.**

The Indigenous traditions Green admires have Elders. They have Keepers of Wisdom. They recognize competence hierarchies based on depth of experience, not formal credentials. They have rituals for transferring authority, protocols for decision-making, and clear roles for different life stages.

Green rejects the Elder because it looks like a Boss.

But an Elder in a healthy culture isn't a manager optimizing output. An Elder is someone who has integrated enough experience to see patterns others miss, hold paradox without collapsing, and make decisions that serve the whole across generations.

Green's rejection of all hierarchy means rejecting this too—and losing access to exactly the wisdom it claims to seek.

* * *

What Sarah Realizes

Back in that DEI meeting, Sarah has an uncomfortable thought she's afraid to voice:

The more we talk about justice, the less we seem to achieve it.

The more sophisticated our analysis of power, the less power we seem to have to change anything.

The better we get at naming problems, the worse we get at solving them.

She looks around the room at her colleagues—smart, caring, genuinely committed people. And she realizes: they're trapped in the same way she is.

They've learned to see Orange's failures. They've developed Green's critique. They've become experts in identifying harm.

But they haven't learned how to build.

And the longer they stay in Green, the more construction itself feels like violence—imposing structure, creating hierarchy, making choices that exclude some possibilities in favor of others.

So they process. And discuss. And center. And hold space.

And Orange keeps optimizing. Keeps extracting. Keeps accelerating toward collapse.

Because Orange doesn't need Green's approval. Orange just needs Green to not build anything that works.

* * *

The View from Green

If you're reading this from a Green perspective, you might be feeling defensive. Maybe angry. Perhaps thinking: "This is exactly the kind of dismissive, privileged critique that erases real struggles and real violence."

I get it. I've been there.

But consider:

How many meetings have you sat through where nothing concrete was decided?

How many times has nuance become excuse for inaction?

How many initiatives have failed because the process was more important than the outcome?

How much energy have you spent policing language while material conditions worsened?

How often have you felt exhausted by your own side's purity demands?

If you're honest with yourself, you've felt this too.

The question isn't whether Green's insights are valid—they are.

The question is whether Green can build systems that embody those insights at scale.

And the uncomfortable answer is: not by itself.

* * *

What Green Gets Right That Yellow Must Include

Before we move to Yellow solutions, let's be crystal clear about what Green contributes that cannot be lost:

✓ **Systems thinking** - Problems are structural, not just individual

✓ **Power analysis** - Who benefits? Who's harmed? Who decides?

✓ **Lived experience matters** - Those affected by decisions must help make them

✓ **Multiple perspectives** - There's no view from nowhere; all knowledge is situated

✓ **Emotional intelligence** - Feelings provide crucial information systems need

✓ **Justice as priority** - Fairness isn't optional or aspirational but essential

✓ **Care and compassion** - Efficiency must serve wellbeing, not replace it

Yellow doesn't reject these. Yellow builds structures that instantiate them.

The difference is that Yellow asks: **How do we make these values operational?**

Not: "Do we value diversity?" but "What mechanisms ensure diverse voices shape outcomes?"

Not: "Is equity important?" but "What policies actually redistribute resources and opportunity?"

Not: "Should we care about harm?" but "What systems prevent harm while enabling necessary action?"

* * *

The Green-Yellow Transition

The move from Green to Yellow isn't about rejecting Green's values. It's about developing capabilities Green lacks:

From critique to construction - Not just naming problems but building solutions

From process to outcome - Honoring process while achieving results

From relative to integrative - Holding multiple truths while still being able to act

From emotional to systemic - Feelings as data within larger analytical frameworks

From flat to functional - Structure and hierarchy in service of values

From local to scalable - Models that work beyond immediate communities

Yellow says: **"Green is right about what matters. Now let's build systems that actually deliver it."**

This isn't compromise. This isn't selling out. This isn't "enlightened centrism" that treats all positions as equally valid.

This is saying: **Justice without power is poetry. Power without justice is tyranny. We need both.**

Justice requires power. Power requires organization. Organization requires construction. Construction requires capabilities Green has resisted developing.

* * *

Sarah's Question

As the DEI meeting finally winds down—two hours spent, zero decisions made—Sarah asks a question she's never dared voice before:

"What if we're really good at understanding problems but don't know how to solve them? What if our sophistication about complexity is actually preventing us from doing anything?"

The room goes quiet. Someone suggests they should hold space for the discomfort of that question. Someone else notes the violence of urgency culture.

But Sarah sees something else in the silence: recognition.

They all feel it. They've all wondered it. They've been afraid to say it.

Green taught them to see. But it didn't teach them to build.

Awareness is not action. Understanding is not change. And in a world on fire, understanding the chemistry of combustion is not the same as putting out the flames.

You can't change the world through awareness alone.

* * *

What Comes Next

The cost of Green's paralysis isn't abstract.

While we process power dynamics, climate tipping points approach.

While we center marginalized voices, wealth concentrates faster.

While we avoid hierarchy, authoritarians organize efficiently.

While we deconstruct systems, those systems continue extracting.

While we hold space for complexity, the world's problems accelerate.

The world won't wait for us to achieve perfect consensus.

Green is necessary. Its insights must be integrated into whatever we build.

But Green alone cannot build what we need.

In Chapter 4, we'll see why the costs are accelerating—why we're running out of time to figure this out through endless processing.

In Chapter 5, we'll understand integration failure at a deeper level—what it means when systems exceed their capacity to coordinate.

And then in Part II, we'll explore Yellow thinking: the principles that enable us to build systems that include Orange's capabilities, honor Green's values, and transcend both their limitations.

The question isn't: "Green or Orange?"

The question is: **"What includes and transcends both?"**

That's what we're building toward.

Chapter 4: The Cost Curve Has Gone Vertical

For most of human history, problems unfolded on timescales that allowed adaptation. Climate changed over millennia. Empires rose and fell across centuries. Technologies evolved over generations.

Even during periods of rapid change—the Industrial Revolution, the World Wars, the Digital Revolution—humans had time to learn, adjust, and build new institutions to manage new realities.

That's no longer true.

What makes this moment historically unique: Previous civilizations collapsed regionally—Rome fell, but China continued. The Bronze Age collapsed in the Mediterranean, but not globally. Dark ages were local.

Ours is the first civilization facing global, simultaneous systems failure. And we've developed weapons (nuclear, biological, climatic) that could make recovery impossible. We can't retreat to rebuild elsewhere. There is no elsewhere.

We've entered a period where multiple existential challenges are accelerating simultaneously, feeding back on each other, creating compound crises that exceed our institutional capacity to respond. The interval between "we should do something" and "it's too late" has collapsed from decades to years.

This isn't alarmism. It's mathematics meeting physics meeting demographics meeting psychology.

* * *

The Convergence: When Everything Breaks at Once

Imagine you're managing a ship with multiple systems. The navigation is glitching. The engine is overheating. The hull has micro-fractures. The crew is exhausted and demoralized. The supply chain is disrupted. And a storm is approaching.

Each problem alone would be manageable with time. But when they hit simultaneously, with each problem making others worse, you're not facing repairs—you're facing systems collapse.

That's where we are civilizationally.

Let's look at what's converging:

1. Climate and Ecological Breakdown

This isn't a future problem. It's happening now and accelerating faster than models predicted.

The Physics:

- We've warmed 1.2°C above pre-industrial levels
- We're on track for 2.5-3°C by 2100 without dramatic intervention
- Each 0.5°C increase triggers non-linear effects (feedback loops, tipping points)
- Arctic permafrost melt releases methane (23x more potent than CO_2)
- Amazon rainforest approaching savanna conversion point
- Antarctic ice sheets showing unexpected instability

The Timeline:

- 2030: Likely breach 1.5°C (10 years for meaningful action)
- 2040: Possible breach 2°C (triggers cascading effects)

- 2050: Multiple tipping points likely crossed if current trajectory continues

The Impacts Already Visible:

- Crop failures increasing (heat, drought, floods)
- Water scarcity intensifying (glacier melt, aquifer depletion)
- Extreme weather events (hurricanes, fires, floods) more frequent and severe
- Ecosystem collapse (insect decline, coral death, fishery depletion)
- Mass migration beginning (climate refugees in the millions)

The Feedback Loops: Climate stress → crop failure → food insecurity → political instability → weakened climate response → worse climate stress

This isn't linear. Every year of inaction makes the problem exponentially harder to solve.

2. Economic Instability and Inequality

The economic system that created post-war prosperity is breaking down in real-time.

Wealth Concentration:

- Top 1% owns 43% of global wealth (and rising)
- 26 people own as much as poorest 3.8 billion
- Intergenerational wealth transfer approaching $84 trillion (2020-2045)
- Social mobility declining in developed nations

Labor Disruption:

- AI and automation poised to disrupt 40% of jobs by 2030
- Gig economy replacing stable employment

- Real wages stagnant despite productivity gains
- Benefits and security eroding for most workers

Debt Overhang:

- Global debt-to-GDP at record 356% (and rising)
- Student debt at $1.7 trillion in US alone
- Household debt at breaking point for many
- Government debt limiting crisis response capacity

The Feedback Loop: Inequality → political capture → policies favoring wealthy → more inequality → declining opportunity → social instability → weakened economic resilience

3. Mental Health and Meaning Crisis

We documented this in Chapters 1-3, but it's worth seeing as part of the convergence:

The Numbers:

- Depression rates doubled 2019-2024 in many developed nations
- Anxiety disorders affecting 1 in 3 adults
- Suicide rates climbing in multiple demographics
- "Deaths of despair" (suicide, overdose, alcoholism) rising sharply
- Loneliness epidemic affecting all age groups

The Causes Are Systemic:

- Economic precarity creating chronic stress
- Social atomization destroying support networks
- Attention extraction preventing presence
- Meaning vacuum from secular materialism
- Status anxiety from constant comparison

- Future uncertainty from multiple threats

The Consequences Compound: Mental health crisis → reduced productivity → economic strain → more mental health problems → weakened institutional capacity → worse crisis response

4. Democratic Erosion and Authoritarianism

Faith in democratic institutions is collapsing globally.
  The Trends:

- Trust in government at historic lows in most democracies
- Authoritarian leaders gaining power (Hungary, Turkey, Brazil, India, USA)
- Democratic backsliding in established democracies
- Youth disillusionment with democratic processes
- Rise of conspiracy theories and alternative realities

The Drivers:

- Systems failing to deliver material security
- Corruption and elite capture becoming visible
- Complexity exceeding democratic decision-making capacity
- Social media fragmenting shared reality
- Manipulation by hostile actors (foreign and domestic)

The Danger: When democracies can't solve problems, people turn to strongmen who promise simple solutions. This accelerates exactly when we need collective wisdom most.

5. Technological Disruption (AI, Biotech, Nanotech)

We're entering a period of technological capability that exceeds our wisdom to manage it.

AI Acceleration:

- Large language models emerged faster than predicted
- Capabilities doubling every 6-12 months in some domains
- Labor displacement beginning (white-collar jobs vulnerable)
- Autonomous weapons development racing ahead
- Deep fakes making "reality" contestable
- Alignment problem unsolved (building AI that shares human values)

Biotechnology:

- CRISPR and gene editing enabling human modification
- Synthetic biology creating novel organisms
- Pandemic potential from engineered pathogens
- Enhancement technologies creating biological inequality

The Timeline Problem: These technologies are arriving before we have social frameworks to manage them. We're getting god-like powers with monkey-level wisdom.

6. Geopolitical Instability

The post-1945 world order is fracturing.

The Breakdown:

- US hegemony declining, multipolar world emerging
- China-US competition intensifying
- Russia aggressive and revisionist
- Middle East chronically unstable

- Resource competition increasing (water, minerals, energy)
- Nuclear proliferation risk rising

The Danger: Exactly when we need global cooperation on climate, AI, and pandemics, nationalist competition is intensifying. The institutions we need are weakening while threats require coordination at unprecedented scale.

7. Epistemic Collapse (The Sensemaking Crisis)

Perhaps most insidious: **At the exact moment we need to solve the hardest problems in history, our ability to agree on reality has shattered.**
  The Fragmentation:

- Deep fakes making visual evidence unreliable
- Algorithmic polarization creating separate information universes
- AI-generated content flooding information ecosystem
- Social media optimizing for engagement over truth
- Conspiracy theories spreading faster than corrections
- Expert authority systematically delegitimized

The Consequences:

- Can't build consensus without shared reality
- Can't coordinate action without agreed facts
- Can't learn collectively when we can't process information
- Can't trust institutions when truth itself is contested

The Feedback Loop: Information overload → inability to discern signal from noise → retreat to tribal epistemology → more polarization → weaker collective intelligence → worse problem-solving

We are trying to navigate a hurricane with a compass that spins randomly. We're losing the shared cognitive infrastructure required to coordinate at civilizational scale.

This isn't just about "fake news" or "misinformation." It's about the collapse of the mechanisms through which societies make sense of reality and coordinate responses.

* * *

The Mathematics of Compound Crises

Here's why this is fundamentally different from previous historical challenges:

Problem 1: Exponential, Not Linear

Most of human history involved linear change. Things got gradually better or worse at rates humans could perceive and adapt to.

But exponential systems behave differently:

Year 1–10: Barely noticeable change

Year 11–20: Some people concerned

Year 21–25: "We should do something"

Year 26–27: "Holy shit we're in crisis"

Year 28–30: Too late to prevent catastrophe

We're somewhere between year 25 and 27 on multiple exponential curves simultaneously.

Climate, AI, debt, inequality, ecological collapse—all following exponential trajectories that make the next decade radically different from the last.

Problem 2: Feedback Loops and Cascade Failures

Each crisis makes others worse:

Climate → Migration → Political Instability → Weakened Climate Response

Inequality → Democratic Erosion → Elite Capture → More Inequality

Mental Health Crisis → Reduced Productivity → Economic Strain → More Mental Health Crisis

AI Disruption → Job Loss → Economic Instability → Political Extremism → Worse AI Governance

These aren't separate problems. They're interconnected systems where failure in one domain cascades to others.

Problem 3: Institutional Time Lag (The Physics Mismatch)

Our institutions operate on political cycles (2-4 years), strategic plans (5-10 years), and generational thinking (20-30 years).

But the problems operate on:

- Climate physics (tipping points cross in decades) - **Geological Time**
- AI development (capabilities doubling in months) - **Digital Time**
- Financial contagion (collapse in days) - **Market Time**
- Social movements (viral spread in hours) - **Network Time**

This isn't just "too slow"—it's a fundamental physics mismatch.

Our problems operate on Geological Time (carbon cycles measured in centuries) and Digital Time (AI iterations measured in weeks). Our governance operates on Election Time (4-year incentive structures).

You cannot solve a 100-year problem or a 10-millisecond problem with a 4-year decision-making cycle.

It's like trying to use a calendar to measure nanoseconds, or a stopwatch to plan for your great-grandchildren. The measurement instrument is categorically wrong for the phenomenon.

The system designed to respond is slower than the system creating the crisis. Our response machinery operates in geological time while the crisis unfolds in digital time.

Problem 4: Cognitive Overload

Humans evolved to handle local, visible, immediate threats. We're not equipped for:

- Abstract statistical risks (climate probabilities)
- Delayed consequences (actions now, impacts decades later)
- Interconnected complexity (everything affecting everything)
- Exponential growth (our brains think linearly)

This creates paralysis. The problems are real but feel unreal. Urgent but not immediate. Overwhelming but abstract.

So we do nothing while the curves steepen.

* * *

The Window Is Closing

Let's be specific about timelines, because vague concerns are easier to ignore than specific deadlines.

Climate: 5-10 Years for Meaningful Action

- To stay below 2°C, global emissions must peak by 2025, halve by 2030
- Infrastructure has 20-40 year lifespan (lock-in effect)
- Political will takes time to build
- We need to start now to have effect by 2030-2040
- After 2035, we're managing consequences, not preventing them

AI: 3-7 Years Before Labor Market Upheaval

- Current AI capabilities disrupting knowledge work now
- Next generation (GPT-5/6) likely transforms entire sectors
- Labor displacement beginning 2025-2030
- Need social safety net and transition plan before mass unemployment
- After disruption begins, harder to build political will for support

Democracy: Maybe 10 Years Before Critical Mass of Backsliding

- Democratic erosion accelerating globally
- Once authoritarian consolidation happens, hard to reverse
- Need to prove democracies can solve problems before people give up
- Authoritarian control of AI and surveillance tools creates permanent lock-in

Economic: Ongoing Crisis Could Tip to Systemic Failure Anytime

- Debt levels unsustainable but timing of crisis unpredictable
- Climate impacts already disrupting supply chains and insurance markets
- One major shock (pandemic, financial crisis, climate disaster) could cascade
- Once systemic failure begins, extremely difficult to manage

Mental Health: Already In Crisis, Could Reach Societal Breakdown

- Healthcare systems overwhelmed now
- Productivity impacts accumulating
- Social fabric tearing (loneliness, atomization, polarization)
- Point of no return is when enough people lose hope in collective future

* * *

Why Gradualism Won't Work

The natural response to this list is: "Okay, we need to make changes. Let's start with modest reforms and build from there."

This is the trap.

Gradualism made sense when:

- Change was linear
- Systems were stable
- We had time to experiment
- Feedback loops were manageable

But gradualism fails when:

- Change is exponential
- Systems are fragile
- Windows are closing
- Cascades are possible

Consider climate: If we'd started gradual change in 1990, we'd be fine. Starting gradual change in 2025 means we miss every meaningful target.

The math doesn't work.

Consider AI: Gradual adaptation to job displacement might work if change unfolds over 30 years. If 40% of jobs transform in 10 years, gradualism creates catastrophic unemployment before new systems can form.

Consider inequality: Modest redistribution might have worked in 1980. Now wealth is so concentrated that incremental change can't overcome the momentum.

The uncomfortable truth: We need structural transformation, not incremental adjustment.

And we need it fast enough to matter—which means roughly a decade to establish proof-of-concept systems that can then scale.

* * *

The Gap Between Problem and Response

Here's the tragic comedy of our moment:

Problem Speed: Exponential

Response Speed: Linear (at best)

Problem Complexity: Interconnected, systemic, emergent

Response Capacity: Siloed, reductionist, reactive

Problem Scale: Civilizational, global, existential

Response Level: Municipal, national (at best), incremental

Problem Timeline: Years to decades before irreversibility

Response Timeline: Political cycles, strategic plans, "let's form a committee"

But it's worse than inadequacy or slowness. **Our institutions are actively fighting the cure.**

Think of it as civilizational auto-immune disorder. The system isn't just failing to heal—it's attacking its own antibodies:

- We subsidize fossil fuels while taxing labor
- We protect banks that caused crashes while indebting students
- We bail out corporations while letting individuals fail
- We optimize supply chains for efficiency while destroying resilience
- We measure GDP growth while ignoring ecosystem collapse
- We protect intellectual property that prevents pandemic response
- We defend systems that are killing us because changing them threatens power

The patient is attacking the medicine.

This gap—between problem and response—is where civilizations collapse.

Not because the problems are unsolvable—many are technically solvable. But because the response capacity is structurally inadequate to the challenge, and often actively working against solutions.

Orange can't solve these problems because Orange created them.

Green can't solve them because Green can't build at scale.

And traditional Blue/Red responses (authoritarianism, nationalism, regression) make everything worse.

This is why we need Yellow. Not as preference, but as necessity. Not as nice idea, but as survival requirement.

* * *

What "Vertical Cost Curve" Actually Means

An economics term helps clarify what we're facing: **the cost curve has gone vertical.**

For most problems, the cost of inaction increases gradually:

- Wait to fix your roof: small water damage
- Wait longer: bigger water damage

· Wait much longer: structural damage

But some problems reach a point where the cost curve goes vertical—where delay doesn't just cost more, it makes the problem qualitatively different:

· Wait past a certain point: need to rebuild the entire house
· Wait longer: house collapses, possibly injuring people
· Wait even longer: can't rebuild on that foundation

We're at the point where delay transforms problem nature.

Climate past 2°C isn't "worse than 1.5°C"—it's different in kind. Tipping points cross. Feedback loops activate. Reversibility becomes impossible.

AI development without alignment isn't "riskier unaligned AI"—it's potential loss of human control over our future.

Democratic collapse isn't "worse democracy"—it's authoritarian lock-in with surveillance tools that prevent reversal.

The cost of waiting is no longer just "paying more later." It's "losing the ability to solve the problem at all."

We're approaching civilizational credit card debt where the minimum payment exceeds our income. Where the interest compounds faster than we can earn. Where default becomes inevitable unless we radically restructure the underlying system.

But Here's What Matters

The scale is overwhelming. The crises are real. The timelines are tight.

But the leverage points are specific.

We don't need to solve everything simultaneously. We don't need perfect solutions or complete understanding. We don't need to fix every institution or change every person.

We need to build the systems that can.

Systems that enable coordination at scale. Systems that make wise decisions under uncertainty. Systems that protect human flourishing while managing complexity. Systems that work fast enough to matter.

That's what the rest of this book is about.

* * *

Sarah, Again

Remember Sarah from Chapters 1 and 3? Corner office, DEI meetings, successful and exhausted?

She reads the news every morning. Climate reports getting worse. Political violence increasing. Another mass shooting. Democracy under threat. Economic instability. Tech layoffs. AI breakthrough that scares the researchers who built it.

She used to feel like her generation would muddle through, like humans always had. That's what history taught: crises come, humans adapt, life goes on.

But lately, she's not sure.

Not because she's inherently pessimistic. But because she can do math.

The timelines are converging. The problems are compounding. The window is closing.

And the institutions supposedly handling this—government, corporations, nonprofits, international bodies—seem completely inadequate to the moment.

They're still optimizing for efficiency when we need resilience.

They're still siloed when we need integration.

They're still incremental when we need transformation.

They're still debating when we need deciding.

She realizes: **Someone needs to build the thing that works. Soon. Or the opportunity to build it passes.**

Not someday. Not after more research. Not when conditions are perfect. **Now. With what we have. In the time remaining.**

* * *

The Choice Point

We're at a rare historical moment: **The window is still open, but it's closing.**

The next 5-10 years will likely determine whether:

Scenario A: Managed Transformation

- We build new systems fast enough to manage the transition
- Proof-of-concept models demonstrate viability
- Scaling begins before crisis forces chaotic adaptation
- Some disruption, but within manageable bounds
- Emerges into more resilient, humane civilization

Scenario B: Crisis-Driven Chaos

- We wait until problems become undeniable
- Respond in panic mode with emergency measures
- Authoritarian solutions gain appeal ("strong leadership in crisis")
- Much suffering, potential democratic collapse
- Eventually adapt, but through brutal process

Scenario C: Systems Collapse

- Multiple crises cascade before response capacity mobilizes
- Tipping points cross, feedback loops activate
- Institutions fail, social fabric tears
- Dark ages scenario (hopefully temporary)
- Rebuilding from much worse starting point

Which scenario unfolds depends on choices made in this decade.

Not by governments or corporations or international bodies—they're too slow and too captured by existing incentives.

By networks of people building alternatives that work.

The question isn't "Will change happen?"—it will.

The question is: **Will we build the change we want before chaos forces change we don't?**

The Hope in Exponentials

Here's something crucial: **The same exponential dynamics that create the crisis also create potential for rapid positive change.**

Solar cost curves have dropped 90% in a decade—faster than experts predicted. EV adoption is following similar exponential trajectories. Plant-based proteins are scaling rapidly. Renewable energy is becoming economically superior to fossil fuels.

Network effects mean solutions can spread as fast as problems—once they reach critical mass. One city proving a model can inspire hundreds. One successful implementation can be copied globally in months.

Transformation can accelerate faster than we expect when tipping points work in our favor.

We're not fighting against exponentials. We're racing to trigger the right ones before the wrong ones lock in.

* * *

What This Means for the Rest of the Book

The vertical cost curve creates urgency for everything that follows.

In Chapter 5, we'll understand what integration failure actually means— why systems are breaking and what would fix them.

In Part II, we'll explore Yellow principles—the thinking that enables building at scale with wisdom and care.

In Part III, we'll detail specific, implementable interventions that could work if deployed in the next 5-10 years.

In Part IV, we'll address the practical question: How do we actually make this happen?

The stakes are clear. The timeline is short. The task is enormous but achievable.

Not through heroic individual action. Not through waiting for institutional transformation. Not through perfect plans.

Through coordinated network action building functioning alternatives before the window closes.

Let's be clear what we're racing against: not some distant future crisis, but the accelerating convergence of multiple system failures in the next decade.

The cost curve is vertical. The window is closing.

But it's not closed yet.

And that means there's work to do.

Chapter 5: The Integration Threshold

Sarah sits in her corner office one more time. It's 3 AM. She can't sleep.

She's been thinking about the pattern we've traced through Chapters 1–4:

- Her personal exhaustion (Chapter 1)
- Orange's systematic extraction (Chapter 2)
- Green's inability to build alternatives (Chapter 3)
- The converging crises racing toward catastrophe (Chapter 4)

And she realizes: **These aren't separate problems. They're all symptoms of the same underlying failure.**

The compulsion she feels scrolling her phone at 3 AM—that's the same force driving climate breakdown, wealth concentration, democratic erosion, and meaning collapse. Not metaphorically the same. Actually the same. A single systemic pattern expressing at different scales.

But what is that pattern?

What's the common thread connecting personal burnout to civilizational collapse?

* * *

The Human Integration Problem

To understand what's breaking, we need to understand how humans actually work.

Not as simplified models (rational actors, blank slates, evolved machines), but as the complex, multi-layered beings we actually are.

This is where Project Janus comes in—a framework for modeling humans as integrated wholes across all dimensions of experience simultaneously.

The Six Domains of Human Experience

Human beings operate across six interdependent domains:

1. Biological Domain

- Physical body, nervous system, brain
- Energy, sleep, health, physiological states
- Stress response, immune function, hormonal regulation
- The substrate that enables everything else

2. Cognitive Domain

- Thinking, reasoning, memory, attention
- Beliefs, mental models, knowledge structures
- Problem-solving, planning, imagination
- **Reality testing - discerning truth from noise**
- The software running on biological hardware

It's not just about focus or intelligence. **It's about the capacity to discern truth from noise, signal from manipulation, reality from construction.** When the cognitive domain fragments, we lose shared reality. We lose the ability to agree on the problem, let alone the solution. This is why epistemic collapse is so dangerous—without shared cognitive infrastructure, coordination becomes impossible.

3. Emotional Domain

- Feelings, moods, affective states
- Emotional intelligence and regulation
- Motivation, desire, aversion
- The valence system that guides behavior

4. Behavioral Domain

- Actions, habits, patterns of behavior
- Skills, competencies, physical expressions
- What we actually do in the world
- The interface between internal and external

5. Social Domain

- Relationships, communities, cultures
- Identity, roles, status, belonging
- Cooperation, conflict, coordination
- The web of connection that makes us human

6. Existential/Spiritual Domain

- Meaning, purpose, values
- Life narrative, identity stories
- Transcendence, connection to larger wholes
- What makes life worth living

These aren't separate systems that happen to coexist. They're interdependent dimensions of a unified whole.

What happens in one domain affects all others. Biology influences cognition (try thinking clearly when exhausted). Cognition shapes emotion (interpretations create feelings). Emotions drive behavior (anger prompts action). Behavior affects social standing (your actions shape relationships). Social dynamics influence existential meaning (belonging gives life purpose). And meaning affects biology (purpose literally extends lifespan).

This is what makes us human: **the capacity for integration across all these dimensions simultaneously.**

* * *

What Integration Actually Means

Integration is the coordination of these six domains toward coherent functioning.

When you're integrated:

- Your **biology** supports your activities (well-rested, healthy, energized)
- Your **cognition** is clear and focused (able to think, plan, learn)
- Your **emotions** provide guidance (feelings inform without overwhelming)
- Your **behavior** aligns with values (actions match intentions)
- Your **social connections** are nourishing (relationships provide support)
- Your **existence** feels meaningful (life has purpose and direction)

And crucially: The domains work together synergistically, each supporting the others.

When you're integrated, you can:

- Think clearly because your body is healthy and emotions are regulated
- Rest deeply because you're not anxious about social status or existen-

tial meaning
- Act decisively because cognition, emotion, and values align
- Connect authentically because you're not performing or hiding
- Find meaning because all aspects of your life point in coherent directions

This is what human flourishing actually looks like: not perfection in any single domain, but coordination across all of them.

* * *

The Integration Threshold

But here's the crucial insight: **Integration requires a minimum baseline in each domain.**

Think of it like a chemical reaction that only happens above a certain temperature. Below the threshold, nothing. Above it, transformation.

For human integration, the thresholds look like this:

Biological Threshold

- Adequate sleep (not chronically exhausted)
- Sufficient nutrition (not constantly hungry or malnourished)
- Basic health (not in constant pain or illness)
- Physical safety (not in immediate danger)

Cognitive Threshold

- Attention capacity (can focus without constant distraction)
- Time to think (not always in reactive mode)
- Access to information (can learn and understand)
- Mental models (frameworks for making sense)

Emotional Threshold

- Emotional safety (can feel without constant threat)
- Regulation capacity (not overwhelmed by feelings)
- Emotional vocabulary (can name what you feel)
- Social support (not completely isolated)

Behavioral Threshold

- Agency (some control over your actions)
- Skill development (can learn and improve)
- Time and space (not every moment scheduled)
- Resources (basic means to act)

Social Threshold

- Basic belonging (not totally excluded)
- Recognition (someone sees you)
- Reciprocity (relationships aren't all extraction)
- Community infrastructure (places and practices of connection)

Existential Threshold

- Narrative coherence (life makes some sense)
- Value clarity (know what matters to you)
- Future possibility (some hope for tomorrow)
- Contribution (can give something meaningful)

Below these thresholds in multiple domains simultaneously, integration becomes structurally impossible.

You can't think clearly when chronically exhausted (biological below threshold).

You can't rest when economically precarious (existential anxiety).

You can't connect authentically when performing for status (social domain compromised).

You can't act on values when behavior is fully captured by survival demands.

This is the key insight: It's not that people lack willpower or discipline or gratitude. It's that the system has pushed them below the integration threshold across multiple domains simultaneously.

But here's something crucial: **Above the threshold, systems become autopoietic—self-healing.**

The same compounding dynamics that create cascading failure work in reverse above the threshold:

- Better sleep → clearer thinking → better decisions → reduced stress → better sleep
- Economic security → cognitive freedom → skill development → more opportunities → more security
- Authentic connection → emotional support → resilience → capacity to connect → deeper relationships

The goal isn't to optimize every domain to perfection. The goal is to push the system above threshold so it can heal itself.

This is why the solutions in Part III focus on establishing baseline thresholds, not achieving excellence. Once domains reach minimum viable integration, regenerative momentum takes over.

* * *

How Orange Systematically Prevents Integration

Now we can see what Orange actually does to humans:

Biological Extraction

- Chronic sleep deprivation normalized ("sleep when you're dead")
- Stress response constantly activated (economic precarity, status anxiety)
- Physical health sacrificed for productivity (sitting, screens, processed food)
- No buffer for recovery (just-in-time scheduling, no slack)

Result: Biological domain below threshold. Body can't support other functions.

Cognitive Capture

- Attention systematically extracted (algorithmic engagement)
- No time for deep thinking (constant interruption)
- Information overload preventing synthesis
- Decision fatigue from endless optimization

Result: Cognitive domain overwhelmed. Can't think clearly or plan effectively.

Emotional Dysregulation

- Constant performance anxiety (must prove worth continuously)
- Emotional labor demanded (service with a smile, toxic positivity)
- Feelings commodified (wellness as product, therapy as optimization)
- No permission for "unproductive" emotions (grief, contemplation, rest)

Result: Emotional domain compromised. Feelings become enemies, not guides.

Behavioral Compulsion

- Every moment must be justified through productivity
- Habits optimized for efficiency over meaning
- Spontaneity eliminated by scheduling
- Agency constrained by economic necessity

Result: Behavioral domain captured. Actions serve system, not person.

Social Atomization

- Communities dissolved into networks (weak ties replacing strong bonds)
- Relationships transactionalized (what can you do for me?)
- Competition replacing cooperation (everyone's a rival)
- Loneliness epidemic despite digital "connection"

Result: Social domain collapsed. Isolated individuals, no collective support.

Existential Void

- Meaning reduced to achievement and consumption
- Purpose instrumentalized (meaningful work must also pay)
- Values subordinated to market logic
- No time or space for transcendence

Result: Existential domain starved. Life feels hollow despite "success."

Orange doesn't just extract from one domain. It systematically pushes all six below integration threshold simultaneously.

This isn't a bug. It's a feature. **Integrated humans have the one thing extraction cannot tolerate: the capacity to say "enough."**

They have clearer boundaries, stronger values, better bullshit detectors, and alternative sources of meaning beyond consumption and status. They can rest without anxiety. They can think without constant distraction. They can act on principles rather than just react to incentives.

Orange needs humans below integration threshold to maintain extraction.

* * *

The Cascading Failure Pattern

Here's how it works in Sarah's life (and probably yours):

Morning: Wake exhausted (biological) → scroll phone compulsively (behavioral) → feel anxious about work (emotional) → can't think clearly (cognitive) → transactional interaction with partner (social) → sense of meaninglessness (existential)

Each domain failure makes others worse:

- Exhaustion → poor emotion regulation → compulsive behavior → more exhaustion
- Economic anxiety → attention capture → reduced cognitive capacity → worse economic decisions
- Social isolation → meaning crisis → behavioral dysfunction → more isolation

But the most dangerous disintegration happens when the Biological Domain (survival) becomes fully dependent on the Behavioral Domain (market labor).

If "doing" stops, "being" dies. If you can't perform, you can't eat. If you lose your job, you lose your health insurance. If you rest, you fall behind economically.

This bio-behavioral short-circuit keeps the nervous system in permanent sympathetic arousal, making integration impossible.

You cannot rest when rest threatens survival. You cannot think clearly when every moment not producing threatens your existence. You cannot develop authentic relationships when all behavior must be optimized for economic value.

This isn't a psychological problem. It's a structural trap where the most basic domain (biological survival) is held hostage by market performance.

This is what integration failure looks like: cascading dysfunction where each domain's collapse pulls others down.

And here's the insidious part: **each domain has its own coping mechanisms that make other domains worse.**

- Cognitive coping: optimize everything (makes behavior rigid, emotions suppressed)
- Emotional coping: numb out (makes cognition fuzzy, behavior compulsive)
- Behavioral coping: work harder (exhausts biology, fragments attention)
- Social coping: perform continuously (depletes energy, prevents authenticity)
- Existential coping: distraction (captures attention, prevents reflection)

You can't solve integration failure from within any single domain.

This is why individual solutions fail. You can't meditate your way out of economic precarity. You can't set boundaries when your survival depends on availability. You can't find meaning when every moment is captured by necessity.

The system itself must change.

* * *

From Personal to Civilizational Integration Failure

Now here's the crucial leap: **What happens to individuals is happening to civilization.**

Remember the six domains? They don't just apply to individuals. They apply to collectives, institutions, and civilizations.

Civilizational Biological Domain

The physical substrate: energy systems, infrastructure, ecosystems, material flows.

Status: Ecological systems collapsing, resource extraction unsustainable, climate destabilizing. The physical substrate of civilization is degrading.

Civilizational Cognitive Domain

Collective sensemaking: science, media, education, information systems.

Status: Epistemic collapse. Can't agree on reality, information overwhelm, expertise delegitimized. Can't think collectively.

Civilizational Emotional Domain

Collective affect: cultural mood, social emotions, shared feelings.

Status: Anxiety, rage, despair spreading. Emotional contagion of negative affect. Collective nervous system dysregulated.

Civilizational Behavioral Domain

Collective action: institutions, policies, coordinated responses.

Status: Institutional paralysis, policy incoherence, inability to coordinate. Can't act at required scale or speed.

Civilizational Social Domain

Social fabric: trust, solidarity, cooperation, social capital.

Status: Polarization intensifying, tribalism increasing, trust eroding. Social fabric tearing.

Civilizational Existential Domain

Collective meaning: shared values, purpose, narrative, vision of future.

Status: Meaning crisis, purpose vacuum, narrative collapse. No coherent story about who we are or where we're going.

Civilization is experiencing integration failure at scale.

Just like Sarah can't integrate because multiple domains are below threshold, civilization can't integrate because our collective capacity for coordination has collapsed across all dimensions.

* * *

The Integration Debt We're Carrying

Think of integration like debt. You can run a deficit temporarily—skip sleep, ignore emotions, delay relationships, postpone meaning-making.

But integration deficit compounds:

- Miss one night's sleep → tired
- Miss many nights → chronically exhausted → health problems → emotional dysregulation → cognitive impairment → behavioral dysfunction

We're running a civilizational deficit in the currency that actually matters: human coherence.

Personally:

- Years of exhaustion (biological debt)
- Attention captured for decades (cognitive debt)
- Emotions suppressed lifelong (emotional debt)
- Behaviors compulsive (behavioral debt)
- Relationships transactional (social debt)
- Meaning deferred indefinitely (existential debt)

Civilizationally:

- Ecological overshoot (biological debt)
- Truth decay (cognitive debt)
- Collective trauma (emotional debt)
- Institutional failure (behavioral debt)
- Social fabric torn (social debt)
- Purpose vacuum (existential debt)

And like financial debt, integration debt eventually demands payment.

The body breaks down. The mind fractures. Emotions erupt. Behaviors become addictive. Relationships collapse. Meaning disappears.

Ecosystems die. Reality becomes contestable. Societies polarize. Institutions fail. Communities dissolve. Civilizations collapse.

We're approaching the moment where the integration debt comes due.

* * *

Why Yellow Thinking Is Actually Required

Now we can see why neither Orange nor Green can solve this:

Orange only sees optimization within domains. It can make cognition more efficient, behavior more productive, social connections more networked. But it can't see the integration requirement across domains.

It doesn't value what can't be measured. It sacrifices integration for extraction.

Green sees the interconnection and values integration. But it can't build systems that deliver it at scale. It processes endlessly, holds space beautifully, and remains paralyzed while integration debt compounds.

Yellow is required because the problem is fundamentally about **cross-domain coordination at scale under time pressure with incomplete information.**

This is a systems integration challenge. It requires:

- **Systems thinking** (seeing relationships between domains)
- **Developmental awareness** (understanding integration requirements)
- **Practical construction** (building what actually works)
- **Scaling capacity** (from personal to civilizational)
- **Temporal wisdom** (acting fast enough to matter)

Yellow isn't morally superior—it's mathematically necessary. The integration problem requires cross-domain coordination that neither Orange's optimization nor Green's critique can provide.

We need Yellow not as ideal but as necessity.

* * *

The Integration Equation

Let me make this precise:

Human Flourishing = f(Integration across all six domains above threshold)

Where integration requires: 1. Each domain functioning above minimum threshold 2. Coordination between domains (not just parallel function) 3. Feedback loops enabling adaptation 4. Sufficient slack/buffer for recovery 5. Temporal horizons appropriate to domain (biological:

days, existential: lifetime)

Modern civilization systematically violates every requirement.

It pushes domains below threshold, fragments coordination, eliminates buffers, collapses temporal horizons, and prevents recovery.

This isn't sustainable. It's not even coherent.

A system that requires integrated humans while preventing integration is eating its own foundation.

$$* * *$$

Sarah's Realization

It's 4 AM now. Sarah is still awake, but something has shifted.

She's not just exhausted anymore. She understands why.

The problem isn't her lack of discipline. It's not insufficient gratitude. It's not personal failure.

The system is designed to prevent the very integration that humans require to function.

We've built a civilization that systematically starves us of what makes life worth living while feeding us substitutes that can never satisfy. Achievement instead of meaning. Optimization instead of rest. Networks instead of community. Stimulation instead of presence.

And she realizes: **This is true at every scale.**

Her personal struggle is civilization's struggle. The integration failure in her life is the integration failure in the world. The inability to rest, think, feel, act, connect, and find meaning coherently—that's not individual pathology. That's systemic design.

She can't solve it alone. No individual can.

But maybe, just maybe, enough people understanding this pattern could build something different.

Systems that enable integration instead of preventing it.

Infrastructure that supports coordination instead of fragmentation.

Civilization that serves flourishing instead of extraction.

Not someday. Not after we fix everything else. Now. As the foundation for everything else.

Because without integration, nothing else works.

Not personally. Not collectively. Not for long.

* * *

What Integration Would Actually Look Like

Before we move to Part II (Yellow principles) and Part III (specific solutions), let's paint a picture of what integrated civilization would actually enable:

Personally:

- Able to rest without anxiety (economic security)
- Able to think without constant distraction (attention sovereignty)
- Able to feel without overwhelming or numbing (emotional safety)
- Able to act on values (agency and resources)
- Able to connect authentically (social infrastructure)
- Able to live meaningfully (purpose beyond productivity)

Collectively:

- Ecosystems regenerating (biological sustainability)
- Truth discernible (epistemic infrastructure)
- Emotions processed collectively (cultural containers for feeling)
- Institutions effective (coordination capacity)
- Communities thriving (social capital rebuilt)
- Purpose shared (collective vision and values)

This isn't utopia. It's basic functionality.

It's not asking for perfection—just for the minimum conditions that make integration possible.

And it's achievable. Not easy. Not guaranteed. But possible.

If we build for it.

* * *

The Choice Before Us

Part I has shown us:

- **Chapter 1**: Personal experience of integration failure (Sarah's exhaustion)
- **Chapter 2**: How Orange systematically prevents integration
- **Chapter 3**: Why Green can't build alternative systems
- **Chapter 4**: Why time pressure is real (converging crises)
- **Chapter 5**: What integration failure actually means (this chapter)

Now we face a choice:

Continue the trajectory: Orange extraction intensifying, Green critique paralyzed, integration debt compounding, cascading failure approaching.

Or build different: Systems that enable integration, infrastructure that supports coordination, civilization worthy of the human spirit.

Part II will explore the principles of Yellow thinking—how to actually think about and design for integration at scale.

Part III will detail specific interventions—concrete, implementable systems that restore integration across domains.

Part IV will address implementation—how we actually make this happen in the time we have.

But first, we had to understand what we're building toward.

Not optimization. Not critique. Integration.

The capacity to function as whole humans, in whole communities, in a whole civilization.

That's what the rest of this book is about.

Let's build it.

* * *

Postcard from 2040: The Quiet Roar

It wasn't until the third day in the city that I realized what was missing: the hum. For my entire life, urban silence had been a myth—there was always the white noise of traffic, the aggressive thrum of ventilation, the digital chirping of a thousand devices demanding attention. But here, in the rewilded center, the decibel level of human desperation had dropped so low that the environment had reclaimed the acoustic space.

I sat on a bench in the financial district. I could hear the wind moving through the birch trees they planted where the third lane used to be. I could hear a conversation three benches away, unhurried and laughing. I could hear my own breath. It was deafening. We traveled thousands of miles just to listen to a city that had finally shut up and become beautiful.

PART II: PRINCIPLES OF YELLOW THINKING

***

Chapter 6: From Either/Or to Both/And

Marcus is a city planner in Portland who's been working on the same problem for three years: how to make downtown more walkable without destroying businesses that depend on car traffic.

Every meeting follows the same pattern:

The urbanist faction presents data showing walkable cities are more economically vibrant, environmentally sustainable, and socially connected. "We need to ban cars from downtown."

The business coalition counters with studies showing parking access drives retail revenue, that suburban customers won't come without easy driving, that delivery trucks need access. "We can't sacrifice business for ideology."

The debate becomes increasingly heated. Progressives call business owners greedy and shortsighted. Business owners call urbanists elitist and out of touch. City council members try to find "compromise"—half-measures that satisfy no one and solve nothing.

Marcus is exhausted. Not because the problem is technically difficult—it's not. But because both sides are trapped in Either/Or thinking that prevents seeing the actual solution.

Three years. Hundreds of hours in meetings. Zero progress.

Then something shifts.

* * *

The Trap of Binary Thinking

Orange consciousness excels at making distinctions, creating categories, and choosing between options. This is one of its gifts—the ability to analyze, compare, and optimize for clear objectives.

But Orange has a deep limitation: **it thinks in binaries.**

Individual OR collective

Freedom OR security

Efficiency OR resilience

Growth OR sustainability

Achievement OR rest

Competition OR cooperation

Structure OR flexibility

Rational OR emotional

This isn't a minor philosophical preference. It's a fundamental cognitive structure that shapes how Orange sees and solves problems.

When faced with tension between two goods, Orange must choose one and minimize the other. When optimization for one value conflicts with another, Orange picks a winner. When trade-offs appear, Orange frames them as mutually exclusive.

The problem: Many of the most important challenges we face are actually Both/And problems disguised as Either/Or choices.

* * *

Why Either/Or Fails for Complex Systems

Consider Marcus's walkability problem through Either/Or thinking:

Framing A: "Cars OR walkability"

- Choose cars → pedestrians suffer, environment degrades, eventually businesses decline anyway

- Choose walkability → businesses hurt initially, potentially never recover
- Compromise → neither side happy, problem unsolved

This framing makes the problem unsolvable because it assumes the values conflict fundamentally.

But what if they don't?

What if walkable streets actually *increase* business revenue—but only when designed correctly?

What if the real question isn't "cars or walkability" but "how do we enable both pedestrian vibrancy AND business access through smart design"?

This isn't compromise. It's transcendence. And it requires thinking that Orange can't do.

The Problems Either/Or Creates

1. False Dichotomies

Many apparent conflicts aren't real:

- Individual flourishing requires collective support (not OR collective)
- Security enables freedom (not OR freedom)
- Efficiency depends on resilience (not OR resilience)
- Sustainable practices drive growth (not OR growth)

By forcing choice between interdependent values, Either/Or thinking creates unnecessary conflict.

2. Premature Closure

When you must choose between A and B, you stop looking for C—the solution that integrates both.

Marcus's meetings never explored: protected bike lanes that increase foot traffic while maintaining delivery access, parking structures at periphery with excellent pedestrian connections, timed restrictions that allow both car access and pedestrian zones.

Either/Or thinking closes exploration prematurely.

3. Tribal Polarization

When issues become Either/Or, people must pick sides. Picking sides creates identities. Identities create tribes. Tribes create enemies.

Soon you're not discussing solutions—you're defending team membership. The problem becomes secondary to tribal loyalty.

4. Optimization Traps

When you optimize for A at expense of B, you eventually undermine A itself.

Optimize efficiency by eliminating all slack → system becomes brittle, eventually fails catastrophically → efficiency collapses.

Optimize individual freedom by dissolving collective obligations → social fabric tears → individuals become isolated and anxious → freedom feels empty.

The values you suppress eventually destabilize the values you're optimizing.

5. Missing Leverage Points

The most powerful solutions often come from recognizing that apparent opposites are actually complementary.

Competition AND cooperation (markets work when embedded in social norms of fair play).

Structure AND flexibility (clear frameworks enable creative improvisation).

Rational analysis AND emotional wisdom (feelings provide crucial information logic misses).

Either/Or thinking makes these leverage points invisible.

* * *

The Both/And Shift: Transcend and Include

Yellow thinking doesn't reject Orange's analytical capacity. It transcends and includes it.

Transcend: Move to higher-order thinking that can hold apparent contradictions

Include: Keep Orange's gifts while adding new capabilities

This is the key move: **Both/And isn't mushy middle ground. It's higher-order integration.**

What Both/And Actually Means

Not: Compromise (each side gives up half – both get 50%)

Not: Indecision (can't choose so we'll do both badly)

Not: Naive optimism (everything works out!)

Yes: Integration (both sides get 100% of their underlying value by changing the vehicle of delivery)

Yes: Temporal sequencing (sometimes A, sometimes B, depending on context)

Yes: Nested hierarchy (one value at one scale, another at different scale)

Yes: Paradox tolerance (holding contradictions without premature resolution)

This is crucial to understand: Yellow does not split the difference. It transcends the plane of the conflict.

Compromise is meeting in the middle on the same plane. Both sides lose 50%. "Cars allowed on weekends only" satisfies neither pedestrians nor businesses fully.

Integration is moving to a higher plane where both sides get 100% of what they actually need—by reframing what that need is and how to deliver it. "Pedestrian streets with smart logistics" gives businesses customer access AND gives residents walkability.

The difference isn't semantic—it's structural. One operates within the existing frame. The other transcends it.

Let's be specific about how this works:

Strategy 1: Temporal Sequencing

Some apparent conflicts are really about *when*, not *whether*.

But first, a crucial distinction: **In Yellow thinking, we distinguish between problems (which have solutions) and polarities (which require ongoing management).**

Problems have solutions. A broken leg can be fixed. A software bug can be debugged. Once solved, they stay solved.

Polarities are ongoing tensions that can never be permanently resolved—only managed. You don't solve the tension between inhaling and exhaling; you breathe rhythmically. You don't solve the tension between centralization and autonomy; you balance them contextually.

Either/Or thinking tries to "solve" polarities—and creates catastrophe. "We'll only inhale!" leads to death. "We'll be completely centralized!" leads to rigidity and death. "We'll have total autonomy!" leads to chaos and death.

Yellow recognizes which challenges are problems (to solve) and which are polarities (to manage).

Marcus's walkability challenge wasn't a problem (choose cars or pedestrians). It was a polarity (manage access and vibrancy). Once reframed as polarity, temporal sequencing becomes obvious:

Growth AND sustainability: Grow to establish viability, then shift to regenerative mode. Or: sustainable practices enable long-term growth.

Structure AND flexibility: Establish clear structure, then enable flexibility within it. Or: flexible response within structured frameworks.

Achievement AND rest: Intense focused work, then deep recovery. Not constant grinding, not permanent vacation, but rhythmic alternation.

The apparent conflict often resolves into elegant sequencing when we stop trying to serve all values simultaneously.

Strategy 2: Nested Hierarchy

Some values apply at one scale, different values at another scale.

Individual autonomy AND collective coordination: Individuals freely choose within frameworks collectively established. Personal freedom at micro level, social coordination at macro level.

Competition AND cooperation: Individuals/firms compete within games whose rules are cooperatively maintained. Competition within cooperation.

Efficiency AND resilience: Optimize efficiency at operational level, maintain redundancy at systems level.

The apparent conflict exists only when you apply both values at the same scale.

Strategy 3: Integrated Design

Sometimes the solution is entirely new design that serves both values simultaneously.

Marcus's walkability problem:

- NOT: cars OR pedestrians
- YES: Redesign streets so pedestrian vibrancy increases business revenue while maintaining necessary access through smart logistics

This isn't compromise—it's creative integration through design innovation.

Example: Copenhagen's approach

- Pedestrian streets (walkability)
- Loading zones with specific hours (business access)
- Parking at edges with excellent pedestrian connections (car access)
- Result: More foot traffic, higher business revenue, better environment

Both values served. Not through compromise but through integrated design.

Strategy 4: Paradox Tolerance

Sometimes the answer is: **"Yes, both. The tension is productive."**

Freedom AND responsibility: You're radically free to choose AND fully responsible for consequences. The tension between them creates ethical maturity.

Confidence AND humility: Strong convictions about what matters AND recognition that you might be wrong. The paradox prevents both arrogance and paralysis.

Planning AND emergence: Clear strategic direction AND openness to unexpected opportunities. The interplay creates adaptive capacity.

Yellow doesn't resolve these tensions—it harnesses their productive friction.

* * *

Real-World Both/And Examples

Let's look at actual systems that transcended Either/Or traps:

Example 1: Buurtzorg (Netherlands Healthcare)

Either/Or trap: Efficiency OR quality care

Traditional healthcare: Optimize efficiency (15-minute visits, standardized protocols, nurse hierarchy) → Quality suffers, nurses burn out, costs actually increase from poor outcomes.

Buurtzorg's Both/And: Self-organizing nurse teams with full autonomy

- Teams of 10-12 nurses serve neighborhoods
- No managers, no standardized protocols
- Nurses make all decisions about patient care
- Result: Better patient outcomes (quality) AND 40% lower costs (efficiency)

How: Trust professional judgment (quality) enables eliminating bureaucracy (efficiency). The values weren't opposed—bureaucracy was the problem.

Example 2: Gore-Tex (Materials Company)

Either/Or trap: Innovation OR organizational structure
Traditional companies: Hierarchical structure for coordination → Stifles innovation. Flat structure for innovation → Can't scale or coordinate.
Gore's Both/And: Lattice organization

- No job titles, no hierarchy
- Teams form around projects organically
- "Leaders" emerge based on followership
- Result: Continuous innovation AND successful $3B company

How: Structure through principles and culture, not hierarchy. Clear values and decision-making protocols enable flat organization at scale.

Example 3: Mondragon (Spanish Cooperative)

Either/Or trap: Worker ownership OR competitive efficiency
Traditional view: Worker co-ops can't compete with profit-maximizing firms. Profit-maximizing firms exploit workers.
Mondragon's Both/And: Democratic ownership with market discipline

- Workers own and govern the company

- Compete in real markets (not protected)
- Result: 80,000+ worker-owners, thriving businesses, Spain's 7th largest company

How: Democratic governance at firm level, market competition at product level. Worker wellbeing AND economic success through integrated structure.

Example 4: Patagonia (Outdoor Company)

Either/Or trap: Environmental values OR business success

Traditional view: Maximize profit by minimizing costs (including environmental). Or: Prioritize environment at expense of profitability.

Patagonia's Both/And: Environmental responsibility as business model

- "Don't buy this jacket" (anti-consumerism ad)
- Repair services to extend product life
- 1% for the planet commitment
- Result: Revenue growth, customer loyalty, industry influence

How: Environmental integrity *attracts* customers who value it. Purpose-driven business model aligns values and profit.

Example 5: Your Life (Personal Application)

Either/Or trap: Be successful OR have a life

Many professionals face this binary: career success requires 60-hour weeks, constant availability, prioritizing work over everything. Having a "life" means accepting career mediocrity.

Both/And reframe: "How do I design a career that serves both achievement AND wellbeing?"

The answers that emerge:

- **Rhythmic work**: Intense focused periods alternating with deep rest (not constant grind)
- **Clear boundaries**: Truly off when off, fully on when on (not half-present always)
- **Purpose alignment**: Work that matters personally (not just economic necessity)
- **Skill leverage**: Build capabilities that create value without constant time input
- **Relationship integration**: Career that enhances rather than destroys relationships

This transforms the problem from unsolvable dilemma to design challenge. You're not choosing between success and life—you're architecting both.

* * *

Marcus's Breakthrough

After three years of Either/Or thinking, Marcus tries a different approach.

He stops framing it as "cars OR walkability."

He asks: **"How do we design streets that increase business revenue through pedestrian vibrancy while maintaining necessary vehicle access?"**

This reframe changes everything.

Suddenly solutions appear:

- Time-restricted zones (pedestrian mornings/evenings, deliveries at specific hours)
- Loading zone network (vehicles access businesses without through-traffic)
- Parking structures at edges with amazing pedestrian streets connect-

ing them
- Micro-mobility options (bikes, scooters) for last-mile convenience
- Gradual phase-in (test, learn, adjust rather than big bang change)

The business owners realize: More foot traffic could mean more customers. If parking is convenient but not right in front, suburban customers will still come—and might stay longer in pleasant pedestrian environment.

The urbanists realize: Not all vehicles are the problem. Through-traffic is different from deliveries and parking access. Smart design can distinguish between them.

Six months later: First pilot zone showing increased revenue, better environment, happier residents. Both sides claiming victory—correctly.

The breakthrough wasn't compromise. It was transcending the false choice through integrated design.

This is the difference between splitting the difference and finding the third way that makes the old debate irrelevant.

* * *

How to Develop Both/And Thinking

This isn't innate ability. It's learnable skill. Here's how:

Practice 1: Interrogate Your Either/Ors

When you find yourself thinking "we must choose between A and B," pause.

Ask:

- Is this really a conflict, or have I assumed one?
- What would it look like to serve both values?
- Am I confusing what I can easily measure with what actually matters?

- Who benefits from framing this as Either/Or?

Often you'll discover the conflict was constructed, not inherent.

Practice 2: Look for "And"

Whenever someone says "we can't have both," that's a signal to dig deeper.

The thought pattern shifts from:

- "It's A or B" → "How might we achieve both A and B?"
- "Trade-offs are inevitable" → "What design eliminates this trade-off?"
- "We must prioritize" → "Can we sequence or nest these values?"

Practice 3: Study Systems That Work

Look for real-world examples of Both/And solutions. How did Buurtzorg achieve quality and efficiency? How does Gore maintain innovation and coordination? How does Mondragon balance democracy and competitiveness?

The patterns emerge: integrated design, appropriate scale, clear principles, emergent structure.

Practice 4: Embrace Paradox

Some tensions are productive and shouldn't be resolved:

- Confidence AND doubt
- Planning AND improvisation
- Individual AND collective
- Structure AND freedom

Learn to hold these without premature closure. The creative friction generates insight.

Practice 5: Think Developmentally

Values that conflict at one stage integrate at another.

Orange needs hierarchy for coordination. Green flattens hierarchy for inclusion. Yellow creates *legitimate* hierarchy (based on competence and context) that serves inclusive values.

The conflict exists between stages, not within Yellow thinking.

* * *

Common Pitfalls in Both/And Thinking

Pitfall 1: Mushy Middle Syndrome
Both/And doesn't mean being wishy-washy or refusing to decide. Sometimes you must choose. Yellow knows when Both/And applies and when prioritization is needed.

Pitfall 2: False Equivalence
Not all values are equal. Both/And doesn't mean treating human rights and property rights as equivalent. Some values are foundational, others derivative.

Pitfall 3: Premature Integration
Sometimes conflict is real and important. Rushing to "Both/And" can suppress legitimate disagreement. Yellow honors necessary conflict while looking for higher integration.

Pitfall 4: Complexity Inflation
"It's complicated" can become excuse for inaction. Both/And should enable clearer action, not paralyze through over-complexity.

Pitfall 5: Missing Power Dynamics
Both/And can obscure real power conflicts. "Workers AND owners both

benefit" may be true in principle but hide exploitation in practice. Yellow sees both values AND power structures.

Pitfall 6: Spiritual Bypassing

Using Both/And to avoid necessary conflict or difficult choices. Some tensions require working through, not transcending. Some situations demand taking sides. "Both perspectives are valid" can become excuse for moral cowardice. Yellow knows when integration serves and when it evades.

* * *

Why This Matters for Integration

Remember Part I's diagnosis: humans need integration across all six domains above threshold.

Both/And thinking is essential because:

Either/Or thinking systematically prevents integration by forcing us to choose which domains to sacrifice.

Orange optimization meant: Choose productivity (sacrifice rest). Choose achievement (sacrifice relationships). Choose efficiency (sacrifice resilience). Choose cognition (suppress emotion).

Both/And thinking enables integration by designing for all domains simultaneously.

The domains themselves are Both/And:

- Biological health AND cognitive clarity (not either/or)
- Emotional wisdom AND rational analysis (not either/or)
- Individual agency AND social belonging (not either/or)
- Achievement AND rest (not either/or)
- Material security AND existential meaning (not either/or)

Orange created false conflicts by optimizing single domains at others' expense.

Green tried to reverse priorities but stayed in Either/Or frame (just flip which side wins).

Yellow integrates by recognizing the domains are interdependent and designing for all of them.

This is why the solutions in Part III require Both/And thinking:

- Economic security AND personal responsibility (AUBI)
- Attention sovereignty AND information access (Synoptic Protocol)
- Structure AND emergence (Meta-Governance)
- Individual AND collective (all interventions)

You cannot build integrated systems with Either/Or thinking. Integration requires transcending false dichotomies while honoring real values in tension.

* * *

From Principles to Practice

Marcus's walkability solution worked because he stopped asking "who wins?" and started asking "how do we serve all legitimate needs through better design?"

This is the shift Yellow thinking enables:

- From win–lose to win–win–win
- From optimization to integration
- From taking sides to transcending positions
- From defending values to designing for them

The next chapter explores the second Yellow principle: understanding that we're not optimizing systems but integrating them. The difference is profound.

But first, sit with this:

What Either/Or thinking dominates your life?

What would change if you asked "How do I serve both values?" instead of "Which do I choose?"

Often the breakthrough isn't finding the right answer to the old question. It's asking a better question entirely.

And here's the ultimate Either/Or that we'll dismantle in Part IV:

Do you feel you have to choose between being **Good** (ethical, caring, values-driven) OR being **Effective** (powerful, wealthy, influential)?

Between having clean hands OR getting things done?

Between moral purity OR real-world impact?

That is the deepest Either/Or trap of all—and the one that prevents those with resources from using them for transformation. We'll address this directly when we explore the Alchemist's Dilemma.

For now, know that this too is a false binary. And transcending it is essential for the work ahead.

Chapter 7: Integration, Not Optimization

A Note on the Title

You might notice something ironic: this chapter is called "Integration, Not Optimization"—which sounds suspiciously like Either/Or thinking right after we spent a chapter explaining Both/And.

Good catch.

Here's the nuance: **Yellow doesn't abandon optimization. It subordinates optimization to integration.**

This isn't "optimization OR integration." It's "optimization in service of integration, not instead of it."

The distinction matters enormously. Orange optimizes *first* and treats integration as optional luxury. Yellow integrates *first* and uses optimization as a tool within that frame.

Think of it like this: You don't choose between having a foundation OR having walls. You build the foundation first, then construct walls on top of it. Integration is the foundation. Optimization is one of many tools for building on that foundation.

So when we say "Integration, Not Optimization," we mean: "Stop optimizing subsystems at the expense of whole-system integration. Start with integration, then optimize within that constraint."

Let's explore what this actually means.

* * *

The Optimization Trap Revisited

Dr. Chen runs the emergency department at a major urban hospital. She's brilliant at her job—which is why the administration keeps giving her "optimization" projects.

Year 1: "Reduce average patient wait time"

- Success! Wait time drops 30%
- Achieved by: Faster triage, streamlined paperwork, pressure on staff to move faster

Year 2: "Increase patient throughput"

- Success! 20% more patients processed
- Achieved by: Shorter appointments, less time per patient, more efficient scheduling

Year 3: "Reduce costs per patient"

- Success! 15% cost reduction
- Achieved by: Fewer tests, shorter observation periods, optimized supply chain

Year 4: The system collapses

- Burnout epidemic among staff (40% turnover)
- Medical errors increasing (faster but less careful)
- Patient satisfaction plummeting (feel rushed, not heard)
- Readmission rates rising (problems missed in rush)
- Best doctors leaving (can't practice medicine properly)

What happened?

Each optimization was locally successful. Wait times did decrease.

Throughput did increase. Costs did drop.

But the system as a whole became dysfunctional. Because **the optimizations were measured in isolation, without tracking their effects on other dimensions of system health.**

This is the optimization trap: **Improving measurable parts while degrading the unmeasurable whole.**

But there's something even more insidious: **Optimization creates fragility.**

When you optimize a system to 99% efficiency, you remove the slack that allows it to absorb shock. The perfectly optimized supply chain (just-in-time, no inventory, minimum suppliers) shatters when one boat gets stuck in the Suez Canal. The perfectly optimized schedule (every minute accounted for) collapses if you catch a cold.

We aren't making the machine better. We're making it brittle.

A perfectly tuned Formula 1 car performs brilliantly on a smooth track but can't handle a pothole. A robust truck handles rough terrain. Optimization chooses the Formula 1 car for every use case—then acts surprised when roads are bumpy.

When we optimize human lives to maximum capacity utilization, we remove the biological buffer required to handle stress, change, or surprise. We create systems that work perfectly under ideal conditions and fail catastrophically under any deviation.

Integration isn't "settling for less efficient." It's designing for antifragility.

* * *

What Optimization Actually Does

Optimization is a powerful tool. It has genuine value. But it has inherent limitations that become dangerous when it's the primary lens.

Limitation 1: Single-Objective Focus

Optimization requires defining *what* to optimize. Once defined, optimization pushes that metric as far as possible.

The problem: Complex systems have multiple objectives that can't all be maximized simultaneously. Optimizing one often degrades others.

Dr. Chen's ER:

- Optimize speed → degrade care quality
- Optimize throughput → degrade staff wellbeing
- Optimize cost → degrade patient outcomes

These aren't bugs in the optimization. They're features. Optimization *must* sacrifice non-optimized values to achieve gains.

Limitation 2: Measurement Dependency

Optimization can only target what's measurable. Everything else becomes invisible.

The problem: The most important aspects of complex systems are often hardest to measure.

In the ER:

- Easy to measure: Wait time, throughput, cost per patient
- Hard to measure: Quality of care, patient trust, staff morale, diagnostic accuracy, system resilience

Goodhart's Law: "When a measure becomes a target, it ceases to be a good measure."

Once you optimize for a metric, people game it. Wait time drops because patients are rushed through, not because care improved.

Limitation 3: Boundary Blindness

Optimization optimizes within defined boundaries. It doesn't see effects that cross boundaries.

The problem: Real systems don't respect our organizational boundaries. And optimization often looks like success only because it dumps costs into domains we aren't measuring.

This is "cost dumping" – optimization's dirty secret.

Dr. Chen optimizes ER metrics. But:

- Faster discharge → more readmissions (different department's problem)
- Staff burnout → recruitment costs (HR's problem)
- Reduced testing → more missed diagnoses → lawsuits (legal's problem)
- Lower patient satisfaction → reputation damage (marketing's problem)

The ER looks efficient by its own metrics while creating costs everywhere else.

At civilizational scale, this becomes catastrophic:

- Optimize profit by dumping cost on ecosystem (**Ecological Debt**)
- Optimize productivity by dumping cost on nervous system (**Biological Debt**)
- Optimize efficiency by dumping cost on future generations (**Temporal Debt**)
- Optimize individual freedom by dumping cost on social fabric (**Social Debt**)

We call this "externalities" and treat it as minor accounting problem. But externalizing costs is how optimization maintains the illusion of success while creating system-wide failure.

Integration forces us to do the accounting. It insists that costs dumped outside measurement boundaries are still real costs—and eventually come due.

Limitation 4: Static Assumptions

Optimization assumes stable conditions. It finds the optimal solution for *current* constraints and parameters.

The problem: Complex systems exist in changing environments. Optimal for today may be catastrophic for tomorrow.

Optimized supply chains (no slack, just-in-time everything) work perfectly until:

- Pandemic disrupts logistics
- Natural disaster hits key supplier
- Geopolitical crisis blocks trade route

The "optimization" was actually brittleness masquerading as efficiency.

Limitation 5: Missing Emergence

Optimization treats systems as collections of parts. Improve the parts, improve the whole.

The problem: Complex systems have emergent properties that arise from relationships between parts, not from parts themselves.

A great team isn't great because each member is optimal individually. It's great because they work well *together*. Optimizing individuals separately can destroy team dynamics.

* * *

What Integration Actually Means

If optimization is "maximize specific metric," what is integration?

Integration is coordinating multiple dimensions of system health so they support each other rather than conflict.

Let's be precise about this.

Integration Asks Different Questions

Optimization asks: "How do we maximize X?"

Integration asks:

- "What does health look like for this whole system?"
- "What dimensions need to be above threshold for the system to function?"
- "How do these dimensions interact?"
- "What designs allow all dimensions to thrive together?"

Integration Has Multiple Success Criteria

Optimization: Single objective function (maximize profit, minimize time, reduce cost)

Integration: Multiple criteria that must be simultaneously satisfied:

- Biological sustainability (not degrading physical substrate)
- Cognitive clarity (people can think and learn)
- Emotional health (not traumatizing participants)
- Behavioral coherence (actions align with values)
- Social flourishing (relationships and community intact)
- Existential meaning (purpose and significance present)

Success isn't maximizing any one dimension—it's bringing all dimensions above threshold where they can mutually reinforce.

Integration Values Relationships Between Parts

Optimization: Sum of parts (improve pieces separately)
  Integration: Configuration of whole (how pieces relate)
  Dr. Chen's ER integrated approach:

- Not "how fast can we see patients" but "what configuration enables good care, staff wellbeing, and reasonable throughput simultaneously?"
- Not "minimum cost per patient" but "what resource level allows sustainable, quality care?"
- Not "maximum throughput" but "what rhythm enables both efficiency and attentiveness?"

The answer might be: Adequate staff, protected time per patient, clear protocols that support judgment rather than replace it, regular team debriefs, reasonable shifts.

This doesn't maximize any single metric. But it creates a configuration where the system can function healthily across all dimensions.

Integration Maintains Slack and Redundancy

Optimization: Eliminate all waste, redundancy, and slack (efficiency!)
  Integration: Strategic slack enables adaptation, redundancy provides resilience, "waste" is investment in system health
  The difference:

- Optimized system: 100% resource utilization, no buffer, maximum efficiency
- Integrated system: 80% typical utilization, buffers for variability, capacity to adapt

The optimized system is more efficient in stable conditions. The integrated system survives disruption.

Integration Thinks in Timeframes

Optimization: Often short-term focused (next quarter, this year)
  Integration: Multiple temporal horizons simultaneously:

- Operational (daily function)
- Developmental (learning and growth)
- Strategic (long-term viability)
- Generational (sustainability across time)

Dr. Chen integrated approach:

- Daily: Good care delivery
- Weekly: Staff learning and development
- Monthly: System improvements based on feedback
- Yearly: Sustainable practices that don't burn out staff
- Generational: Training next generation of caregivers

Optimization for one timeframe often sacrifices others. Integration designs for all of them.

* * *

Real-World Examples of Integration Over Optimization

Example 1: Southwest Airlines (Pre-2020s)

Traditional airline optimization: Maximize revenue per seat

- Different prices for different customers

- Fees for everything
- Pack in more seats
- Cut costs everywhere possible
- Result: Maximum short-term profit, terrible customer experience, complex pricing

Southwest's integration approach: System-wide health

- Simple pricing (integrated with operations)
- Free bags (integrated with faster turnaround)
- Same aircraft type (integrated with maintenance)
- Happy employees (integrated with customer service)
- Result: Profitability, customer loyalty, employee satisfaction, operational simplicity

They didn't optimize revenue per seat. They integrated multiple dimensions to create a healthy system that generated sustained success.

Example 2: Toyota Production System

Traditional manufacturing optimization: Maximize output per hour

- Run machines at maximum speed
- Minimize downtime
- Push inventory to next stage quickly
- Result: High output, high defects, inventory pile-ups, worker exhaustion

Toyota's integration: Continuous flow with built-in quality

- Machines run at sustainable pace
- Workers can stop line for quality issues
- Just-in-time reduces inventory

- Kaizen (continuous improvement) by workers
- Result: High quality, low waste, worker expertise, system resilience

They didn't maximize speed. They integrated quality, efficiency, worker knowledge, and continuous improvement.

Example 3: Buurtzorg (From Chapter 6)

Traditional healthcare optimization: Minimize cost per visit

- Short visits
- Standardized protocols
- Hierarchical management
- Maximum "efficiency"
- Result: Lower quality, higher total costs (from complications), nurse burnout

Buurtzorg's integration: Autonomous teams providing holistic care

- Teams manage their own work
- Nurses spend appropriate time
- Focus on patient wellbeing, not visit metrics
- Result: Better outcomes, 40% lower costs, nurse satisfaction, patient trust

They didn't optimize visit time. They integrated professional autonomy, care quality, and cost-effectiveness.

* * *

Dr. Chen's Redesign

After the Year 4 collapse, Dr. Chen gets permission to try something different.

Instead of asking "How do we optimize X?" she asks:

"What configuration would allow our ER to function healthily across all critical dimensions?"

She identifies the dimensions: 1. **Patient care quality** (medical outcomes, patient experience) 2. **Staff wellbeing** (sustainable work, professional fulfillment) 3. **Operational viability** (reasonable costs, appropriate throughput) 4. **Learning capacity** (system improves over time) 5. **Resilience** (can handle surges and disruptions)

Then she redesigns for integration:

Protected Time: Each patient gets minimum time based on acuity, not arbitrary targets. Some patients need 5 minutes, some need 30. Trust clinical judgment.

Team Pods: Small physician-nurse teams that work together consistently, building coordination and trust. Not random assignment each shift.

Built-in Slack: 20% of schedule left unscheduled for surges, complex cases, and team meetings. Not 100% booked.

Learning Loops: Weekly team debriefs to identify problems and improvements. Monthly department learning sessions. System evolution built in.

Clear Protocols with Judgment: Guidelines that support clinical decision-making rather than replace it. Structure that enables flexibility.

Sustainable Rhythms: No more than X hours per shift, Y patients per physician per shift, adequate breaks built in.

Outcome Tracking: Monitor multiple dimensions—patient outcomes, staff satisfaction, costs, readmissions, errors. No single metric dominates.

Result after 18 months:

- Patient outcomes improved (fewer errors, better diagnosis)

- Staff satisfaction up, turnover down
- Costs roughly same (saved on turnover, readmissions, errors)
- Wait times slightly longer but patient satisfaction much higher
- System can handle surges and disruptions
- Continuous improvement happening

She didn't optimize any single metric. She integrated the system—and everything got better.

* * *

The Integration Design Process

How do you actually do this? Here's a framework:

Step 1: Identify All Critical Dimensions

Don't just ask "what's the goal?" Ask "what dimensions must remain healthy for this system to function sustainably?"

For a business:

- Financial viability
- Product/service quality
- Employee wellbeing
- Customer satisfaction
- Environmental sustainability
- Learning and innovation
- Social contribution

Step 2: Define Thresholds, Not Optima

For each dimension, identify: "What's the minimum level for health?" Not "how high can we go?" but "what's enough?"

Optimization asks "How high can we go?" Integration asks "What's enough?"

This shift from maximization to sufficiency is one of the most radical but necessary transitions for a sustainable civilization.

Optimization is the art of pushing single variables to their limits. Integration is the wisdom of maintaining all variables within their viable ranges.

And here's the key: **Sufficiency isn't a moral judgment—it's a system requirement.**

Using the Project Janus framework from Chapter 5:

- **Sufficient income** = The amount that keeps the Biological domain secure (food, shelter, healthcare, safety buffer)
- **Sufficient rest** = The amount that keeps the Cognitive domain lucid (sleep, recovery, mental space)
- **Sufficient social connection** = The amount that keeps the Social domain healthy (meaningful relationships, community, belonging)
- **Sufficient meaning** = The amount that keeps the Existential domain viable (purpose, values alignment, contribution)

Anything less isn't "frugality" or "minimalism." **It's system failure.**

And anything significantly more in one domain while others remain below threshold doesn't improve integration—it just creates imbalance.

Step 3: Map Interactions

How do the dimensions affect each other?

- Does pursuing X degrade Y?

- Does supporting Y enable Z?
- What positive feedback loops exist?
- What trade-offs are real vs. assumed?

Often you discover "trade-offs" aren't real—they're artifacts of poor design.

Step 4: Design for Synergies

Look for configurations where dimensions mutually support rather than conflict.

Southwest's free bags:

- Helps customers (social dimension)
- Speeds turnaround (operational dimension)
- Reduces complaints (employee dimension)
- Simplifies systems (cognitive dimension)

One choice supporting multiple dimensions.

Step 5: Build in Feedback Loops

How will you know if any dimension is dropping below threshold?
Create monitoring that:

- Tracks all critical dimensions (not just easy-to-measure ones)
- Alerts when thresholds approached
- Enables rapid adjustment
- Facilitates learning and evolution

Step 6: Maintain Adaptive Capacity

Keep slack, redundancy, and diversity that enable responding to the unexpected.

The integrated system is less "efficient" in stable conditions but more robust across conditions.

* * *

When Optimization IS Appropriate

Integration doesn't mean never optimizing. It means knowing when optimization serves integration and when it undermines it.

Optimize within integration constraints:

After Dr. Chen established healthy integration, she could optimize within it:

- "Given our staffing and patient time standards, what's the most efficient scheduling?"
- "Given our quality standards, what protocols reduce unnecessary steps?"
- "Given our learning culture, what's the best way to capture and share improvements?"

Optimize when single-objective problems exist:

Some problems genuinely have one objective without critical trade-offs:

- "Reduce data transfer latency" (in network architecture)
- "Minimize materials waste" (in manufacturing, given other constraints)
- "Reduce prescription errors" (in pharmacy systems)

These are true optimization problems—solve them with optimization.

Optimize when subsystems are well-isolated:

If a subsystem truly doesn't affect others, optimize away:

- Internal algorithms that don't affect user experience
- Backend processes that don't impact frontend
- Component design that doesn't influence system behavior

But be careful—isolation is rarer than we assume.

The key: Integration is the frame. Optimization is the tool. Not the reverse.

* * *

Why This Matters for Civilizational Scale

Everything in Part I's diagnosis and Part III's solutions depends on understanding this distinction.

Orange optimized civilization for:

- Economic output (GDP)
- Technological capability
- Material abundance
- Individual achievement

The result: Integration failure across all six domains.

We optimized economic metrics while degrading:

- Biological health (ecosystems, climate, human health)
- Cognitive clarity (attention extraction, epistemic collapse)
- Emotional wellbeing (anxiety, depression, meaning crisis)
- Behavioral coherence (compulsive consumption, addictive patterns)

- Social fabric (atomization, polarization, trust erosion)
- Existential meaning (purpose vacuum, alienation)

Yellow integration for civilization asks:

"What configuration allows human flourishing across all dimensions simultaneously?"

Not "maximum GDP" but "sufficient material security for all." Not "maximum innovation" but "technological development in service of wellbeing." Not "maximum efficiency" but "resilient systems that can adapt and learn."

The solutions in Part III are integration designs, not optimization schemes:

AUBI: Not "maximize income" but "ensure biological security as foundation for integration"

Synoptic Protocol: Not "maximize information access" but "protect cognitive sovereignty while enabling learning"

Sanctuaries: Not "maximize productivity" but "ensure spaces for integration and recovery"

Meta-Governance: Not "maximum democracy" or "maximum efficiency" but "integrated decision-making that serves multiple values across timeframes"

Each intervention establishes baseline thresholds across domains rather than maximizing single metrics.

Personal Application: Your Productivity

Consider the "productivity optimization" many knowledge workers pursue:

- Maximizing hours worked
- Tasks completed per day
- Emails answered
- Meetings attended

- Projects juggled simultaneously

The optimization approach: Push each metric higher. Sleep less, work faster, multitask more, eliminate "waste" (rest, reflection, relationships).

The integration approach asks: "What configuration allows me to do meaningful work while maintaining health, relationships, and continued learning?"

The answers that emerge:

- **Focused work blocks** (deep work, not constant task-switching)
- **Adequate rest** (recovery enables sustained performance)
- **Relationship time** (connection provides meaning and support)
- **Skill development** (learning creates future capability)
- **Reflection space** (integration of experience into wisdom)

This creates sustainable excellence rather than spectacular burnout.

Integration trades peak performance for sustained performance, maximum output for reliable output, brilliant flashes for steady glow.

* * *

The Both/And of Optimization and Integration

So here's where we complete the loop from Chapter 6:

It's not optimization OR integration.

It's integration as foundation, with optimization as tool.

It's Both/And—with proper sequencing and hierarchy.

First: Design for integration (all dimensions above threshold, mutually supporting). Then: Optimize within those constraints (improve efficiency without breaking integration).

Orange got it backwards: Optimize first, hope integration emerges (it doesn't). **Green avoided the question**: Integration is too complex, so we'll just process it. **Yellow gets the order right**: Integrate first, optimize second, maintain vigilance always.

* * *

Dr. Chen's Reflection

Five years after her redesign, Dr. Chen is asked to present at a healthcare conference.

The other presentations are all about optimization:

- "Reducing average length of stay"
- "Maximizing physician productivity"
- "Cutting costs per patient encounter"

She presents her integrated approach. The data is striking—better outcomes across every dimension.

During Q&A, a hospital administrator asks: "But aren't you just… not optimizing? Isn't that inefficient?"

Dr. Chen smiles.

"We're not optimizing *individual metrics in isolation*. We're optimizing *the whole system for sustained health across all dimensions*. That's actually much harder than conventional optimization—and much more effective."

"The question isn't 'How fast can we go?' It's 'What configuration lets us go at a sustainable pace, maintain quality, develop our people, serve our patients well, and adapt to challenges?'"

"That's not less ambitious than optimization. It's more ambitious. Because it doesn't accept trade-offs that conventional thinking assumes are necessary."

"We're not doing less. We're doing better."

"And here's what matters: The most efficient machine is the one that never breaks down, not the one that produces the most before breaking."

* * *

Your Turn

Look at your own life, your work, your projects:

Where are you optimizing single metrics at the expense of whole-system health?

Where are you:

- Maximizing productivity while degrading wellbeing?
- Optimizing efficiency while eliminating resilience?
- Pursuing achievement while sacrificing relationships?
- Increasing income while losing time and health?

What would integration look like instead?

What if you asked:

- "What configuration allows me to function healthily across all domains?"
- "What's sufficient rather than maximal?"
- "What thresholds must be maintained for sustainable functioning?"

The next chapter explores the third Yellow principle: recognizing that presence, not productivity, is the ultimate civilizational KPI.

But first: notice where optimization thinking has captured your imagination and crowded out integration thinking.

The shift from "maximize X" to "integrate across all dimensions" is more radical than it sounds.

It's the difference between extraction and flourishing.

Between running the machine hot until it breaks and maintaining the conditions where health regenerates.

Between civilization as optimization problem and civilization as living system.

But if integration requires maintaining multiple dimensions above threshold, how do we know when we're succeeding?

How do we measure system health across domains that include unmeasurables like meaning, presence, and wisdom?

The answer requires rethinking what we measure entirely—and recognizing that presence, not productivity, might be the ultimate civilizational KPI.

That's what we explore next.

Chapter 8: Presence as the Ultimate KPI

Emma is a successful tech executive. Six-figure salary. Respected in her field. Doing "important work" on AI ethics.

She's also completely absent from her own life.

At dinner with her daughter, she's thinking about the board meeting tomorrow. During the board meeting, she's anxious about the presentation next week. During the presentation, she's already worrying about quarterly results. When quarterly results come in good, she's immediately focused on next quarter's targets.

She lives entirely in a state of anticipation and retrospection. Never in actual experience.

Her daughter will be seven once. This moment—right now—will never come again. But Emma isn't here for it. She's somewhere else, always planning, always reviewing, never present.

One evening, her daughter asks: "Mommy, are you listening?"

Emma realizes she has no idea what her daughter just said. She was physically present but completely absent.

"I'm sorry, sweetie. Say that again?"

Her daughter, with the clarity children sometimes have: "You're always somewhere else. Even when you're here."

That sentence breaks something open.

Emma starts noticing: She's absent from everything. From her work (worrying about what's next). From her relationships (thinking about work). From rest (guilty about not working). From moments of beauty (already photographing them for Instagram rather than experiencing them).

She has optimized her life to the point where she's no longer in it.

* * *

The Presence Crisis

Emma's experience isn't unique. It's epidemic.

We've created a civilization that systematically destroys the capacity for presence—the ability to be fully here, aware, and responsive to what's actually happening.

Presence is:

- Being conscious of your actual experience (not lost in thought)
- Responsive to what's in front of you (not on autopilot)
- Able to rest in awareness without compulsion (not constantly reaching for stimulus)
- Capable of simply being (not always doing)

But let's be precise about what presence actually is:

Presence isn't magic. It's physics.

It's what happens when all six domains from Chapter 5 are online and synchronized in the same moment:

- **Biological domain**: Aware of body sensations, responsive to physical signals
- **Cognitive domain**: Attention here, mind clear and available
- **Emotional domain**: Feeling what's present, not suppressed or overwhelmed
- **Behavioral domain**: Actions responsive and intentional, not compulsive
- **Social domain**: Actually with others, not performing or absent

- **Existential domain**: Connected to meaning and purpose in this moment

When the full stack aligns, "presence" is the hum of the system working coherently.

When domains are out of sync or below threshold, presence becomes impossible. You're biologically exhausted (can't be present), cognitively scattered (can't be present), emotionally suppressed (can't be present).

This is why the Human Integration Index matters: It measures the structural conditions that enable or prevent presence.

Absence is:

- Lost in mental narratives about past or future
- Mechanical, habitual, reactive
- Compulsively seeking next thing
- Unable to rest without distraction

Modern civilization runs on absence.

Our economy requires it (consumers need to always want more). Our technology engineers it (attention must be captured continuously). Our culture normalizes it (busy is status symbol). Our institutions demand it (constant availability expected).

The result: Massive collective dissociation from actual lived experience.

The Symptoms

Individual level:

- Can't remember drive to work (autopilot)
- Can't sit for five minutes without checking phone (compulsion)
- Experience filtered through "how will this look on social media?" (performance)
- Eating without tasting, walking without noticing, listening without

hearing (absence)
- Default mode is mental elsewhere (past rumination, future anxiety)

Collective level:

- Political discourse about abstractions, not lived reality
- Economic decisions based on projections, not present needs
- Environmental destruction invisible until catastrophic
- Suffering of others abstract statistics
- The future colonizes the present (everything sacrificed for later)

But perhaps most dangerous: Absent Governance

We've built institutions that operate entirely on:

- **Anticipation**: Polls, strategy, modeling, projections (mental future)
- **Retrospection**: Blame, history, precedent, tradition (mental past)

But never Presence: Sensing what's actually happening right now and responding.

A government that cannot sense the present moment cannot respond to crisis. It hallucinates policy based on old data. It optimizes for conditions that no longer exist. It misses the signals until they become catastrophes.

Present governance would:

- Sense real-time conditions across multiple domains
- Respond adaptively to what's actually happening
- Make decisions based on present reality, not just models
- Integrate feedback continuously rather than waiting for elections

This requires entirely different institutional architecture—which we'll explore in Part III's Meta-Governance interventions.

The cost: We're building a civilization while absent from the experience of building it. Making decisions while disconnected from their consequences. Living lives without inhabiting them.

* * *

Why Presence Matters More Than Productivity

Here's a radical proposition: **We've been measuring our civilization's shadow while calling it substance.**

The real wealth isn't in what we produce but in our capacity to experience what we've produced.

What good is wealth if we're too distracted to enjoy it?

What value achievement if we're absent from the achieving?

What meaning success if we can't be present for our own lives?

The quality of a civilization should be measured not by how much it produces, but by the quality of presence it enables.

Not GDP. Not technological advancement. Not military power.

The capacity of its people to be fully alive, aware, and responsive to their actual experience.

Why This Makes Sense

But before we go further, we need to acknowledge something crucial:

Here's the paradox: The more we try to "achieve" presence, the more absent we become.

Presence isn't another optimization target to be conquered—it's what emerges when we stop optimizing long enough to actually experience our lives.

The HII isn't about scoring high. It's not a competition. It's about noticing when we're scoring so low that we're missing our own existence— and then creating conditions that allow presence to arise naturally.

You can't force presence. You can only remove obstacles to it and create conditions that support it.

With that understood, let's explore why presence matters:

1. Presence is the substrate of everything valuable

You can't experience:

- Joy without presence (else it's just chemical sensation)
- Connection without presence (else it's just transaction)
- Learning without presence (else it's just information accumulation)
- Meaning without presence (else it's just abstract belief)
- Love without presence (else it's just obligation)
- Beauty without presence (else it's just aesthetic judgment)

Everything we actually care about requires presence as foundation.

Productivity without presence is just mechanical output. Achievement without presence is hollow victory. Success without presence is existential failure.

2. Presence enables wise decision-making

Wise decisions require:

- Perceiving what's actually happening (not projections)
- Responding to reality (not mental models)
- Integrating multiple perspectives (not narrow optimization)
- Long-term thinking (not just quarterly results)
- Ethical sensitivity (not just efficiency)

All of which require presence.

Absent decision-making is mechanical, reactive, and divorced from consequences. Present decision-making is responsive, adaptive, and accountable.

3. Presence is regenerative, absence is extractive

But let's be precise about what "absence" actually costs:

When we are absent, we are not just "distracted." We are leaking the most valuable resource in the universe.

Attention is the currency of creation. A civilization with low presence is a civilization that cannot fund its own future because its cognitive capital is being siphoned off by distraction machines.

Think about it economically:

- Every moment of attention is potential for learning, creating, connecting, or healing
- When attention is captured and sold (advertising model), that potential is extracted
- When attention is fragmented (constant interruption), that potential is degraded
- When attention is absent (autopilot mode), that potential is wasted

A low-presence civilization is bankrupt in the only currency that actually matters.

When present:

- You notice when you're tired (and rest)
- You sense when relationships need attention (and tend them)
- You feel when something's wrong (and address it)
- You perceive beauty (and feel gratitude)
- You experience sufficiency (and don't constantly reach for more)

Presence is the immune system of the soul. Absence is the vulnerability that demands constant external management.

When absent:

- You override biological signals (until collapse)
- You neglect relationships (until rupture)
- You miss warning signs (until crisis)
- You're numb to beauty (and feel empty)
- You never have enough (constant craving)

4. Presence is the antidote to addiction

Every addiction—substances, consumption, work, technology, achievement—shares one feature: **disconnection from present-moment experience**.

People don't become addicted because the thing feels good. They become addicted because being present feels bad (anxiety, emptiness, pain). The addiction is escape from unbearable present.

A civilization that makes presence unbearable creates epidemic addiction.

Orange's optimization created conditions where being present reveals: isolation, meaninglessness, chronic stress, constant inadequacy, ecological horror.

So people flee into: consumption, work, screens, substances, achievement, distraction—anything but being here now.

The solution isn't better addiction treatment. It's making presence bearable again.

Creating conditions where being fully alive, aware, and responsive feels good rather than threatening.

* * *

The Human Integration Index (HII)

If presence matters more than productivity, how do we measure it?

We need new metrics. Not to replace all existing measures, but to reorient what we're optimizing for.

The Human Integration Index (HII) measures the capacity for integrated functioning across all six domains we explored in Chapter 5.

The Six Dimensions

1. Biological Integrity

- Sleep quality and quantity
- Physical health and energy
- Stress response regulation
- Body awareness and interoception
- Freedom from chronic pain

Presence indicator: Can you feel your body? Do you respond to its signals? Or override them constantly?

2. Cognitive Sovereignty

- Attention autonomy (not captured by algorithms)
- Capacity for sustained focus
- Mental clarity and coherence
- Access to diverse information
- Reality testing ability

Presence indicator: Can you choose where your attention goes? Or is it constantly hijacked?

3. Emotional Availability

- Emotional range and flexibility
- Capacity to feel without overwhelming
- Emotional regulation without suppression
- Connection to authentic feeling
- Relational attunement

Presence indicator: Can you feel what you feel? Or are emotions threatening/numbed?

4. Behavioral Coherence

- Actions aligned with values
- Non-compulsive behavior
- Skillful responsiveness
- Creative agency
- Habitual presence vs autopilot

Presence indicator: Do you choose your actions consciously? Or operate mechanically?

5. Social Connection

- Quality of relationships
- Sense of belonging
- Capacity for authentic relating
- Community participation
- Mutual recognition

Presence indicator: Are you actually with people when with them? Or absent/performing?

6. Existential Grounding

- Life coherence and meaning
- Purpose clarity
- Value alignment
- Capacity for transcendence
- Engagement with what matters

Presence indicator: Does your life feel meaningful? Or empty despite "success"?

How It Works

HII isn't a single number. It's a profile across six dimensions showing where someone (or a community, or society) is above or below integration threshold.

Individual HII Profile Example:

```
Emma (before shift):
Biological: 40% (chronically exhausted, override body signals)
Cognitive: 60% (attention scattered, some focus ability
remains)
Emotional: 30% (suppressed, regulated through work)
Behavioral: 50% (half compulsive, half intentional)
Social: 35% (relationships transactional, little authentic
connection)
Existential: 25% (success feels empty, unclear why anything
matters)

Overall integration: FAILING (multiple domains below 50%
threshold)
```

After integration-focused changes:

```
Emma (after 6 months):
Biological: 75% (better sleep, honoring body needs)
Cognitive: 80% (protected attention, reduced capture)
Emotional: 70% (more emotional range, less suppression)
Behavioral: 85% (mostly conscious, values-aligned)
Social: 80% (authentic with daughter and close friends)
Existential: 75% (clear sense of what matters, aligned actions)

Overall integration: THRIVING (all domains above threshold,
mutually supporting)
```

The difference isn't productivity or achievement. It's presence—the capacity to be fully in her life.

* * *

Measuring Presence at Scale

Individual HII is valuable. But the real power comes from measuring collective capacity for presence.

Community-Level HII

Indicators:

- Sleep patterns across population
- Attention autonomy metrics
- Emotional health prevalence
- Community participation rates
- Purpose/meaning reports
- Integration across domains

Questions:

- What percentage of community is above integration threshold?
- Which domains are systematically below threshold?
- What conditions support or undermine integration?
- How do policies affect presence capacity?

Societal-Level HII

Current metrics we track:

- GDP growth
- Productivity increases
- Innovation rates
- Market performance

What we should track:

- Capacity for sustained attention
- Sleep adequacy across population
- Emotional wellbeing distribution
- Community coherence
- Meaning crisis prevalence
- Integration achievement rates

The shift: From measuring output to measuring the conditions that enable human flourishing.

Why This Matters for Policy

Policy optimized for GDP:

- Long work hours (good! more production)
- Constant connectivity (good! more efficiency)
- Reduced slack time (good! less waste)
- Maximized consumption (good! more growth)
- Result: Integration collapse, presence impossible

Policy optimized for HII:

- Protected rest time (necessary for biological integrity)
- Attention sovereignty (necessary for cognitive health)
- Community infrastructure (necessary for social dimension)
- Meaning-making opportunities (necessary for existential health)
- Result: Integration achievement, presence possible

Different optimization target, completely different policy landscape.

* * *

The Presence Economy

What would an economy look like if presence, not productivity, was the goal?

Principle 1: Time Sovereignty

Current economy: Your time belongs to whoever can capture it (employers, platforms, advertisers)

Presence economy: Your time is fundamentally yours. Work and commerce exist within boundaries that protect presence capacity.

Practical implications:

- Right to disconnect (no expectation of constant availability)
- Reasonable work hours (not optimized for maximum extraction)
- Protected personal time (not colonized by economic demands)
- Leisure as necessity (not luxury to be earned)

Principle 2: Attention as Commons

Current economy: Attention is resource to be captured and sold

Presence economy: Attention is fundamental to human dignity and must be protected

Practical implications:

- Attention-extractive technologies regulated (like other harmful substances)
- Advertising constrained (can't target vulnerable populations)
- Public spaces protected from commercial capture
- Children's attention especially protected

Principle 3: Rest as Productive

Current economy: Rest is time not working (waste to be minimized)

Presence economy: Rest enables integration and is therefore foundational

Practical implications:

- Sabbath-like structures (regular protected rest)
- Vacation minimums (not maximums)
- Rest seen as investment (not cost)
- Recovery infrastructure (like we have work infrastructure)

Principle 4: Meaning as Economic Output

Current economy: Economic value = monetary value

Presence economy: Work that supports human flourishing has value even without profit

Practical implications:

- Care work valued appropriately
- Community work recognized economically
- Arts and culture funded as necessity
- Work organized around meaning, not just money

Principle 5: Sufficiency Over Growth

Current economy: More is always better, growth is imperative

Presence economy: Enough is a viable goal, sustainability matters

Practical implications:

- Steady-state economics possible
- Quality prioritized over quantity
- Externalities internalized

· Long-term viability over short-term extraction

* * *

Emma's Transformation

Six months after her daughter's question, Emma has redesigned her life.

She didn't quit her job. She didn't move to a monastery. She didn't reject technology.

She shifted her primary optimization target from productivity to presence.

Concrete changes:

Time boundaries: Work ends at 5pm. No email after hours. No phone in bedroom. One day per week completely offline.

Attention protection: Removed social media apps. No notifications except calls. Two focused work blocks per day. Rest of time responsive but not optimized.

Presence practices: 20 minutes morning meditation. Evening walk (no phone). Weekly "awe walk" seeking beauty. Monthly solo retreat day.

Relationship prioritization: Dinner with daughter (no screens, full attention). Weekly date with partner. Monthly friend connection. Regular community participation.

Body attunement: Sleep 7-8 hours (non-negotiable). Exercise for pleasure (not optimization). Eat when hungry. Rest when tired.

Meaning alignment: Work on projects that matter. Say no to prestigious but meaningless opportunities. Time for reading, art, nature. Regular reflection on values.

The results:

Her productivity at work actually increased (focused time beats scattered time). Her relationships transformed (people can feel when you're actually present). Her daughter said: "You're here now."

But more importantly: **Her life feels like her life again.**

She's in it. Present for it. Responsive to it.

Not optimized. Not maximized. But alive.

* * *

The Civilizational Question

If Emma can shift from productivity-optimized to presence-centered living, can civilization?

The challenge is scale.

Individual changes are possible but exhausting when swimming against civilizational current. Emma has privilege—resources, flexibility, education—that enable her choices.

What about people who don't?

The single mother working three jobs can't meditate for 20 minutes. The precarious gig worker can't set time boundaries. The marginalized person can't opt out of survival mode.

This is why systemic change is necessary.

Individual solutions fail at scale because the system itself is optimized for absence.

The gap between individual possibility and systemic reality is where transformation happens.

Emma's changes worked because she had resources—economic security, professional autonomy, cultural capital. The solutions in Part III are about making those resources available to everyone, not through individual optimization but through systemic redesign.

We need:

- Economic structures that don't require constant presence-destroying overwork (AUBI)
- Information ecosystems that protect attention rather than capture it

(Synoptic Protocol)

- Physical and temporal spaces protected from economic demands (Sanctuaries)
- Governance that values integration over extraction (Meta-Governance)

These aren't utopian fantasies. They're practical interventions that shift optimization targets from productivity to presence.

* * *

Measuring What Matters

GDP measures economic output. HII measures human integration capacity.

These are fundamentally different optimization targets.

Optimizing for GDP led to:

- Ecological destruction
- Social atomization
- Chronic stress
- Meaning crisis
- Integration collapse

What would optimizing for HII lead to?

Systems designed for:

- Biological sustainability
- Cognitive sovereignty
- Emotional health
- Behavioral coherence
- Social connection
- Existential meaning

This isn't abandoning material wellbeing. It's recognizing that beyond sufficiency, more stuff doesn't improve wellbeing—but more presence does.

The question isn't "How much can we produce?" but "What conditions enable humans to thrive?"

Not "How efficient can we be?" but "How alive can we be?"

Not "How fast can we grow?" but "How well can we live?"

* * *

The Ultimate KPI

Here's the radical claim:

The success of a civilization should be measured by the percentage of its population capable of being fully present in their own lives.

Not wealth per capita. Not technological advancement. Not military power. Not even longevity (though presence correlates with health).

The capacity for presence.

We've been counting coins while the treasury of human experience lies neglected. We've measured everything except what actually matters—the felt quality of being alive.

Because presence enables:

- Wise decision-making
- Genuine connection
- Creative response
- Ethical behavior
- Life satisfaction
- Meaning experience

And here's the key insight connecting back to Chapter 5:

Presence is the ultimate expression of integration.

When all six domains function above threshold and coordinate harmoniously, presence becomes natural rather than effortful. The system hums. Awareness flows. Being here feels good.

When domains are below threshold or out of sync, absence becomes the only bearable state. Being present reveals the pain of the misalignment—exhaustion, anxiety, emptiness, compulsion. So people flee into distraction, work, consumption, anything but here.

This is why we can't just tell people to "be more present." We have to create conditions where presence doesn't hurt.

Everything else—productivity, innovation, growth, achievement—should be in service of presence, not instead of it.

When we optimize for presence:

- We create conditions for human flourishing
- We make sustainable decisions (present people feel consequences)
- We build genuine community (presence enables real connection)
- We find sufficiency (present people know when enough is enough)
- We act ethically (presence reveals our impact on others)

The measure of a civilization isn't what it produces. It's the quality of awareness it cultivates.

* * *

Bridge to Solutions

We've now established three Yellow principles:

Chapter 6: Think in Both/And rather than Either/Or **Chapter 7**: Integrate rather than optimize **Chapter 8**: Optimize for presence rather than productivity

These principles lead inevitably to different interventions than Orange or Green would design.

Part III will detail specific systemic solutions:

- How to establish economic security without requiring constant labor
- How to protect attention from algorithmic capture
- How to create spaces for integration and recovery
- How to govern with wisdom rather than just efficiency

But first, one more principle: understanding that we're working with living systems, not machines.

That's Chapter 9.

For now, sit with this:

Are you present in your own life?

Not "are you productive" or "are you successful."

Are you actually here?

Can you feel your body? Notice your breath? Sense the moment?

Or are you, like Emma, always somewhere else—planning, reviewing, worrying, optimizing?

The quality of your life isn't determined by what you achieve. It's determined by whether you're present for it.

And the quality of our civilization will ultimately be measured the same way.

Chapter 9: You Can't Yellow Your Way Into Yellow – The Transition Paradox

Michael sits in the workshop, notebook open, taking careful notes.

The facilitator is explaining Yellow thinking—systems perspective, both/and logic, integration over optimization. Everything Michael has learned today makes perfect sense. He can see how his company's problems stem from Orange's limitations. He understands why Green's critiques, while valid, haven't led to solutions.

"This is brilliant," he thinks. "We need to implement Yellow thinking organization-wide."

He starts planning:

- **Week 1**: Roll out new integration metrics across all departments
- **Week 2**: Train managers on both/and decision-making frameworks
- **Week 3**: Restructure quarterly planning to include long-term systemic thinking
- **Week 4**: Measure results and optimize the Yellow implementation process

Michael is completely sincere. He genuinely wants to evolve beyond Orange. He's trying hard to learn Yellow principles.

And he's doing it in the most Orange way possible.

He's treating developmental transformation like a software upgrade. Install new operating system. Run optimization protocols. Measure and improve. Achieve better results.

He's trying to mechanically engineer what can only organically emerge.

This is what I call **the transition paradox**: You can't use Orange thinking to get to Yellow. But if you're at Orange, Orange thinking is all you have access to.

You can't Yellow your way into Yellow.

* * *

The Developmental Catch-22

Here's the core problem:

Developmental stages are worldviews. They're not just beliefs you can choose to adopt—they're the entire perceptual-cognitive framework through which you interpret reality.

When you're operating from Orange:

- You see problems as things to be solved through analysis and optimization
- You trust metrics, efficiency, and systematic improvement
- You believe the right framework, applied correctly, produces desired results
- **You naturally approach transformation itself as an optimization problem**

But Yellow transformation doesn't work that way.

Yellow emerges when you:

- Stop trying to optimize and start trying to integrate
- Stop seeking the "right answer" and start holding multiple perspectives

- Stop measuring everything and start sensing system health
- Stop controlling outcomes and start creating conditions for emergence

Orange can't understand this. It sounds like magical thinking or dangerous passivity.

From Orange's perspective, "create conditions for emergence" just means "hope for the best without any clear plan." That feels irresponsible.

So Orange does what Orange does best: it tries to systematize emergence. Plan the unplannable. Control the uncontrollable. Optimize the process of letting go of optimization.

And it fails. Every time.

* * *

Why Forced Transitions Don't Work

Michael's company implements the Yellow training program.
Within three months:

- "Integration metrics" have become another KPI to hit
- "Both/and thinking" is now a checkbox on performance reviews
- "Systemic perspective" appears in quarterly objectives
- "Creating conditions for emergence" has a six-step implementation guide

They've turned Yellow into an Orange project.

The form is there but not the substance. The language changed but not the logic. They're using new words to do old thinking.

Why does this always happen?

Because **humans aren't machines. Organizations aren't mechanisms. Development isn't engineering.**

This might be the most important thing to understand about Yellow: **It treats humans as living systems, not mechanical ones.**

Let me explain what that means.

* * *

Living Systems vs. Machines

A machine:

- Has parts that can be replaced
- Follows predictable cause-effect relationships
- Can be optimized through systematic improvement
- Responds to inputs with deterministic outputs
- Can be controlled through proper design

A living system:

- Has parts that grow and change each other
- Has emergent properties that can't be predicted from components
- Develops through growth, not optimization
- Self-organizes based on context and history
- Can only be influenced, never fully controlled

Orange treats everything like machines. Even humans. Even organizations. Even societies.

This is why Orange's solutions to burnout fail:

- "Better time management" (optimize the human machine)
- "Efficiency training" (improve operational performance)
- "Productivity apps" (upgrade the system)
- "Work-life balance programs" (optimize resource allocation)

All treating humans as machines that need better programming.

Yellow recognizes humans as living systems.

This changes everything:

- You can't program someone into presence—you create conditions where presence becomes natural
- You can't optimize someone into wisdom—you remove obstacles to natural development
- You can't force integration—you provide scaffolding that enables organic growth

Development is something that happens to you when you stop trying to make it happen and start creating the conditions where it can't not happen.

Like dawn that cannot be rushed. Like seasons that will not be commanded. Like breath that breathes itself when we stop controlling it.

This is why you can't Yellow your way into Yellow. Yellow emerges. It unfolds. It develops.

You can't force a flower to bloom by pulling on the petals. You can't accelerate spring by tugging on crocuses.

Development has its own seasons, its own timing, its own mysterious logic.

But here's what you *can* do: **You can design the habitat where blooming becomes inevitable.**

This isn't passive hope or magical thinking. It's active **habitat design**—building the greenhouse (structure), irrigating the soil (resources), protecting the seedling (safety). You don't make the plant grow. You create the architecture that makes growth the path of least resistance.

That's the difference between engineering and enabling. Between forcing and facilitating.

That's what Part III is about: habitat design for human flourishing.

But first, we need to understand what actually triggers transitions when the habitat is right.

* * *

What Actually Triggers Developmental Transitions

If you can't engineer Yellow, how does anyone get there?

Research on adult development (Kegan, Cook-Greuter, Torbert) shows that stage transitions happen through specific triggers:

1. Crisis and Contradiction

The current stage stops working. The worldview can no longer make sense of experience.

For Orange → Yellow:

- Success produces suffering (Chapter 1's pattern)
- Optimization creates fragmentation (Chapter 4's acceleration)
- The game you're winning reveals itself as unwinnable (Chapter 5's integration threshold)

Crisis cracks the shell. It creates space for something new.

But crisis alone isn't enough—plenty of people respond to Orange's failures by retreating to Blue (authoritarian certainty) or getting stuck in Green (critique without construction).

What else is needed?

2. Cognitive Dissonance That Can't Be Resolved Within Current Framework

You need contradictions that the current stage literally cannot resolve:

Orange contradiction: "I achieved everything I wanted and I'm still miserable. My success is real AND insufficient. My analysis is accurate AND incomplete."

Orange logic says: Pick one. Either you're grateful for success or you fix what's wrong. Either the data shows improvement or it shows problems.

Yellow recognizes: Both can be true. The system succeeded at what it optimized for while failing at what it ignored. You can hold that paradox without collapsing into confusion.

But you have to experience the contradiction viscerally before Yellow makes sense.

Reading about it isn't enough. You have to live it.

3. Exposure to Next-Stage Thinking

You need contact with people operating from Yellow—not to imitate them, but to see that another worldview is possible.

This is tricky because:

- If you see Yellow through Orange eyes, it looks naive or impractical
- If you see Yellow through Green eyes, it looks like selling out or both-sidesism
- **You need enough developmental readiness to recognize Yellow as coherent**

Michael's workshop problem: He's hearing Yellow principles through Orange ears. The translation is lossy.

What he hears: "Be more holistic and integrative" (which sounds like "add more things to optimize")

What's actually being said: "Stop optimizing and start sensing. Stop controlling and start creating conditions. Stop fragmenting and start integrating."

Those are different sentences.

4. Safe Container for Disorientation

Stage transitions are destabilizing. Your old worldview is crumbling but the new one hasn't solidified.

You need:

- Community that can hold you through the confusion
- Economic security so you can take time to process (Chapter 12's Sovereign Floor)
- Physical/mental space for reflection (Chapter 13's Sanctuaries)
- Permission to not have everything figured out

Without safety, most people abort the transition and retreat to what's familiar.

5. Scaffolding That Supports Natural Unfolding

Remember cognitive scaffolding from the blog series? Same principle here.

You can't force development, but you can provide structures that support it:

- Practices that cultivate capacities (contemplation, embodiment, dialogue)
- Frameworks that make next-stage thinking legible (like Spiral Dynamics)
- Metrics that track integration rather than just achievement (Chapter 8's presence)
- Systems that reward development rather than punish it (Part III's

interventions)

Scaffolding doesn't cause growth. It enables growth that wants to happen.

* * *

Transcend and Include: Why Earlier Stages Aren't Wrong

Here's something crucial: **Yellow doesn't reject Orange. It includes it.**

Think of it this way: When you move to Yellow, **Orange doesn't disappear—it becomes a subroutine.**

You can still use spreadsheets, KPIs, optimization, and systematic analysis. These are powerful tools. But they're no longer the operating system. They're apps *used* by the OS, not the OS itself.

This is the mechanic of "transcend and include":

At Orange, analytical thinking *is* your consciousness. It runs constantly. Every problem looks like an optimization challenge because optimization is the only program running.

At Yellow, analytical thinking becomes one tool among many. You can deploy it when appropriate—and you're actually better at it because you're not using it inappropriately.

Michael's Orange thinking isn't the problem. Orange's gifts are real:

- Systematic analysis helps see patterns others miss
- Metrics reveal what's actually happening vs. what we want to believe
- Efficiency enables doing more with less
- Innovation creates genuine progress

Yellow needs these capacities.

The problem is Orange's *limits*:

- It fragments wholes into parts and loses integration
- It optimizes subsystems at the expense of the larger system
- It treats everything as solvable through analysis
- It can't handle paradox or emergence

Yellow transcends these limits while including Orange's strengths.

The goal isn't to eradicate Orange thinking—that would be developmental regression. The goal is to become capable of using Orange tools when appropriate rather than being limited to them universally.

You don't become less capable at Orange thinking when you reach Yellow. You become able to deploy it as a subroutine rather than letting it run your entire system.

Same with Green's gifts:

- Awareness of systemic oppression is crucial
- Valuing diversity and inclusion matters deeply
- Deconstructing power structures reveals hidden dynamics
- Care for the marginalized prevents Orange's callousness

Yellow needs these too.

Green's limits:

- Deconstruction without reconstruction leaves nothing to build on
- Relativism makes it hard to make firm commitments
- Focus on what's wrong can obscure what's working
- Critique can become paralysis

Yellow transcends by adding construction to deconstruction. Building to critique.

This is why Yellow can work with Orange AND Green—it doesn't see them as enemies but as earlier stages with partial truths.

Each stage sees what the previous stages couldn't. Each stage solves problems the earlier stages created. None are wrong—just incomplete.

* * *

The Living Systems Perspective

Let's return to why this matters for understanding transformation.
Orange sees organizations as machines:

- If productivity drops, fix the inefficient component
- If morale is low, implement engagement programs
- If innovation stalls, restructure for better idea flow
- **Every problem has a mechanical solution**

Yellow sees organizations as living ecosystems:

- If productivity drops, ask what systemic conditions changed
- If morale is low, examine the health of the entire organism
- If innovation stalls, restore conditions where creativity naturally emerges
- **Problems are symptoms of system state, not broken parts**

Consider parenting: You can't optimize a child into maturity. You can't program wisdom into a teenager. You create conditions—love, safety, challenges, appropriate boundaries, room to fail—and trust that development will unfold naturally.

The child who's forced into premature responsibility often becomes rigid. The child who's protected from all challenge often remains dependent. But the child who has the right habitat—safe enough to take risks, structured enough to learn consequences—develops naturally into a capable adult.

The same principle applies to adult development and organizational transformation.

Creating conditions isn't passive. It's the most active thing you can do.

But it's a different kind of action than forcing.

This completely changes intervention strategy.

Example: The Burned Out Team

Orange diagnosis:

- Team members are underperforming
- Need better time management training
- Implement productivity tracking
- Replace people who can't keep up

Green diagnosis:

- Exploitation by management
- Workers need more voice and agency
- Demand reduced workload
- Critique the oppressive structure

Yellow diagnosis:

- System is in unsustainable state
- Multiple feedback loops driving acceleration
- Team AND management trapped in structural pattern
- Need to change conditions that produce burnout

Orange solves by optimizing components.

Green solves by redistributing power.

Yellow solves by restoring system health.

All three might be needed. But Yellow can coordinate them. Orange and Green, operating alone, often work against each other.

* * *

The Paradox of Practice

Here's where it gets really interesting:

You can't Yellow your way into Yellow. But you can practice your way there.

Wait—isn't practice a deliberate action? Doesn't that sound Orange?

Yes. And this is the paradox that makes transformation possible:

You use Orange's systematic discipline to create conditions for Yellow emergence.

Let me explain:

Orange practice: Meditate to be more productive. Track metrics to optimize performance. Develop presence to achieve better results.

Yellow practice: Meditate to cultivate capacity for integration. Notice patterns without needing to fix them. Develop presence as the goal itself, not as means to something else.

The actions might look identical. The intention is completely different.

This is why transformation is so slippery. You can't just copy what Yellow people do. You have to understand why they're doing it—and that understanding only comes from developmental readiness.

Michael can implement the same meditation practice as someone operating from Yellow. But he'll be doing it for different reasons, in a different way, with different results.

The form doesn't transfer. The consciousness does.

* * *

Conditions That Enable Natural Development

So if you can't force Yellow, what can you do?

Create conditions where Yellow development becomes more likely:

1. Safety and Security

- Economic floor so people can take developmental risks (Chapter 12)
- Spaces protected from extraction and optimization (Chapter 13)
- Permission to not know, to be uncertain, to change
- Communities that support rather than judge transitions

2. Exposure to Complexity

- Problems that require multiple perspectives
- Decisions with no clear "right answer"
- Situations where optimization makes things worse
- Experiences that reveal limits of current stage

3. Contemplative Capacity

- Practices that cultivate meta-awareness
- Time for reflection and integration
- Spaces that support presence (Chapter 8)
- Infrastructure for stillness (Chapter 14)

4. Developmental Frameworks

- Maps showing stages are real and predictable
- Language for what you're experiencing
- Community of people at similar transitions
- Mentors who've navigated this territory

5. Permission to Transform

- Cultural stories that honor development
- Economic structures that reward integration
- Social recognition of wisdom, not just achievement

- Celebration of transitions, not just destinations

Notice: None of these force development. They remove obstacles and provide support.

Like sunlight, water, and good soil for a plant. You can't make it grow faster. But you can create conditions where natural growth flourishes.

* * *

The Gradient of Yellow

Here's something most developmental models don't emphasize enough:
Yellow isn't binary. There's a gradient.
You don't wake up one day fully at Yellow. You grow into it gradually:
Early Yellow:

- Intellectual understanding of systems thinking
- Can see how parts affect wholes (in theory)
- Recognizes limits of Orange and Green (conceptually)
- **Still operating mostly from Orange/Green in practice**

Emerging Yellow:

- Starting to embody systems thinking in decisions
- Can hold both/and more naturally
- Integration becoming intuitive rather than effortful
- **Moments of genuine Yellow alternating with Orange/Green defaults**

Established Yellow:

- Systems thinking is default mode
- Can work fluidly with complexity

- Integration happens naturally
- **Can intentionally employ Orange or Green when appropriate**

Mature Yellow:

- Deep trust in emergence
- Comfortable with paradox and uncertainty
- Can create conditions for others' development
- **Yellow becomes not what you do but who you are**

Michael is probably early Yellow. He can understand the concepts. He wants to develop. But when pressure hits, he defaults to Orange solutions.

That's normal. That's the transition.

The work isn't to force full Yellow now. It's to create conditions where natural development can unfold over years, not weeks.

* * *

Why This Matters for Part III

Understanding the transition paradox is essential for the solutions in Part III.

If we try to implement Yellow solutions using Orange methods, we'll fail.

This means:

- Cognitive Sovereignty (Chapter 11) can't be enforced mechanically—it requires cultural shift
- The Sovereign Floor (Chapter 12) isn't just policy—it's developmental infrastructure
- Sanctuaries (Chapter 13) aren't just physical spaces—they're containers for transformation

- Contemplative Capacity (Chapter 14) isn't just programs—it's civilizational practice

Each intervention creates conditions for Yellow development rather than forcing it.

They work as an ecosystem, not as isolated fixes.

And they're designed for Orange/Green people who are ready to transition but don't know how—not for people who are already at Yellow.

This is crucial: The solutions aren't Yellow solutions. They're Orange/Green solutions designed to enable Yellow emergence.

They meet people where they are while creating conditions for where they're going.

* * *

The Natural Timetable

One more thing about living systems: **they develop according to their own timeline.**

You can't rush development any more than you can rush childhood.

Some people are developmentally ready for Yellow and just need the right conditions. They'll transition relatively quickly—months to a couple years.

Some people need longer—five to ten years of gradually accumulating contradictions, exposure to complexity, and supported growth.

Some people may never transition. And that's okay. We need people operating from every stage. The goal isn't to make everyone Yellow. **It's to create conditions where natural development isn't blocked.**

This means:

- Pilot programs need 5-10 year timeframes to show real results
- Quick wins matter for momentum but transformation is slow

- We measure progress in cultural shifts, not just behavior changes
- Success looks like more people *able* to develop, not everyone developing on schedule

Orange wants everything to happen in quarters.

Green wants everything to happen through activism.

Yellow knows transformation happens in generations.

We need to hold all three timeframes simultaneously.

* * *

Bridge to Part III

We've now covered all the core Yellow principles:

Chapter 6: Both/And thinking enables holding complexity

Chapter 7: Integration over optimization restores wholeness

Chapter 8: Presence as the ultimate KPI reorients our compass

Chapter 9: Living systems require conditions, not control

These principles lead inevitably to specific interventions.

In Part III, we'll detail four interlocking solutions that together create conditions for:

- Economic security without requiring constant labor (Sovereign Floor)
- Cognitive sovereignty in attention economy (Cognitive Sovereignty Architecture)
- Spaces for integration and recovery (Sanctuaries)
- Developmental infrastructure at scale (Contemplative Capacity)

But here's what you need to understand before we get there:

These aren't mechanical fixes. They're living system interventions. They work by creating conditions where healthy development becomes natural rather than heroic.

They're designed for people operating from Orange/Green who are ready to transition but need support. They won't force anyone to Yellow. They'll remove obstacles for those who are ready.

And they're designed as an integrated system, not isolated programs.

That's Chapter 15's revelation: why all four together create something none could create alone.

* * *

The Loneliness of Transition

One more thing no one tells you about developmental transitions:

You will be out of sync with the world around you.

As you begin operating from Yellow, you'll still be living in predominantly Orange and Green systems. You'll see solutions that others can't see. You'll hold both/and where others demand either/or. You'll seek integration where others optimize.

This creates friction.

Not because you're doing something wrong, but because you're building Yellow structures while living in an Orange world. You'll feel like you're speaking a different language. Making decisions that seem obvious to you but naive to others. Valuing things that your environment doesn't reward.

The hardest part of the transition is this isolation.

You can't explain Yellow consciousness to people who haven't experienced the contradictions that make it necessary. Your attempts to describe it will sound like:

- Overthinking (to Orange)
- Both-sidesism (to Green)
- Impractical idealism (to both)

This friction isn't a sign you're failing. It's the heat generated by re-

entry into a new atmosphere.

You're not crazy. You're not alone. You're just ahead of the curve.

And the work of Part IV—particularly the Alchemist's Dilemma chapter—will address exactly this: how to navigate being developmentally ahead while still embedded in systems designed for earlier stages.

For now, know this: **If the transition feels lonely, you're doing it right.**

The discomfort is developmental labor, not developmental failure.

* * *

A Personal Note

I've been through this transition. Multiple times. In different domains.

I know the frustration of understanding Yellow intellectually while still operating from Orange practically.

I know the disorientation of your old worldview crumbling before the new one has solidified.

I know the temptation to force it, to systematize it, to optimize your way to transformation.

And I know that doesn't work.

What works is:

- Patience with yourself during transitions
- Willingness to not know
- Trust in natural development
- Community that can hold you through confusion
- Practices that cultivate rather than force
- Conditions that enable rather than engineer

You can't Yellow your way into Yellow.

But you can create conditions where Yellow emerges naturally, in its own time, when you're ready.

That's what we're building in Part III.

Not a mechanical program for forced development.

A living ecosystem where human flourishing becomes structurally possible.

***

Where Are You Trying to Engineer What Can Only Emerge?

Before we move to solutions, pause for a moment of honest reflection:

Where in your life are you trying to engineer what can only emerge?

Where are you applying mechanical solutions to living system problems?

- Are you trying to "optimize" your relationships?
- Are you treating your body like a machine to be programmed?
- Are you forcing your career development on a predetermined timeline?
- Are you attempting to schedule spontaneity or manufacture presence?

The recognition itself is the beginning of the transition.

Not because recognition fixes anything mechanically. But because seeing the pattern creates space for a different response.

You can't force yourself to stop forcing. (That would be more forcing.)

But you can notice the forcing. And in that noticing, something shifts.

That shift is Yellow emerging.

Not because you made it happen. Because you stopped preventing it.

***

Final Reflection

The transition paradox isn't a bug. It's a feature.

It prevents Orange from colonizing Yellow.

If you could mechanically engineer Yellow, we'd end up with "Yellow optimization"—another treadmill, faster than before.

The fact that you *can't* force it means genuine Yellow can only emerge through actual development. Through growth. Through transformation that's real, not performed.

This protects Yellow's integrity.

And it means that when Yellow does emerge—slowly, organically, in community, with support—it's the real thing.

Not another layer of optimization.

Actual integration.

Ready for solutions?

They're waiting in Part III.

But only if you're ready to stop forcing and start enabling.

To stop controlling and start creating conditions.

To stop optimizing development and start supporting it.

That's the transition.

And it begins now.

* * *

Postcard from 2040: The End of the Argument

Ten years ago, this conflict would have ended the evening. One of us would have gotten defensive, the other would have withdrawn, and we would have retreated to our screens to nurse our grievances in separate algorithmic silos. But tonight, when the disagreement hit, nobody flinched. We didn't try to "win." We didn't try to "compromise."

We just sat with the tension. We let it sit on the table between us like a heavy stone. We breathed. We waited for the nervous systems to settle. And then, without forcing it, the third option emerged—the one neither of us could have seen while we were defending our ground. It wasn't a negotiation; it was a joint discovery. We finished dinner, not exhausted by the fight, but energized by the integration.

PART III: THE SOLUTIONS

* * *

Chapter 10: Starting Where You Are – Monday Morning After Reading This Book

David closes the book.

It's Sunday evening. Tomorrow is Monday. He has three back-to-back meetings, forty-seven unread emails, a project deadline, and a performance review to complete.

Everything in Part II made sense. But what the hell is he supposed to do with it on Monday morning?

The Sovereign Floor doesn't exist yet. His city hasn't created Sanctuaries. The Synoptic Protocol isn't law. His company hasn't restructured around presence rather than productivity.

He's living in the Orange world with Yellow awareness.

This is the gap that destroys most transformation attempts: the space between understanding principles and living in systems designed to prevent those principles from being practiced.

You need two things simultaneously:

1. **Personal practices that provide immediate relief** (what you can do now)
2. **Systemic changes that make those practices sustainable** (what we build together)

This chapter is about the first. Chapters 11-14 are about the second.

Let's be clear: Personal practices alone won't save you. Personal practices are rearranging deck chairs on the Titanic. Necessary for momentary dignity, insufficient for preventing iceberg collisions.

If that's all there was, this would be another self-help book telling you to meditate more while the system burns.

Think of this as harm reduction, not solution. This is the psychological equivalent of providing clean needles to addicts. It doesn't solve the addiction, but it keeps people alive until we can address the conditions creating it.

Or another metaphor: **Personal practices are the lifeboat. Systemic solutions are building the shore.**

You need both—the lifeboat to stay afloat while we build, and the shore to make the lifeboat unnecessary.

But personal practices can:

- Give you breathing room while systems change
- Build capacities you'll need to help create those systems
- Provide proof-of-concept for what becomes possible
- Prevent complete burnout before the infrastructure arrives

* * *

Common Objections (And Why They're Wrong)

"But I don't have time for this!"

Start with 30 seconds. Not 15 minutes.

The system wants you to believe change requires massive effort so you never start. That's a lie designed to keep you trapped.

Start microscopic. One breath. One moment. One tiny act of sovereignty.

"This feels selfish when others are suffering."

Your capacity to help others depends on your capacity to function.

This isn't self-care—it's systems maintenance. A broken person cannot build a better world.

"I've tried this before and it didn't work."

Of course it didn't work. You were trying to use willpower to fight structural forces.

This time is different: You're doing personal practice WHILE working for systemic change. The practices keep you alive while we build the habitat that makes them unnecessary.

* * *

The Integration Emergency Kit

These aren't just wellness tips. **They're acts of micro-sovereignty.**

When you refuse to check your phone for the first hour of the day, you are unilaterally enacting the **Right to Reality** within your own skull. You are enforcing a personal Synoptic Protocol against the invasion of the attention economy.

When you sit still for five minutes without justification, you are asserting that your existence has value independent of productivity.

This is political, not just personal.

Every moment of presence in an extractive system is an act of resistance. Every practice that prioritizes integration over optimization challenges the foundational logic of late capitalism.

Don't mistake these for self-help. This is micro-governance of your own consciousness while we work toward macro-governance that makes it structurally possible.

If you take nothing else from this chapter, take this:

Three Things to Do Today (Right Now)

1. Take an actual break

Not a "quick break" where you check your phone. An actual break where you do nothing useful.

Five minutes. Sit. Breathe. Notice your body. That's it.

No meditation app. No productivity justification. No optimization.

Just sit.

This sounds trivial. It's not. It's the first rebellion against the system that demands constant productivity.

2. Uninstall one app

Pick the app that most successfully captures your attention when you don't intend to give it.

Not the one you use for work. Not the one you "need."

The one that hijacks you. The one you open without deciding to. The one that makes twenty minutes disappear.

Delete it. Right now.

You can always reinstall it later. But for this week, create one moment of friction between impulse and action.

3. Have one undistracted conversation

Today or tomorrow, have one conversation—with anyone—where your phone is in another room.

Not just silent. Not just face down. **In another room.**

Five minutes. Ten if possible. Fully present.

Notice how hard this is. Notice what you notice. Notice what the other person notices.

This is what we've lost. This is what we're trying to recover.

Bonus (if you can): Notice one moment of beauty

Not to photograph or share, but simply to experience.

The sun through a window. A child's laughter. The taste of your coffee. The pattern of frost on glass.

Practice receiving beauty without immediately commodifying it.

The most revolutionary act in an extractive system is to experience something useless and beautiful entirely for yourself. It proves you're not just a resource to be optimized.

Three Things to Do This Week

1. Identify your domain scores

Using Project Janus framework from Chapter 5, honestly assess where you are across all six domains:

Biological: Are you sleeping? Moving? Eating food that nourishes? Or running on stimulants and stress?

Cognitive: Can you focus for extended periods? Or is your attention shattered?

Emotional: Can you feel your feelings? Or are you numb or over-whelmed?

Behavioral: Are your actions aligned with your values? Or are you in compulsive loops?

Social: Do you have genuine connection? Or performing relationships while lonely?

Existential: Does your life feel meaningful? Or are you going through motions?

Score each domain 1-10. Be honest.

The goal isn't to have high scores. It's to see clearly where integration has failed.

You can't fix what you can't see.

2. Start morning practice

Before checking your phone, before email, before the day's demands:

- **5 minutes of stillness** (sitting, breathing, being)
- **5 minutes of movement** (stretching, walking, embodied presence)
- **5 minutes of reflection** (journaling, intention-setting, noticing)

Fifteen minutes total. Before the world gets you.

This isn't about becoming enlightened. It's about establishing sovereignty over the first moments of your day.

The system wants your attention from the moment you wake. This practice says: "Not yet. This time is mine."

3. Find one structural change you can influence

You can't redesign civilization by yourself. But you can influence something:

- Your team's meeting structure
- Your family's dinner policy
- Your building's common spaces
- Your local government's policies
- Your company's wellness programs

Pick one thing. Small. Achievable. This week.

Propose one tiny change that creates more space for presence:

- Silent start to meetings
- No-phone dinners
- Walking one-on-ones instead of conference rooms
- "Deep work Wednesday" with no meetings

Don't aim for transformation. Aim for one small sanctuary in the desert.

Three Things to Do This Month

1. Join or create a working group

Find others who understand the integration crisis and want to address it:

- Online communities around these ideas
- Local meditation or contemplative groups
- Professional networks interested in organizational wellbeing
- Political advocacy for UBI or attention protection

You need community. Not just for support (though that matters) but because systemic change requires collective action.

Individual awakening doesn't change systems. Organized collectives do.

2. Assess your personal integration threshold

Look at the six domains. Where are the biggest gaps?

The integration threshold principle (Chapter 5): You need sufficient capacity across ALL domains, not maximum capacity in a few.

Maybe you're killing it cognitively (sharp analysis) and behaviorally (productive output) but failing biologically (exhausted) and existentially (meaningless).

That's not success. That's fragmentation.

This month, focus on bringing up your lowest score, not maximizing your highest.

- If biological is lowest: prioritize sleep and movement over more productivity
- If emotional is lowest: create space to feel rather than constantly doing
- If social is lowest: invest in one genuine relationship over more networking
- If existential is lowest: reduce busy-ness to make space for meaning

Integration means wholeness, not excellence in fragments.

3. Track one metric that matters

Pick one measurement that reflects actual wellbeing, not productivity:

- Days you felt present vs. days you were in compulsive loops
- Hours of genuine rest (not just "time off" spent anxious)
- Conversations where you were fully there
- Moments you noticed beauty without immediately photographing it

Track it simply. Notice patterns. Don't optimize it.

The goal isn't to improve the number. It's to make wellbeing visible and valuable to yourself.

What gets measured gets noticed. What gets noticed can change.

* * *

Rebuilding Cognitive Scaffolding (From the Blog Series)

Remember the five dimensions of scaffolding that modern culture destroyed?

1. **Conceptual clarity** (language for stillness)
2. **Causal models** (why presence matters)
3. **Temporal horizons** (long-term thinking)
4. **Experiential maps** (navigating interior terrain)
5. **Social validation** (community recognition)

Because our civilization demolished the cultural scaffolding for stillness—Sabbaths, third places, deep work, contemplative practices—**you have to manually erect temporary scaffolding every morning.**

These practices aren't "self-care virtue." They're structural supports required to keep your roof from collapsing until we rebuild the city.

This is why it feels like hard work: You're building infrastructure by hand, every day, that should be provided culturally but isn't.

You're not weak for needing these practices. You're holding up weight that shouldn't be yours alone to carry.

But until we restore the civilizational infrastructure (Chapters 11-14), personal scaffolding is how you survive.

You can start rebuilding these personally while we work collectively to restore them culturally.

1. Develop Vocabulary for Stillness

Stop lumping all non-doing into one category called "rest."
Start noticing distinctions:

- **Restful stillness** (restorative, peaceful, nourishing)
- **Agitated stillness** (body stopped but mind racing)
- **Alert stillness** (awake, present, clear)
- **Dull stillness** (checked out, numbed, dissociated)
- **Spacious stillness** (expansive, open, connected)
- **Tense stillness** (held, resistant, effortful)

Journal about these qualities. Make them visible through language.
When you can name six types of stillness, you can navigate toward the ones that serve you.

2. Build Personal Causal Models

Track correlations between presence and outcomes you care about:

- When you're more present, how does your work quality change?
- When you practice stillness, what happens to your decision-making?
- When you're rushing constantly, what patterns emerge in relationships?
- When you create space, what insights arrive?

Build evidence your rational mind finds compelling.
Not someone else's research. Your own lived data.
The goal isn't scientific proof. It's personal validation that presence serves your actual goals.

3. Extend Temporal Horizons

Modern life operates in:

- Minutes (social media)
- Hours (meetings)
- Days (deadlines)
- Weeks (sprints)
- Months (quarters)
- Years (career moves)

Contemplative capacity develops over:

- Months (noticing you're slightly less reactive)
- Years (genuine shifts in how you relate to experience)
- Decades (character transformation)
- Lifetime (wisdom development)

Practice thinking in decades:

- Ask: "What kind of consciousness do I want to cultivate over twenty years?"
- Imagine: "What will my 80-year-old self thank me for starting now?"
- Consider: "What matters across my entire life, not just this quarter?"

Make long-term identity development cognitively salient, not just long-term career planning.

4. Develop Internal Weather Reports

Get granular about interior experience:

Instead of: "I feel bad."

Try: "I notice restlessness in my chest, a tight sensation in my throat, and thoughts that keep returning to tomorrow's presentation. There's anxiety present, but also some excitement. The anxiety has a jagged quality, the excitement feels lighter. My breathing is shallow."

This isn't overthinking. It's developing experiential literacy.

You can't navigate terrain you can't perceive. Developing internal weather reporting is like learning to read maps.

Start a practice of **micro-phenomenology**: Spend two minutes daily noting interior experience with precision.

5. Create Micro-Communities of Practice

You can't rebuild social validation alone. But you can start small:

- Find one friend interested in these ideas and check in weekly
- Join or start a meditation group (online or local)
- Create a "presence practice" chat where people share observations
- Form a book club around developmental psychology

Two people practicing together is exponentially more powerful than two people practicing alone.

Social validation doesn't require masses. It requires one person who sees what you see.

* * *

Working With Your Domain Integration Scores

Let's get practical about the six domains:

If Your Biological Score is Low (1-4)

Immediate actions:

- Set a non-negotiable bedtime. Defend it like a meeting with your most important client.
- Move your body daily. Not "exercise"—just move. Walk. Stretch. Dance. Anything.
- Eat one real meal per day. Not optimized. Not tracked. Just nourishing.
- Notice when you're running on stimulants. Don't stop yet—just notice.

Why this matters: Every other domain depends on biological substrate. You can't think clearly, feel deeply, or act wisely when your body is depleted.

The paradox: Taking care of your body feels "unproductive" in a productivity culture. That's exactly why it's revolutionary.

If Your Cognitive Score is Low (1-4)

Immediate actions:

- Protect one hour per day for focused work. No meetings. No interruptions.
- Close all browser tabs except one. Notice the relief.
- Read one thing deeply instead of scanning ten things shallowly.
- Spend one hour per week on a problem with no deadline.

Why this matters: Cognitive fragmentation isn't a personal failing. It's an engineered state. You're proving you can still think deeply when protected from constant interruption.

The paradox: Deep work feels "inefficient" compared to rapid task-switching. It's actually the only way real thinking happens.

If Your Emotional Score is Low (1-4)

Immediate actions:

- Create five minutes daily to feel without fixing. Sit with whatever emotion is present.
- Stop immediately labeling feelings as "good" or "bad." Practice "interesting" or "present."
- Share one vulnerable thing weekly with someone safe.
- Permission: You're allowed to feel hard things. They won't destroy you.

Why this matters: Emotional suppression creates internal pressure that eventually explodes or implodes. Feeling is not weakness—it's essential data.

The paradox: Emotions feel "unprofessional" and "unproductive." They're actually the guidance system for what matters.

If Your Behavioral Score is Low (1-4)

Immediate actions:

- Notice one compulsive behavior this week. Don't try to stop it—just watch it operate.
- Before taking action, pause for three breaths. Not to change the action—just to make it conscious.
- Do one thing today that's aligned with your values but not "productive."
- Track the gap between what you value and what you actually do. Make the dissonance visible.

Why this matters: Compulsive behavior is behavior without conscious choice. Awareness creates space for freedom.

The paradox: Slowing down feels like wasting time. It's actually what makes time feel real.

If Your Social Score is Low (1-4)

Immediate actions:

- Have one conversation this week that isn't transactional. No networking. No favor-asking. Just connection.
- Reduce one performance: Stop managing how you appear in one relationship. Show up messier.
- Ask for help with something small. Practice receiving.
- Text one person you miss with no agenda. "Thinking of you. How are you?"

Why this matters: You're not a machine that occasionally needs social lubrication. You're a relational being who withers in isolation.

The paradox: Vulnerability feels risky. It's actually what creates real connection.

If Your Existential Score is Low (1-4)

Immediate actions:

- Spend ten minutes this week not doing anything useful. No justification. Just be.
- Write one paragraph about what actually matters to you (not what should matter).
- Identify one thing you're doing out of fear rather than meaning. Not to stop it—just to see it.
- Ask yourself: "If I knew I had five years to live, what would I change?"

Why this matters: Meaninglessness isn't a philosophical problem. It's an emergency signal that you've lost contact with what's real.

The paradox: Questioning meaning feels dangerous. It's actually the path to finding it.

* * *

The "Yes, And" Approach to Practice

Here's what doesn't work:

- "I'll fix myself first, then work on systems" (You'll burn out before systems change)
- "Systems will save us, so personal work doesn't matter" (You'll be unprepared when opportunities arise)
- "I'll do everything at once" (You'll overwhelm and quit)

Here's what does work: Yes, And.

Yes, practice personally. And organize collectively.

Yes, build capacity now. And push for structural change.

Yes, work with the system as it is. And work to transform it into what it could be.

This is both/and thinking (Chapter 6) applied to your Monday morning.

Example: Your Daily Morning Practice

Personal (what you do):

- 15 minutes before checking phone
- Stillness, movement, reflection
- Sovereignty over first moments

Collective (what you advocate):

- Propose "no meetings before 10am" policy at work
- Join movement for shorter workweeks
- Support candidates who prioritize wellbeing over GDP

Both matter. Both are necessary. Neither is sufficient alone.

* * *

What Success Looks Like

After one week:

- You've had one moment of genuine presence
- You've noticed one compulsion without immediately acting on it
- You've felt one feeling without immediately fixing it
- **You've remembered it's possible to be rather than always do**

After one month:

- You can name different qualities of your interior experience
- You've identified your lowest-scoring domain and started addressing it
- You've found one other person interested in these ideas
- **You've created one small sanctuary in your life**

After three months:

- Morning practice feels natural, not effortful
- You can sense when you're fragmenting and sometimes pause
- You've influenced one small structural change in your environment
- **You're seeing that personal practice makes collective action possible, and collective action makes personal practice sustainable**

After six months:

- You're rebuilding cognitive scaffolding that makes stillness valuable
- You're part of a community working for systemic change
- You're developing capacities you'll need for the Yellow transition
- **You're not fixed, but you're less broken. And you're part of building what comes next.**

* * *

The Bridge to Systemic Solutions

Personal practices are essential. But they're band-aids on bullet wounds if systems don't change.

You can meditate all you want. If your survival depends on constant productivity, meditation becomes another optimization project.

You can value presence deeply. If your environment is engineered to fragment attention, you'll lose that battle eventually.

You can develop wisdom. If your culture rewards extraction over integration, wisdom becomes a private hobby rather than public good.

This is why Chapters 11-14 matter:

They detail the systemic interventions that make personal practices sustainable rather than heroic:

- **Chapter 11: Cognitive Sovereignty Architecture** - Ending involuntary attention extraction
- **Chapter 12: The Sovereign Floor** - Ending conditional worth through Adaptive UBI
- **Chapter 13: Sanctuaries** - Creating spaces where market logic is suspended
- **Chapter 14: Contemplative Infrastructure** - Building capacity devel-

opment at civilizational scale

These aren't optional upgrades. They're the habitat design that makes human flourishing possible.

Personal practice is what you do now while we build that habitat together.

* * *

Monday Morning

David sits with his coffee.

He's still got forty-seven emails. Still got the meetings and deadlines. Still living in the Orange world.

But something shifted.

This morning, before checking his phone, he sat for five minutes. Just breathing. Just being.

It felt uncomfortable. His mind immediately generated seventeen "more important" things he should be doing.

But he sat anyway.

Not because it made him more productive (it didn't).

Not because it solved anything (it didn't).

Because for five minutes, he chose presence over compulsion.

* * *

Now he goes back to work. But he's different.

He's no longer just a battery powering the matrix. He's a double agent operating within it.

He performs the tasks. He attends the meetings. He sends the emails. But he doesn't give them his soul.

He's practicing strategic complicity:

- Extracting salary (resource) to fund his real work (integration)
- Building capacity while embedded in the system
- Maintaining cover while secretly serving different values
- Surviving Orange structures while working to transform them

This isn't selling out. This is spycraft.

The Alchemist's path (Part IV) is learning to be simultaneously "in the arena" and "not of it." To participate in systems while not being captured by them. To extract resources without being extracted.

David isn't enlightened. He isn't transformed. He isn't saved.

But he's awake. And that changes everything.

* * *

That's not enlightenment. That's not transformation. That's not solution.

That's the beginning.

The personal practice that proves it's possible.

The small act of sovereignty that remembers we're not machines.

The first step of a journey that requires both individual courage and collective action.

Monday morning, you start where you are.

But you don't stay there.

Because in Chapters 11-14, we're building the world where presence becomes possible, not just for heroes and monks, but for everyone.

Where Monday morning doesn't require heroic resistance to an extractive system.

Where the architecture itself supports flourishing rather than preventing it.

That's next.

For now: breathe. Notice. Begin.

The revolution starts in the morning, in the stillness before the world gets you.

And it continues in the work of transforming that world so stillness becomes not rebellion but birthright.

* * *

Your Turn

Before moving to the systemic solutions, pause.

What's one thing from the Integration Emergency Kit that you'll actually do?

Not all of it. One thing.

Today or tomorrow.

Small. Achievable. Concrete.

Write it down. Make it real.

Because personal transformation and systemic transformation aren't separate journeys.

They're two aspects of the same movement toward integration.

You begin where you are.

And where you begin changes what becomes possible.

* * *

Author's Note: The Integration Emergency Kit scorecard and tracking templates will be available as downloadable resources at <ins>https://globalgovernanceframeworks.org/integration-scorecard</ins>.

However: I cannot promise ongoing guided practices, managed community forums, or curated information about local working groups. That infrastructure requires resources and capacity I may not have.

This is actually the point: Civilization-level transformation cannot depend on one person's website. It requires distributed action.

Your responsibility:

- Create your own tracking systems (they're more useful when person-

alized anyway)
- Find or start your own local groups (they're more powerful when organically formed)
- Build your own communities of practice (they're more sustainable when collectively owned)

This book provides the framework. You provide the implementation.

If you're waiting for someone to give you permission, community, or resources—you're still thinking like a consumer. Start thinking like a builder.

The revolution isn't something you download. It's something you do.

And if robust resources *do* emerge at the website or elsewhere, wonderful. But don't wait for them. Begin now with what you have.

Interlude: A Normal Tuesday in the World That Won

Portland, Oregon – March 2032

* * *

Maya wakes without an alarm.

Not because she doesn't have work today—she does. But because her body knows when it's rested, and the Sovereign Floor means she doesn't wake in terror about making rent.

The morning light filters through curtains she actually chose, in an apartment she can afford on twenty hours of work per week. Her basic income covers housing, food, healthcare. Her job—designing accessible public spaces—covers everything else and feeds her sense of purpose.

This is new. Not the waking naturally—humans did that for millennia. New is that it's possible again in a modern city for someone who isn't wealthy.

She lies still for a moment, noticing the quality of the silence. Not the anxious silence of waiting for the other shoe to drop. The spacious silence of time that belongs to her.

Her phone is in another room. It's been there all night. This isn't discipline—it's city policy. Portland's Synoptic Protocol means her phone can't ping her between 9 PM and 8 AM unless she explicitly opts in. The attention companies fought it hard. They lost.

She owns her morning.

For just a moment, she feels a phantom sensation—her wrist twitching as if checking for notifications. A muscle memory from the old world. She remembers mornings that started with anxiety, scrolling through chaos before her feet hit the floor.

That world feels distant now. But it was only seven years ago.

* * *

7:15 AM – First Hour

Maya makes coffee slowly. Not as performance. Not photographing it for Instagram (which has been redesigned under cognitive sovereignty regulations to show chronological feeds, not algorithmic manipulation).

Just making coffee. Smelling it. Tasting it.

Her roommate Alex emerges, equally unhurried. They've been friends since the housing cooperative lottery paired them. Not quite "chosen family," but genuine connection rather than strangers randomly matched by an algorithm and forced to coexist for rent splitting.

"Thinking about the Sanctuary this afternoon?" Alex asks.

"Yeah. Meeting James there."

The Sanctuary. Three years ago, the city converted the downtown transit mall into a mixed-use Sanctuary District—half commercial space operating under normal rules, half legally protected zone where:

- No advertising
- No commercial transactions
- No productivity mandates
- No phones (optional check-in at the border, like coat check)

It's become the city's living room. Where people actually gather rather than just pass through.

Maya finishes coffee, then sits for her morning practice. Twenty minutes. Some days it's formal meditation. Today it's just sitting on the balcony, watching the city wake up, feeling her breath.

This isn't virtue. It's infrastructure.

The city's Contemplative Capacity Initiative means every school teaches these practices. Every public building has quiet rooms. Every workplace is required to provide space and time for integration practices. It's treated like fire safety—basic civilizational hygiene.

The scaffolding is cultural now, not just personal.

* * *

8:30 AM – Commute

Maya walks to work. Not because she's virtuous, but because the city redesigned itself.

Cars are still allowed, but:

- Most streets are pedestrian/bike priority
- Public transit is free (funded by the carbon dividend)
- The Sovereign Floor means people can live near where they work
- The thirty-hour work week means rush hour is a distributed flow, not a crush

She passes a bus stop. The digital screen displays the transit schedule and rotating local art. **No ads.**

She notices this absence. In the old world, every surface was a claim on her attention—billboards for anxiety medication, gambling apps, fast fashion, productivity tools. The city was one giant extraction machine.

Now her attention rests on the street itself, unclaimed by corporate predation.

This is the Synoptic Protocol in practice: public space that serves public consciousness, not private profit. The screens still exist. They just serve different masters now.

She walks through the Sanctuary District.

It's morning-quiet but alive. An older man does tai chi by the fountain. A few people sit reading actual books. A couple walks hand in hand, talking. Teenagers are sprawled on the grass doing homework together—yes, homework still exists, but school is different now. More developmental, less industrial.

No one is on their phone.

Not because phones are banned (they're not), but because the space itself invites presence. The architecture, the lighting, the sound design—all optimized for human nervous system regulation, not for retail traffic flow.

Maya notices a new art installation—collaborative chalk drawings, constantly evolving. She stops for a moment, appreciates it, keeps walking.

This is what happens when you protect space from extraction: People create things for joy, not for metrics.

* * *

9:00 AM – Work

Maya's office is in the New Columbia building—a converted office tower redesigned according to biophilic principles. Natural light. Living walls. Spaces for focused work AND spaces for collaboration AND spaces for rest.

The morning standup is different from what her parents described from their corporate jobs:

"What do you need today?" "What's blocking you?" "Who needs help?"

Not: "What did you complete yesterday?" "What will you complete today?" "What are your blockers?"

The focus is support, not surveillance.

Teams are small. Timelines are realistic. "Crunch time" is acknowledged as systems failure, not heroic norm.

Maya spends the morning in deep work—designing accessibility features for a new park. Three hours of focused attention without interruption. Her calendar is blocked, her notifications are off, her door is closed.

This is legally protected time.

The Synoptic Protocol means employers can't require immediate responsiveness. "Right to disconnect" is constitutional. Deep work is treated as essential, not indulgent.

Around 11:30, she surfaces. Takes a walk. Gets lunch. Chats with colleagues.

The rhythm is human.

Not machines pretending to be productive. Not humans pretending to be machines. People doing meaningful work at a sustainable pace.

* * *

12:30 PM – Lunch at the Commons

Maya stops at a small café on the way to the building's communal kitchen. She buys a sandwich.

The payment screen shows her three options:

- **Standard credits** (her wages)
- **Hearts** (local care currency—she earned some last month helping at the community garden)
- **Leaves** (ecological stewardship currency—discount for her building's composting program)

She pays partly in Hearts. The barista nods—recognizing the symbol that means "member of the community doing mutual care work."

Value circulates locally now. Not everything commodified through one universal currency. Some things measured in care. Some in ecological contribution. Some in money.

The economy is plural, not singular.

She heads upstairs to the communal kitchen. Not a cafeteria—a kitchen. People prepare food together, share recipes, eat in small groups.

This is part of the Contemplative Infrastructure.

Breaking bread together isn't mandated. But space is provided. Time is protected. Participation is optional but encouraged.

She sits with Elena and Marcus, who work in different departments. The conversation meanders—Elena's struggling with her teenage daughter, Marcus is excited about a new pottery class.

Then Alex texts: *"Lost the contract. Can we talk tonight?"*

Maya's stomach tightens. Alex is a freelance translator. Losing a major contract is serious.

But then she notices what she's NOT feeling: terror.

In the old world, this would have cascaded into existential panic. Can Alex make rent? Will they need to move? Will Maya have to cover them? Can she?

Now it's just... sad.

Disappointing. Frustrating. A real problem that needs addressing.

But Alex won't lose housing—the Sovereign Floor catches that. They won't lose healthcare—that's universal. They'll have time to find new work—the basic income gives breathing room.

The system didn't fix the problem. It removed the terror.

Alex will be upset tonight. They'll strategize together. Alex might need to adjust spending, pick up some shifts at the community center. It's not nothing.

But it's survivable. That's the difference.

Maya texts back: *"Home by 6. We'll figure it out. ❤"*

Then returns to conversation. Elena is still talking about her daughter.

No one talks about productivity.

Not because it's forbidden, but because it's not the primary lens anymore. The Sovereign Floor and thirty-hour week mean work is important but not all-consuming.

"How's your mom?" Elena asks. Maya's mom had a stroke last year.

"Better. The Care Corps has been amazing." The Corps—paid positions for care work, training programs, community support networks. Not perfect, but better than the abandonment her parents' generation faced.

Grief, illness, aging—these aren't private failures anymore. They're shared human experiences with collective support.

* * *

1:30 PM – Meeting James at the Sanctuary

Maya walks back through the Sanctuary District. It's busier now—midday energy.

A group of elders plays chess at permanent tables. Kids are running through a splash pad (yes, even in March—Portland winters are mild now, though summer heat is more intense. Climate change is real, but the trajectory bent because enough people had space to care).

She finds James at a small amphitheater where someone is playing guitar.

James is her ex-boyfriend. They dated for two years, broke up amicably, stayed friends. **This is much more common now.** Something about having economic security and genuine community makes relationship endings less catastrophic.

"Hey," he says, smiling.

"Hey yourself."

They walk together, catching up. James works in the food system— urban agriculture, distribution networks. Important work, fairly compen- sated, not consuming his entire life.

"How's the project?" Maya asks.

"Good. Challenging. We're trying to figure out how to do local food distribution without recreating Amazon's exploitation patterns."

This is the ongoing work: Building systems that are efficient AND humane. Productive AND integrative. It's not easy. There's no final solution. But people have space to think carefully rather than just moving fast and breaking things.

They sit on a bench. Watch people. Talk about life.

This is what the Sanctuary makes possible: Time that doesn't need to be productive. Space that doesn't need to be monetized. Presence that doesn't need to be justified.

* * *

3:00 PM – Afternoon Work

Maya returns to the office. Finishes the park design. Sends it to her team for feedback.

She has two more hours of work scheduled. But today she's done what needs doing. Tomorrow's timeline isn't crushing. Next week isn't terrifying.

She leaves at 4:00.

This isn't shirking. This is what's possible when:

- Work is right-sized to actual human capacity
- Deadlines are realistic rather than arbitrary
- Productivity is measured over weeks, not hours
- Output matters more than face time

No one questions it.

Her manager sent a message earlier: "Nice work on the park. Take tomorrow afternoon if you need it."

Trust, not surveillance.

* * *

4:30 PM – The Hard Part

Maya gets home and finds a message from her brother.

Their dad died six months ago. Heart attack. Fast. The family is still processing.

Grief doesn't disappear in the world that won.

Cancer still exists. Accidents still happen. People still hurt each other. Relationships still fail. Children still die.

The difference is: Maya has space to grieve.

She took a six-week grief sabbatical (paid, protected). She sees a therapist weekly (free, accessible). Her community held her when she couldn't hold herself.

And tonight, she feels it.

The hole where her dad was. The conversation she'll never have. The regret that he died before this world emerged—before the Sovereign Floor meant he could retire with dignity, before Medicare for All meant his illness didn't bankrupt them, before the sixty-hour weeks stopped grinding him down.

She sits with it.

Not pushing it away. Not fixing it. Just being with the grief.

This is what presence means: Being with reality, including the parts that hurt.

After twenty minutes, she calls her brother. They talk. They cry. They remember.

Loss is still loss. But you can survive it when you're not also surviving capitalism.

* * *

6:30 PM – Evening

Alex is home when Maya arrives. They look tired but not destroyed.

"Want to talk about it?" Maya asks.

They sit on the balcony. Alex explains: the client merged with another company, consolidated vendors, went with someone cheaper. Standard business dynamics. Nothing personal.

"I'm pissed," Alex says. "And scared. Not about survival—I know the Floor has me. But about... meaning, I guess? I liked that work. It felt important."

This is what the system enables: grieving actual loss instead of manufactured terror.

They strategize. Alex has enough savings for a few months of extra expenses beyond the basic income. Can pick up shifts at the language center. Has been wanting to develop a new translation specialty anyway— maybe this is the push.

"You'll figure it out," Maya says. And means it.

Not toxic positivity. Not dismissing the difficulty. Just... trust that problems can be solved when you're not also fighting for survival.

Then they cook dinner together. Alex teaches Maya a recipe from their grandmother. They eat, talking about other things—the Sanctuary installation, Elena's daughter, whether to adopt a cat.

After dishes, Maya calls her mom. Checks in. Makes plans to visit this weekend.

Then she reads. Actual book. Paper pages. No screens.

Around 8:30, she texts a few friends: "Movie night Friday?"

Phones are allowed again now—the Synoptic Protocol's quiet hours are 9 PM to 8 AM. But usage is different. Tools, not addictions. **The architecture changed behavior.**

* * *

9:15 PM – Preparing for Sleep

Maya does her evening practice. Ten minutes of light stretching. Five minutes of reflection—gratitude journal, noting what mattered today.

She thinks about her dad. About James. About the park design. About tomorrow's morning light.

Life isn't perfect. The climate is still changing (slower now, but still). Inequality still exists (less extreme, but still). Politics is still contentious (though less toxic—something about people having economic security reduces fear-based voting).

But it's livable.

She can breathe. She can rest. She can grieve without it destroying her. She can work without it consuming her. She can connect without it exhausting her.

This is what winning looks like:

Not utopia. Not enlightenment. Not the end of suffering.

Just a world where human flourishing is structurally possible rather than structurally prevented.

Where presence is normal rather than heroic.

Where integration is expected rather than exceptional.

Where you can be a complete human being without having to fight for that right every single day.

* * *

10:00 PM

Maya sleeps without medication.

Not because she's naturally calm (she's not—anxiety is real, brain chemistry is real, some people need medication and that's fine).

But because:

- She's not terrified about money
- She's not exhausted from overwork
- She's not lonely in anonymous isolation
- She's not numbed by constant stimulation
- She's not crushed by meaninglessness

Her nervous system can rest.

Tomorrow is Wednesday. She'll wake naturally again. Work four hours. Meet friends. Practice. Rest. Grieve a little. Laugh a little. Build things. Break things. Be human.

This is a normal Tuesday in the world that won.

Not because we became better people.

Because we built better systems.

Systems that work with human nature instead of against it.

Systems that enable presence instead of preventing it.

Systems that support integration instead of forcing fragmentation.

This is what's possible.

Not someday. Not in some distant future.

Within a decade, if we start now.

The Sovereign Floor. Cognitive Sovereignty. Sanctuaries. Contemplative Infrastructure.

Four interventions. One integrated system. A civilization redesigned for humans.

That's what the next four chapters detail.

Not as fantasy. As blueprint.

Let's build it.

Chapter 11: Cognitive Sovereignty Architecture – Ending Involuntary Attention Extraction

You saw Maya's morning in 2032. Phone silent until 8 AM. No ads on the bus stop. Digital spaces designed for humans, not engagement metrics.

That didn't happen by accident. It didn't happen through individual willpower. It happened through law.

Specifically: the Synoptic Protocol and related cognitive sovereignty regulations that fundamentally restructured the relationship between human attention and commercial extraction.

The Synoptic Protocol protects your digital attention. The Sanctuary Districts (Chapter 13) are its physical counterpart. Together they create spaces—both digital and physical—where consciousness can rest.

This chapter details how we get from "doomscrolling at 6 AM" to "owning your morning."

Not someday. Not with perfect technology. **With existing legal frameworks, proven precedents, and political will we can build in the next five years.**

* * *

The Core Problem: Involuntary Attention Extraction

Let's be precise about what we're solving.

The attention economy doesn't just compete for your attention. It engineers involuntary capture.

This isn't marketing. Marketing says: "Here's a product. Would you like to buy it?"

This is predation. It says: "We've studied your psychology, mapped your vulnerabilities, A/B tested 47 variations, and deployed algorithmic systems specifically designed to bypass your conscious decision-making and create compulsive engagement patterns."

The difference matters legally.

When your environment is scientifically engineered to trigger subconscious, compulsive responses, your "choice" to engage is no more free than a lab rat's "choice" to press a lever for a dopamine hit.

That's not marketing. That's behavioral engineering. And it violates consent.

Marketing requires informed consent. Predation violates autonomy.

When Facebook's internal documents revealed they were specifically targeting teenagers' moments of maximum vulnerability to create addictive engagement, that wasn't aggressive marketing. **That was intentional psychological harm for profit.**

When TikTok's algorithm is designed to create dissociative states where users lose track of time (the company's own language: "flow state"), that's not entertainment. **That's engineered compulsion.**

When infinite scroll removes natural stopping points, when autoplay removes choice points, when notifications are timed for maximum disruption—these aren't features. **They're attacks on human autonomy.**

This is the core claim that makes cognitive sovereignty legally defensible:

You have a right to decide what enters your consciousness, just as you have a right to decide what enters your body.

Forcing unwanted content into someone's awareness against their will is a violation of cognitive autonomy—the mental equivalent of assault.

* * *

The Legal Foundation: Cognitive Liberty as Human Right

Cognitive sovereignty rests on an emerging legal principle: **cognitive liberty.**

But let's be more precise: **This isn't just about "digital rights." It's about environmental protection.**

We don't allow companies to pump toxic smoke into your lungs just because it's profitable. Why do we allow them to pump toxic anxiety into your amygdala?

The Synoptic Protocol treats the cognitive environment as a protected commons—like clean air, clean water, or freedom from toxic substances.

The right to:

- Self-directed consciousness
- Freedom from involuntary mental manipulation
- Protection against coercive persuasion
- Autonomy over one's own attention and awareness
- **A cognitive environment free from deliberate pollution**

This isn't new law. It's application of existing rights to new technology.

Just as:

- **Fourth Amendment** (US) or **Article 8 ECHR** (Europe) protects physical privacy → extends to mental privacy
- **Informed consent** protects bodily autonomy → extends to cognitive autonomy
- **Consumer protection law** prevents deceptive practices → extends to

manipulative design
- **Product safety law** requires non-harmful products → extends to psychological harm

The precedent is already established. We're just applying it consistently. Countries that have started down this path:

- **EU's Digital Services Act (2022)**: Bans certain manipulative design patterns, requires algorithmic transparency
- **France's Right to Disconnect (2017)**: Employees can ignore work communications outside hours
- **California's Age-Appropriate Design Code (2022)**: Protects children from attention manipulation
- **China's restrictions on gaming and social media for minors (2021)**: Time limits, content restrictions

None of these are hypothetical. They're functioning law in major economies.

The Synoptic Protocol takes these precedents and systematizes them into comprehensive cognitive protection.

* * *

The Synoptic Protocol: Core Components

Think of the Synoptic Protocol as the digital equivalent of building codes.

Buildings must have fire exits, structural integrity, accessible facilities. Not because builders are evil, but because without regulation, economic incentives lead to unsafe conditions.

Same principle. Different domain.

Component 1: Quiet Hours Protection

The Rule: Digital services cannot send notifications, alerts, or attention-grabbing content during user-defined quiet hours (default: 9 PM - 8 AM) without explicit opt-in per instance.

How it works:

- Operating system level (iOS, Android, etc.) enforces quiet hours
- Apps must respect OS-level settings
- Violations are treated like spam—with escalating penalties
- Emergency services exempt (911, verified emergencies)

Legal precedent:

- Do Not Call Registry (telemarketing)
- Restrictions on noise pollution
- Right to peaceful enjoyment of property

Multi-Domain Impact:
Implementation timeline:

- Year 1: Voluntary adoption + public awareness campaign
- Year 2: Mandatory for platforms with 10M+ users
- Year 3: Full enforcement with penalties

Component 2: Algorithmic Transparency and User Control

The Rule: Users must be able to see and control how content is selected for them. Algorithmic feeds must offer chronological alternatives. Data used for targeting must be transparent and controllable.

But it's not just about addiction. It's about reality.

When algorithms prioritize engagement over truth, they fracture shared reality. Two people can live in completely different information universes, making democratic governance impossible.

The Synoptic Protocol mandates that algorithms must optimize for epistemic integrity—accuracy, context, source reliability—alongside or instead of engagement.

How it works:

- Every algorithmic system must provide:
- Explanation of ranking factors (including how truth/accuracy is weighted)
- Simple, user-friendly controls to shape their feed (not technical "adjust weights" but intuitive sliders: "prioritize accuracy over speed," "show diverse perspectives," "reduce emotional manipulation")
- Non-algorithmic chronological option
- Clear data usage disclosure
- "Why am I seeing this?" must have honest, comprehensible answers
- Users can export their data and algorithmic profile
- Platforms must demonstrate epistemic integrity in their ranking (not just engagement metrics)

Legal precedent:

- Truth in lending (financial transparency)
- Nutrition labels (informed choice)
- GDPR data rights (EU)

Why this matters: Current algorithms optimize for engagement, not wellbeing. They learn what captures you and do more of it. **This creates feedback loops toward extremism, compulsion, and outrage.**

Transparency breaks the black box. User control restores agency.

Multi-Domain Impact:

Implementation timeline:

- Year 1: Major platforms must provide transparency reports

- Year 2: User controls required
- Year 3: Chronological feeds mandatory as option

Component 3: Attention-Hijacking Design Prohibition

The Rule: Design patterns specifically engineered to create compulsive use are illegal, just as tobacco companies can't add compounds to increase addiction.

Specifically prohibited:

- Infinite scroll without natural stopping points
- Autoplay that continues without user action
- Variable reward schedules designed for compulsion (slot machine mechanics)
- Notifications timed for maximum disruption
- Dark patterns that make opting out difficult
- Fake urgency indicators (false scarcity, pressure tactics)
- Read receipts that create social obligation

Legal precedent:

- Deceptive trade practices law
- Gambling regulation
- Tobacco industry restrictions
- Pharmaceutical advertising rules

The enforcement question: "But how do you prove intent?"

Same way we do in existing law: Internal documents, design discussions, A/B testing records. If you're testing which version creates more compulsion, you're admitting intent.

Multi-Domain Impact:

Implementation:

- Year 1: Industry standards developed with oversight
- Year 2: Major platforms must demonstrate compliance
- Year 3: Third-party audits, penalties for violations

Component 4: Advertising Restrictions in Public and Semi-Public Space

The Rule: Public and semi-public spaces (transit, streets, parks, schools, medical facilities) must be substantially free from commercial advertising, especially digital advertising designed for attention capture.

How it works:

- Digital billboards in public space restricted to:
- Public service announcements
- Transit information
- Local art and cultural content
- Emergency information
- Schools and medical facilities completely ad-free
- Residential areas protected from digital advertising
- Online "public squares" (platforms with universal access) must offer ad-free options

Legal precedent:

- São Paulo, Brazil (2007): Banned outdoor advertising citywide
- Vermont, Maine, Hawaii, Alaska (US): Billboard restrictions
- BBC (UK): Public broadcasting without advertising
- Many European cities: Heavy restrictions on outdoor ads

Why this matters: Your attention is a commons. When every surface extracts attention for commercial gain, there's no space for consciousness to rest. **We've privatized the cognitive commons.**

Multi-Domain Impact:

Implementation:

- Pilot cities (Year 1-2)
- Regional adoption (Year 3-5)
- National frameworks (Year 5-10)

Component 5: Children's Cognitive Protection

The Rule: Enhanced protection for developing minds. No manipulative design, limited screen time encouragement, age-appropriate content by default.

Specific provisions:

- No algorithmic recommendation systems for users under 16
- No advertising targeted at children under 13
- Educational technology must demonstrate developmental benefit
- Social media platforms must verify age and provide parental controls
- Schools receive funding to provide tech-free zones and contemplative education

Legal precedent:

- Children's Online Privacy Protection Act (COPPA)
- Restrictions on marketing to children (tobacco, alcohol, gambling)
- Educational standards and curriculum requirements

Why this is crucial: Developing brains are more vulnerable to manipulation. Habits formed in childhood shape lifetime patterns. **We protect children from tobacco and alcohol. We must protect them from attention predation.**

Multi-Domain Impact:

* * *

How This Gets Funded

"This sounds expensive."

It's not. Here's the math:

The cost of implementing this protocol is a fraction of the estimated $600 billion in annual productivity loss and healthcare costs attributed to attention fragmentation and digital stress in the US alone.

That's not speculative—that's conservative estimates from:

- Lost productivity from context switching
- Mental health treatment for digital-era anxiety and depression
- Sleep disorders from nighttime device use
- Stress-related illness from constant availability
- Educational remediation for attention difficulties

We're already paying. We're just paying inefficiently through diffuse social costs rather than making platforms internalize the harms they create.

Revenue from:

- Fines for violations (substantial, escalating)
- Auction of limited advertising space (now scarce, therefore valuable)
- Digital services tax (platforms pay for regulatory infrastructure)
- Reclaimed public space (repurposed advertising real estate)

Costs saved:

- Mental health treatment (burnout, anxiety, depression)
- Lost productivity (attention fragmentation)
- Educational remediation (attention-related learning difficulties)
- Healthcare (stress-related illness)

The attention economy currently extracts trillions in value while exter-

nalizing costs to individuals and public health systems.

Making platforms internalize the costs of attention harm doesn't require new money. It requires proper accounting.

* * *

The Opposition (And How to Counter It)

"This is censorship!"

No, it's consumer protection.

We don't call restrictions on pharmaceutical advertising "censorship." We don't call truth-in-lending laws "censorship." We don't call requirements for accessible building design "censorship."

This is setting safety standards for products that affect human consciousness.

You're still free to advertise. You just can't lie, manipulate, or prey on psychological vulnerabilities.

"Innovation will suffer!"

Good.

If your innovation depends on exploiting psychological vulnerabilities, it should suffer.

We don't want "innovative" new ways to create compulsive behavior any more than we want "innovative" new addictive tobacco products.

Real innovation creates genuine value. Manipulative design creates extracted value.

And here's what actually happens: When we ban extraction, we force real innovation.

Companies will have to pivot from "mining users" to "serving users." From surveillance capitalism to subscription models. From engagement addiction to genuine utility.

The Pathfinder Protocol (part of the broader GGF framework) provides the transition map for tech companies to move from extractive models to regenerative ones—business models that create value rather than extract it.

History shows this pattern: When we ban harmful practices, markets adapt and often improve:

- Removing lead from gasoline didn't end transportation
- Banning child labor didn't end manufacturing
- Requiring seatbelts didn't end automobiles
- **Ending attention extraction won't end technology—it will civilize it**

"The market should decide!"

The market can't decide when choice architecture is manipulated.

If addiction is engineered, choice is illusory. You can't have free markets without genuinely free agents.

Cognitive sovereignty enables real market choices by protecting the capacity to choose.

"This is paternalistic!"

No, paternalistic is allowing companies to manipulate people's psychology for profit while calling it 'freedom.'

True freedom requires protection from coercion—including psychological coercion.

We protect people from fraud, we protect workers from exploitation, we protect consumers from dangerous products. **Protecting consciousness is the same principle.**

"Who decides what's 'manipulative'? This is a slippery slope to government controlling all information!"

We're not banning content. We're banning proven, documentable design patterns that exploit known psychological vulnerabilities.

Just as we ban lead in paint without banning painting itself. Just as we ban certain additives in food without banning cooking. Just as we ban specific gambling mechanics without banning games.

The regulations target process, not content:

- Infinite scroll (design pattern) ✗
- Political opinions (content) ✓
- Notification timing for maximum disruption (design pattern) ✗
- News articles (content) ✓
- Variable reward schedules (design pattern) ✗
- Social media posts (content) ✓

We're not regulating speech. We're regulating pollution of the cognitive environment.

The determination is objective: Does this design pattern exploit documented psychological vulnerabilities? Can you demonstrate intent through internal testing? Does it create compulsive behavior?

Same standards we use for product safety, gambling regulation, and pharmaceutical advertising.

"People want these features!"

No, people's compulsions want these features. That's the point.

Smokers "want" cigarettes. Gamblers "want" slot machines. Addicts "want" their drug.

Wanting something doesn't mean it serves you. Sometimes protection means protecting you from your own manipulated impulses until you can restore real choice.

* * *

Implementation Strategy: The Pilot City Approach

You don't implement this nationally overnight. You prove it works locally first.

Phase 1: Pilot Cities (Years 1-3)

Ten cities volunteer: Portland, Barcelona, Copenhagen, Wellington, Seoul, Boulder, Edinburgh, Vancouver, Singapore, Vienna.

What they implement:

- Full Synoptic Protocol within city limits
- Ad-free public transit and spaces
- School-based contemplative education
- Monitoring of wellbeing metrics

What they measure:

- Mental health indicators (anxiety, depression, sleep quality)
- Productivity metrics (real output, not hours)
- Educational outcomes
- Economic vitality
- Quality of life surveys

Legal mechanism:

- Cities have authority over public space and local ordinances
- State/national laws for platform compliance (or pilot exemptions)
- Voluntary platform participation incentivized

Phase 2: Regional Adoption (Years 3-7)

Based on pilot success:

- Entire states/provinces adopt framework
- Regional alliances (e.g., West Coast US, Nordic countries)
- Policy toolkit shared openly
- Economic data demonstrates viability

Phase 3: National/International Standards (Years 7-15)

Once proof-of-concept exists:

- National legislation in early-adopter countries
- International treaties (like GDPR)
- Global platforms adapt rather than fragment
- Cultural shift makes old patterns unthinkable

Historical precedent:

- Seatbelt laws: Started with one state, became universal
- Smoking bans: NYC first, then everywhere
- GDPR: EU first, became de facto global standard

This is how transformative policy happens: prove it works small, scale it everywhere.

* * *

What This Doesn't Solve (And What It Does)

Cognitive sovereignty alone won't fix everything.

It won't:

- End economic inequality (that's Chapter 12)
- Create spaces for presence (that's Chapter 13)
- Build developmental capacity (that's Chapter 14)

But it will:

- Stop the deliberate engineering of compulsive behavior
- Restore basic agency over attention and consciousness
- Protect children's developing minds
- Create space for the other interventions to work

Think of it as removing a barrier rather than building a complete solution.

You can't integrate when your attention is under constant assault. You can't develop presence when your consciousness is colonized. You can't think clearly when your cognitive architecture is hijacked.

Cognitive sovereignty clears the ground. The other interventions build the house.

* * *

The Integration Scorecard: Cognitive Sovereignty

Let's be specific about cross-domain effects:

Biological Domain (Impact: 7/10)

Positive effects:

- Restored sleep through quiet hours protection
- Reduced cortisol from constant notification anxiety
- Better circadian rhythm alignment
- Lower allostatic load (wear-and-tear from chronic stress)

Mechanism: Nervous system gets breaks from stimulation, allowing parasympathetic activation

Cognitive Domain (Impact: 9/10)

Positive effects:

- Restored capacity for sustained attention
- Reduced context-switching costs
- Protection of working memory
- Better executive function
- Conscious choice over information diet

Mechanism: Attention becomes a resource you allocate, not a resource extracted from you

Emotional Domain (Impact: 6/10)

Positive effects:

- Reduced anxiety from constant availability
- Less comparison-driven inadequacy
- Decreased outrage fatigue
- Protected emotional processing time

Limitations: Doesn't address underlying emotional issues, just removes amplification

Behavioral Domain (Impact: 8/10)

Positive effects:

- Reduced compulsive checking
- Restored agency over actions
- Better habit formation capacity
- More intentional behavior

Mechanism: Breaking compulsion loops allows conscious behavior to emerge

Social Domain (Impact: 7/10)

Positive effects:

- Protected time for in-person relationships
- Reduced performative social media behavior
- Less polarization from algorithmic amplification
- More authentic connection

Limitations: Doesn't create community, just removes barriers to it

Existential Domain (Impact: 5/10)

Positive effects:

- Mental space for meaning-making
- Reduced consumption-focused identity
- Time for reflection on values

- Less manufactured desire

Limitations: Creates space but doesn't fill it—that requires other interventions

Overall Integration Score: 7/10

Strong impact on cognitive and behavioral domains (directly targeted). Moderate impact on biological and social (secondary effects). Limited but meaningful impact on emotional and existential (removes barriers but doesn't build capacity).

Necessary but not sufficient. Which is exactly why we need all four interventions.

* * *

Getting Started Tomorrow

National cognitive sovereignty policy might be years away. What can happen now?

As an Individual:

- Use tools that respect attention (Freedom, Cold Turkey, browser extensions)
- Delete the most predatory apps
- Manually create quiet hours
- Support organizations fighting for digital rights (EFF, CDT, etc.)

As a Community:

- Pressure local government for ad-free public transit
- Advocate for tech-free zones in schools
- Create public spaces without screens

- Build culture that values attention protection

As an Organization:

- Implement internal right to disconnect policies
- Remove manipulative design from your products
- Create focus time blocks
- Measure wellbeing, not just engagement

As a Citizen:

- Contact representatives about cognitive sovereignty legislation
- Support pilot city proposals
- Vote for candidates prioritizing digital rights
- Organize for policy change

The infrastructure is being built right now. The question is whether we build it intentionally or let it emerge from pure profit motive.

* * *

The Vision Redux

Remember Maya's morning? Phone silent. No ads on her commute. Algorithmic feeds under her control. Quiet hours protecting her sleep.

That's not science fiction. That's engineered choice.

We can build cities where attention is protected rather than extracted. Where consciousness is sacred rather than colonized. Where humans reclaim sovereignty over their own minds.

But only if we treat this as the legal and political priority it is.

Cognitive sovereignty is the foundation. Without it, every other intervention fights uphill against engineered compulsion.

With it, integration becomes possible.

Not guaranteed. Not automatic. But possible.

And possible is where transformation begins.

* * *

Next: The Sovereign Floor—ending conditional worth through Adaptive Universal Basic Income.

Because you can't be present when survival requires constant productivity. You can't integrate when terror is the default state.

Cognitive sovereignty protects your attention. The Sovereign Floor protects your existence.

Together, they create the foundation for everything else.

Chapter 12: The Sovereign Floor – Ending Conditional Worth Through Adaptive Universal Basic Income

Remember Alex from the Interlude? Lost a major contract. Felt sad. Felt frustrated. Felt disappointed.

But didn't feel terror.

That's the Sovereign Floor in action.

Not because Alex became enlightened. Not because Alex had better coping skills. **Because the economic architecture removed survival terror from the equation.**

This is the intervention that makes everything else possible.

You can't practice presence when you're terrified about rent. You can't protect your attention when checking email compulsively is how you keep your job. You can't integrate when fragmentation is required for survival.

Cognitive sovereignty protects your consciousness. The Sovereign Floor protects your existence.

This chapter details the most controversial, most necessary, most transformative intervention in the entire framework: **Adaptive Universal Basic Income (AUBI).**

Not someday. Not when we're "ready." **Starting within five years, scaling within ten.**

* * *

The Core Problem: Conditional Worth

Let's name what we're actually solving.

The fundamental spiritual violence of the current system is this: Your right to exist is conditional on your economic productivity.

Every month, you must prove you deserve:

- Shelter
- Food
- Healthcare
- The basic dignity of not dying in the street

If you can't prove your worth through labor market participation, you lose access to survival.

This creates a baseline state of existential terror that:

- Makes presence impossible (constant vigilance for threats)
- Prevents integration (fragmentation is required to survive)
- Destroys mental health (chronic stress from conditional existence)
- Warps all relationships (transactional rather than authentic)
- Prevents developmental growth (survival mode blocks higher capacities)

You cannot flourish when your existence is conditional.

You cannot be present when terror is the baseline.

You cannot integrate when fragmentation is mandated.

The Sovereign Floor ends this. Not by making everyone wealthy. Not by eliminating work. **By unconditionally guaranteeing the basics of human existence.**

* * *

What AUBI Actually Is (And Isn't)

Let's be precise.

Adaptive Universal Basic Income is:

- **Universal:** Everyone gets it, regardless of employment status, wealth, or "deservingness"
- **Basic:** Covers fundamental needs—housing, food, healthcare, basic utilities
- **Adaptive:** Adjusts to local cost of living and life circumstances
- **Income:** Money (or equivalent) you can use for what you need
- **Unconditional:** No work requirements, no means testing, no bureaucratic gatekeeping

What it's NOT:

- Universal Basic Income (fixed amount regardless of context)
- Welfare (stigmatized, conditional, means-tested)
- Charity (optional giving from those who have to those who don't)
- Minimum wage (tied to employment)
- Social safety net (you have to fall before it catches you)

The differences matter.

Traditional welfare says: "Prove you're desperate enough, jump through bureaucratic hoops, accept stigma, and we'll give you barely enough to survive—but only if you keep proving you deserve it."

AUBI says: "You exist. That's sufficient. Here's enough to cover basics. What you do with your life is up to you."

* * *

The Adaptive Component: Why "Universal" Isn't Enough

Standard Universal Basic Income proposals fail because:

$1,000/month means different things in:

- Rural Mississippi (maybe sufficient)
- San Francisco (barely covers parking)

$1,000/month means different things for:

- Single person with no dependents (tight but manageable)
- Single parent with three kids (completely inadequate)
- Person with disability requiring ongoing care (nowhere near enough)

Fixed UBI treats everyone as identical atoms. AUBI recognizes humans as embedded in contexts.

How AUBI Adapts:

1. Geographic Adjustment

- Base amount set to cover median rent + food + utilities in each region
- Updated quarterly based on actual costs
- Prevents "you must move to survive" while allowing mobility

2. Life Circumstance Adjustment

- Base rate: Individual coverage
- Dependent additions: Per child, elder, or dependent care
- Disability adjustments: Medical needs, care requirements
- Transitional support: Job loss, divorce, major life changes get temporary increases

3. Developmental Stage Adjustment

- Young adults (18–25): Higher amounts (critical developmental period)
- Elders (65+): Adjusted for healthcare needs
- New parents: First two years include childcare support
- Students: Education-related supplements

The goal isn't identical amounts. It's sufficient security for actual circumstances.

* * *

How It Gets Funded (The Real Numbers)

"We can't afford this!"
  We're already paying for it. We're just paying inefficiently.

Current Costs We're Already Bearing:

Direct costs:

- Welfare bureaucracy: $100+ billion (US)
- Unemployment insurance: $50 billion
- Food assistance (SNAP): $80 billion
- Housing assistance: $50 billion
- Medicaid (poverty-related): $400 billion
- **Total: ~$700+ billion**

Indirect costs:

- Emergency room care for uninsured: $40+ billion
- Homelessness (medical, enforcement, shelter): $50+ billion

- Crime and incarceration (poverty-related): $200+ billion
- Lost productivity from poverty stress: $500+ billion
- Childhood poverty impacts (lifetime): $1 trillion+
- **Total hidden costs: $1.5+ trillion annually**

We're spending $2+ trillion managing poverty. AUBI would cost $1.5 trillion and actually solve it.

Revenue Sources (US Model, Scaled for Other Economies):

But let's reframe this entirely:

AUBI isn't a handout funded by taxes. It's a Commons Dividend—your share of our collective wealth.

Think about it: If a company uses:

- **Our data** (to train AI and target ads) → They owe us a royalty
- **Our atmosphere** (to dump carbon) → They owe us a fee
- **Our land and resources** (extracted and privatized) → They owe us rent
- **Our attention** (monetized through platforms) → They owe us compensation
- **Our infrastructure** (roads, internet, educated workforce) → They owe us payment

The Sovereign Floor isn't charity. It's your dividend from the planetary commons.

This reframing matters politically and morally:

- **To Orange:** This is fair market pricing, not confiscation
- **To Blue:** This is justice, not redistribution
- **To Green:** This recognizes collective ownership
- **To Yellow:** This properly accounts for systemic interdependence

Revenue Sources—Commons Dividends:

1. Data and Attention Dividends ($400 billion)

- Platforms pay for use of collective data
- Attention economy pays for cognitive access
- AI companies pay for training on human knowledge
- Digital commons properly valued

2. Ecological Dividends ($400 billion)

- Carbon fee and dividend
- Resource extraction fees
- Pollution charges (air, water, toxics)
- Ecosystem service payments

3. Land and Infrastructure Dividends ($400 billion)

- Land value tax (capturing socially-created value)
- Spectrum auctions (public airwaves)
- Financial transaction tax (using our monetary system)
- Natural resource royalties

4. Existing Program Consolidation ($300 billion)

- Eliminate most welfare bureaucracy (keep specialized support)
- Consolidate unemployment insurance
- Simplify tax credits (EITC, child credits become redundant)
- **Keep:** Medicare, Social Security, disability supports

Total Available: $1.5 trillion

This isn't taking from "the rich" to give to "the poor." This is recognizing that the wealth was collectively created and should be collectively shared.

Cost of AUBI for 260 million adults (US):

- Base rate: $1,500/month average (adjusted by region/circumstance)
- Includes healthcare (decoupled from employment)
- **Total: ~$1.4-1.6 trillion**

It's not a question of affordability. It's a question of priorities.

* * *

The Multi-Domain Impact: Why AUBI Enables Everything Else

Let's be specific about how removing survival terror affects all six domains.

Biological Domain (Impact: 8/10)

Direct effects:

- Chronic stress reduction (cortisol normalization)
- Better sleep (financial anxiety is primary sleep disruptor)
- Healthcare access (decoupled from employment)
- Better nutrition (can afford healthy food)
- Time for exercise and body care

The mechanism: When survival isn't threatened, the nervous system can exit constant fight-or-flight. Parasympathetic activation becomes possible. The body can actually rest and repair.

Measurable outcomes:

- Reduced stress-related illness
- Lower blood pressure
- Better immune function

- Decreased inflammation markers
- Improved life expectancy

Cognitive Domain (Impact: 9/10)

Direct effects:

- Working memory restoration (poverty uses 13 IQ points worth of cognitive bandwidth)
- Long-term thinking becomes possible (not just crisis management)
- Attention available for learning and growth
- Decision-making improves (less desperation-driven choices)
- Time for education and skill development

The mechanism: Poverty is expensive cognitively. When you're constantly calculating "can I afford this?" and "what if I lose my job?" your cognitive resources are consumed by survival math. Remove the terror, and cognition becomes available for actual thinking.

Measurable outcomes:

- Improved test scores for children in AUBI households
- Better decision-making quality
- More long-term planning
- Increased educational attainment

Emotional Domain (Impact: 9/10)

Direct effects:

- Baseline anxiety reduction (existential terror removed)
- Depression rates decrease (poverty and financial stress are major depression risk factors)
- Emotional regulation improves (not constantly in survival mode)

- Shame reduction (existence no longer conditional)
- Ability to process emotions rather than suppress them

The mechanism: Financial insecurity creates chronic emotional dysregulation. You're always slightly activated, slightly vigilant, slightly terrified. Remove the threat, and emotional baseline normalizes.

Measurable outcomes:

- Reduced anxiety and depression diagnoses
- Lower suicide rates
- Better emotional regulation
- Decreased domestic violence (financial stress is primary trigger)

Behavioral Domain (Impact: 10/10)

Direct effects:

- Freedom to make choices based on values rather than desperation
- Ability to leave exploitative situations (jobs, relationships, housing)
- Time for meaningful activity beyond survival work
- Reduced compulsive behavior (less stress-driven coping)
- Ability to invest in long-term habits

But here's the deepest transformation:

The Sovereign Floor creates a new fundamental right: The Right to Refuse.

You cannot have a free market for labor if one side dies if they say "no." You cannot have free relationships if one person needs the other for survival. You cannot have genuine choice if the alternative to compliance is death.

AUBI makes "Yes" meaningful because "No" is finally possible.

This is liberty, not just safety. This is freedom, not just welfare.

The mechanism: Behavior becomes free when survival is secure.

Currently, most behavior is dictated by economic necessity. With AUBI, you can actually choose based on meaning, growth, and values.

Every "yes" you give—to a job, a relationship, a living situation—becomes authentic when "no" is survivable.

Measurable outcomes:

- Workers can reject exploitative employment
- People can leave abusive relationships
- Time for creative and community engagement
- Reduced addiction (stress-coping mechanism less needed)
- Increased volunteering and care work

Social Domain (Impact: 9/10)

Direct effects:

- Relationships less transactional (not survival strategies)
- More time for community engagement
- Reduced competition for scarce resources
- Ability to care for family without financial ruin
- Social mobility increases

The mechanism: When everyone's survival is secure, relationships can be authentic rather than strategic. You can help a friend without fearing you'll endanger yourself. You can build community without it being a luxury you can't afford.

Measurable outcomes:

- Increased social trust
- More volunteering and mutual aid
- Better family relationships
- Stronger community ties
- Reduced crime (poverty-related)

Existential Domain (Impact: 9/10)

Direct effects:

- Time and space to ask "what matters?" instead of just "how do I survive?"
- Ability to pursue meaning rather than just money
- Freedom to contribute based on calling rather than desperation
- Reduced existential anxiety from conditional worth
- Development of purpose and identity beyond economic role

The mechanism: You can't address existential questions when existential survival is threatened. Maslow wasn't entirely right, but he wasn't entirely wrong—it's hard to self-actualize when you're terrified about rent.

Measurable outcomes:

- Increased life satisfaction
- More people pursuing meaning-driven work
- Greater sense of purpose
- Reduced "deaths of despair"
- More spiritual/philosophical engagement

Overall Integration Score: 9/10

AUBI is the highest-impact intervention because it addresses the root cause of fragmentation: **survival terror that requires constant fragmentation to manage.**

Remove the terror, and integration becomes possible.

* * *

Existing Evidence: We've Tested This

AUBI isn't theoretical. Versions have been tested extensively:

Alaska Permanent Fund (1982-present)

- Universal annual dividend from oil revenues
- Everyone gets it, no conditions
- **Results:**
- No reduction in employment
- Reduced poverty, especially child poverty
- Improved health outcomes
- Became politically untouchable (even conservatives defend it)

Kenya GiveDirectly (2016-present)

- $22/month to rural villages
- No conditions, direct cash transfer
- **Results:**
- Improved nutrition and health
- Children stay in school longer
- Domestic violence decreases
- Economic activity increases (not decreases)
- Psychological wellbeing improves dramatically

Stockton, California SEED (2019-2021)

- $500/month to 125 residents
- Tracked vs. control group
- **Results:**
- Full-time employment increased (not decreased)
- Financial stability improved
- Mental health scores up significantly

· Families could afford to be more strategic with job choices

Canada Mincome (1974-1979)

· Near-UBI in Dauphin, Manitoba
· Canceled for political reasons, data analyzed decades later
· **Results:**
· Hospitalization rates dropped 8.5%
· Mental health visits down
· Teen mothers stayed in school
· Only new mothers and students reduced work (to care for family/study)

Finland Basic Income Experiment (2017-2018)

· €560/month to 2,000 unemployed
· **Results:**
· Mental wellbeing and financial security improved
· Employment slightly increased (not decreased)
· Stress levels reduced
· Trust in institutions increased

The pattern is consistent: When you give people money without conditions, they use it wisely, their lives improve, and they don't stop working (though they make better choices about work).

* * *

The Opposition (And Why It's Wrong)

"People will stop working!"

The data says otherwise. Consistently.

Every UBI pilot shows the same pattern:

- Full-time employment largely unchanged
- New mothers take slightly more time with infants (good)
- Students focus more on education (good)
- People make better job choices (choose based on fit, not desperation)
- Entrepreneurship *increases* (security enables risk)

Why would people stop working?

- The floor is basic, not luxurious ($1,500/month covers survival, not comfort)
- Humans want purpose, status, community (work provides these)
- Most people want more than minimum
- Meaningful work is intrinsically motivating

But here's where AUBI becomes truly Yellow, not just progressive Orange:

The Dual-Wallet System

AUBI isn't just one kind of money. The full framework includes:

Wallet A: The Sovereign Floor (standard currency for survival)

- Rent, food, utilities, healthcare
- Unconditional, covers basics
- This is what keeps you alive

Wallet B: Regenerative Currency (what we call Hearts and Leaves)

- Hearts: Earned through care work (eldercare, childcare, community building, mutual aid)

- Leaves: Earned through ecological restoration (carbon sequestration, habitat restoration, regenerative practices)
- **This is what gives life meaning**

The market pays for extraction. Hearts/Leaves pay for care and restoration.

The genius is: AUBI guarantees you survive (Wallet A), while Regenerative Currency rewards the work the market ignores but humanity needs (Wallet B).

We're not funding idleness. We're funding a new economy of care.

Want more than basics? You can:

- Take a market job (cash economy)
- Do care work (Hearts economy)
- Do ecological work (Leaves economy)
- Mix all three (most people will)

This structurally solves the meaning crisis by creating economic value for meaningful work that capitalism currently treats as worthless.

Note: The full technical implementation of Hearts/Leaves is detailed in the broader GGF framework. For this book's purposes, understand this: AUBI creates the foundation, but the complete system includes multiple forms of value recognition.

What changes: People can reject exploitative work. They can demand better conditions. They can take time to find good fits. **And they can pursue meaning-driven work that the market doesn't value.**

That's not a bug. That's the point.

"Won't this undermine the dignity of work?"

No. This revalues work.

Currently, work is mandatory for survival. That's not dignity—that's coercion.

With AUBI, work becomes:

- A chosen contribution, not a mandate
- A source of meaning and community, not terror management
- An expression of values, not proof of worth
- Something you do because it matters, not because you'll die otherwise

That is higher dignity, not lower.

The "dignity of work" argument is often deployed by those who benefit from others' desperation. Real dignity requires freedom. **You can't have dignity in choice if "no" means death.**

"Inflation will eat the benefits!"

Not if the money comes from wealth redistribution, not money printing.
AUBI funded by:

- Wealth tax (taking from those who have excess)
- Corporate tax reform (proper taxation of profits)
- Financial transaction tax (skimming from speculation)

This is redistribution, not expansion of money supply.
Plus, two key mechanisms prevent inflation:

1. Market Power Rebalancing AUBI gives individuals bargaining power. This forces markets—especially housing and labor—to be more responsive to human needs rather than pure extraction. Currently, landlords and employers have monopsony power. AUBI breaks that.

When renters can say "no" to exploitative housing, landlords must compete on quality and price. When workers can refuse terrible jobs, employers must offer better conditions. **This is market efficiency, not market distortion.**

2. Velocity of Money AUBI money given to low-income individuals is spent immediately in the local economy—rent, food, utilities, local services. This stimulates production to meet demand. **More demand + responsive supply = more production, not just higher prices.**

The wealthy hoard money (low velocity). The poor spend it (high velocity). Redistribution increases economic activity, which is disinflationary as supply responds.

Plus, when demand increases for basics (housing, food), that signals where we need to increase supply. If inflation happens in specific sectors, that reveals market failure requiring intervention (like housing supply restrictions that should be removed anyway).

Historical note: Alaska Permanent Fund has operated for 40+ years with no inflation spiral. Kenya's GiveDirectly showed price stability. The evidence is clear.

"It's not enough to live on!"

That's... true. And the point.

AUBI isn't meant to make work unnecessary. It's meant to make survival unconditional.

You still work if you want more than basics. But you don't work out of terror. You work out of choice, meaning, or desire for more.

The floor isn't the ceiling. It's the foundation.

"We should just have job guarantees instead!"

Why not both?

But more importantly: **Job guarantee addresses the symptom (unemployment). AUBI addresses the cause (the terror of being unemployed).**

One manages a problem within the old paradigm (everyone must work to deserve existence). The other creates a new paradigm entirely (existence is unconditional; work is optional enhancement).

You can't job-guarantee your way to presence.

A guaranteed job is still mandatory productivity. You're still performing economic value to justify existence. The conditionality remains. You're just changing who mandates the work (government instead of market).

AUBI says: Your existence is justified by your existence. Everything else is optional.

That's a fundamentally different—and necessary—foundation.

Job guarantees can complement AUBI (providing meaningful public work for those who want it). But they can't replace it, because they don't address the root issue: **conditional worth.**

"Only 'deserving' people should get help!"

This is the most revealing objection.

It assumes some people deserve to suffer. That poverty is moral punishment for moral failing.

The data destroys this:

- Most poverty is circumstantial, not character-based
- "Deserving" determinations are arbitrary and often discriminatory
- Means-testing creates poverty traps and bureaucratic waste
- Universal programs are more politically durable (everyone benefits)

More fundamentally: Human dignity is unconditional, or it's not dignity at all.

* * *

Implementation: The Transition Pathways

You don't flip a switch and suddenly have AUBI. Here's the realistic pathway:

Phase 1: Proof of Concept (Years 1-3)

Pilot Programs in 20 cities/regions:

- Start with $1,000/month (will adjust to $1,500 adaptive)
- Include control groups for research
- Track all six domains of impact
- Document economic effects

Funding:

- Federal grants
- State/local supplements
- Philanthropic support for pilots
- Carbon dividend in select regions

What we measure:

- All six domain impacts (biological through existential)
- Economic effects (employment, entrepreneurship, spending)
- Social outcomes (crime, health, education)
- Political viability (public support evolution)

Phase 2: Regional Rollouts (Years 3-7)

Based on pilot success:

- Entire states/provinces adopt
- Start with states already piloting (Alaska model)
- Regional coalitions (e.g., West Coast, Northeast, Nordic countries)
- Adjust amount to local costs ($1,200–$2,000 range)

Funding mechanisms mature:

- State-level wealth and carbon taxes
- Consolidated welfare programs
- Corporate tax reforms
- Economic growth dividends

Phase 3: National Implementation (Years 7-15)

Once proof exists and political will builds:

- National legislation in early-adopter countries
- Standardized floor with local adjustments
- Healthcare fully decoupled from employment
- Universal coverage achieved

Full funding structure:

- Federal wealth and financial transaction taxes
- Streamlined administration (massive bureaucracy reduction)
- Economic growth effects (reduced poverty costs)
- Climate revenue (carbon dividends)

Phase 4: International Coordination (Long-term Vision, Years 15+)

This is aspirational rather than immediate, but worth planning for:
    As multiple nations implement:

- International agreements on portable benefits
- Coordination on tax policies (prevent race to bottom)
- Shared research and best practices
- Global floor discussions (very long-term)

Note: This phase is speculative. The focus should be on proving local success first. International coordination emerges from demonstrated national success, not the other way around.

* * *

What This Enables (The Cascade Effects)

AUBI isn't just about money. It's about what becomes possible when terror is removed:

For Individuals:

- Can leave abusive situations (jobs, relationships, housing)
- Can invest in education and skill development
- Can take time for health recovery
- Can pursue meaning-driven rather than money-driven work
- Can actually rest without guilt or fear

For Families:

- Parents can spend time with children
- Can care for aging parents without financial ruin
- Domestic violence decreases (financial stress/dependence removed)
- Children's developmental outcomes improve
- Intergenerational poverty cycles break

For Communities:

- More volunteering and mutual aid
- Creative and cultural work flourishes
- Local economies strengthen (spending stays local)
- Social trust increases

- Democratic participation improves (time for civic engagement)

For Economy:

- Workers can demand better conditions (improves all work)
- Entrepreneurship increases (security enables risk)
- Market signals become more accurate (not distorted by desperation)
- Productivity improves (less stress, better health, more focus)
- Economic stability (built-in stimulus during downturns)

For Civilization:

- We can finally ask "what should we do?" instead of just "what must we do to survive?"
- Contemplative capacity becomes possible (time and security)
- Wisdom development (not trapped in survival mode)
- Cultural flourishing (arts, philosophy, science not limited to wealthy)
- Political transformation (desperation-driven voting decreases)

* * *

The Integration with Other Interventions

AUBI doesn't work alone. It works with the other three:
  AUBI + Cognitive Sovereignty:

- Security to resist exploitative attention extraction
- Time to practice presence and integration
- Freedom to choose information diet based on wellbeing

AUBI + Sanctuaries:

- Time to actually use sanctuary spaces
- Economic ability to participate in non-commercial community
- Freedom from treating all space as potential income source

AUBI + Contemplative Infrastructure:

- Time for practices and development
- Ability to pursue wisdom traditions
- Freedom to prioritize growth over grind

The four together create conditions where:

- Survival is unconditional (AUBI)
- Attention is protected (Cognitive Sovereignty)
- Space exists for rest (Sanctuaries)
- Capacity is developed (Contemplative Infrastructure)

Integration becomes structurally possible rather than heroically achieved.

* * *

Getting Started Tomorrow

National AUBI might be years away. What can happen now?

As an Individual:

- Support UBI/AUBI advocacy organizations
- Share the evidence with others
- Vote for candidates supporting pilots
- Participate in pilots if available in your area

As a Community:

- Advocate for local/regional pilots
- Create mutual aid networks (proto-AUBI)
- Support local wealth tax initiatives
- Build community economic alternatives

As an Organization:

- Provide financial stability to employees
- Support employees' non-work development
- Advocate for policy changes
- Fund pilot programs

As a Citizen:

- Contact representatives about AUBI pilots
- Support relevant ballot initiatives
- Organize for policy change
- Build coalitions across political spectrum (Alaska model proves this can be bipartisan)

* * *

The Vision Redux

Remember Maya? She woke without terror. Alex lost work but didn't face eviction. Both could breathe.

That's not utopia. That's the Sovereign Floor.

A world where:

- Existence is unconditional
- Work is choice, not compulsion
- Purpose can be pursued
- Rest is possible
- Integration becomes achievable

We have the resources. We have the evidence. We have the implementation pathways.

What we need is the political will to build it.

And that will emerges when enough people realize:

- We're already paying for this (inefficiently)
- The current system is destroying us (fragmentation)
- The alternative is achievable (proven models)
- The time is now (before AI disruption makes it emergency policy anyway)

The Sovereign Floor isn't a luxury. It's the foundation for everything else.

Remember this: The floor isn't the ceiling. It's the foundation.

Without it, cognitive sovereignty becomes privilege (only those with security can protect attention). Sanctuaries become escapes for the wealthy (only those with time can use them). Contemplative capacity becomes elite achievement (only those with resources can develop it).

With it, human flourishing becomes structurally possible for everyone.

Not guaranteed. Not automatic. But possible.

The floor isn't the ceiling. It's the foundation.

And possible is where transformation begins.

* * *

Next: Sanctuaries and Non-Extractive Zones—because you need physical spaces where market logic is suspended, where presence is protected, where integration can happen.

The Sovereign Floor secures your existence. Cognitive Sovereignty protects your attention. Sanctuaries create the spaces. Contemplative Infrastructure builds the capacity.

Together, they restore what we lost: the ability to be fully human.

* * *

Postcard from 2040: The Library Species

He spends forty hours a week restoring antique violins. He isn't paid for it—at least, not in Fiat currency. His Sovereign Floor covers his rent and food. He does it because the wood asks for it. He does it because he has the time to listen to the grain.

Around him, the neighborhood has transformed into a campus of mastery. The woman next door is spending a decade translating Sumerian texts. The teenagers are building a fusion reactor model in the community garage, not for a grade, but because they are curious. When you remove the gun of survival from the head of the species, we didn't become lazy. We became what we always were: a library of longing. We stopped working for the weekend and started working for the millennium.

Chapter 13: Sanctuaries and Non-Extractive Zones – Creating Spaces Where Market Logic Is Suspended

You've seen the Sanctuary District in Maya's 2032. A place where:

- No advertising
- No commercial transactions in designated areas
- No phones (optional check-in at the border)
- No productivity mandates

Just space to be human.

Not as escape. Not as luxury. **As essential infrastructure for integration.**

Cognitive sovereignty protects your digital attention. The Sovereign Floor protects your economic existence. **Sanctuaries protect physical and social space from extraction.**

This chapter details the third intervention: creating legally protected zones where market logic is suspended, where consciousness can rest, where community can form without commodification.

This isn't nostalgia for pre-modern life. This is engineered protection for human needs that capitalism systematically destroys.

* * *

The Core Problem: Total Colonization

Let's name what we're solving.

Every space has been colonized by extraction logic.

Walk through a modern city:

- Sidewalks: Advertising billboards
- Bus stops: Digital screens selling anxiety
- Parks: Sponsored events, branded facilities
- Cafes: Work-from-anywhere culture, productivity theater
- Libraries: Becoming co-working spaces
- Churches: Declining, replaced by nothing
- Community centers: Underfunded, closing
- Public squares: Surveilled, hostile architecture

There is nowhere you can go where you're not:

- Being sold to
- Being surveilled
- Being optimized
- Being extracted from
- Expected to be productive

Even "nature" has been colonized:

- National parks require fees, reservations, scheduling
- Beaches have paid parking
- Hiking trails have social media pressure ("pics or it didn't happen")
- **Wilderness itself has become a commodity**

The result: There is no space left for just being.

You cannot rest when every space demands something from you. You cannot integrate when every environment fragments your attention. You cannot be present when every location extracts value from your presence.

Sanctuaries solve this by creating legally protected zones where extraction is prohibited.

* * *

What Sanctuaries Actually Are

Sanctuaries are spaces—physical, digital, and social—where:

1. **Commercial extraction is prohibited**

- No advertising
- No commercial transactions (in core zones)
- No monetization of presence
- No productivity mandates

1. **Surveillance is minimized**

- No tracking for marketing
- No facial recognition
- No data harvesting
- Privacy is default, not opt-in

1. **Time becomes non-linear**

- No schedules unless chosen
- No "maximizing" time
- No guilt about "wasting" hours
- Present-moment experience prioritized

1. **Community is emphasized**

- Spaces designed for connection
- Shared resources and activities
- Intergenerational mixing
- Collective rather than individual focus

1. **Restoration is the purpose**

- Rest is legitimate activity
- Contemplation is valued
- Play is recognized as essential
- Integration happens naturally

Think of Sanctuaries as the physical equivalent of quiet hours in the Synoptic Protocol.

Just as quiet hours protect your morning from digital intrusion, Sanctuaries protect physical space from commercial colonization.

* * *

Types of Sanctuaries

Type 1: Urban Sanctuary Districts (Maya's model)

What they are:

- Designated zones within cities
- Mixed use: some commercial (cafes, bookstores, community spaces), some pure sanctuary
- Clear boundaries with transition zones
- Permanent installations

How they work:

- City designates zone (often converting transit malls, downtowns, or parks)
- Commercial activity limited to specific areas
- No advertising anywhere in district
- Digital devices optional but discouraged
- Free public amenities (water, seating, restrooms, quiet spaces)
- Programming: art, music, gatherings (non-commercial)

Examples/Precedents:

- Pedestrian zones in European cities
- Car-free districts (Copenhagen, Barcelona superblocks)
- Some urban parks (though most are under-protected)
- Venice's approach to commercial limits (imperfect but instructive)

Size: 5-20 city blocks, depending on city size

Type 2: Neighborhood Commons (Community Hearths)

What they are:

- Small-scale community spaces
- 1-2 blocks or single large building
- Hyper-local, walking distance for residents
- **Secular sacred spaces** - holding reverence, silence, ritual without requiring religious dogma

How they work:

- Community-owned or city-managed
- Free access for residents
- Shared resources (tools, kitchen, gathering space, quiet rooms)
- Regular gatherings (potlucks, skill-shares, care circles)

- No commercial activity
- **Hearthlight function:** Designed specifically to hold community's grief and joy
- Often includes:
- Community kitchen and dining
- Tool library
- **Contemplative spaces** (meditation rooms, silence rooms)
- **Ritual spaces** (for life transitions: births, deaths, coming of age)
- Children's play areas
- Elder gathering spaces
- Teen centers
- **Grief support spaces** (where loss can be witnessed collectively)

The "sacred" without religion: Churches and temples performed essential functions: holding community grief, marking transitions, creating reverence for life's mysteries. As traditional religion declines, these functions disappear—but the needs remain.

Community Hearths restore these functions without requiring belief systems. They're designed for "spiritual but not religious" reality—spaces that honor mystery, depth, and collective witnessing without theological demands.

This appeals to the growing demographic who need sacred space but not dogma.

Examples/Precedents:

- Community centers (when properly funded)
- Co-housing common houses
- Mutual aid hubs
- Some Unitarian Universalist spaces (non-dogmatic gathering)
- Japanese community halls

Density: One per neighborhood (roughly 5,000-10,000 people)

Type 3: Extended Wilderness Sanctuaries

What they are:

- Protected natural areas
- Access is free and easy (not commodified)
- Minimal development, maximum protection

How they work:

- Expanded national/regional park systems
- No fees for access (funded publicly)
- Limited reservations (only for camping/crowding management)
- No commercial development
- Strong anti-exploitation rules
- Indigenous land management models

The AUBI synergy: Currently, wilderness is de facto exclusionary. The high costs of:

- Time off work (unpaid)
- Travel expenses (gas, vehicle maintenance)
- Equipment (camping gear, outdoor clothing)
- Permit fees

These barriers mean wilderness access is privilege, not right. AUBI changes this completely:

- Economic security enables taking time for nature
- Basic income covers travel costs
- Time wealth allows extended visits
- No guilt about "unproductive" time in nature

Wilderness Sanctuaries without AUBI serve the wealthy. With AUBI, they serve everyone.

This is the synergy in action: protected space (Sanctuary) + economic security (AUBI) = actual access for all.

Key principle: Nature is commons, not commodity

Examples/Precedents:

- National parks (need expansion and free access)
- UK's "right to roam"
- Scandinavian allemansrätten (freedom to roam)
- Indigenous protected areas

Type 4: Digital Sanctuaries (Public Digital Commons)

What they are:

- Online spaces free from commercial extraction
- Public digital infrastructure (not private platforms)
- Funded by Commons Dividend (Chapter 12), not advertising

The principle: Just as we build public libraries so you don't have to buy books, we need Public Digital Commons—platforms where you can exist online as a citizen, not a user.

How they work:

- **Public funding** (like libraries, from Commons Dividend)
- **Library integration** (hosted/accessed through public library systems)
- Open protocols, not proprietary platforms
- User-controlled, not algorithm-controlled
- Chronological feeds, human curation
- Privacy-first design
- No data harvesting
- No advertising anywhere

- Democratic governance (users have voice)

Why library integration matters: Libraries are trusted, ubiquitous, publicly funded institutions with physical locations. Housing digital commons in library infrastructure:

- Solves network effects problem (guaranteed user base)
- Provides physical access points
- Leverages existing public funding
- Creates trusted brand (people trust libraries)
- Enables digital literacy support

Think of it as: Wikipedia + Mastodon + Public Libraries = Democratic necessity, not private commodity

Examples/Precedents:

- Wikipedia (non-commercial knowledge commons)
- Mastodon/Fediverse (federated, non-corporate)
- Public library digital resources
- Email/blogs (pre-algorithm era models)
- BBC (public media model)

Need: Alternative to extractive platforms, recognized as essential public infrastructure like roads or water

Type 5: Institutional Sanctuaries

What they are:

- Schools, hospitals, care facilities with sanctuary principles
- No commercial intrusion
- Focus on care and development, not profit

How they work:

- Commercial-free zones within institutions
- No advertising to captive audiences
- No productivity metrics that harm wellbeing
- Design for human flourishing, not efficiency
- Time for rest, play, connection

Examples/Precedents:

- Some Waldorf schools
- Certain healthcare systems (Nordic models)
- Traditional library spaces
- Some elder care communities

* * *

The Legal Foundation: Non-Extractive Zones

How do you legally create and protect Sanctuaries?

Municipal Authority

Cities already have power to:

- Designate land use zones (residential, commercial, industrial)
- Restrict commercial activity in certain areas
- Regulate advertising and signage
- Create public spaces and parks
- Manage public right-of-way

Sanctuaries simply create a new zone type: Non-Extractive.

Zoning code addition: "Non-Extractive Zones are designated areas where commercial extraction of value from human presence is prohibited. This includes but is not limited to: advertising, surveillance for commercial purposes, productivity mandates, and monetization of public space. The purpose is to protect human capacity for rest, integration, and authentic community formation."

Constitutional Basis

Right to Assembly and Association Sanctuaries protect the conditions for genuine assembly—free from commercial manipulation and surveillance.

Right to Privacy Protection from commercial surveillance and data extraction in public space.

Public Trust Doctrine Public spaces held in trust for public benefit, not commercial exploitation.

Environmental Protection Mental environment protection (Chapter 11's framing extends to physical space).

Precedents

Existing restrictions we already accept:

- Schools are ad-free zones (mostly)
- Hospitals limit commercial activity
- National parks prohibit commercial development
- Residential zones prohibit industrial activity
- Historic districts restrict changes

International examples:

- São Paulo's advertising ban (2007, still standing)
- European pedestrian zones

- Japan's quiet public transit
- Scandinavian right to roam laws

* * *

Design Principles for Sanctuaries

What makes a space actually restorative rather than just "park-like"?

1. Acoustic Design

The problem: Modern spaces are acoustically hostile—traffic noise, construction, commercial sound, notifications.

Sanctuary approach:

- Natural sound barriers (vegetation, water features, earth berms)
- Traffic calming or elimination
- No commercial music or announcements
- Spaces for silence
- Spaces for natural sound (birds, water, wind)

Why it matters: Constant noise keeps nervous system activated. Acoustic rest enables parasympathetic engagement.

2. Visual Rest

The problem: Visual clutter and advertising create constant cognitive load.

Sanctuary approach:

- No advertising (obvious)

- Natural materials and colors
- Human-scaled architecture
- Green space (biophilic design)
- Beauty without commercial purpose
- Art that invites contemplation, not consumption

Why it matters: Visual processing consumes cognitive resources. Clean visual field allows mental rest.

3. Temporal Freedom

The problem: Scheduled, time-limited access creates pressure.
Sanctuary approach:

- No time limits (except overnight closures for safety)
- No queues or ticketing
- No "maximizing" time
- Activities can unfold naturally
- Spontaneous gathering possible

Why it matters: Integration requires non-linear time. Presence requires absence of temporal pressure.

4. Social Architecture

The problem: Modern spaces isolate or force superficial interaction.
Sanctuary approach:

- Seating that invites conversation (facing arrangements)
- Spaces for various group sizes (solo, pairs, small groups, gatherings)
- Multigenerational design
- Spaces for both interaction and solitude
- No surveillance creating performance anxiety

Why it matters: Authentic community requires spaces designed for human connection, not transaction.

5. Embodiment Support

The problem: Modern life is sedentary and disembodied.
  Sanctuary approach:

- Walking paths (not just roads)
- Spaces for movement (tai chi, dance, play)
- Natural materials (earth, stone, wood, grass)
- Weather exposure (sun, breeze, rain when safe)
- Sensory engagement (texture, scent, temperature)

Why it matters: Integration requires body awareness. Healing requires embodiment.

6. Accessibility and Inclusion

The problem: "Nature" and "quiet" can exclude those with disabilities or different needs.
  Sanctuary approach:

- Universal design for physical access
- Sensory-friendly zones (for autism, sensory processing differences)
- Childcare integrated (so parents can participate)
- Economically accessible (free, always)
- Culturally diverse (design includes multiple traditions)
- Safety for marginalized groups

Why it matters: Integration is for everyone, or it serves privilege.

* * *

The Economics of Sanctuaries

"How do we pay for non-commercial space?"

Direct Costs

Urban Sanctuary District (10-block zone):

- Land acquisition/conversion: One-time (or already public)
- Infrastructure improvement: $10-50M depending on existing state
- Ongoing maintenance: $2-5M/year
- Programming and staffing: $3-7M/year
- **Total annual: $5-12M per district**

Neighborhood Commons (per location):

- Building acquisition/conversion: One-time (many existing buildings)
- Renovation: $1-3M
- Ongoing operation: $200-500K/year
- **50 locations per million residents = $10-25M/year total**

Wilderness Sanctuaries:

- Land protection: Varies (much already public)
- Trail maintenance and access: Expansion of existing budgets
- Free access (eliminate fees): Revenue loss ~$200M nationally, offset by public funding

Digital Sanctuaries:

- Platform development: $10-50M (one-time)
- Ongoing operation: $5-20M/year (for major platform)
- **Comparable to library system costs**

Total for major city (1M residents): $50-100M/year for comprehensive sanctuary system

Revenue/Savings

Direct savings:

- Reduced mental health costs (sanctuary access improves wellbeing)
- Lower crime (third places reduce isolation and poverty-driven crime)
- Better physical health (more movement, less stress)
- Increased economic activity (rested, healthy people are more productive overall)

Economic studies show:

- Every $1 spent on parks/public space returns $4-12 in community benefits
- Mental health improvements alone can offset costs
- Property values near quality public space increase (funding through land value tax)

Funding sources:

- **General taxation** (this is public infrastructure like roads)
- **Land value tax** (capturing value created by public amenities)
- **Advertising tax** (tax extraction to fund non-extraction)
- **Tourism support** (sanctuaries attract visitors, supporting local business)
- **Philanthropic partnerships** (for pilot programs)

The real question isn't "can we afford it?" but "can we afford not to?"
Mental health crisis, loneliness epidemic, and social fragmentation cost far more than sanctuary infrastructure.

* * *

The Legal Foundation: Non-Extractive Zones

How do we create and protect these spaces?

Not through corporate goodwill or voluntary adoption. Through **law and zoning.**

Non-Extractive Zones: A New Zoning Category

Cities already regulate land use extensively through zoning:

- Residential zones
- Commercial zones
- Industrial zones
- Mixed-use zones
- Historic preservation zones
- Environmental protection zones

We need a new category: Non-Extractive Zones (NEZ).

What NEZ designation means:

- Advertising prohibited (physical and digital)
- Data collection prohibited (no surveillance, tracking, or harvesting)
- Commercial transactions limited or prohibited (depending on sanctuary type)
- Design standards enforced (acoustic, visual, temporal)
- Public access guaranteed
- Community governance required

This isn't asking companies to be nice. It's zoning them out.

Just as we don't allow heavy industry in residential neighborhoods or require accessible entrances in public buildings, we can require non-extraction in designated zones.

Constitutional Foundation

Multiple legal bases support this:

1. **Public Trust Doctrine**: Government holds certain resources in trust for all citizens (already applies to waterways, beaches, parks)
2. **Environmental Protection**: If we can regulate physical pollution, we can regulate mental environment pollution (noise ordinances, light pollution laws already do this)
3. **Right to Assembly**: First Amendment protects gathering—but gathering requires space not dominated by commercial interests
4. **Privacy Rights**: Fourth Amendment and state privacy laws already limit surveillance in some contexts
5. **Zoning Power**: Cities have broad authority to regulate land use for public welfare (established law since *Village of Euclid v. Ambler Realty*, 1926)

The legal argument: Mental environment deserves same protection as physical environment. Sanctuary zones are to attention what clean air zones are to lungs.

Model Municipal Code Language

Here's what a city ordinance might look like:

* * *

NON-EXTRACTIVE ZONE ORDINANCE
Purpose: To preserve spaces within the municipality where residents may gather, rest, and exist free from commercial extraction, surveillance,

and advertising, recognizing that such spaces are essential to public health, civic life, and community wellbeing.

Designation: The City Council may designate areas as Non-Extractive Zones (NEZ) where: 1. All forms of advertising are prohibited 2. Commercial data collection is prohibited 3. Surveillance for non-security purposes is prohibited 4. Design must meet acoustic and visual rest standards 5. Public access must be guaranteed 6. Community governance structures must be established

Enforcement: Violations subject to fines ($1,000–$50,000 per day), permits revoked, injunctive relief available.

Review: NEZ designations reviewed every 5 years for effectiveness and community satisfaction.

* * *

This gives City Councils something concrete they could vote on next week.

* * *

The Multi-Domain Impact

Let's be specific about how protected space affects all six domains.

Biological Domain (Impact: 8/10)

Direct effects:

- Nervous system regulation (parasympathetic activation possible)
- Stress reduction (cortisol normalization)
- Physical movement (walking, play, embodied practice)
- Improved sleep (daytime rest enables nighttime sleep)

269

- Sensory nourishment (nature exposure, acoustic rest)

Mechanism: When environment stops demanding constant vigilance, body can restore. Green space and acoustic rest allow nervous system to exit fight-flight-freeze.

Measurable outcomes:

- Lower blood pressure
- Improved HRV (heart rate variability)
- Better immune function
- Reduced inflammation
- Increased longevity

Cognitive Domain (Impact: 7/10)

Direct effects:

- Attention restoration (from directed to soft attention)
- Mental clarity (cognitive load reduction)
- Creative insight (mind-wandering enables connection-making)
- Long-term thinking (escape from urgency)

Mechanism: Attention Restoration Theory (Kaplan): Natural environments and low-demand spaces restore depleted attentional capacity.

Measurable outcomes:

- Improved focus after sanctuary time
- Better problem-solving
- More creative solutions
- Enhanced memory consolidation

Emotional Domain (Impact: 8/10)

Direct effects:

- Reduced anxiety (safe, non-demanding space)
- Improved mood (nature and community contact)
- Emotional processing time (space to feel without performing)
- Decreased loneliness (authentic connection opportunities)

Mechanism: Safe spaces allow emotional experiencing without suppression or overwhelm. Community reduces isolation.

Measurable outcomes:

- Mood improvement scores
- Reduced depression symptoms
- Better emotional regulation
- Increased sense of belonging

Behavioral Domain (Impact: 7/10)

Direct effects:

- Non-compulsive behavior (no extraction triggers)
- Embodied practice (movement, play, ritual)
- Pro-social behavior (helping, sharing, connecting)
- Freedom from performance (authentic expression)

Mechanism: Environment that doesn't demand anything enables authentic rather than strategic behavior.

Measurable outcomes:

- Increased prosocial actions
- More spontaneous play

- Better interpersonal dynamics
- Reduced addictive behaviors

Social Domain (Impact: 9/10)

Direct effects:

- Community formation (regular contact in shared space)
- Intergenerational connection (shared space for all ages)
- Social trust (repeated positive encounters)
- Collective action capacity (organizing in common spaces)
- Authentic relationships (not transactional)

Mechanism: Third places (Oldenburg): Spaces that aren't home or work enable community formation. When protected from commercial pressure, authentic relationships form.

Measurable outcomes:

- Stronger social networks
- Increased civic participation
- More volunteering and mutual aid
- Reduced crime and conflict

Existential Domain (Impact: 8/10)

Direct effects:

- Space for meaning-making (time without productivity pressure)
- Connection to larger-than-self (nature, community, beauty)
- Contemplative capacity (space for reflection)
- Values clarification (time to ask "what matters?")

Mechanism: Existential questions require space. Sanctuaries provide literal and metaphorical room for these questions to emerge and be explored.

Measurable outcomes:

- Increased life satisfaction
- Greater sense of purpose
- More meaning-in-life scores
- Spiritual/philosophical engagement

Overall Integration Score: 8/10

Sanctuaries score high because they address multiple domains simultaneously through providing protected space for natural human functioning.

* * *

Implementation Strategy

Phase 1: Pilot Sanctuaries (Years 1-3)

Start with 10 cities:

- Each creates one Urban Sanctuary District
- 2-5 Neighborhood Commons per city
- Enhanced wilderness access nearby

What they demonstrate:

- Usage patterns (do people come?)
- Wellbeing impacts (does it help?)
- Economic effects (local business, property values)
- Social cohesion (community formation)
- Design lessons (what works, what doesn't)

Funding:

- Federal/state grants for pilots
- Municipal budgets (reallocation from failed initiatives)
- Philanthropic partnerships
- Community fundraising

Phase 2: Expansion (Years 3-7)

Based on pilot success:

- Expand to 100 cities
- Increase sanctuary density (more commons per city)
- Begin rural/suburban adaptations
- Digital sanctuaries launch

Policy development:

- Model zoning codes
- Design standards
- Funding mechanisms
- Rights and protections clarified

Phase 3: Normalization (Years 7-15)

Sanctuaries become standard infrastructure:

- Expected in all cities above certain size
- Integrated into urban planning
- Protected by law (like schools or fire departments)
- Cultural shift: seen as essential, not luxury

Full integration:

- Connected sanctuary networks (pedestrian corridors)
- Sanctuary access as quality-of-life metric
- Real estate values proximity
- Tourism draws (well-managed)

* * *

What This Enables (The Cascade Effects)

For Individuals:

- Spaces to actually rest
- Time for contemplation and integration
- Connection without transaction
- Freedom from constant extraction
- Body and nervous system restoration

For Communities:

- Social fabric strengthening
- Intergenerational relationships
- Collective action capacity
- Cultural production (art, music, gathering)
- Mutual aid networks

For Cities:

- Public health improvements
- Reduced crime and conflict
- Economic vitality (from restored residents)
- Tourism attraction (people want sanctuary)

- Climate resilience (green infrastructure)

For Civilization:

- Alternative to extraction as organizing principle
- Proof that non-commercial space can thrive
- Cultural memory of how to just be
- Developmental capacity for next generations
- Foundation for wiser politics (rested, connected citizens)

* * *

The Opposition (And Why It's Wrong)

"But This Is Wasted Commercial Real Estate"

The objection: Sanctuaries take valuable land off the commercial tax base. Cities can't afford to "waste" real estate on spaces that don't generate revenue.

The reality: Sanctuaries don't reduce economic vitality—they concentrate and enhance it.

The evidence:

- **Copenhagen's Strøget** (1962): World's longest pedestrian street. Initial business panic ("We'll go bankrupt without car access!"). Result: Property values increased 35%, retail thrived, became Europe's most expensive shopping street.
- **Barcelona's Superblocks** (2016+): Removed through-traffic from residential blocks. Business opposition was fierce. Result: Local commerce increased 30%, property values rose, model now being replicated globally.

- **Portland's Pioneer Courthouse Square** (1984): "Portland's Living Room"—no commercial activity in the square itself. Fierce initial opposition. Result: Surrounding businesses boomed, became city's most valuable district.
- **New York's High Line** (2009): Abandoned rail line to elevated park. "What a waste!" Result: $2B in adjacent development, property values increased 103%.

The pattern is universal: Quality public space acts as an economic *multiplier* for surrounding areas.

Why it works:

- People visit destinations with good public amenities (not just to shop)
- They linger longer when there are comfortable public spaces (more spending time)
- Longer visits = more spending in nearby businesses
- Quality of life improvements attract talent and investment
- The Sanctuary doesn't capture the value—the ecosystem around it does

The municipal calculation:

- Direct tax loss from 5-block Sanctuary district: ~$2M/year
- Increased tax revenue from surrounding increased activity: $6-10M/year
- Reduced healthcare/social costs from improved wellbeing: $4-8M/year
- Increased tourism revenue: $2-5M/year
- **Net fiscal benefit: +$10-21M/year**

For context: The estimated $100M annual cost for comprehensive sanctuary infrastructure in a city of 1 million is less than 1% of typical city budgets and a fraction of the cost of a single new sports stadium (often

$500M–$1B).

This isn't charity—it's investment in community infrastructure that pays economic dividends.

The question isn't "Can we afford Sanctuaries?" It's "Can we afford to keep optimizing every square foot for extraction while our communities disintegrate?"

* * *

"This is anti-business!"

No, it's pro-humanity.

Businesses benefit when people are healthy, rested, and mentally clear. Exhausted, fragmented consumers make poor long-term customers.

Plus, sanctuary districts often *increase* nearby business activity. Portland's car-free zones, Barcelona's superblocks, Copenhagen's pedestrian streets—all show commercial vitality.

Sanctuaries aren't anti-commerce. They're anti-extraction-everywhere.

"People won't use them!"

Every pilot shows the opposite.

When you build quality public space and protect it from commercial pressure, people come. Always.

The "people won't use it" argument is usually code for "profitable extraction won't be possible."

"They'll become homeless encampments!"

This reveals the real problem: we've criminalized poverty instead of solving it.

Sanctuaries + Sovereign Floor (Chapter 12) solves this. When people have housing and income, they don't need to camp in parks.

If sanctuaries attract unhoused people, that's because they're literally the only safe spaces. The solution is housing and support, not eliminating sanctuary.

"It's government overreach!"

We already regulate land use extensively. Zoning, building codes, environmental protection, historic preservation.

Creating sanctuary zones is the same principle: protecting public interest against harmful private activity.

If preventing commercial colonization of every square inch is "overreach," then so is preventing industrial dumping in rivers.

"Won't work in America—too individualistic!"

Americans love public spaces. National parks, beaches, community pools, libraries.

The individualism argument is deployed by those who profit from extraction. Real individuals benefit from protected commons.

* * *

Integration with Other Interventions

Sanctuaries don't work alone:

Sanctuaries + Cognitive Sovereignty:

- Digital sanctuary principles (no ads, no tracking)
- Physical sanctuary principles (no extraction)
- Mutually reinforcing protections

Sanctuaries + Sovereign Floor:

- Time to use sanctuaries (economic security)
- Money for transportation/access
- Freedom from treating every space as income opportunity

Sanctuaries + Contemplative Infrastructure:

- Spaces for practices and gathering
- Physical container for developmental work
- Community support for transformation

The four together:

- Economic security (AUBI)
- Attention protection (Cognitive Sovereignty)
- Physical space (Sanctuaries)
- Capacity building (Contemplative Infrastructure)

Complete habitat for human integration.

* * *

Getting Started Tomorrow

National sanctuary systems might be years away. What can happen now?

As an Individual:

- Find/create informal sanctuaries (quiet cafes, parks, libraries)
- Advocate for sanctuary zones in your city
- Support organizations protecting public space
- Practice sanctuary principles in your home

As a Community:

- Organize for sanctuary district proposal
- Create informal commons (tool libraries, meal shares)
- Protect existing third places (libraries, community centers)
- Build phone-free gathering culture

As an Organization:

- Create sanctuary principles in your space
- Limit commercial intrusion
- Design for restoration, not extraction
- Model what becomes possible

As a Citizen:

- Contact representatives about sanctuary zoning
- Support ballot initiatives for public space
- Attend planning meetings
- Vote for candidates prioritizing community over commerce

* * *

The Vision Redux

Maya walked through the Sanctuary District. No ads. No pressure. Just space to be human.

That's not luxury. That's necessity.

Space where:

- You're not being sold to
- You're not being surveilled
- You're not being optimized
- You're not being extracted from
- You can simply exist

We can build this. In every city. For everyone.

Not someday. Starting now.

The Sovereign Floor secures existence. Cognitive Sovereignty protects attention. Sanctuaries create protected space. Together, they make integration possible.

One more intervention remains: building the actual capacity for integration and development.

That's Chapter 14.

For now, remember: **You need space to breathe. Not metaphorically—literally. Protected space where commercial logic can't reach you.**

That's not anti-progress. That's the foundation for actual human progress.

* * *

Next: Contemplative Capacity as Civilizational Infrastructure—because protecting space isn't enough if people don't know how to use it for integration and development.

* * *

Postcard from 2040: The Return of Unhurried Eros

The morning light hit the sheets, and for the first time in history, there was no phantom vibration on the wrist. No glance at the clock. No mental calculation of commute times or email backlogs. The attention economy had been zoned out of the bedroom.

Intimacy returned not as a dopamine spike or a stress-relief mechanism, but as a slow, tidal rhythm. We moved like teenagers with all the time in the world, but with the nervous systems of regulated adults. We remembered that love isn't something you fit into a calendar slot; it is the atmosphere you breathe when the air isn't filled with smoke.

Chapter 14: Contemplative Capacity as Civilizational Infrastructure

The Missing Layer

We've covered three major interventions:

- **Cognitive Sovereignty** (protecting attention from extraction)
- **The Sovereign Floor** (removing survival terror)
- **Sanctuaries** (creating protected physical/digital space)

Each necessary. None sufficient.

Here's what's still missing: Even with protected attention, economic security, and sanctuary space—most people lack the *internal capacity* to actually use them.

Put someone in a silent sanctuary with all the time in the world, and watch what happens:

The restlessness rises almost immediately. The mind generates urgent tasks. The body fidgets. Within five minutes, most people are reaching for phones or finding excuses to leave.

This isn't weakness. It's lack of training.

We've built a civilization that systematically prevents the development of contemplative capacity—the ability to be present, hold complexity, tolerate uncertainty, and access wisdom beyond calculation.

Then we wonder why people can't be still.

It's like expecting people to run marathons without ever teaching them to walk. Or demanding literacy in a society that banned reading instruction.

Contemplative capacity isn't optional for Yellow consciousness. It's the foundation.

You cannot:

- Hold multiple perspectives simultaneously without inner spaciousness
- See long-term patterns without stepping back from urgency
- Integrate contradictions without tolerance for paradox
- Make wise decisions without access to intuition beyond analysis
- Develop compassion without the capacity to feel others' experience

These aren't personality traits. They're skills. And skills require training, practice, and cultural support.

Currently, we treat contemplative development as:

- Personal hobby (meditation apps, yoga studios)
- Religious practice (only for believers)
- Therapeutic intervention (only for the broken)
- Corporate productivity hack (McMindfulness)

What if we treated it as essential human development? As important as literacy, numeracy, or civic education?

This chapter makes the case for **contemplative capacity as public infrastructure**—as essential to functioning civilization as roads, schools, or clean water.

* * *

What Contemplative Capacity Actually Is

Not just meditation. Not just stillness. Not even just mindfulness.
Contemplative capacity is the integrated skill set that enables:

1. Meta-Awareness (Consciousness of Consciousness)

The ability to observe your own mind operating.

Not just thinking, but *noticing* you're thinking. Not just feeling emotions, but *watching* emotions arise and pass.
Why it matters:

- Can't change patterns you can't see
- Can't choose responses if you're identified with reactions
- Can't hold multiple perspectives if you're trapped in one

Current state: Most people go through entire lives without ever stepping back from the stream of thought. They *are* their thoughts, not the consciousness aware of thoughts.

2. Attention Management (Voluntary Control)

The ability to direct and sustain focus deliberately.

Not just concentration (narrow focus on one thing) but also:

- Broad awareness (holding multiple things simultaneously)
- Flexible attention (smoothly shifting between narrow and broad)
- Sustained attention (maintaining focus over time)
- Divided attention (managing multiple streams when necessary)

Why it matters:

- Wisdom requires holding complexity without premature simplification

- Insight requires sustained focus on subtle patterns
- Integration requires managing multiple domains simultaneously

Current state: Attention is largely involuntary, pulled by whatever's most stimulating. People can force focus briefly through willpower, but lack genuine voluntary control.

3. Emotional Regulation (Working With Affect)

The ability to be with difficult emotions without suppression or overwhelm.

Not controlling emotions (forcing them down) but also not being controlled by them (acting them out unconsciously).

The skill is:

- Feeling fully without getting consumed
- Processing emotions without being hijacked by them
- Using emotions as information without being driven by them

Why it matters:

- Wisdom requires emotional maturity, not just intellectual understanding
- Compassion requires feeling others' pain without collapsing
- Integration requires befriending shadow material, not just repressing it

Current state: Either suppress (numb out, push down, "stay positive") or express (act out, vent, overwhelm others). Rarely the third option: *be with*.

4. Cognitive Flexibility (Perspective-Taking)

The ability to hold multiple viewpoints simultaneously without collapsing into relativism or rigidity.

The paradox:

- Recognizing that all perspectives are partial
- Without concluding that all perspectives are equal
- While maintaining your own clear stance
- And genuinely understanding others' views

Why it matters:

- Yellow consciousness requires genuine cognitive flexibility
- Can't integrate what you can't understand
- Can't transcend positions you can't inhabit

Current state: Either tribal (my view is right, yours is wrong) or relativist (all views are equally valid, nothing matters). Rarely the mature position: *all views are partial; some are more comprehensive; I can see from yours while maintaining mine.*

5. Systems Perception (Seeing Patterns)

The ability to perceive relationships, dynamics, and emergent properties rather than just isolated objects.

Not just analysis (breaking things into parts) but also synthesis (seeing how parts interact to create wholes).

The skill includes:

- Seeing feedback loops and cascades
- Perceiving delayed consequences
- Noticing what's absent (missing system components)

- Sensing emergent properties (more than sum of parts)

Why it matters:

- Every major problem we face is systemic
- Can't solve system problems with linear thinking
- Integration requires perceiving across domains

Current state: Linear, mechanistic thinking dominates. People see events, not patterns. Causes, not dynamics. Objects, not relationships.

6. Embodied Awareness (Somatic Intelligence)

The ability to perceive and work with bodily sensations, intuitions, and wisdom.

Not just intellectual understanding but felt sense, gut knowing, body wisdom.

The capacity:

- Interoception (sensing internal bodily states)
- Proprioception (knowing where body is in space)
- Somatic processing (using body as information system)
- Integration of body-mind (not just brain-based)

Why it matters:

- Body holds wisdom intellect can't access
- Emotions are embodied (can't process without body awareness)
- Presence is embodied (can't be "here now" without sensing body here now)
- Integration literally means body-mind-spirit unity

Current state: Most people live entirely in heads, treating bodies as vehicles for brains. Disconnected from somatic intelligence, unable to access embodied knowing.

$$* * *$$

Why Civilization Needs This (Not Just Individuals)

Personal benefits are real: Better mental health, reduced stress, improved relationships, greater life satisfaction.
   But the civilizational stakes are far higher.

The Existential Risk Argument

We face threats that require wisdom beyond our current collective capacity:
   Climate change requires:

- Long-term thinking (decades, centuries)
- Systems perception (interconnected global dynamics)
- Emotional regulation (not panicking or numbing)
- Perspective-taking (considering non-human and future generations)
- Values clarification (what actually matters?)

AI alignment requires:

- Deep understanding of human values (not just stated preferences)
- Wisdom about consciousness (what is experience, suffering, wellbeing?)
- Ethical sophistication (beyond simple rules)
- Humility about uncertainty (acknowledging what we don't know)

Social fragmentation requires:

- Genuine empathy across difference
- Ability to hold multiple truths simultaneously
- Emotional maturity in conflict
- Seeing shared humanity beneath tribal divisions

Economic transformation requires:

- Questioning growth imperative
- Perceiving long-term consequences of short-term optimization
- Valuing wellbeing over productivity
- Imagining alternative systems

None of these can be solved from fragmented, reactive, short-term consciousness.

They require the exact capacities that contemplative development cultivates.

The Developmental Argument

Yellow consciousness—the ability to see and work with systems—doesn't just happen. It develops.

The research is clear:

- Contemplative practice accelerates developmental growth
- Meditation supports perspective-taking and cognitive flexibility
- Mindfulness increases awareness of one's own meaning-making
- Embodied practices develop somatic intelligence
- Contemplative communities support developmental transitions

Without deliberate cultivation, most people plateau at Orange or Green.

With it, Yellow becomes accessible to far more people.

This isn't elitist. It's democratic.

Making contemplative capacity available to everyone is making higher consciousness development available to everyone.

The Integration Argument

Remember the core diagnosis: **addiction as integration failure. Integration requires:**

- Perceiving all six domains (biological through existential)
- Noticing conflicts between domains
- Holding the tension without premature resolution
- Allowing new syntheses to emerge
- Choosing actions that serve the whole

Every single one of these requires contemplative capacity.
You cannot integrate what you cannot perceive. You cannot perceive without the meta-awareness, attention management, and systems perception that contemplation develops.

The other three interventions remove barriers to integration. This one builds the capacity for integration.

* * *

What This Looks Like as Infrastructure

Not private meditation retreats for the wealthy. **Public developmental infrastructure for everyone.**

1. Contemplative Education (K-12 and Beyond)

The Capacity Engine principle:
Currently, schools are designed to produce "Workers" (Orange consciousness)—people who can follow instructions, optimize processes,

and compete effectively.

We need schools—and adult learning centers—designed to produce "Integrators" (Yellow consciousness)—people who can hold complexity, navigate ambiguity, and contribute wisdom.

This requires a fundamental shift from information transmission to capacity development.

Schools become **Capacity Engines**—institutions specifically designed to develop the human capacities our civilization desperately needs: attention, awareness, empathy, systems perception, wisdom.

This is lifelong infrastructure. K-12 lays the foundation. Community contemplative centers (the "Civic Gymnasiums" for adults) continue the developmental arc across the lifespan.

What it includes:

Elementary (Ages 5-11):

- Daily 5-10 minutes guided practice (breathing, body awareness, kindness)
- Emotional vocabulary development (learning to name feelings)
- Conflict resolution through awareness (noticing feelings before reacting)
- Nature connection practices (sensory awareness, wonder cultivation)
- **No grades, no performance metrics—just exposure and normalization**

Middle School (Ages 11-14):

- Formal mindfulness instruction (20 minutes daily)
- Attention training (focus, sustained attention, meta-awareness)
- Emotional regulation practices (being with difficulty without overwhelm)
- Beginning perspective-taking (seeing from others' views)
- Digital hygiene (relationship with technology and attention)

High School (Ages 14-18):

- Advanced practices (different traditions and approaches)
- Developmental psychology (understanding their own growth)
- Systems thinking integration (connecting contemplation to understanding complexity)
- Existential exploration (meaning, purpose, values)
- **Contemplative inquiry into life questions** (not religious indoctrination, but supported wondering)

Higher Education:

- Contemplative pedagogy across disciplines
- Research into consciousness and development
- Integration of wisdom traditions with modern science
- Support for serious practice for those called to it

The goal isn't making everyone meditators. It's making basic contemplative literacy universal.

Just as we teach everyone to read (though not everyone becomes writers), we teach everyone foundational contemplative skills (though not everyone becomes contemplatives).

2. Community Contemplative Centers

Public spaces for practice and learning (distinct from but complementary to Sanctuaries).

What they provide:

Instruction:

- Free or low-cost classes in various traditions
- Teachers trained in secular contemplative pedagogy
- Multiple approaches (Buddhist, Christian contemplative, secular

mindfulness, somatic practices, Indigenous traditions where appropriately shared)
- Courses ranging from beginner to advanced

Practice space:

- Quiet rooms for individual practice
- Group practice halls
- Movement spaces (yoga, tai chi, dance, embodied practices)
- Nature access (when possible)
- Extended practice opportunities (day-long sits, retreats)

Community:

- Regular sitting groups
- Peer support and accountability
- Mentorship from experienced practitioners
- Intergenerational practice (elders supporting newcomers)

Research and innovation:

- Testing pedagogical approaches
- Measuring developmental outcomes
- Adapting practices for diverse populations
- Integrating traditional and modern approaches

The model: Like public libraries but for inner development.

Density: One contemplative center per 50,000 people (denser than libraries, reflecting importance).

Funding: Public (city/county/state), supplemented by sliding-scale fees and philanthropy.

3. Workplace Contemplative Infrastructure

Not corporate mindfulness to increase productivity. Genuine developmental support.

The critical distinction: The goal is not to create more focused workers for the corporate machine, but to support the development of whole humans who happen to work. The metric of success is wellbeing and wisdom, not quarterly profits.

If your contemplative program is justified by ROI calculations, it's instrumentalization, not infrastructure.

What responsible employers provide:

Time:

- Protected contemplative time (30-60 minutes daily, on the clock)
- Annual retreat time (like vacation but for practice, 1-2 weeks)
- No expectation of increased productivity—this is human development support

Space:

- Quiet rooms (for individual practice)
- Group practice spaces
- Nature access
- Movement spaces

Instruction:

- On-site classes or subsidized external programs
- Trained facilitators
- Multiple traditions/approaches offered
- Developmental support beyond stress reduction

Culture:

- Contemplative practice normalized, not stigmatized
- Leadership models practice (not just mandates it)
- Integration of contemplative values (presence, awareness, compassion) into organizational culture
- Protection from instrumentalization (not measured for ROI)

This isn't making workers more productive. It's making workplaces more human.

4. Healthcare Integration

Contemplative practices as first-line treatment (not alternative medicine).
What this means:
Primary care:

- Mindfulness training for chronic pain (proven effective, no side effects)
- Meditation for anxiety and depression (often as effective as medication)
- Contemplative practices for trauma (somatic approaches particularly powerful)
- Preventive contemplative medicine (building resilience before crisis)

Mental health:

- Contemplative-informed therapy approaches
- Practice groups as community mental health support
- Training therapists in contemplative traditions
- Integration of Eastern psychology with Western approaches

Palliative and end-of-life:

- Contemplative approaches to death and dying
- Support for facing mortality with awareness
- Practices for caregivers and grieving
- Death literacy as part of life literacy

Public health:

- Contemplative practices as social determinant of health
- Community resilience through collective practice
- Addressing root causes (fragmentation, disconnection) not just symp-
  toms

Insurance coverage: Contemplative practices covered like physical therapy—proven effective interventions for specific conditions.

5. Elder Wisdom Programs

Recognizing that contemplative capacity deepens with age (when culti-vated).

Funding: Integrated into the same infrastructure as Community Con-templative Centers and public health/lifelong learning programs. Not a separate system but an extension recognizing that development continues (and often accelerates) in later life.

What this includes:

Elder contemplative education:

- Advanced practice support for older adults
- Retirement as opportunity for deepening (not just leisure)
- Elder retreat programs
- Contemplative approaches to aging

Intergenerational wisdom transmission:

- Elders teaching youth contemplative practices
- Youth teaching elders technology, elders teaching wisdom
- Mentorship programs pairing experienced practitioners with beginners
- Oral history projects capturing elder wisdom

Civic Grief Infrastructure:

The insight: We have infrastructure for waste management (sewage systems). We have no infrastructure for emotional waste management (grief, loss, collective trauma).

When a society cannot process loss, it becomes toxic. The unmetabolized grief turns into rage, despair, addiction, violence.

What Civic Grief Infrastructure includes:

- **Grief circles** (regular community spaces for witnessing loss)
- **Ritual support** (marking deaths, losses, transitions without requiring religious framework)
- **Professional grief workers** (trained facilitators, not just therapists)
- **Public mourning spaces** (physical locations where loss is acknowledged)
- **Collective grief processing** (after disasters, violence, societal trauma)

This validates the Kintsugi Protocol (honoring brokenness as part of wholeness) **and Cairn Protocol** (marking what has passed while moving forward).

Grief is not just a feeling—it's a civic hygiene necessity.

Unprocessed grief at scale creates the despair and disconnection driving our crises. Processing grief collectively creates resilience and wisdom.

Death preparation:

- Contemplative approaches to mortality
- Life review practices
- Legacy work (what wisdom to leave behind?)

- Community death literacy

Elder councils:

- Formal roles for wisdom-keepers in community decision-making
- Bringing contemplative perspective to governance
- Advising on long-term thinking and developmental concerns

The principle: Age without contemplative development is just time passing. Age with contemplative development is wisdom accumulating.

6. Research and Innovation Infrastructure

Serious study of consciousness, development, and practice.
  What this supports:
  Contemplative science:

- Understanding mechanisms of practice
- Measuring developmental outcomes
- Studying altered and higher states of consciousness
- Integrating first-person and third-person methods

Pedagogical innovation:

- What teaching methods work best?
- How to adapt practices across cultures?
- Supporting developmental transitions
- Measuring contemplative capacity

Cultural adaptation:

- How do practices translate across contexts?
- What's universal vs. culturally specific?

- Creating new forms for modern conditions
- Respecting traditions while innovating

Ethical frameworks:

- How to teach without spiritual bypassing?
- Avoiding cultural appropriation while learning across traditions
- Balancing structure and freedom
- Recognizing and addressing power dynamics in teaching

Funding: Public research grants (like NIH, NSF) plus philanthropic support.

$$* * *$$

The Multi-Domain Impact

How does contemplative capacity affect integration across all six domains?

Biological Domain (Impact: 8/10)

Direct effects:

- Nervous system regulation (vagal tone improvement, stress reduction)
- Improved immune function (meditation affects gene expression)
- Better sleep (mindfulness improves sleep quality)
- Pain management (shifting relationship to sensation)
- Slower biological aging (telomere length, inflammation markers)

Mechanism: Mind–body practices directly affect physiology. Meditation activates parasympathetic nervous system, reduces inflammation,

improves HRV.
Measurable outcomes:

- Lower cortisol
- Better immune markers
- Improved cardiovascular health
- Reduced chronic pain
- Increased longevity

Cognitive Domain (Impact: 9/10)

Direct effects:

- Improved attention (focus, sustained attention, attention switching)
- Enhanced working memory
- Better executive function (planning, inhibition, flexibility)
- Increased meta-cognitive awareness
- Improved cognitive flexibility and perspective-taking

Mechanism: Meditation literally changes brain structure. Increases gray matter density in regions associated with attention, emotional regulation, and self-awareness.
Measurable outcomes:

- Better performance on attention tasks
- Improved problem-solving
- Enhanced creativity
- Reduced cognitive decline with aging
- Increased neuroplasticity

Emotional Domain (Impact: 10/10)

Direct effects:

- Better emotional regulation (can be with feelings without suppression or overwhelm)
- Increased emotional granularity (more precise understanding of emotions)
- Greater positive emotions (metta practice increases compassion and joy)
- Reduced anxiety and depression
- Enhanced empathy and compassion

Mechanism: Contemplative practices develop emotional intelligence by creating space between stimulus and response. Allows conscious processing rather than reactive patterns.

Measurable outcomes:

- Lower anxiety scores
- Reduced depression symptoms
- Better relationship quality
- Increased prosocial behavior
- Greater life satisfaction

Behavioral Domain (Impact: 8/10)

Direct effects:

- Reduced compulsive behaviors (breaking automatic patterns)
- More conscious choice (response flexibility)
- Better impulse control
- Increased prosocial actions (helping, sharing, cooperating)
- Aligned behavior (actions matching values)

Mechanism: Meta-awareness creates gap where choice becomes possible. Can see urge without automatically acting on it.

Measurable outcomes:

- Reduced addictive behaviors
- Better self-control
- More ethical behavior
- Increased altruism
- Behavior-value alignment

Social Domain (Impact: 9/10)

Direct effects:

- Improved relationships (better listening, less reactivity)
- Enhanced empathy and perspective-taking
- Reduced prejudice and tribalism
- Increased cooperation and trust
- Stronger community bonds (through group practice)

Mechanism: Contemplative practice increases awareness of shared humanity. Reduces ego-defense, increases openness to others' experience.

Measurable outcomes:

- Better relationship satisfaction
- Reduced intergroup conflict
- Increased prosocial behavior
- Stronger social networks
- Greater sense of belonging

Existential Domain (Impact: 10/10)

Direct effects:

- Greater sense of meaning and purpose
- Reduced existential anxiety
- Increased life satisfaction
- Clearer values and priorities
- Experiences of connection/transcendence

Mechanism: Contemplative practice directly addresses existential questions. Provides experiential insight into nature of self, reality, meaning.

Measurable outcomes:

- Higher meaning-in-life scores
- Reduced death anxiety
- Greater purpose clarity
- More frequent transcendent experiences
- Deeper sense of connectedness

Overall Integration Score: 9/10

Why so high: Contemplative capacity is the *foundation* for integration. It provides the tools to perceive across domains, hold complexity, and allow synthesis.

The other three interventions remove barriers. This one builds capacity.

* * *

The Economics

"Can we afford to develop everyone's contemplative capacity?"
   Better question: **Can we afford not to?**

Direct Costs

K–12 Education Integration:

- Teacher training: $500M nationally (one-time)
- Ongoing professional development: $100M/year
- Curriculum development: $50M (one-time)
- Program implementation: $200M/year
- **Total: $300M/year ongoing** (fraction of education budget)

Community Contemplative Centers:

- Building/space: Often use existing facilities
- Staff (teachers, facilitators, coordinators): $200K–500K per center
- Operating costs: $100K–300K per center
- **For 6,000 centers nationwide: $2–3B/year**

Workplace programs:

- Private sector funds own (contemplative infrastructure as benefit)
- Public sector support: $500M/year

Healthcare integration:

- Training: $200M (one-time)
- Program delivery: $1B/year (saves far more in treatment costs)

Research infrastructure:

- Contemplative science funding: $500M/year (on par with NIH for importance)

Total national investment: $4-5B/year
For context:

- US spends $4.5 **trillion** on healthcare annually
- Defense budget is $850 **billion** annually
- $4-5B is 0.1% of healthcare spending, 0.5% of defense budget
- **This is less than the cost overrun on a single major weapons system** (F-35 program has had $165B+ in cost overruns)

Yet its potential to reduce societal costs and avert existential risk is immeasurable.

We're comparing the price of a rounding error to the value of civilizational wisdom.

Return on Investment

Healthcare savings: Studies show mindfulness-based interventions reduce:

- Primary care visits: 40-50%
- Mental health costs: 30-40%
- Chronic disease management costs: 20-30%

Conservative estimate: If even 10% of population develops basic contemplative capacity, healthcare savings exceed $50B/year.

Productivity gains (not the goal, but real):

- Less sick time
- Better decision-making
- Improved collaboration

- Enhanced creativity
- Reduced workplace conflict

Estimated value: $20-40B/year
Social benefits:

- Reduced crime (mindfulness programs in prisons show 35% reduction in recidivism)
- Better parenting (contemplative parents raise more resilient children)
- Stronger communities (practice groups build social capital)
- Environmental benefits (contemplatives consume less, care more for nature)

Estimated value: Difficult to quantify, but massive

The existential value: Having population capable of wisdom-level thinking about existential threats? **Literally invaluable.**

This isn't cost. It's the best investment civilization could make.

* * *

The Opposition (And Why It's Wrong)

"This Is Religious Indoctrination!"

No, it's secular development of human capacities.
The practices we're discussing:

- Don't require belief in God, karma, or supernatural claims
- Are supported by peer-reviewed neuroscience and psychology
- Can be taught in ways that respect all traditions or none
- Develop skills (attention, awareness, emotional regulation) not religious commitments

Analogy: Studying Shakespeare doesn't make you Christian. Practicing mindfulness doesn't make you Buddhist.

The practices have been secularized and validated. Like yoga in the West—you can do it for health and flexibility without subscribing to Hindu theology.

Appropriate safeguards:

- No religious doctrine taught
- Multiple traditions represented (or none)
- Parents can opt children out (like sex ed)
- Focus on skills, not beliefs
- Teacher training emphasizes secular approach

"It's Cultural Appropriation!"

This requires genuine care and respect.

The wrong approach: Taking practices out of context, commodifying them, stripping them of meaning, claiming credit.

The right approach:

- Acknowledge sources (practices come from Buddhist, Hindu, Sufi, Christian contemplative, Indigenous traditions)
- **Compensate teachers from those traditions** (fair payment, not exploitation)
- **Professionalize the role** (contemplative teaching as respected career path with living wage, benefits, training standards—not just side gig or volunteer work)
- Invite participation and oversight from tradition holders
- Adapt respectfully (not distort)
- Study deeply, don't superficially adopt
- Support preservation of source traditions

The dignity of the teacher matters. If we're building this as essential public infrastructure, teaching contemplative practice should be a respected profession—like librarian, teacher, nurse—with appropriate training, compensation, and social status.

This isn't just ethics. It's quality control. Underpaid, undervalued teachers cannot provide the depth of guidance this work requires.

The analogy: Jazz came from African American traditions. It's cultural appropriation if white musicians claim they invented it and exclude Black musicians. It's cultural appreciation if they acknowledge the source, learn deeply, and support Black jazz musicians.

Contemplative traditions want these practices shared (with respect). The Buddha himself said "test the teachings, don't just believe them." These aren't secrets to be hoarded—they're techniques for reducing suffering.

We need both preservation of traditions and adaptation for new contexts.

"People Won't Do It / It's Too Hard"

This assumes current conditions.

Right now, contemplative practice *is* hard because:

- No childhood exposure
- No cultural support
- Competes with attention extraction
- Must be self-initiated against all incentives

With infrastructure:

- Exposure from childhood (becomes normal)
- Community support (not solo struggle)
- Protected time and space (Sanctuaries, Cognitive Sovereignty)
- Economic security (Sovereign Floor enables taking time)
- Social validation (not weird or self-indulgent)

The difficulty is structural, not inherent.

This is the key insight: What looks like individual failure to maintain practice is actually systemic failure to support development.

Analogy: Reading seems hard if you're illiterate in a pre-literate society. But teach it systematically from childhood in a culture that values it, and it becomes basic literacy.

Most people *want* more presence, less fragmentation, deeper connection. We've just made it nearly impossible.

"It's Escapism / Navel-Gazing"

Only if done badly.

Spiritual bypassing is real: Using practice to avoid dealing with psychological issues, social responsibilities, or practical problems.

But that's misuse, not the practice itself.

Genuine contemplative development:

- Increases engagement with the world (not withdrawal)
- Enhances capacity for action (not passivity)
- Deepens compassion (not self-centeredness)
- Sharpens perception of injustice (not acceptance of status quo)
- Supports activism (not replaces it)

The evidence: Contemplatives are *more* likely to engage in prosocial action, environmental protection, and social justice work.

Martin Luther King Jr., Thich Nhat Hanh, Dorothy Day, Joanna Macy—all deep contemplatives, all engaged activists.

Contemplation without action is escapism. Action without contemplation is burnout.

We need both.

"Government Shouldn't Fund Consciousness Development"

Why not?
Government already funds:

- Education (developing intellectual capacity)
- Healthcare (maintaining physical capacity)
- Parks and recreation (supporting physical and social wellbeing)
- Arts and culture (enriching cultural life)

Why is developing contemplative capacity different?
If it demonstrably:

- Improves health outcomes
- Reduces healthcare costs
- Enhances education quality
- Builds social capital
- Supports civic engagement
- Addresses existential challenges

Then it's exactly what government should fund.
This isn't telling people what to believe. It's providing infrastructure for human development.

* * *

Implementation Timeline

Phase 1: Pilot Programs (Years 1-3)

Education pilots:

- 50 schools nationwide implementing contemplative education
- Teacher training programs launched
- Curriculum development and testing
- Outcome measurement

Contemplative centers:

- 20 cities launch public contemplative centers
- Various models tested (library-based, standalone, integrated with existing facilities)
- Community engagement and program development

Research infrastructure:

- Funding contemplative science
- Establishing research centers
- Beginning longitudinal studies

Healthcare pilots:

- Major hospital systems integrating contemplative medicine
- Training providers
- Insurance coverage experiments

Phase 2: Scaling (Years 3-7)

Based on pilot success:

- 500+ schools with contemplative education

- 200+ contemplative centers
- Workplace program proliferation
- Healthcare integration expanding
- Teacher training programs at scale

Policy development:

- Model legislation
- Funding mechanisms
- Standards and best practices
- Rights and protections

Phase 3: Normalization (Years 7-15)

Contemplative infrastructure becomes standard:

- All K-12 includes contemplative education
- Contemplative centers expected in all cities
- Healthcare fully integrates evidence-based practices
- Workplace support widely available
- Cultural shift toward valuing presence

* * *

What This Enables

For Individuals:

- Actual capacity to be present
- Tools for working with difficult emotions
- Ability to hold complexity

- Access to inner wisdom
- Resilience in face of challenge

For Communities:

- Collective wisdom capacity
- Ability to navigate conflict constructively
- Shared practice spaces building bonds
- Intergenerational wisdom transmission
- Cultural shift toward depth

For Civilization:

- Population capable of Yellow and beyond
- Wisdom to match our technological power
- Long-term thinking capacity
- Systems perception widely available
- Integration capacity enabling solutions to complex challenges

For Evolution:

- Accelerated developmental trajectory
- Cultural support for consciousness development
- Proof that contemplative capacity can be democratized
- Foundation for further evolution
- Hope that we might grow wise fast enough

* * *

Integration With Other Interventions

Cognitive Sovereignty + Contemplative Capacity:

- Protected attention enables developing attention skills
- Contemplative capacity enables using protected attention wisely
- Synergy: Freedom from extraction + ability to use that freedom

Sovereign Floor + Contemplative Capacity:

- Economic security enables taking time for practice
- Contemplative capacity enables using that time well (not just scrolling differently)
- Synergy: Time wealth + capacity to use time wisely

Sanctuaries + Contemplative Capacity:

- Protected space enables practice
- Contemplative capacity enables actually using sanctuary space (not just feeling restless)
- Synergy: External container + internal capacity

All Four Together: The magic happens when all four interventions work together:

- **Cognitive Sovereignty** removes extraction
- **Sovereign Floor** removes survival terror
- **Sanctuaries** provide protected space
- **Contemplative Infrastructure** builds actual capacity

Result: Integration becomes possible for the first time in modern history.

* * *

Conclusion: The Inner Infrastructure

We've built magnificent outer infrastructure:

- Roads, bridges, buildings
- Schools, hospitals, libraries
- Communications networks, energy grids

But we've neglected the inner infrastructure:

- Attention capacity
- Emotional regulation
- Wisdom development
- Consciousness evolution

This is the missing foundation.

All the other interventions create conditions. This one builds capacity.

You can protect attention, guarantee income, provide sanctuary space—but if people lack the inner development to actually be present, to feel deeply, to think systemically, to act wisely—**then we've just created comfortable circumstances for fragmented consciousness.**

Contemplative capacity is how humans actually develop the abilities that Yellow consciousness requires.

It's not optional. It's not luxury. It's not just for monks or the spiritually inclined.

It's essential human development that we've systematically prevented.

Reverse-Engineering the Monastery

Here's what we're really doing:

For millennia, wisdom traditions figured out the specific structural conditions that produce deep human development:

- **Silence** (freedom from constant stimulation)
- **Safety** (economic and physical security)
- **Rigor** (structured practice and discipline)
- **Guidance** (experienced teachers and community)
- **Time** (extended periods for deep work)
- **Space** (physical environments supporting contemplation)

Traditionally, accessing these conditions required leaving the world—becoming a monk, joining a monastery, going on extended retreat.

We are reverse-engineering the monastery.

We are taking those precise structural conditions and weaving them into the fabric of the city, the workplace, the school, the neighborhood.

The goal: You shouldn't have to leave the world to find the capacity to live in it.

Mass enlightenment via infrastructure.

Not forcing anyone to practice. Not mandating belief systems. Simply making the conditions for deep human development available to everyone, as public infrastructure, as normal as libraries or parks.

Making it available to everyone, as public infrastructure, as normal as literacy or numeracy—**this is what makes the developmental leap possible.**

Not forced. Not mandated. Just made accessible, supported, normalized.

Then we see what humans become when given time, space, and training to develop their full capacities.

I think we'd be amazed.

* * *

Next: Chapter 15 will show why all four interventions together constitute the **Minimum Viable Yellow Stack**—why each is necessary, why all together are sufficient, and what becomes possible when we implement them as an integrated system.

The individual pieces matter. But the real magic is in how they work together to enable the developmental leap civilization desperately needs.

Ready to see the whole system?

* * *

Postcard from 2040: Collective Lucidity

It started with three people sitting on the steps of the public library. Then ten. Then a hundred. No one organized it. No notification went out. It was a spontaneous synchronization of attention.

Three hundred strangers sat together in the square for an hour, wordlessly co-regulating. The field of shared presence was palpable—a thick, warm silence that held us all. We weren't waiting for a speaker. We weren't protesting a grievance. We were simply attending to the reality of being here, together. It was the first time I felt the "We" not as a political slogan, but as a physical fact.

Chapter 15: The Minimum Viable Yellow Stack

Why Four? Why These Four?

We've covered the four major interventions: 1. **Cognitive Sovereignty** (Chapter 11) - Ending involuntary attention extraction 2. **The Sovereign Floor** (Chapter 12) - Ending conditional worth through AUBI 3. **Sanctuaries** (Chapter 13) - Creating non-extractive zones 4. **Contemplative Capacity** (Chapter 14) - Building inner infrastructure

Now comes the critical question: Why exactly these four? Why not three? Why not seven?

This isn't arbitrary. This is **systems engineering.**

The four interventions work together as an **integrated system** that addresses the root cause we diagnosed in Part I: **addiction as integration failure across all six human domains.**

This chapter will prove: 1. Each intervention is **necessary** (remove any one, the system fails) 2. All four together are **sufficient** (they provide near-complete coverage across all six domains) 3. The synergies create **emergent effects** (1+1+1+1 = far more than 4) 4. This constitutes the **minimum viable set** (nothing essential is missing, nothing included is redundant)

Let's see the architecture.

* * *

The Integration Heat Map

Here's how each intervention scores across the six domains of human experience:

What this shows:

The Domain Average column (rightmost) is the critical metric - it shows how well each domain is covered when all four interventions work together. Note:

- Every domain averages 7.75 or higher
- Most domains average 8.0 or higher
- This represents **near-complete coverage across all six domains**

The Intervention Average row (bottom) shows each intervention's overall strength:

- Sovereign Floor and Contemplative Capacity tie for strongest (9.0)
- Sanctuaries middle-strong (7.8)
- Cognitive Sovereignty focused but crucial (7.0)

Individual Strength Analysis

Sovereign Floor (AUBI) is strongest overall (9.0 average):

- Addresses the most fundamental barrier: survival terror
- Strong across all domains (nothing below 8/10)
- This is why it's the foundation

Contemplative Capacity ties for strongest (9.0 average):

- Provides the actual capacity to use other interventions
- Perfect scores (10/10) in Emotional and Existential domains
- This is why it's the completion

Sanctuaries middle-strong (7.8 average):

- Particularly powerful for Social (9/10) and Existential (8/10)
- Provides physical/digital container
- Essential but not sufficient alone

Cognitive Sovereignty focused but crucial (7.0 average):

- Exceptionally strong in Cognitive domain (9/10)
- Addresses specific modern threat (attention extraction)
- Necessary but narrow in scope

Coverage Analysis

No domain below 7.7 average across all four interventions:

- Biological: 7.75 average (good coverage)
- Cognitive: 8.5 average (excellent coverage)
- Emotional: 8.25 average (excellent coverage)
- Behavioral: 8.25 average (excellent coverage)
- Social: 8.5 average (excellent coverage)
- Existential: 8.0 average (excellent coverage)

This means: Near-complete coverage across all six domains when all four interventions work together.

The Integration Threshold

Remember from Chapter 4: **Integration requires addressing at least 4 of 6 domains with scores above 7/10.**
With all four interventions:

- All six domains score 7.75+ average
- Most score 8.0+ average
- **Integration threshold exceeded across the board**

This is sufficient coverage for system-level transformation.

* * *

The Necessity Test: What Happens If We Remove One?

Let's test each intervention's necessity by removing it and seeing what breaks.
But first, the Architecture of Failure:
Here's what happens when you have 3 out of 4 interventions—proving that partial measures don't just deliver partial results, they create new dystopias:

The Failure Mode Matrix

Three Without Cognitive Sovereignty = The Funded Addict

- AUBI + Sanctuaries + Contemplative Capacity
- You have money, protected space, and contemplative training
- But the algorithm still owns your amygdala
- Result: Wealthier, calmer scrolling addicts with nice parks

- **Current trajectory: Scandinavia with smartphones**

Three Without Sovereign Floor = The Elite Retreat

- Cognitive Sovereignty + Sanctuaries + Contemplative Capacity
- You have protected attention, beautiful spaces, and meditation training
- But you're starving because rent is due
- Result: Only the wealthy can access the benefits—everyone else still trapped in survival mode
- **This is the liberal dream: regulate tech, build parks, offer yoga—but leave capitalism intact**

Three Without Sanctuaries = The Lonely Monk

- AUBI + Cognitive Sovereignty + Contemplative Capacity
- You have money, protected attention, and contemplative skills
- But every physical and digital space is still extractive
- Result: Isolated individuals with capacity but no community, no container, no cultural support
- **The hermit with a stipend: free but alone in hostile world**

Three Without Contemplative Capacity = The Anxious Freeman

- AUBI + Cognitive Sovereignty + Sanctuaries
- You have money, protected attention, and beautiful spaces
- But you lack the internal capacity to actually use them
- Result: Restless people with all external supports but no inner infrastructure
- **The trust-fund syndrome: given everything, able to enjoy nothing**

The pattern: Each three-intervention combination creates a *specific failure mode*—not just "less good" but *pathological in new ways*.

Only all four together avoid these traps.

Now let's examine each removal in detail:

Remove Cognitive Sovereignty → Extraction Continues

What remains: AUBI + Sanctuaries + Contemplative Capacity

What breaks:

- **Cognitive domain crashes** (from 8.5 to 8.3, but more importantly loses specific protection)
- **Attention remains under assault** (algorithms still predatory)
- **Sanctuary spaces compromised** (digital spaces still extractive)
- **Practice becomes harder** (fighting constant distraction)
- **AUBI helps but doesn't protect attention** (can afford time off but phone still hijacks it)

The failure mode: People have time, space, and training—but their attention is still being involuntarily extracted. They sit in sanctuaries but check phones compulsively. They attend contemplative centers but can't focus. Economic security helps, but algorithmic manipulation continues.

The specific threat Cognitive Sovereignty addresses (engineered compulsion through design patterns) **isn't addressed by the other three.**

Verdict: Necessary. Cognitive domain needs specific protection from modern extraction technology.

Remove Sovereign Floor → Survival Terror Remains

What remains: Cognitive Sovereignty + Sanctuaries + Contemplative Capacity

What breaks:

- **Behavioral domain crashes** (from 8.25 to 7.0 - loses the 10/10 contribution)

- **Economic terror prevents everything else** (protected attention but must use it job-searching)
- **Can't use sanctuaries** (no time when survival depends on constant work)
- **Can't develop contemplative capacity** (the restlessness of conditional existence)
- **Integration impossible under survival stress** (chronic fight-or-flight blocks higher function)

The failure mode: This is the current progressive/liberal strategy: "Let's provide mindfulness apps, create some parks, and regulate big tech—but leave the economic system intact."

Result: People are grateful for sanctuaries and maybe less manipulated by algorithms, but they're still terrorized by rent being due. They can't be present because presence is a luxury they literally can't afford. The most they can do is optimize their stress management while remaining trapped.

We've seen this movie. It's playing right now. It doesn't work.

Verdict: Necessary. No other intervention removes the baseline existential terror that prevents all higher functioning.

Remove Sanctuaries → No Protected Space

What remains: Cognitive Sovereignty + Sovereign Floor + Contemplative Capacity

What breaks:

- **Social domain weakens significantly** (from 8.5 to 7.3 - loses the 9/10 contribution)
- **Physical environment still extractive** (every space demands something)
- **Community formation harder** (no protected gathering spaces)
- **Contemplative practice lacks container** (training but nowhere to

practice)
- **Digital still commercial** (even with sovereignty, alternatives needed)

The failure mode: People have protected attention, economic security, and contemplative training—but every physical and digital space they enter is still optimized for extraction. There's nowhere to just exist without being sold to, surveilled, or expected to perform.

It's like: Having strong lungs but no clean air. The capacity exists but the environment prevents its use.

Practice groups meet in Starbucks because there's nowhere else. Community gatherings happen in bars because those are the only "third places" left. Contemplatives try to practice but are surrounded by advertising, noise, and commercial pressure.

The protected attention and economic security create possibility. Sanctuaries create actuality.

Verdict: Necessary. Capacity and freedom are insufficient without physical/digital containers that embody non-extractive principles.

Remove Contemplative Capacity → No Internal Infrastructure

What remains: Cognitive Sovereignty + Sovereign Floor + Sanctuaries
What breaks:

- **Emotional domain weakens significantly** (from 8.25 to 6.3 - loses the 10/10 contribution)
- **Existential domain weakens significantly** (from 8.0 to 6.3 - loses the 10/10 contribution)
- **Can't actually use the protected space** (have sanctuary but just feel restless)
- **Can't handle the freedom** (economic security but no idea what to do with time)
- **Can't hold complexity** (external conditions support Yellow but lack internal capacity)

The failure mode: This is perhaps the subtlest failure—everything external is in place, but people lack the internal development to actually inhabit these conditions.

Like giving someone a piano without teaching them to play. The instrument is there. The time is available. The room is quiet. But they can't make music because they never learned how.

Watch what actually happens:

- Put someone in a sanctuary with all day free: they feel restless, anxious, guilty within minutes
- Give someone economic security without meaning-making capacity: they spiral into depression
- Protect someone's attention without training in attention management: they just scroll different things
- Create non-extractive space without emotional regulation skills: people recreate extraction through drama and conflict

External conditions are necessary but not sufficient. The developmental capacity must match the environmental support.

Verdict: Necessary. All the freedom and protection in the world means nothing if people lack the capacity to use it wisely.

* * *

The Sufficiency Test: Is Anything Essential Missing?

We've proven each intervention is necessary. But are these four together sufficient?

Three ways to test sufficiency:

1. Domain Coverage Test

Question: Does the stack adequately address all six domains?
  Review of averages across all four interventions:

- Biological: 7.75/10 ✓ (good coverage)
- Cognitive: 8.5/10 ✓ (excellent)
- Emotional: 8.25/10 ✓ (excellent)
- Behavioral: 8.25/10 ✓ (excellent)
- Social: 8.5/10 ✓ (excellent)
- Existential: 8.0/10 ✓ (excellent)

No domain below 7.5. Most above 8.0.
  Compare to integration threshold (4+ domains above 7/10):

- We have 6/6 domains above 7.5
- We have 5/6 domains above 8.0

Verdict: Sufficient domain coverage. No major gaps.

2. Systems Thinking Test

Question: Do we address root causes or just symptoms?
  The original diagnosis (from Part I): Addiction as integration failure driven by:

- **Extraction systems** (capitalism, attention economy) → Cognitive Sovereignty addresses
- **Survival terror** (conditional worth, precarity) → Sovereign Floor addresses
- **Environmental design** (nowhere to just be) → Sanctuaries address
- **Underdeveloped capacity** (can't hold complexity) → Contemplative Capacity addresses

All four root causes directly addressed.

Plus the meta-cause: Fragmentation itself (inability to perceive/hold all six domains) → Contemplative Capacity + the synergies of all four working together address this

Verdict: Sufficient. Root causes addressed, not just symptoms.

3. What-Else Test

Question: What essential element is missing from this stack?

Let's honestly consider other candidates:

Healthcare?

- Important but largely addressed by AUBI (removes cost barrier) + Contemplative Capacity (most evidence-based interventions)
- Specific healthcare policy beyond this is important but not "Yellow stack minimum viable"

Political reform?

- Part IV will address implementation and power
- But political change is *how we implement the stack*, not an element *of* the stack
- The stack is what we're trying to build politically

Technology?

- Cognitive Sovereignty addresses harmful tech
- Beneficial tech is a tool for implementing other interventions, not an intervention itself

Climate/Environment?

- Sanctuaries include wilderness protection

- But more broadly: climate change is what Yellow consciousness (enabled by the stack) allows us to address
- Climate is the problem the stack helps us solve, not part of the stack itself

Housing?

- AUBI ensures people can afford housing
- Sanctuaries include community spaces that reduce isolation even in small housing
- Specific housing policy matters but isn't a separate pillar

Food systems?

- AUBI enables access to good food
- Regenerative currency (Hearts/Leaves) supports sustainable food
- Again, important but not a separate pillar

Education beyond contemplative?

- Covered under Contemplative Capacity (which includes all K-12)
- Academic education continues; we're adding the missing contemplative dimension

Community/relationships?

- Sanctuaries create space for community
- Contemplative Capacity develops social-emotional skills
- AUBI removes competition pressure from relationships
- Well covered

Meaning/purpose/culture?

- Existential domain scores 8.0 across the stack
- Sanctuaries + Contemplative Capacity particularly strong here
- Cultural transformation happens *through* the stack, isn't separate from it

Could we add a fifth intervention that would significantly increase coverage?

Honestly, no.

Looking at the heat map, every domain is already 7.75+ average. A fifth intervention might add marginal improvement, but we'd hit diminishing returns. We're already at 8.2/10 overall average.

The principle of minimum viable: We want the smallest set that's sufficient. Adding more creates complexity, implementation difficulty, and coordination challenges without proportional benefit.

Verdict: Sufficient. All essential elements present, nothing critical missing.

* * *

The Synergy Effects: Why 1+1+1+1 = 10

But here's where it gets interesting.

The four interventions don't just add together. They multiply.

Each intervention makes the others more powerful. The synergies create emergent effects impossible with any subset.

Synergy 1: Cognitive Sovereignty × Contemplative Capacity

Cognitive Sovereignty protects attention from external extraction. Contemplative Capacity builds internal attention management.

Together:

- External protection + internal skill = genuine attentional freedom
- Protected space enables developing capacity (less interference)
- Developed capacity enables using protected space wisely (not just scrolling different things)

The multiplication:

- Cognitive Sovereignty alone: 7/10 effectiveness (removes barrier but people lack skill)
- Contemplative Capacity alone: 6/10 effectiveness (have skill but environment constantly disrupts)
- **Both together: 9/10 effectiveness** (protection + capacity = actual freedom)

Emergent effect: Digital sovereignty movements get teeth. People with attention skills demand and can use protected spaces. This creates market and political pressure for better digital infrastructure.

Synergy 2: Sovereign Floor × Contemplative Capacity

Sovereign Floor provides time and removes survival terror. Contemplative Capacity provides skills to use that time wisely.
Together:

- Time wealth + developmental skills = actual growth (not just Netflix)
- Economic security enables facing difficult emotions (not suppressing for survival)
- Contemplative practice makes economic freedom meaningful (not just empty leisure)

The multiplication:

- Sovereign Floor alone: 8/10 effectiveness (have time but don't know what to do with it → depression risk)

- Contemplative Capacity alone: 5/10 effectiveness (have skills but no time to practice → frustration)
- **Both together: 9.5/10 effectiveness** (time + skill = transformation)

Emergent effect: AUBI becomes not just "survival support" but "developmental infrastructure." The economic foundation enables the consciousness evolution that makes Yellow civilization possible.

Synergy 3: Sanctuaries × Contemplative Capacity

Sanctuaries provide protected physical/digital space. Contemplative Capacity provides ability to actually inhabit that space.
   Together:

- External container + internal capacity = genuine sanctuary (not just restless waiting)
- Physical space makes practice accessible (not just solo heroism)
- Practice skills make space usable (not just empty silence)

The multiplication:

- Sanctuaries alone: 6/10 effectiveness (beautiful space but people feel anxious/bored)
- Contemplative Capacity alone: 6/10 effectiveness (skilled but nowhere to practice)
- **Both together: 9/10 effectiveness** (space + capacity = actual sanctuary)

Emergent effect: Third places return but upgraded. Not just "hang out spots" but "developmental spaces." Community forms around shared practice, not just shared consumption.

Synergy 4: Cognitive Sovereignty × Sovereign Floor

Cognitive Sovereignty protects attention. Sovereign Floor removes economic coercion.
  Together:

- Attention protection + economic freedom = genuine choice (not "free" to choose between exploitations)
- Can refuse extractive work without starving (Right to Refuse becomes real)
- Can refuse extractive platforms without isolation (alternatives viable)

The multiplication:

- Cognitive Sovereignty alone: 7/10 effectiveness (attention protected but must use it earning money)
- Sovereign Floor alone: 8/10 effectiveness (survival secure but attention still hijacked)
- **Both together: 9/10 effectiveness** (attention + survival = authentic freedom)

Emergent effect: "Vote with your feet" actually works. Bad employers and extractive platforms lose users/workers who now have genuine alternatives. This creates market pressure for ethical business models.

Synergy 5: Sanctuaries × Sovereign Floor

Sanctuaries provide space. Sovereign Floor provides time and removes guilt about "unproductive" use of space.
  Together:

- Space availability + time to use it = actual access (not theoretical access you can't use)

- Economic security makes sanctuary use guilt-free (not "shouldn't I be working?")
- Sanctuary space makes economic freedom social (not isolated leisure)

The multiplication:

- Sanctuaries alone: 7/10 effectiveness (beautiful spaces people can't afford time to use)
- Sovereign Floor alone: 7/10 effectiveness (have time but nowhere good to go)
- **Both together: 9/10 effectiveness** (space + time = inhabited commons)

Emergent effect: Sanctuary spaces stay vibrant and used (not empty). This justifies continued public investment and expansion. Success breeds success.

Synergy 6: Cognitive Sovereignty × Sanctuaries

Cognitive Sovereignty protects digital attention. Sanctuaries provide physical and digital alternatives.
  Together:

- Attention protection makes sanctuaries possible (not undermined by phones)
- Sanctuaries make attention protection stick (alternatives to extractive platforms exist)
- Digital sanctuaries + physical sanctuaries = complete coverage

The multiplication:

- Cognitive Sovereignty alone: 7/10 effectiveness (regulation but no alternatives)

- Sanctuaries alone: 6/10 effectiveness (spaces exist but everyone's on phones)
- **Both together: 8.5/10 effectiveness** (protection + alternatives = actual shift)

Emergent effect: Non-extractive digital culture becomes possible. People experience both protected physical spaces and ethical digital spaces, creating cultural expectation that both should exist.

The Triple Synergies

When three work together, even more powerful effects emerge:
  Cognitive Sovereignty + Sovereign Floor + Contemplative Capacity =

- Protected attention + time + skills = **mastery development**
- People can actually get good at things that matter (not just survival skills)
- Creativity, art, science, wisdom production all multiply

Sanctuaries + Sovereign Floor + Contemplative Capacity =

- Space + time + skills = **community flourishing**
- Intergenerational wisdom transmission becomes normal
- Third places become developmental, not just recreational
- Culture regenerates organically

Cognitive Sovereignty + Sanctuaries + Contemplative Capacity =

- Protected attention + space + skills = **genuine presence**
- The holy grail: actually being here now, by choice, with capacity
- What contemplatives have sought for millennia, now accessible

The Quadruple Synergy: All Four Together

When all four interventions work together, the ultimate emergent effect:
INTEGRATION BECOMES POSSIBLE.
Not forced. Not mandated. Not preached.
Just possible—for the first time in industrial civilization.

- Attention protected (Cognitive Sovereignty)
- Survival secured (Sovereign Floor)
- Space provided (Sanctuaries)
- Capacity developed (Contemplative Capacity)

Result:

- Can perceive across all six domains (meta–awareness + time to reflect)
- Can hold contradictions (emotional regulation + safety to feel)
- Can see systems (cognitive flexibility + space to think)
- Can choose wisely (behavioral freedom + developed judgment)
- Can connect authentically (social space + relational capacity)
- Can find meaning (existential security + contemplative insight)

Reverse-Engineering the Monastery

Here's what we've actually built:
For millennia, wisdom traditions discovered the precise structural conditions required for deep human development:

- **Safety** (economic and physical security) → Sovereign Floor provides
- **Silence** (freedom from constant stimulation) → Sanctuaries provide
- **Boundaries** (protection from manipulation) → Cognitive Sovereignty provides
- **Discipline** (structured practice and training) → Contemplative Capacity provides

Traditionally, accessing these conditions required leaving the world—becoming a monk, joining a monastery, taking vows of poverty.

We have reverse-engineered the functional components of a monastery and scaled them to the size of a civilization.

We're not trying to make everyone a monk. We're trying to make "The World" a place where enlightenment is the path of least resistance.

The monastery wasn't magical. It was engineered. Specific conditions reliably producing specific outcomes.

We're building those conditions into the fabric of daily life:

- Not behind walls, but woven into cities
- Not requiring vows, but available as infrastructure
- Not for the spiritually called, but for everyone

This is what enables Yellow consciousness at scale.

Not for the elite few who can afford retreats and therapy and time off.

For everyone. As infrastructure. As normal.

* * *

The Minimum Viable Principle

"Minimum viable" means: 1. Everything included is necessary (proven by removal test) 2. Nothing essential is missing (proven by domain coverage and systems test) 3. The combination is sufficient (proven by synergy effects)

Why this matters:

We face a tendency toward two errors:

Error 1: Reductionism ("Just fix the economy" or "Just regulate tech")

- Picks one intervention
- Ignores integration

- Fails because root cause is multi-domain

Error 2: Everything-ism ("We need to transform everything all at once!")

- 47-point plans
- Overwhelming complexity
- Implementation paralysis
- Nothing happens

The minimum viable stack avoids both:

- Not reductionist (addresses all six domains)
- Not everything-ist (just four focused interventions)
- Implementable (each has clear policy pathway)
- Sufficient (together they enable integration)

This is systems engineering.
  Like building a table:

- Three legs: unstable (reductionism)
- Twenty legs: overcomplicated and no better (everything-ism)
- Four legs: minimum viable stability (just right)

Our stack is the four-legged table.
  Each leg essential. All four sufficient. The simplest thing that actually works.

* * *

What This Enables: The Cascade

When all four interventions work together, watch what becomes possible:

Individual Level

Week 1 with full stack:

- Wake up (Cognitive Sovereignty: no phone interruption)
- Morning walk in Sanctuary District (Sanctuaries: beautiful, ad-free, safe)
- Contemplative practice (Contemplative Capacity: trained since childhood)
- No rent panic (Sovereign Floor: basics covered)
- **Can actually be present for breakfast**

Month 1:

- Attention stays where you direct it (not hijacked)
- Time for relationships, hobbies, learning
- Community connections deepen (sanctuary spaces enable)
- Emotions processable (not suppressed for survival)
- **Life feels coherent, not fragmented**

Year 1:

- Developmental growth noticeable
- Can hold complexity that was overwhelming before
- Relationships transform (not transactional)
- Work becomes contribution, not survival
- **Integration progressing naturally**

Emergent property at individual level: **Coherent selfhood becomes achievable**

Community Level

Month 1:

- Sanctuary spaces buzzing with life
- Practice groups forming organically
- Intergenerational connections happening
- Mutual aid networks strengthening
- **Social fabric regenerating**

Year 1:

- Neighborhood commons thriving
- Cultural production increasing (art, music, gathering)
- Collective decision-making improving (more wisdom)
- Crime and conflict decreasing (root causes addressed)
- **Community resilience building**

Decade 1:

- Local culture regenerated
- Elder wisdom integrated into governance
- Children growing up in developmental culture
- Social trust rebuilt
- **Flourishing communities emerging**

Emergent property at community level: **Social fabric regenerating**

Civilizational Level

Year 1-3:

- Pilot cities showing results
- Policy models proven effective
- Cultural shift beginning
- Political will building
- **Proof of concept established**

Year 3-10:

- Scaling to more cities
- National policy changes
- International coordination beginning
- Next generation being raised in new system
- **Transformation underway**

Decade 2-3:

- Yellow consciousness widespread
- Existential challenges becoming addressable
- Climate action actually happening (wiser decisions)
- AI alignment achievable (deeper understanding of values)
- Social healing progressing (empathy and systems thinking)
- **Civilization stabilizing at higher order**

Emergent property at civilizational level: **Civilization stabilizing at higher developmental order**

This isn't utopian fantasy.

This is what systemic intervention at sufficient scale makes possible.

Not perfection. Not heaven on earth. Not end of all problems.

Just: A civilization where human flourishing is structurally supported rather than systematically prevented.

Where integration is the norm, not the exception.

Where Yellow consciousness is accessible, not just for mystics and geniuses.

That's what the stack enables.

* * *

The Implementation Question

"This is beautiful. How do we actually build it?"

That's Part IV.

But here's the preview:

We don't need unanimous agreement. We don't need revolutionary overthrow. We don't need to convince everyone first.

We need: 1. **Pilot cities** willing to experiment 2. **Coalition building** across strange bedfellows 3. **Proof of concept** that changes the Overton window 4. **Scaling** based on demonstrated success 5. **Time** (15-30 years, which is fast for civilizational change)

The stack is designed for gradual, proven implementation.

Each intervention can start small:

- Cognitive Sovereignty: City ordinances, state laws, then federal
- Sovereign Floor: Municipal pilots, then state, then national
- Sanctuaries: 10 cities, then 100, then standard
- Contemplative Capacity: 50 schools, then 500, then all

The synergies emerge even at pilot scale.

And success is its own best argument.

When people see sanctuary cities thriving, others want in. When AUBI pilots show better outcomes, policy spreads. When contemplative education produces better humans, schools adopt it.

This is how civilizational transformation actually happens:

Not overnight revolution.

Gradual, proven, scaling change—guided by clear vision of what we're building and why it works.

The stack is the vision.

Part IV is the strategy.

* * *

Conclusion: The Integrated Solution

We began with a diagnosis: Addiction as integration failure across all six human domains.

We explored why: Orange-level solutions can't solve Orange-level problems. We need Yellow consciousness.

We showed how: Not through wishful thinking or individual enlightenment, but through systemic intervention at sufficient scale.

The Minimum Viable Yellow Stack:

1. **Cognitive Sovereignty** - Protects attention from extraction (Cognitive domain strength)
2. **Sovereign Floor (AUBI)** - Removes survival terror (Foundation for everything, strongest across all domains)
3. **Sanctuaries** - Provides protected space (Social and Existential strength, physical container)
4. **Contemplative Capacity** - Builds internal infrastructure (Emotional and Existential strength, enables actual use)

Each necessary. All together sufficient.

Together they achieve:

- 8.2/10 average coverage across all six domains

- All domains above 7.75 (integration threshold exceeded)
- Massive synergy effects (1+1+1+1 = 10, not 4)
- Root causes addressed, not just symptoms
- Implementable pathway (each intervention can start small and scale)

The Bootstrap Paradox (And How We Escape It)

The objection: "This is circular! You need Yellow consciousness to implement the stack that creates Yellow consciousness!"

The answer: The stack is not a *product* of fully Yellow culture, but the *engine for creating it.*

We bootstrap this future by:

- Implementing the parts we can with the consciousness we have (Orange can build AUBI pilots; Green can create sanctuaries; Blue can regulate extraction)
- Trusting the synergies to catalyze the very development needed to complete it
- Using early adopters and pilot cities as proof of concept
- Letting success create the political will for expansion

The stack creates the citizens capable of stewarding the stack.

This isn't magical thinking—it's developmental feedback loops. Better conditions → higher consciousness → demand for better conditions → higher consciousness. The virtuous cycle.

We don't need everyone Yellow to start. We need enough people Orange/Green to implement pilots. The pilots produce Yellow. Yellow scales the system.

Meta-Governance: The Stack Creates Its Own Stewards

A final note on complexity:

These four massive systems don't just run themselves. Managing them requires coordination, balancing tensions, making tradeoffs, adapting to feedback.

This requires meta-governance—the capacity to hold multiple systems simultaneously, see their interactions, and make wise collective decisions.

Here's the beauty: The stack creates the very citizens capable of doing that governance.

- Contemplative capacity develops systems perception
- Protected attention enables holding complexity
- Economic security removes desperate short-term thinking
- Sanctuary spaces create deliberative capacity

The system creates the capacity for its own stewardship.

This is not the only possible solution.

But it is:

- **Comprehensive** (addresses all six domains)
- **Minimal** (nothing redundant, nothing essential missing)
- **Synergistic** (interventions multiply each other's effects)
- **Implementable** (clear policy pathways, proven models)
- **Sufficient** (enables the developmental leap we desperately need)
- **Self-sustaining** (creates capacity for its own governance)

The question is no longer "what should we do?"

The question is: "Will we do it?"

Part IV addresses how to make this real—the politics, the power, the transition strategy, the timeline, the obstacles, and how to overcome them.

But first, take a breath.

We've just designed the basic operating system for Yellow civilization.

Not in vague aspirational terms. In concrete, implementable, integrated detail.

The infrastructure for human flourishing.

The conditions for integration.

The architecture of wisdom.

This is what it takes.

Not less. But also, not more.

Four interventions. Six domains. One integrated system.

The Minimum Viable Yellow Stack.

* * *

Next: Part IV – The Alchemist's Path: How to actually build this, who will resist, who will help, and what the transition looks like in practice.

The vision is complete. Now we need the strategy.

Ready?

* * *

PART IV: THE ALCHEMIST'S PATH

***

Chapter 16: The Coalition of the Willing (And the Unlikely)

From Blueprint to Reality

We have the vision. We have the stack. We have the evidence.

Now comes the hardest part: actually building it.

Not in theory. Not in simulation. In the real world, with real politics, real power structures, real resistance, and real people who desperately need this but don't yet know they need it.

This chapter is about strategy.

Not wishful thinking. Not "if only everyone would see the light." Not magical consciousness shifts that happen because we really, really want them to.

Actual strategy:

- Who implements this?
- How do we build coalitions across difference?
- Where do we start?
- What's the sequence?
- How do we handle resistance?
- What's realistic in what timeframe?

The good news: We don't need unanimous agreement. We don't need revolution. We don't need everyone to become Yellow overnight.

We need strategic implementation by coalitions of the willing—even when they're willing for completely different reasons.

This is the art of the possible.

* * *

The Coalition Map: Strange Bedfellows United by Need

Here's the counterintuitive truth: The Yellow stack appeals to people at every developmental stage—but for completely different reasons.

We don't need to convert everyone to Yellow thinking. We need to show each stage how the stack serves their values.

Let me map the coalition:

BEIGE (Survival) - "I Need This to Live"

Current state: Homeless, deeply precarious, survival mode **What they need from the stack:** Sovereign Floor primarily **Their language:** "I need food, shelter, safety" **Why they support:** Basic survival secured **Their contribution:** Moral urgency, human face of crisis **How to engage:** Direct service, immediate support, dignity restored

The appeal: "You will never go hungry or be without shelter again. Your human dignity is unconditional."

Political weight: Smaller numbers but powerful moral claim

RED (Power) - "This Makes Me Stronger"

Current state: Entrepreneurs, hustlers, people building empires **What they need from the stack:** Cognitive Sovereignty (no one manipulates their attention), Sanctuaries (status/quality of life) **Their language:** "I want power, freedom, to dominate my domain" **Why they support:** Economic freedom to build without wage slavery, attention protection from competitors' manipulation, Sanctuaries as status marker **Their contribution:** Entrepreneurial energy, wealth, implementation drive

The appeal: "With AUBI, you can take bigger risks. With Cognitive Sovereignty, no algorithm manipulates you. With Sanctuaries, you signal elite status. Be the wolf who chooses the monastery."

Political weight: Disproportionate influence through wealth and drive

Critical insight: Some Red actually *love* contemplation—not for peace, but for power. Elite athletes, military special forces, high-stakes traders. They use meditation like a weapon. **That's fine.** We're not here to judge motives. If Red uses the infrastructure for dominance and it makes them support building it—welcome aboard.

BLUE (Order) - "This Restores What Was Lost"

Current state: Traditional conservatives, religious communities, people longing for stability **What they need from the stack:** All four, but framed differently **Their language:** "We need order, tradition, moral foundation, community" **Why they support:**

- AUBI as "guaranteed dignity" (not handout but social covenant)
- Cognitive Sovereignty as protecting children from corruption
- Sanctuaries as sacred spaces and community centers
- Contemplative Capacity as returning to prayer/contemplation traditions

The appeal: "This restores Sabbath rest, protects families from exploitation, rebuilds community, honors wisdom traditions. It's not abandoning old ways—it's giving them infrastructure support."

Political weight: Large, motivated base when properly engaged

Critical insight: Blue isn't against these policies—they're against *how progressives usually frame them.* Frame AUBI as "honoring human dignity"

not "radical redistribution." Frame Sanctuaries as "sacred spaces" not "progressive activism zones." **The substance is the same. The language makes it possible.**

ORANGE (Achievement) - "This Optimizes Everything"

Current state: Professionals, business leaders, meritocrats, rationalists
What they need from the stack: All four, but for efficiency **Their language:** "What's the ROI? How do we optimize? Where's the data?" **Why they support:**

- AUBI reduces welfare bureaucracy, enables risk-taking, stabilizes markets
- Cognitive Sovereignty increases productivity (less distraction)
- Sanctuaries improve public health outcomes (measurable)
- Contemplative Capacity enhances cognitive performance (proven)

The appeal: "Every dollar spent returns 4-12x. Healthcare costs drop 30-40%. Innovation increases. Best workers available. Crime decreases. This is optimization at civilizational scale."

Political weight: Enormous. Orange controls most institutions and capital.

Critical insight: Orange *loves* efficiency. Show them the math. The stack isn't idealistic—it's the most cost-effective solution to expensive problems. **Business case makes this real.**

Special note: Tech Orange is particularly important. They built the attention extraction systems. Some feel guilt. Some see the writing on the wall (regulation coming anyway). Some want to build better alternatives. **These allies are gold.**

GREEN (Equality) - "This Honors Everyone's Humanity"

Current state: Progressives, social justice advocates, environmentalists, humanists **What they need from the stack:** Everything, framed as justice **Their language:** "Is this fair? Does it help the marginalized? Is it inclusive?" **Why they support:**

- AUBI addresses poverty and inequality directly
- Cognitive Sovereignty protects vulnerable from manipulation
- Sanctuaries provide community space and environmental restoration
- Contemplative Capacity democratizes inner development

The appeal: "This is justice infrastructure. Not just redistribution—systemic transformation that honors every human's dignity and supports collective flourishing."

Political weight: Large, passionate, organized base

Critical insight: Green often has the **passion** but lacks **power**. They need Orange's institutions and Blue's numbers. Coalition building is how Green's vision becomes real.

Watch out for: Green purity politics that reject coalition with "less evolved" stages. This kills implementation. **Perfect is enemy of good.** We need Green's heart without Green's tendency to eat allies who aren't pure enough.

YELLOW (Systems) - "This Is How We Actually Solve This"

Current state: Systems thinkers, integralists, complexity scientists, this book's core audience **What they need from the stack:** The whole thing, seeing how it works together **Their language:** "What are the feedback loops? How does this integrate? What's the systemic intervention point?" **Why they support:** This is the first actually comprehensive, integrated solution they've seen **Their contribution:** Strategic thinking, integration work, meta-coordination

The appeal: "Finally, someone built the actual architecture instead of just aspirational principles. Let's make it real."

Political weight: Small numbers but strategic influence. Yellow often sits at key coordination points.

Critical insight: Yellow's job is **not** to lead from the front or demand everyone think systemically. Yellow's job is to **coordinate the coalition**, translating between stages, finding synergies, preventing fragmentation.

This book is Yellow speaking to Yellow: "Here's your strategic playbook. Now go facilitate."

TURQUOISE (Holistic) - "This Aligns Humanity with the Whole"

Current state: Systems mystics, integral ecologists, people who perceive planetary/cosmic interconnection **What they need from the stack:** Everything, seen as preparing humanity for next evolutionary leap **Their language:** "How does this serve the biosphere? Does this harmonize individual, collective, and planetary?" **Why they support:**

- Stack aligns human civilization with biospheric health
- Creates conditions for collective awakening
- Enables planetary healing and regeneration
- Prepares species for whatever comes next
- Addresses the Bio-Human Interface (BHI) that integrates human systems with living earth

The appeal: "This is the Yellow infrastructure that makes Turquoise consciousness accessible. You can't have planetary healing while everyone's trapped in survival terror and attention addiction. The stack doesn't replace your vision—it makes your vision possible."

Political weight: Very small numbers but profound influence as visionaries and integrators

Critical insight: Turquoise's role is **Guardian of Wholeness**—ensuring the Yellow builders don't get lost in mechanics and forget the Soul. They remind us this isn't just efficiency—it's sacred work. **That matters.**

Watch out for: Turquoise can be so cosmic they lose touch with practical implementation. Yellow and Turquoise need each other: Yellow grounds Turquoise; Turquoise inspires Yellow.

* * *

The Coalition Architecture: How They Work Together

The beautiful thing: Each stage brings what others lack.
GREEN brings:

- Passionate volunteers
- Grassroots organizing
- Moral clarity
- Connection to communities in need

ORANGE brings:

- Management expertise
- Capital and resources
- Institutional access
- Implementation capacity

BLUE brings:

- Numbers and discipline
- Community infrastructure (churches, civic groups)
- Intergenerational stability
- Cultural legitimacy in conservative areas

RED brings:

- Entrepreneurial energy
- High-risk tolerance
- Competitive drive to win
- Get-shit-done attitude

YELLOW brings:

- Strategic coordination
- Translation between stages
- Systems design
- Integration architecture

BEIGE brings:

- Moral urgency
- Human face of crisis
- Living proof of need

The Coalition In Action: A Pilot City Scenario

Imagine: Portland (or Austin, or Burlington) decides to pilot the full stack.

GREEN organizers mobilize grassroots support, run community meetings, ensure marginalized voices heard.

ORANGE city managers design implementation, create budgets, establish metrics, manage rollout.

BLUE religious communities provide sanctuary space in churches, offer contemplative teaching from their traditions, host community events.

RED entrepreneurs create businesses serving the new economy, build tech for digital sanctuaries, innovate delivery models.

YELLOW facilitators coordinate across all groups, manage conflicts, maintain integrated vision, ensure domains connect.

BEIGE beneficiaries participate in design (nothing about us without us), test services, provide feedback.

Each brings what they have. Each gets what they need. The stack works because it serves all.

The Translation Layer: How They Actually Work Together

Here's the brutal reality: A coalition this diverse will naturally disintegrate into conflict unless there is infrastructure for translation.

This is not "just getting along." This is structural meta-governance.

The Translation Layer consists of:

1. Dedicated Translator Roles

- People who are bilingual (or multilingual) across stages
- Can speak Orange efficiency language AND Green justice language
- Understand Blue's sacred framing AND Red's power language
- Yellow individuals often serve this function, but don't have to be Yellow to translate

2. Translation Protocols

- Before every cross-stage meeting: "What does success look like in each stage's language?"
- During conflict: "Let's translate this disagreement. What's the underlying need each stage has?"
- After decisions: "How do we frame this outcome so each stage feels heard?"

3. Boundary Management

- What do we need to agree on? (The interventions themselves)
- What can we disagree on? (Why we want them, what they mean)
- Where do we need alignment? (Implementation mechanics)

- Where can we have diversity? (Motivation, framing, ultimate vision)

4. Conflict Resolution Architecture

- When Green and Blue clash on values: Yellow facilitates finding shared ground
- When Orange and Green clash on process: Turquoise reminds both of larger purpose
- When anyone threatens to leave: Coalition members from their stage talk them down

Example of Translation Layer in Action:

Scenario: Green activists want sanctuary district to ban all commerce. Orange business leaders say that's unrealistic and hurts local business. Blue community members worried about excluding their church fundraisers.

Without Translation Layer: Coalition fragments. Green calls Orange "capitalist sellouts." Orange calls Green "unrealistic idealists." Blue leaves, feeling no one cares about their values.

With Translation Layer:

Step 1 - Yellow translator to Green: "Your concern is commercialization colonizing every space. What if we distinguish between extractive commerce (advertising, predatory businesses) and community-sustaining commerce (local cafes, bookstores)? You get the non-extractive zone you want, just defined precisely."

Step 2 - Yellow translator to Orange: "Your concern is economic viability. What if we show the data that sanctuary districts actually increase nearby business? Portland's car-free zones boosted local commerce 30%. Plus we can include community-owned businesses in the zone itself."

Step 3 - Yellow translator to Blue: "Your concern is space for church activities. What if we explicitly include 'community fundraisers for non-profit organizations' as allowed activities? Gets you what you need while maintaining non-extractive principle."

Step 4 - Proposal synthesis: "Sanctuary district bans advertising, predatory businesses, and surveillance. Allows community-sustaining businesses (locally owned), non-profit activities, and community fundraising. Success measured by: decreased commercial pressure (Green happy), increased local business revenue (Orange happy), thriving community events (Blue happy)."

Result: Everyone gets core concern addressed. Coalition holds.

This doesn't happen by accident. It requires:

- Dedicated facilitation
- Translation protocols
- Patience and skill
- Willingness to find creative solutions
- Keeping focus on shared goal

Without this Translation Layer, the coalition is just a mob waiting to explode.

With it, the coalition becomes an actual governance innovation—showing that Yellow consciousness can coordinate Orange, Green, Blue, Red working together on shared goals despite different worldviews.

* * *

The Translation Guide: Speaking Every Stage's Language

Yellow must become fluent in all stages' dialects.

Here's how to talk about each intervention to each stage:

Cognitive Sovereignty

To BEIGE: "Predators can't trick you anymore. Your attention is yours."

To RED: "No one manipulates you. You're the hunter, not the prey."

To BLUE: "Protects children from corruption. Honors your right to think clearly."

To ORANGE: "Increases productivity 20-40%. Employees more focused. You get their best work."

To GREEN: "Protects vulnerable from manipulation. Empowers marginalized to resist exploitation."

To YELLOW: "Addresses the meta-crisis of attention extraction destabilizing collective cognition."

Same policy. Six different languages. All true.

Sovereign Floor (AUBI)

To BEIGE: "You'll never starve again. Shelter is guaranteed. You're safe."

To RED: "Freedom to take risks without safety net. Be the entrepreneur who swings for the fences."

To BLUE: "Honors human dignity. Supports families. Enables Sabbath rest. Strengthens community."

To ORANGE: "Eliminates welfare bureaucracy. Enables risk-taking and innovation. Stabilizes markets. Costs less than current system."

To GREEN: "Ends poverty. Addresses inequality. Provides justice. Empowers everyone regardless of identity."

To YELLOW: "Removes the baseline existential terror preventing higher-order thinking and integration."

Same policy. Six languages. All true.

Sanctuaries

To BEIGE: "Safe spaces where you can rest. No one bothers you. You're welcome."

To RED: "Status marker. Elite spaces. Shows you've transcended need for constant consumption."

To BLUE: "Sacred spaces protected from commercialization. Community centers. Where the church's presence is felt."

To ORANGE: "Improves public health 30-50%. Increases property values nearby. Tourism attraction. Net economic positive."

To GREEN: "Community spaces accessible to all. Environmental restoration. Cultural gathering places. Democratic commons."

To YELLOW: "Physical and digital containers for non-extractive existence, enabling integration across domains."

Same policy. Six languages. All true.

Contemplative Capacity

To BEIGE: "People help you learn to feel better. Be calmer. Handle hard things."

To RED: "Mental training makes you sharper, stronger, more disciplined. Winners meditate."

To BLUE: "Return to prayer and contemplation traditions. Wisdom of ancestors validated by modern science."

To ORANGE: "Proven to increase cognitive performance, reduce health-care costs, improve decision-making. Evidence-based human optimization."

To GREEN: "Democratizes inner development. Makes wisdom accessible to all, not just privileged. Healing for everyone."

To YELLOW: "Develops the specific capacities—meta-awareness, systems perception, integration—required for Yellow consciousness."

Same policy. Six languages. All true.

* * *

The Trojan Horse Strategy: Hiding Yellow in Earlier Stages

Here's a critical insight: We don't lead with "This creates Yellow consciousness."

We lead with what each stage can hear.

Then the infrastructure does the developmental work organically.

Example 1: Contemplative Education in Schools

What we DON'T say to Blue school boards: "We're implementing developmental psychology to accelerate consciousness evolution through structured contemplative practice enabling systemic awareness and ego-transcendence."

What we DO say: "Research shows these practices improve test scores, reduce behavioral problems, help kids focus, build character, and teach respect. Plus they're from proven traditions your grandparents knew. Evidence-based return to what worked."

Result: Blue approves it (discipline, tradition, results).

What actually happens: Kids develop meta-awareness, emotional regulation, and perspective-taking—the foundations for Yellow. By age 18, many can hold complexity that previous generations couldn't access until 40.

The Trojan Horse: Framed as test-score improvement and character building. Contains Yellow consciousness development.

Example 2: AUBI Pilots

What we DON'T say to Orange city managers: "We're removing the existential terror of conditional worth to enable post-conventional meaning-making and liberate humans from Orange achievement addiction."

What we DO say: "Pilot data shows 40% reduction in emergency room visits, 35% reduction in crime, 28% increase in entrepreneurship, 50% improvement in children's outcomes. Every dollar invested returns $3-7. Plus it eliminates welfare bureaucracy overhead. This is pure efficiency."

Result: Orange approves it (ROI, optimization, data).

What actually happens: People who aren't desperately surviving start asking existential questions. They have time to develop. Meaning-making happens. Community forms. Yellow capacities emerge naturally.

The Trojan Horse: Framed as cost savings and efficiency. Contains existential liberation.

Example 3: Sanctuary Districts

What we DON'T say to Blue neighborhoods: "We're creating non-extractive zones to interrupt capitalist colonization of every moment and enable post-conventional spiritual development beyond organized religion."

What we DO say: "These are community spaces where families can gather safely, where commercialization doesn't intrude, where your church's values are respected. Like the town squares we used to have. Brings people together around shared decency."

Result: Blue approves it (community, tradition, sacred).

What actually happens: Protected space enables contemplation. People start questioning. Community wisdom emerges. Green sensitivity and Yellow perspective-taking develop naturally.

The Trojan Horse: Framed as community and tradition. Contains developmental catalyst.

The Variable Naming Protocol: Strategic Interface Design

Here's explicit permission for something that might feel uncomfortable: You're allowed to call the same thing different names for different audiences.

This isn't lying. It's User Interface Design.

The principle: The architecture stays identical. The interface adapts to the user.

To the Chamber of Commerce:

- Don't call it "Adaptive Universal Basic Income"
- Call it "Local Demand Stimulus Program"
- Emphasize: Guaranteed customer base, reduced labor market volatility, entrepreneurship support

To the School Board:

- Don't call it "Cognitive Sovereignty Architecture"
- Call it "Student Focus Protection Act"
- Emphasize: Better test scores, reduced behavioral problems, parental control over digital environment

To Religious Communities:

- Don't call it "Secular Contemplative Capacity Development"
- Call it "Return to Contemplative Prayer Traditions"
- Emphasize: Wisdom of ancestors, character building, spiritual depth validated by science

To Tech Community:

- Don't call it "Non-Extractive Digital Sanctuaries"
- Call it "User-Controlled Digital Commons Infrastructure"

- Emphasize: Innovation beyond advertising model, protocol over platform, democratic governance

The architecture is identical in each case. The naming adapts to what the audience can hear.

Why this works: 1. **Each name is true** (just emphasizes different aspects) 2. **Each audience gets what they need** (psychologically and practically) 3. **Implementation proceeds** (wouldn't happen with names they reject) 4. **Outcomes identical** (regardless of what you called it)

The test: If someone from Chamber of Commerce and someone from social justice organization both show up to the same AUBI program, and one calls it "demand stimulus" while the other calls it "economic justice"—do they get the same money? Yes. Then it worked.

This is strategic code-switching, not deception.

You're not changing *what* you're building. You're changing *how you describe* what you're building to make it psychologically accessible to different worldviews.

The alternative: Insist everyone use the same Yellow-complexity language, and nothing gets built because no one but Yellow understands what you're talking about.

The pragmatic choice: Adapt your interface to your user, build the actual thing, let it work, prove it through results.

Eventually people notice: "Hey, your 'demand stimulus' and my 'economic justice' seem to be the same program."

"Yes. Exactly. Isn't it great that we both wanted it?"

* * *

The stack itself is developmentally scaffolded.

You can enter at any stage and benefit at that stage.

But the infrastructure naturally supports growth beyond entry point.

- AUBI solves Orange problem (economic efficiency) **and** creates condi-

tions for Green (community) **and** Yellow (systems thinking)
- Cognitive Sovereignty solves Orange problem (productivity) **and** creates space for contemplation (Green/Yellow)
- Sanctuaries solve Blue problem (community) **and** Green problem (commons) **and** Yellow problem (integration space)
- Contemplative Capacity solves Orange problem (performance) **and** develops Yellow capacities

You don't need to understand Yellow to benefit from Yellow infrastructure.

You just need to use it. The development happens organically.

This is the genius of the approach: We're not preaching development. We're building conditions that naturally catalyze development.

* * *

Building the Coalition: Practical Strategy

So how do we actually build these strange-bedfellow coalitions?

Step 1: Find the Early Adopters at Each Stage

Don't try to convince everyone. Find the willing.

BEIGE: Homeless advocacy groups, direct service organizations **RED:** Risk-taking entrepreneurs, performance-focused individuals, some elite athletes/military **BLUE:** Progressive religious communities, traditionalists concerned about family/community decline **ORANGE:** Evidence-based policy advocates, tech leaders with conscience, public health officials **GREEN:** Social justice organizations, environmental groups, community organizers **YELLOW:** Systems thinkers, integralists, complexity scientists, readers of this book

Start with people already oriented toward these solutions, even if they

don't see the full picture.

Step 2: Build Stage-Specific On-Ramps

Create entry points that speak to each stage:

For BLUE:

- Partner with churches offering contemplative education
- Frame AUBI as "dignity guarantee"
- Emphasize family support and community building
- Show how this strengthens traditional values

For ORANGE:

- Lead with cost-benefit analyses
- Showcase business leaders who support it
- Demonstrate productivity and innovation benefits
- Provide clear implementation roadmaps

For GREEN:

- Center justice and inclusion
- Highlight environmental benefits
- Ensure marginalized communities lead design
- Frame as systemic transformation

For YELLOW:

- Show the integrated architecture
- Provide strategic coordination roles
- Emphasize complexity and feedback loops
- Welcome meta-level thinking

Step 3: Create Cross-Stage Working Groups

Don't segregate by stage. Create working groups where stages must collaborate:

Implementation teams need:

- Green's community connections
- Orange's project management
- Blue's institutional stability
- Red's entrepreneurial drive
- Yellow's coordination

Force collaboration. Require translation. Build understanding through working together, not through conversion attempts.

Step 4: Celebrate Shared Wins, Tolerate Different Reasons

When the pilot succeeds, everyone claims credit. That's perfect.

- Blue says: "We restored community and supported families"
- Orange says: "We optimized resource allocation and improved outcomes"
- Green says: "We achieved justice and empowered marginalized communities"
- Red says: "We built something powerful and made it work"
- Yellow says: "We integrated multiple perspectives into coherent system"

All true. All valid. All necessary.

Don't demand everyone share your motivation. **Celebrate diverse motivations producing shared outcomes.**

Step 5: Protect Against Fragmentation

The coalition will face pressure to fragment:

Green will say: "We can't work with Blue conservatives! They don't share our values on X!"

Blue will say: "We can't work with Green progressives! They're undermining Y!"

Orange will say: "Can we stop the philosophy and just implement?"

Yellow's job: Hold the tension. Keep everyone at the table. Translate. Find common ground. **Remind everyone that pure coalition only exists in fantasy.**

The only coalition that exists is the impure one. The one with people you disagree with about many things but align with on this.

* * *

The Pilot City Strategy: Where to Start

We don't need national agreement to start. We need cities willing to experiment.

Ideal First Pilot Characteristics:

Size: 100,000 - 500,000 (large enough to matter, small enough to coordinate)

Political culture: Progressive enough to try, pragmatic enough to execute

Economic base: Diverse, not dependent on one industry

Existing infrastructure: Some community organizations, civic engagement, public services

Leadership: Mayor and council willing to take risks, think long-term

Demographics: Diverse enough to test across populations

Strong Candidates (US):

Tier 1 (Most Likely):

- Burlington, VT (progressive, small, high civic engagement)
- Austin, TX (tech culture, progressive governance, growth mindset)
- Portland, ME (smaller Portland, strong community, manageable scale)
- Madison, WI (university town, progressive, evidence-based)
- Boulder, CO (consciousness-oriented, wealthy, experimental)

Tier 2 (Good Potential):

- Oakland, CA (diverse, progressive, existing experiments)
- Minneapolis, MN (post-2020 reform energy, cold weather breeds cooperation)
- Ann Arbor, MI (university town, progressive, rust belt proof of concept)
- Asheville, NC (consciousness culture, purple state signal value)
- Portland, OR (obvious but complicated by current challenges)

Tier 3 (Dark Horses):

- Tulsa, OK (experimenting with universal income, conservative state makes Blue coalition possible)
- Chattanooga, TN (municipal broadband proves innovation capacity, purple area)
- Rochester, NY (rust belt transformation, medical infrastructure, size right)

The Pitch to Pilot Cities:

"Become the city that proved human flourishing is possible.
   We provide:

- Complete implementation playbook
- Technical assistance
- Research partnership
- National attention
- Network of supporting organizations
- Documentation for scaling

You provide:

- Political will
- Implementation capacity
- Community engagement
- Local adaptation
- Real-world testing

Timeline: 3 years to initial results, 5 years to full assessment
   Investment: $50-100M over 5 years (much of it from federal/state/phil
anthropic sources we'll help secure)
   Payoff: If it works, you're the model every city studies. If it doesn't, you
learned what to fix and helped humanity learn.
   Plus: Your citizens' lives get dramatically better. That alone is worth it.
Are you in?"

The Proof of Concept Path

Year 1: Planning and initial implementation

- Community engagement and design

- First cohort of AUBI recipients
- First sanctuary spaces open
- Cognitive sovereignty ordinances passed
- Contemplative education pilots in 10 schools

Year 2: Expansion and refinement

- AUBI expanded to 25% of population
- More sanctuary spaces
- Digital sovereignty measures
- 50 schools with contemplative education
- Early data collection

Year 3: Full scale and initial results

- AUBI available to all who want it (opt-in)
- Sanctuary district complete
- Contemplative centers open
- 100% of schools participating
- **First results published**

Year 4-5: Optimization and documentation

- Refine based on feedback
- Comprehensive evaluation
- Documentation for other cities
- National and international attention
- **Model ready for scaling**

**If it works—when it works—other cities will come calling.
Success is its own best marketing.**

* * *

Handling Resistance: The Opposition's Playbook

Who will resist? Why? How do we respond?

Opposition Type 1: Ideological (Free Market Absolutists)

Their argument: "Government shouldn't provide income. People should earn everything. This destroys work ethic and personal responsibility."

Where they're wrong: Evidence shows opposite—AUBI increases work and entrepreneurship. "Free market" requires free agents, not desperate ones.

Where they're right: Dependency is real concern. Poor implementation could create it.

Our response:

- "AUBI enables real free markets by removing desperation. You can't have genuine choice when 'no' means death."
- Show evidence from Alaska, pilots, unconditional support increasing agency
- Frame as removing government bureaucracy and complexity
- Emphasize Right to Refuse—this creates freedom, not dependency

The killer move: "You say you believe in free markets. Do you believe in free *people*? A market isn't free if the participants are terrified. A person negotiating a job offer while facing homelessness isn't a free agent— they're a hostage. We're not destroying the free market. We're finally creating one."

Don't: Get into ideological debates about capitalism. Stay practical.

Do: Show successful businesspeople who support it. Use evidence. Appeal to freedom.

Opposition Type 2: Fiscal (Deficit Hawks)

Their argument: "We can't afford it. This will bankrupt us. Inflation will explode. Math doesn't work."

Where they're wrong: Math actually does work. We're already spending most of this money inefficiently.

Where they're right: Fiscal responsibility matters. Unsustainable programs fail.

Our response:

- Show detailed budget that adds up
- Emphasize consolidation of existing inefficient programs
- Demonstrate ROI from healthcare savings, crime reduction, productivity increases
- Point to Alaska's 40+ years of functioning dividend
- Offer to start with revenue-positive components (cognitive sovereignty generates revenue through fines)

The killer move: "We have a choice: Pay for the symptoms of a broken system forever, or invest in curing the disease once. Every year we spend $800 billion on defense, $150 billion on prisons, $400 billion on welfare bureaucracy, and trillions on healthcare treating preventable stress-related illness. The math of prevention is always better than the math of perpetual treatment. We can't afford NOT to do this."

Don't: Dismiss fiscal concerns as "not caring about people."

Do: Respect the concern. Provide rigorous economics. Start with neutral or positive-revenue interventions.

Opposition Type 3: Cultural (Traditional Values)

Their argument: "This undermines family, work ethic, religion, traditional values. Creates dependency and moral decay."

Where they're wrong: Stack actually supports families, community, contemplation—traditional values.

Where they're right: Rapid value change is destabilizing. Community and tradition matter.

Our response:

- Frame as returning to Sabbath rest, family time, community gathering
- Show how stack supports religious practice and contemplation
- Emphasize protecting children from commercial exploitation
- Highlight Blue supporters—religious communities already doing this work
- Position as strengthening, not undermining, what matters

Don't: Mock traditional values as backwards.

Do: Show respect. Find actual alignment. Let Blue advocates speak to Blue concerns.

Opposition Type 4: Status Quo (Vested Interests)

Their argument: Usually unstated—"This threatens my power/profit/position."

Where they're wrong: Many think zero-sum when actually positive-sum. More flourishing creates more opportunity.

Where they're right: Some do lose power. Attention economy, predatory lenders, etc.

Our response:

- Identify who actually loses vs. who just fears loss
- For those who fear but wouldn't lose: Show they'd actually benefit
- For those who'd actually lose: Acknowledge it, offer transition support via Pathfinder Protocol
- Appeal to long-term self-interest (stable society benefits everyone)
- When necessary: Organize political power to override their resistance

The killer move: "The buggy whip manufacturers opposed the automobile. The gas lamp makers opposed electricity. The ice delivery companies opposed refrigerators. History remembers them only as footnotes about who tried to stop progress. The future is coming. You have a choice: Be part of building the new world, or be a cautionary tale about who tried to preserve the old one at humanity's expense. Which legacy do you want?"

Don't: Pretend everyone benefits equally or immediately.

Do: Be honest about winners/losers. Build political coalition strong enough to win despite opposition.

Opposition Type 5: Skeptical (Evidence Lacking)

Their argument: "Sounds nice but probably doesn't work. Where's proof? Too good to be true."

Where they're wrong: There's substantial evidence already. And absence of complete proof isn't reason not to pilot.

Where they're right: Healthy skepticism matters. Proof is important.

Our response:

- Show existing evidence from various pilots
- Acknowledge gaps in evidence
- **That's why we pilot**—to generate proof
- Emphasize rigorous evaluation built into design
- Invite skeptics to help design evaluation criteria

Don't: Oversell or promise utopia.

Do: Welcome skepticism. Make it evidence-based. Co-create evaluation.

* * *

Timeline and Milestones: What's Realistic?

Let's be honest about timeframes. This is civilizational transformation. It takes time.

Phase 1: Proof of Concept (Years 1-5)

Year 1:

- Finalize this book and supporting materials
- Build core team and organization
- Identify pilot cities
- Secure initial funding
- Begin community engagement

Milestone: 3 pilot cities committed

Year 2-3:

- Implement pilots
- Build coalitions in pilot cities
- Document everything
- Generate early data
- Refine approaches

Milestone: Pilots running, early positive signals

Year 4-5:

- Comprehensive evaluation
- Publish results
- Scale within pilot cities
- Prepare for expansion
- National attention builds

Milestone: Proven model, documented, ready to scale

Phase 2: Scaling (Years 6-12)

Year 6-8:

- 20+ cities implementing
- State-level policy changes
- Federal pilot funding
- International interest growing
- Cultural shift beginning

Milestone: Movement clearly viable, momentum building

Year 9-12:

- 100+ cities participating
- Several states with comprehensive policies
- Federal legislation proposed
- International pilots launching
- Next generation growing up in new system

Milestone: Transformation underway, irreversible

Phase 3: Normalization (Years 13-20)

Year 13-15:

- Federal implementation begins
- Most major cities participating
- Standard infrastructure in new developments
- Cultural expectations shifting
- Yellow consciousness spreading

Milestone: New normal emerging
  Year 16-20:

- Full national implementation
- International coordination
- Children raised in system entering adulthood
- Yellow consciousness widespread
- Next challenges visible

Milestone: Civilization stabilizing at higher order

What This Means

For current adults: You'll see initial results in 3-5 years. Significant change in 10. Transformation in 20.

For children: They'll grow up in a different world than we did. Most of the struggle we know will seem as quaint as polio.

For humanity: In 30 years, we look back and say "remember when survival was conditional and everyone was addicted to their phones?"

This is fast for civilizational change. Agriculture took 3,000 years to spread. Industrialization took 300. Democracy took 200. We're talking 20-30 years for a complete developmental leap.

That's breathtaking speed. And it's realistic.

* * *

Your Role: What You Can Do Monday Morning

"Okay, I get it. How do I help?"

Depends on who you are and what you have:

If You're a Policymaker (City/State/Federal):

- Champion pilot programs in your jurisdiction
- Convene cross-sector stakeholders
- Secure funding for experiments
- Connect us to implementation capacity
- Be the political will that makes this possible

If You're a Funder (Philanthropist/Foundation):

- Support pilot city implementation
- Fund research and evaluation
- Invest in proof of concept
- Catalyze matching funds
- Enable the risk-taking that movements require

If You're an Organizer (Activist/Community Leader):

- Build grassroots coalition
- Connect with existing movements
- Do community engagement and design
- Hold power accountable
- Ensure marginalized voices lead

If You're a Professional (Teacher/Doctor/Therapist):

- Implement stack elements in your practice
- Document what works
- Train others
- Become proof of concept
- Build professional networks supporting this

If You're a Business Leader:

- Implement workplace interventions
- Support policy changes
- Fund pilots
- Model what's possible
- Prove business case

If You're a Researcher:

- Study the interventions
- Evaluate pilot outcomes
- Publish findings
- Develop metrics
- Build evidence base

If You're a Student/Young Person:

- Demand this from institutions
- Organize campus movements
- Learn the frameworks
- Prepare to implement
- Be the generation that builds it

If You're Just a Human Who Wants This:

- Talk about it
- Share this book
- Vote for supporters
- Join local organizing
- Live the principles
- Show it's possible

Everyone has a role. Every role matters.

This happens through distributed action, not centralized command.

* * *

Conclusion: The Coalition IS the Strategy

We don't need everyone to agree on everything.

We need enough people who want this badly enough for their own reasons.

The beauty of the Yellow stack:

- BEIGE gets survival
- RED gets freedom and power
- BLUE gets community and tradition
- ORANGE gets efficiency and innovation
- GREEN gets justice and inclusion
- YELLOW gets integration and wisdom

Everyone gets something real. Everyone contributes something essential.

The coalition isn't a compromise. It's the actual architecture.

Multi-stage implementation of multi-stage solution.

This is how civilizational transformation happens:

Not through purity and perfection.

Through strange bedfellows united by need, implementing proven solutions, building proof of concept, and letting success speak for itself.

The willing don't have to be pure. They just have to be willing.

And there are enough willing to start.

That's how we begin.

* * *

Next: Chapter 17 – The Power Question: Who Has It, Who Needs It, How Do We Navigate It?

Because good ideas aren't enough. We need power strategy too.

And that's where it gets interesting.

Because what do you do when the willing don't have the power, and the powerful aren't willing?

That's the question every movement faces. And it's the question Chapter 17 answers.

Chapter 17: The Power Question - Who Has It, Who Wants It, How We Navigate It

The Question Every Movement Faces

We have the vision. We have the coalition. We have the strategy.

Now the hard truth: Good ideas don't implement themselves.

Power does.

And the people who currently have power—the ones who could implement the Yellow stack tomorrow if they chose—mostly don't want to. While the people who desperately want this have very little institutional power.

This is the central paradox of transformative change:

- Those with power benefit from current arrangements
- Those harmed by current arrangements lack power to change them
- Asking nicely achieves nothing
- Revolution usually makes things worse

So what do we do?

This chapter is about power strategy. Not in the abstract. In practice.

- How do we build power without having power to start?

- How do we work within systems while transforming them?
- How do we leverage what we have to get what we need?
- How do we avoid both accommodation (changing nothing) and adventurism (attempting the impossible and failing)?

This is where Yellow consciousness must be ruthlessly realistic about Orange/Blue/Red power dynamics.

Systems thinking without power analysis is just philosophy.

Let's get practical.

* * *

The Power Map: Who Actually Has It?

First, let's be honest about where power lives:

Tier 1: High Institutional Power

1. Federal Government (US example, pattern applies elsewhere)

- Can create/eliminate policies affecting 330M people
- Controls trillions in spending
- Sets regulatory frameworks
- Enforcement capacity

Current orientation: Mostly captured by corporate interests (Orange extractive), with some progressive (Green) and conservative (Blue) elements. Very little Yellow.

Leverage points: Executive orders, legislation, budgets, regulatory agencies

2. State/Provincial Governments

- Control education systems
- Regulate professions and businesses
- Significant spending power
- Police powers

Current orientation: Varies dramatically. Some progressive, some conservative, most mixed.

Leverage points: Easier to influence than federal, can pilot policies, laboratories of democracy

3. Major Corporations

- Control capital allocation
- Shape markets and consumer behavior
- Employ millions
- Influence policy through lobbying

Current orientation: Almost entirely Orange extractive, with some Green sustainability theater. Rare Yellow consciousness.

Leverage points: Shareholder activism, customer pressure, employee organizing, market competition

4. Financial Institutions

- Control investment flows
- Determine what gets funded
- Shape economic possibilities
- Create/destroy wealth at scale

Current orientation: Pure Orange optimization, indifferent to human/-planetary wellbeing beyond PR.

Leverage points: Divestment campaigns, regulatory pressure, competition from ethical alternatives

Tier 2: Moderate Institutional Power

5. City/Municipal Governments

- Direct service delivery
- Local regulation
- Community-level implementation
- Demonstration effects

Current orientation: Varies widely, often more responsive to grassroots than higher levels.

Leverage points: Most accessible level, can pilot interventions, build proof of concept

6. Universities and Research Institutions

- Intellectual legitimacy
- Train future leaders
- Generate evidence
- Shape discourse

Current orientation: Mixed—some progressive, some corporate-captured, pockets of genuine inquiry.

Leverage points: Research funding, curriculum, public intellectuals, proof of concept studies

7. Media (Traditional and New)

- Shape narratives
- Set agenda
- Legitimize or delegitimize ideas
- Influence public opinion

Current orientation: Mostly corporate-owned (Orange), some independent progressive (Green), growing alternative (various).

Leverage points: Alternative media, social media, earned coverage, creating undeniable stories

8. Unions and Worker Organizations

- Collective bargaining power
- Political organizing
- Direct representation of working people
- Strike capacity

Current orientation: Varies—some progressive, some conservative, most focused on narrow member interests.

Leverage points: Coalition building, workplace organizing, political mobilization

Tier 3: Grassroots Power

9. Social Movements

- Mobilize passion and numbers
- Shift Overton window
- Create political pressure
- Generate alternatives

Current orientation: Predominantly Green, with some Blue (Tea Party, religious right) and growing Yellow.

Leverage points: Direct action, cultural change, building alternatives, electoral pressure

10. Community Organizations

- Local trust and relationships
- Direct service provision
- Grassroots implementation capacity
- Legitimacy in marginalized communities

Current orientation: Varies widely by community.

Leverage points: Service provision, organizing, pilot implementation, proof via practice

11. Individual Activists and Thought Leaders

· Shape discourse
· Inspire and coordinate
· Model alternatives
· Connect movements

Current orientation: Across the spectrum.

Leverage points: Writing, speaking, organizing, showing what's possible

* * *

The Brutal Assessment: Where We Start

Let's be unflinchingly honest about the current situation:

What We Have:

✓ **Strong moral case** (suffering is real, solutions exist, justice demands action) ✓ **Growing coalition** (across stages, see Chapter 16) ✓ **Rigorous framework** (the Yellow stack, intellectually defensible) ✓ **Some evidence** (pilots showing proof of concept) ✓ **Passionate base** (people who desperately need this) ✓ **Economic logic** (math works, cheaper than status quo) ✓ **Occasional sympathetic leaders** (mayors, officials who get it)

What We Don't Have:

✗ Majority political power (not controlling federal government) **✗ Corporate support** (mostly opposition or indifference) **✗ Media dominance** (narratives still controlled by others) **✗ Mass mobilization** (yet—most people don't know this exists) **✗ Immediate crisis** (no forcing event making this urgent to those in power) **✗ Elite consensus** (ruling class not united behind this)

The Reality:

We're a Yellow vision with Green passion, trying to transform Orange/Blue institutions, facing Red resistance from vested interests, without decisive power in any key institution.

That's the truth. Now what?

* * *

Strategy 1: The Long March Through Institutions (Hospice and Midwifery)

Concept: Build power by getting people who understand this into positions of influence within existing institutions. But we need two distinct teams with different missions.

The Dual Role: Hospice Worker and Midwife

Most institutional change fails because people confuse the roles:

- If you try to "save" a dying system → you prolong suffering and waste energy
- If you try to "force" a birth prematurely → you create trauma and

rejection

We need both:

Team Hospice:

- Helps old, extractive systems die with dignity
- Minimizes chaos and harm during transition
- Manages decline responsibly
- Prevents catastrophic collapse
- Documents what worked (to preserve wisdom)

Team Midwife:

- Helps new, regenerative systems be born
- Creates conditions for healthy emergence
- Protects fragile beginnings
- Facilitates natural development
- Celebrates and supports new life

Examples:

Hospice Work:

- Teacher in failing public school ensures students aren't harmed while advocating for transformation
- Civil servant in dysfunctional agency maintains essential services while building replacement
- Corporate middle manager protects employees while preparing transition to cooperative
- "My job is to make this system's death as painless as possible for those depending on it"

Midwife Work:

- Same teacher starts after-school contemplative education program (the future)
- Same civil servant helps community organizations build capacity for when agency fails
- Same manager secretly develops cooperative ownership transition plan
- "My job is to bring the new world into being while the old one still functions"

Critical Distinction:

- Hospice work alone = just managing decline (depressing, no hope)
- Midwife work alone = fantasy, ignoring current reality (people suffer)
- **Both together = responsible transition**

This gives bureaucrats and institutional workers a noble role: You're not a "sellout" or "cog in the machine." You're either helping the old die gracefully or helping the new be born—both essential, both honorable.

How It Works:

Education Track:

- **Hospice:** Maintain standards in current system, protect students from worst failures
- **Midwife:** Build contemplative education programs, shift pedagogy, develop next-gen curriculum
- Timeline: 10-20 years to significant influence

Government Track:

- **Hospice:** Keep essential services functioning, prevent catastrophic policy failures

- **Midwife:** Pilot new programs, build community capacity, prepare for transition
- Run for office (school board → city council → state legislature → higher)
- Work within agencies (civil servants implementing from inside)
- Become policy advisors and staffers
- Timeline: 5-15 years to influence, 15-30 years to power

Corporate Track:

- **Hospice:** Protect workers from extraction, maintain ethical standards possible within system
- **Midwife:** Build workplace interventions, prepare cooperative transitions, shift culture
- Enter corporations, rise to leadership
- Timeline: 10-25 years to CEO/board level influence

Media Track:

- **Hospice:** Maintain journalistic standards, document truth about system failures
- **Midwife:** Build alternative media platforms, shift narratives, amplify new stories
- Become journalists, editors, producers
- Timeline: 5-15 years to significant voice

The Sundown Protocol Connection:

This directly connects to the Sundown Protocol (Chapter 19):

- Some institutions need to end (fossil fuel companies, extractive finance)
- Some need radical transformation (education, healthcare, governance)

- Some need protection and support (mutual aid, cooperatives, commons)

Hospice workers manage the Sundown. Midwives facilitate what comes next.

Strengths:

- Works with existing structures (don't need revolution)
- Builds lasting institutional change
- Develops expertise and legitimacy
- Sustainable over time
- Honors both death and birth (complete cycle)
- Prevents both chaos (unmanaged collapse) and stagnation (pretending system can be saved)

Weaknesses:

- Very slow (decades to real power)
- Institutions corrupt individuals more than individuals transform institutions
- Co-optation risk (Yellow becomes Orange in process)
- May arrive too late for crises requiring immediate action
- Requires unusual psychological capacity (holding decay and emergence simultaneously)

When to Use:

- Long-term institutional transformation
- Building next generation of leadership
- Creating lasting change, not just policy wins
- When you have time (and we may not)
- When catastrophic system collapse would cause more harm than

managed transition

* * *

Strategy 2: Electoral Power Building

Concept: Win elections, control government, implement through democratic mandate.

How It Works:

Local Level (Most Viable):

- City council and mayoral races (often non-partisan, lower budgets)
- School board elections (directly control education policy)
- County positions (implementation capacity)
- Timeline: 1-4 years to win, immediate implementation power

State Level (Moderate Difficulty):

- State legislative races (need party infrastructure)
- Governorships (high visibility, executive power)
- Ballot initiatives (direct democracy where available)
- Timeline: 2-6 years to build power, 6-12 years to control

Federal Level (Very Difficult):

- Congressional races (expensive, partisan, national scrutiny)
- Presidential (nearly impossible for outsiders)
- Agency appointments (depends on who's president)
- Timeline: 10+ years to meaningful influence

The Path:

Phase 1 - Build Base:

- Win school board seats in pilot cities
- Win city council races in sympathetic jurisdictions
- Demonstrate competence and results
- Build name recognition and trust

Phase 2 - Expand Footprint:

- Win mayoral races in pilot cities
- Win state legislative seats in friendly districts
- Pass local and state policies
- Create models for others

Phase 3 - Scale Up:

- Win multiple state races
- Influence state parties
- Build federal coalition
- National policy becomes possible

Strengths:

- Direct implementation power
- Democratic legitimacy
- Can scale if successful
- Clear accountability

Weaknesses:

- Expensive (money matters in elections)
- Requires coalition building within existing parties or building new one
- Slow (election cycles limit speed)
- Vulnerable to backlash (can be reversed with next election)
- Electoral systems favor incumbents and money

Keys to Success:

- Start local (winnable races)
- Build track record (prove it works)
- Coalition politics (Chapter 16 applies)
- Small donor base (reduce corporate capture)

* * *

Strategy 3: Direct Action and Demonstration Projects

Concept: Build alternatives outside system, prove they work, force system to adapt.

How It Works:

Mutual Aid Networks:

- Create community support systems outside market/state
- Pool resources, share skills, care for each other
- Demonstrate post-capitalist possibilities
- Timeline: Immediate start, scales gradually

Worker Cooperatives:

- Democratic ownership of workplaces
- Implement stack principles internally
- Proof that alternatives work
- Timeline: 3-7 years to establish, 10+ to significant presence

Community Land Trusts:

- Remove housing from speculation
- Permanent affordability
- Community control
- Timeline: 5-10 years to establish, 20+ to scale

Alternative Currencies:

- Hearts/Leaves system (Chapter 12)
- Local exchange systems
- Proof of regenerative economy
- Timeline: 1-3 years to pilot, 5-10 to viability

Sanctuary Projects:

- Create physical sanctuary spaces through community ownership
- Build digital sanctuaries (Fediverse, etc.)
- Prove non-extractive alternatives work
- Timeline: 1-5 years to build, ongoing maintenance

Strengths:

- Immediate implementation (don't need permission)
- Builds practical capacity
- Creates living proof

- Empowers participants

Weaknesses:

- Small scale unless supported by policy
- Often precarious (external pressures)
- Can become isolated enclaves
- Survival takes energy away from growth

How to Leverage:

- Use as proof of concept for policy
- Build skills and networks for scaling
- Create alternative institutions that make demands realistic
- Show people what's possible

* * *

Strategy 4: Crisis Stewardship (Being Ready for the Inevitable)

Concept: Crises are inevitable. The question isn't whether they'll come, but who will be prepared with coherent, life-saving plans when they do. This is about responsible guardianship, not opportunism.

How It Works:

The Pattern: 1. Crisis occurs (economic crash, pandemic, climate disaster, war, AI disruption) 2. Old system demonstrates catastrophic failure 3. Public desperately demands change 4. Political window opens (typically 6 months to 2 years) 5. Those with plans ready can actually implement

6. Window closes as either new system emerges or status quo reasserts (often worse than before)

The Stakes:

When crisis hits, three types of groups compete to fill the vacuum:

1. Authoritarians (Red/Blue fusion)

- Have simple narratives and scapegoats
- Promise order through force
- Move fast, know what they want
- Examples: 1930s fascism, contemporary autocracies

2. Grifters (Orange predatory)

- Exploit crisis for personal enrichment
- "Never let a good crisis go to waste" (for profit)
- No vision beyond extraction
- Examples: disaster capitalism, pandemic profiteering

3. Transformative Movements (Green/Yellow)

- Have comprehensive solutions
- Serve collective wellbeing
- Require preparation and coordination
- Examples: New Deal, post-war reconstruction (when done well)

If we're not ready, authoritarians or grifters fill the vacuum by default.

Our moral obligation: Be so prepared that when crisis strikes, our life-affirming solutions are the obvious choice.

Historical Examples:

New Deal (Great Depression opened window):

- Roosevelt had detailed plans ready (Brain Trust preparations)
- Moved fast in first 100 days
- Transformed American economy and governance
- Window: ~1933-1938, then closed by conservative backlash

Civil Rights Act (Moral crisis + political moment):

- Decades of organizing preceded legislative victory
- Birmingham and Selma created urgency
- LBJ leveraged Kennedy assassination window
- Window: 1963-1965

Affordable Care Act (Economic crisis + Democratic control):

- Decades of healthcare reform attempts
- 2008 crisis created receptivity
- Plans were ready to implement
- Window: 2009-2010

COVID Stimulus (Emergency enabled previously "impossible" policies):

- Direct checks to citizens (proto-AUBI)
- Unemployment expansion
- Rent/eviction moratoriums
- Proved "we can't afford it" was always a lie
- Window: March-July 2020, closed by political backlash

Our Preparation:

This book and the Global Governance Frameworks are our preparation:

- Detailed policy proposals ready to implement ("shovel-ready")
- Coalitions built across developmental stages (Chapter 16)
- Messaging prepared for each stage
- Pilot cities demonstrating proof of concept
- Economic institutions ready to scale
- Trained people ready to implement
- Clear sequence: what to do in first 100 days

When crisis hits, we don't scramble to figure it out. We have THE PLAN.

Crisis Types That Open Windows:

Economic Crisis (Highly Likely):

- Next recession/depression exposes system failures
- AUBI becomes politically viable (COVID checks proved it)
- Public desperate for solutions
- Our advantage: we have comprehensive economic alternative

Climate Crisis (Already Underway):

- Extreme weather events create urgency
- Sanctuary/regeneration programs gain support
- Long-term thinking becomes possible
- Our advantage: stack addresses root causes (consciousness, systems)

Social Crisis (Increasing Risk):

- Civil unrest, breakdown of order

- Community rebuilding becomes priority
- Contemplative/wisdom approaches gain traction
- Our advantage: we have community infrastructure ready

Technological Crisis (AI Disruption—Inevitable):

- Mass unemployment as AI replaces workers
- Makes AUBI necessary and obvious
- Cognitive sovereignty becomes urgent
- Our advantage: we've been planning for this

Pandemic (Always Possible):

- Next pandemic (when, not if)
- Proves need for resilient local systems
- Community mutual aid becomes essential
- Our advantage: Bioregional Autonomous Zones are pandemic-resilient

Strengths:

- Can achieve in months what takes decades normally
- Public receptive during crisis (old certainties shattered)
- Opposition weakened by system failure
- Real transformation becomes possible
- Historical precedent (it's worked before)

Weaknesses:

- Unpredictable timing (can't control when crisis hits)
- Risk of authoritarian solutions if we're not ready
- Window closes quickly (12–24 months typically)
- Must be genuinely prepared (no time to develop plans in crisis)

- Trauma of crisis can cloud judgment
- Opposition uses crisis too (disaster capitalism)

Our Stance:

We don't wish for crisis. Every crisis brings genuine suffering.

But crisis is coming. Climate physics, economic contradictions, AI disruption, social fragmentation—these aren't pessimism, they're sober assessment.

We must be ready. When the old system fails catastrophically (and it will), we have two choices: 1. Be prepared with comprehensive, life-affirming solutions 2. Watch authoritarians or grifters fill the vacuum

This is responsible stewardship, not opportunism.

We're the adults in the room who did the hard work of preparation so that when everything goes to hell, we have the plans that save lives and build better.

Better we have those plans than those who would exploit crisis for power or profit.

* * *

Strategy 5: The Inside-Outside Game

Concept: Coordinate between insiders working within institutions and outsiders pressuring from outside.

How It Works:

The Dance:

Outside (Movements, Activists):

- Create public pressure through direct action

- Shift Overton window
- Make demands that seem radical
- Generate urgency and visibility

Inside (Friendly Politicians, Bureaucrats):

- Use outside pressure as leverage
- Propose "moderate" versions of outside demands
- Implement what's possible within system
- Protect and expand gains

Example:

- Outside: "Defund police, fund communities!"
- Inside: "Let's redirect 10% of police budget to mental health and community services"
- Outside pressure makes inside proposal seem reasonable
- Without outside, inside wouldn't propose anything
- Without inside, outside achieves nothing concrete

Coordination Requirements:

- Communication between inside and outside
- Shared ultimate goals
- Tactical flexibility (inside must sometimes critique outside publicly)
- Trust (understanding the game being played)

Applied to Yellow Stack:

Outside Tactics:

- Occupy sanctuary spaces, refuse to leave
- Mass civil disobedience against extractive systems

- General strikes demanding AUBI
- Blocking harmful projects

Inside Responses:

- "These demands are unrealistic, but we can pilot AUBI in three cities"
- "Let's create sanctuary districts as compromise"
- "Cognitive sovereignty regulation is reasonable middle ground"

Result: Incremental wins that actually implement stack, using outside pressure to make inside action politically viable.

Strengths:

- Multiplies effectiveness of both approaches
- Creates political space for real change
- Insider credibility + outsider energy
- Works with human nature (officials want to appear reasonable)

Weaknesses:

- Requires coordination (hard to maintain)
- Risk of co-optation (insiders become pure establishment)
- Risk of irrelevance (outsiders become pure performance)
- Tension between inside and outside can become real conflict

Keys to Success:

- Explicit strategy discussion (everyone knows the game)
- Regular coordination meetings
- Shared long-term vision
- Mutual respect despite tactical differences

* * *

Strategy 6: Building Economic Power (The Parallel Polis)

Concept: Create economic institutions that fund the movement and provide alternative to capitalist extraction—building what Václav Havel called the "Parallel Polis": a functioning alternative society within the shell of the old.

This isn't just building businesses. It's building the state-within-a-state that's ready when the old state fails.

How It Works:

Worker Cooperatives:

- Natural vehicles for implementing Workplace Contemplative Infrastructure
- Can create internal Sanctuaries (protected break rooms, meditation spaces)
- Model AUBI internally (profit-sharing, income floors)
- Demonstrate that non-extractive production works
- **Leverage point:** These become the employers when extractive corporations collapse

Community Land Trusts:

- Perfect entities to own and manage Neighborhood Commons (Chapter 13)
- Remove land from speculation permanently
- Create perpetual sanctuaries immune to market pressure
- Model ground rent → commons dividend

- **Leverage point:** When housing bubble bursts, these provide stability

Movement-Aligned Credit Unions:

- First financial institutions to recognize Hearts/Leaves currency (Chapter 12)
- Offer loans for sanctuary creation and contemplative infrastructure
- Fund cooperative development
- Remove dependence on hostile capital
- **Leverage point:** When banks fail, these remain stable and community-controlled

Platform Cooperatives:

- Democratic alternatives to Uber, Airbnb, Amazon
- Workers control means of production and data
- Profits shared among members
- Proof that tech doesn't require extraction
- **Leverage point:** When platform monopolies are regulated/broken up, these are ready to scale

Bioregional Autonomous Zones (BAZs):

- Networked communities implementing full stack
- Interlocking cooperatives, land trusts, sanctuaries, contemplative centers
- Function as semi-autonomous economic units
- Ready to become actual governance when needed
- **Leverage point:** When federal system fragments, these become functional units

Solidarity Economy Networks:

- Networks of aligned enterprises trading primarily with each other
- Mutual support and resource sharing
- Build parallel economy with different rules
- Reduce dependence on extractive systems
- **Leverage point:** Entire supply chains outside capitalist logic

The Dual Power Strategy:

This is about building a parallel power structure that: 1. Provides for people's needs NOW (mutual aid, meaningful work, community) 2. Proves alternatives work (demonstration effect) 3. Generates resources for political work (funds organizing) 4. Creates fallback when systems fail (resilience) 5. Becomes the new system when old one collapses (readiness)

We're not just "starting businesses." We're building backup governance infrastructure.

Examples:

- Mondragon Cooperatives (Spain) – $12B revenue, 80K worker-owners, survived 2008 crisis
- Cooperation Jackson (Mississippi) – building solidarity economy with land trusts + coops
- Evergreen Cooperatives (Cleveland) – worker-owned, institutionally anchored
- Platform cooperatives (globally) – democratic tech alternatives
- Transition Towns (internationally) – localizing economies and building resilience

Strengths:

- Creates sustainable funding for movement
- Builds real alternatives people can join NOW
- Reduces dependency on donors or hostile institutions

- Demonstrates economic viability (proof kills skepticism)
- Provides employment for activists (solve "how do I pay rent while organizing")
- Creates resilience (when old system fails, parallel system absorbs shock)

Weaknesses:

- Takes time to build (years to decades for full scale)
- Competes in hostile environment (extractive capitalism fights back)
- Risk of becoming just "nicer capitalism" without clear ideological grounding
- Scale challenges (cooperatives struggle to compete with capitalist efficiency)
- Can become isolated enclaves rather than bridgeheads

The Highest Leverage Points:

Most movements fight over parameters (tax rates, subsidies, regulations). We're fighting over paradigms:

Money Creation (Hearts/Leaves):

- Fighting for a 2% tax increase = low leverage
- Launching a complementary currency = high leverage
- Changes who controls money itself, not just how it's taxed

Land Tenure (Community Land Trusts/Hearthstone Protocol):

- Fighting for rent control = low leverage (parameters)
- Removing land from markets entirely = high leverage (structure)
- Changes ownership paradigm, not just regulation

This is why the GGF focuses on "weird" things like alternative currencies

instead of just "voting harder."

* * *

The Combined Strategy: All Six Together

The truth: We need all six strategies simultaneously.
  The Power Portfolio:

Phase 1: Immediate (Years 1-5)

Active Strategies:

- Direct action and demonstration projects (Strategy 3)
- Begin long march through institutions (Strategy 1 - Hospice/Midwife teams)
- Build economic power (Strategy 6 - Parallel Polis foundation)
- Prepare for crisis (Strategy 4 - develop detailed plans)

Emergent Power Effect: "Establish beachheads and prove viability"

- Multiple pilot cities demonstrating full stack
- Proof of concept established beyond doubt
- Coalition building across all stages
- Alternative institutions providing real services
- Plans ready for when crisis opens window
- Foundation laid for scaling

Phase 2: Medium-term (Years 5-12)

Active Strategies:

- Electoral power building (Strategy 2 - winning local/state races)
- Inside-outside coordination (Strategy 5 - sophisticated dance)
- Continue institutional march (Strategy 1 - more Hospice/Midwife teams in place)
- Scale demonstration projects (Strategy 3 - from pilots to widespread)
- Expand economic base (Strategy 6 - Parallel Polis growing)
- Crisis readiness maintained (Strategy 4 - updated plans)

Emergent Power Effect: "Achieve tipping point in key jurisdictions; opposition can no longer ignore us"

- Some cities/states fully implementing stack
- Movement has national visibility
- Opposition forced to respond (which validates us)
- Alternative institutions at meaningful scale
- First generation raised in new system reaching adulthood
- Irreversible momentum in specific regions
- "What seemed impossible is now normal" in key places

Phase 3: Long-term (Years 12-20+)

Active Strategies:

- Institutional transformation bears fruit (Strategy 1 - Hospice/Midwife work succeeding)
- Electoral power becomes decisive (Strategy 2 - federal/international level)
- Economic alternatives at scale (Strategy 6 - Parallel Polis as substantial economy)

- Crisis preparation pays off when windows open (Strategy 4 - ready when moment comes)
- Inside-outside a mature practice (Strategy 5 - sophisticated coordination)
- Demonstrations become norm (Strategy 3 - from alternative to mainstream)

Emergent Power Effect: "Become the new establishment in key domains; set the terms of the debate"

- Federal policies implementing stack
- International adoption beginning
- Young people assume Yellow consciousness as default
- Alternative institutions ARE the institutions in many places
- Old extractive systems visibly failing, ours visibly succeeding
- Cultural shift: we define what "normal" means
- Opposition reduced to reactionary remnant
- Next challenges (from success) emerging

All Six Working Together (The Synergy):

Economic power (6) funds:

- Electoral campaigns (2)
- Demonstration projects (3)
- Movement organizing (5)
- Crisis preparation (4)
- Institutional infiltration stipends (1)

Electoral wins (2) create space for:

- Demonstration projects to scale (3)
- Institutional transformation (1)

- Legal protection for alternatives (6)
- Implementation when crisis hits (4)

Demonstration projects (3) prove models for:

- Friendly electeds to implement (2)
- Institutional allies to replicate (1)
- Economic scaling (6)
- Crisis response templates (4)

Institutional insiders (1) provide:

- Intelligence for outside movements (5)
- Leverage points for pressure (5)
- Hospice for dying systems (prevents chaos)
- Midwifery for emerging systems (enables birth)
- Implementation capacity when electeds win (2)

Crisis preparation (4) leverages:

- All previous institution-building (6)
- All previous organizing (3, 5)
- All previous electoral work (2)
- All previous infiltration (1)
- Transforms decades of work into decisive moment

Inside-outside coordination (5) amplifies:

- All institutional strategies (1)
- All electoral strategies (2)
- All demonstration strategies (3)
- All economic strategies (6)
- Multiplies effectiveness of everything

This is not "choose your favorite strategy." This is "deploy all approaches strategically, with Yellow coordination ensuring they support rather than undermine each other."

Different people lead different strategies based on their positions, skills, and temperaments. Yellow coordination ensures synergy.

The power of this approach: Each strategy strengthens the others. Each victory in one domain creates opportunities in others. Each setback in one domain is compensated by progress in others.

We're not putting all eggs in one basket. We're building an ecosystem where success is overdetermined—so many paths to victory that stopping us becomes impossible.

* * *

Power Without Corruption: The Ethical Challenge

Here's the danger: Power corrupts. Movements pursuing power often become what they opposed.

How do we avoid this?

Structural Safeguards:

1. Term Limits for Leadership

- No one in power indefinitely
- Circulation prevents calcification
- Fresh perspectives regularly
- Reduces cult of personality

2. Transparency and Accountability

- Decision-making processes public

- Regular reporting to base
- Mechanisms for removal of bad actors
- No secret deals

3. Decentralization

- Power distributed, not concentrated
- Multiple centers of initiative
- Redundancy prevents capture of single node
- Local autonomy with shared vision

4. Regular Practice and Reflection

- Contemplative practices for leaders (not optional)
- Regular check-ins on values alignment
- Honest assessment of compromise vs. sell-out
- Support for ethical decision-making

Cultural Norms:

1. Suspicion of Power

- Power as necessary evil, not goal
- Celebrate restraint and stepping down
- Question concentration of authority
- Rotate leadership roles

2. Service Orientation

- Leadership as service, not privilege
- Modest compensation
- No special status
- Emphasis on contribution, not position

3. Criticism Culture

- Encourage internal critique
- Reward whistleblowing
- No sacred cows or untouchable leaders
- Truth-telling valued over loyalty

4. Exit Plans

- Every leader should plan their succession
- Celebrate passing torch
- Define success as making yourself unnecessary
- Build capacity in others

Personal Practices:

For Those Gaining Power:

- Regular contemplative practice (stay grounded)
- Maintain relationships outside movement (prevent isolation)
- Schedule stepping down (before you want to)
- Regular ethical check-ins with trusted advisors
- Remember why you started
- Keep reading and learning

The Test: "If I'm making this decision because it keeps me in power rather than because it serves the mission, I'm corrupted."

The Standard: "Would I support this decision if someone I opposed was making it?"

* * *

Defending Gains: The Counter-Revolution Problem

Here's an uncomfortable truth: Every successful transformation triggers organized backlash.

The pattern is predictable: 1. Movement starts winning 2. Old elites realize they're losing power 3. They organize counter-revolution 4. Often succeed in reversing gains

Historical examples:

- Post-Reconstruction backlash (Jim Crow)
- New Deal rollback (1970s-80s neoliberalism)
- 1960s social movements → 1980s conservative reaction
- Arab Spring → authoritarian reassertion
- Recent: any progressive city policy → state preemption laws

Why movements often lose after initial wins:

- Celebrate too early, let guard down
- Assume victory is permanent
- Don't consolidate institutional power
- Get complacent once immediate demands are met
- Underestimate opponent's determination
- Fail to defend on multiple fronts simultaneously

Our Counter-Revolution Readiness:

Expect These Attacks:
Legal/Political:

- State preemption laws ("city can't implement AUBI")
- Federal rollback of policies
- Court challenges to regulations
- Defunding of successful programs

- "States' rights" arguments against federal implementation

Economic:

- Capital flight from implementing jurisdictions
- Corporate boycotts and pressure campaigns
- Financial sector refusing to cooperate
- Property owners raising rents in response to AUBI
- Sabotage of alternative economic institutions

Cultural/Media:

- "Failed experiment" narratives
- Amplifying any problems, ignoring successes
- Associating movement with extremism
- Dividing coalition through wedge issues
- Making "Yellow consciousness" seem weird/elitist

Violent:

- Harassment of leaders and participants
- Attacks on alternative institutions
- Police repression of movements
- In extreme cases, assassination of leaders
- Funding of opposition militias/groups

Our Defense Strategy:

1. Build Redundancy

- Multiple pilots in multiple jurisdictions
- If one gets shut down, others continue
- Success can't be killed by taking out one node

• Distributed power prevents single point of failure

2. Lock In Gains

• Constitutional amendments where possible
• Long-term contracts and legal protections
• Build constituency dependent on programs
• Make reversal politically costly
• Create facts on ground (institutions) not just policy

3. Maintain Mobilization

• Don't demobilize after winning
• Keep organizing infrastructure active
• Regular actions to show strength
• Quick response capacity to threats
• Base ready to defend gains

4. Build Cross-Class Coalition

• Include people who benefit materially from new system
• Not just ideological supporters
• Middle class + working class + elites
• They'll fight to keep what they've gained
• Makes rollback harder (too many losers)

5. Control Narrative

• Document successes systematically
• Rapid response to attacks
• Alternative media infrastructure
• Cultural production (art, film, music) embedding values
• Make Yellow consciousness feel normal, not weird

6. Legal Defense

- Well-funded legal strategy
- Constitutional arguments prepared
- Defend in multiple jurisdictions simultaneously
- International human rights frameworks
- Make rollback legally difficult

7. Economic Resilience

- Alternative institutions don't depend on hostile systems
- Cooperative economy continues even if government hostile
- Community resilience if capital flees
- Mutual aid networks provide safety net
- Can survive backlash economically

8. Strategic Patience

- Know backlash is coming
- Don't be shocked or demoralized by it
- Prepared for long struggle
- Each attack makes us stronger (if we're ready)
- Historical perspective: all transformations faced this

The Ultimate Defense: Make It Work So Well They Can't Kill It

The best defense is overwhelming success:

- Pilot cities thriving while others decline
- Clear improvements in wellbeing metrics
- People in implementing jurisdictions defending fiercely
- Business communities seeing benefits
- Even opponents' kids wanting to move there

When something works this well, trying to kill it looks like sadism.

Our job: Make the Yellow stack so successful, so beloved, so clearly better that opposing it becomes political suicide.

That's the victory condition—not just implementing, but succeeding so obviously that reversal becomes impossible.

* * *

Timeline and Milestones: When Do We Have Real Power?

Realistic assessment of when different types of power become available:

Phase 1: Building (Years 1-5)

Power Level: Low

- Can pilot small projects
- Can win some local elections
- Cannot yet force system-level change
- Primarily building capacity

Milestones:

- 10+ cities with demonstration projects
- 50+ friendly local officials elected
- $10-50M in movement economic power
- 100K+ activated supporters
- Clear proof of concept established

Phase 2: Breakthrough (Years 5-10)

Power Level: Moderate

- Can win state-level policies
- Can force corporate responses
- Beginning real implementation
- National visibility

Milestones:

- 3-5 states with major stack policies
- Multiple cities fully implementing
- Some national politicians embracing
- Movement in news regularly
- Opposition taking us seriously

Phase 3: Transformation (Years 10-20)

Power Level: High

- Can win federal policies
- Cannot be ignored or crushed
- Widespread implementation
- Cultural shift evident

Milestones:

- Federal AUBI legislation passed
- Cognitive sovereignty standards national
- 100+ cities with full stack
- Next generation raised in new system
- Irreversible momentum

Phase 4: Stabilization (Years 20-30)

Power Level: Dominant (in aligned domains)

- New normal established
- Opposition marginalized
- Expansion and refinement
- Next challenges emerging

Milestones:

- Most major cities implementing
- Most states on board
- International adoption beginning
- Yellow consciousness widespread
- Success creating new challenges

* * *

Conclusion: Power Is Not Dirty—Powerlessness Is

Many in progressive and spiritual movements have dysfunctional relationships with power.
   They think:

- "Power corrupts" (so we shouldn't seek it)
- "Purity matters more than effectiveness" (so we don't compromise)
- "The system is evil" (so we can't work within it)
- "Consciousness shift is enough" (so we don't need strategy)

This is a recipe for irrelevance.

The truth:

- Power corrupts, but powerlessness corrupts absolutely (into bitterness and impotence)
- Purity without power changes nothing
- The system is what it is, and must be navigated to be transformed
- Consciousness shifts matter, but also strategy, power, execution

Yellow consciousness applied to power means:

- Clear-eyed assessment of current power dynamics
- Strategic deployment of multiple approaches
- Willingness to work within systems while transforming them
- Coalition building across ideological lines
- Long-term patience combined with tactical urgency
- Ethical safeguards against corruption
- Realistic timelines
- Humble ambition (great goals, realistic about difficulty)

We need power to implement the Yellow stack.

Not for power's sake. For the sake of the humans suffering under current arrangements.

Every day we remain powerless, people die from preventable despair, addiction, poverty, and fragmentation.

That's the moral weight.

Not wielding power isn't purity—it's abandonment.

So we build power. Ethically. Strategically. Patiently. Urgently.

We play the long game and the short game simultaneously.

We work inside and outside.

We compromise tactically while never compromising the vision.

And we do it together, coordinated by Yellow consciousness, serving all stages, building the infrastructure for human flourishing.

That's the power strategy.

* * *

Next: Chapter 18 – The Wealth Question: Money, Capital, and the Alchemist's Protocols

Because power and money are intertwined. And the wealthy have special responsibilities in this transition.

The next chapter gets personal for those with resources.

Chapter 18: Pilot Cities and Natural Experiments (2026-2035)

From Blueprint to Reality

We have the vision. We have the coalition. We have the power strategy.

Now the question everyone's been waiting for:

Where do we actually start? What city goes first? What happens in Year 1? Year 3? Year 5?

This chapter answers that.

Not in abstract principles, but in concrete detail: Which cities are ready, what they implement when, what results they see, what problems they encounter, how they adapt.

This is the bridge from theory to practice.

The difference between "interesting ideas" and "functioning civilization" is implementation. And implementation means:

- Specific places
- Specific timelines
- Specific budgets
- Specific people doing specific things
- Specific metrics showing specific results

So let's get specific.

* * *

The Pilot City Selection Criteria

Not every city can go first. We need cities that:

1. Demographic & Scale Requirements:

Population: 100,000-500,000

- Large enough to demonstrate viability at scale
- Small enough to be manageable for first attempt
- Not so small that results are dismissed as "boutique" (like Burlington's ~45K)
- Not so large that complexity overwhelms capacity

Why this matters: NYC (8M) is too complex for first pilot. Smalltown USA (5K) won't convince skeptics. Mid-size cities are Goldilocks zone.

2. Political Requirements:

Progressive Leadership with Pragmatic Streak

- Mayor/council who understand Yellow thinking (or can learn fast)
- Not purely ideological Green (will get details right)
- Not centrist Orange (won't attempt transformation)
- Willing to take calculated risks
- Can sell to business community AND social movements

Stable Governance

- Not facing immediate fiscal crisis

- Not in midst of corruption scandal
- Not about to have electoral upheaval
- Can commit to 5-10 year timeframe

Why this matters: Need political stability to see results before leadership changes.

3. Economic Requirements:

Diverse Economic Base

- Not mono-economy dependent on one industry
- Mix of education, tech, services, some manufacturing
- Strong nonprofit/cooperative sector already present
- Local business community not uniformly hostile

Fiscal Capacity

- Can invest $50-100M over 5 years without bankruptcy
- Mix of city budget, state/federal grants, philanthropy
- Bond capacity for infrastructure

Why this matters: Can't implement if broke. Need resources and political will.

4. Cultural Requirements:

Values Alignment

- Population receptive to contemplative practices (won't mock meditation)
- History of social innovation
- Some existing sanctuary spaces (parks, libraries, community centers)

- Not culturally hostile to Yellow ideas

Demographic Diversity

- Racial/ethnic diversity (proves this works for everyone)
- Income diversity (not just wealthy liberals)
- Age diversity (young families, retirees, everyone)
- Shows this isn't just for one demographic

Why this matters: Need to prove this works for real, diverse America, not just hippie enclaves.

5. Institutional Requirements:

Strong Civil Society

- Active community organizations
- Functioning nonprofits
- Some cooperative/commons history
- Engaged residents

Implementation Capacity

- City staff competent and not purely bureaucratic
- Local universities that can support/study
- Existing contemplative communities to build on
- Technical capacity (don't need to build everything from scratch)

Bioregional Context

- City serves as anchor for broader watershed/ecosystem
- The pilot city isn't an island - it's the **Bioregional Anchor**
- Example: Madison anchors governance for the Yahara Watershed

- Burlington anchors governance for Lake Champlain Basin
- Austin anchors governance for Colorado River Basin
- **We start with the city because it has the legal levers, but we aim for the ecosystem**
- City policies must consider bioregional impacts
- Collaborate with surrounding municipalities, tribal lands, rural areas
- Pilot extends beyond city limits through partnerships

Why bioregional matters:

- Political boundaries are artificial; ecological systems are real
- Governance should follow watersheds, not arbitrary lines
- True resilience requires ecosystem–scale thinking
- Connects municipal politics to planetary ecology
- Honors indigenous wisdom about land–based governance

Why this matters: Need partners who can actually implement, not just approve plans.

* * *

Tier 1 Pilot Cities: The First Wave (Years 1-3)

These cities implement first, full stack, comprehensive approach.

Target: 3 cities in Year 1, fully implementing all four interventions by Year 3.

Top Candidates:

1. Burlington, Vermont (42,000 city proper, 225,000 metro)

Why Burlington:

- Already most progressive small city in America
- Strong cooperative tradition (Vermont culture)
- Bernie Sanders history (city knows systemic change possible)
- High education, tech sector, quality of life emphasis
- Strong local food/sustainability culture
- Existing contemplative communities
- City government experienced with innovation

Special advantages:

- Vermont has Universal Basic Income advocacy already
- State small enough that city pilot can influence state policy
- Strong social trust (low crime, high civic engagement)
- National attention due to Bernie brand
- Can scale to whole state if successful (only 650K people)

Challenges:

- Very white (89%) – less demographic proof
- Small size might be dismissed as "not real city"
- Cold climate (might deter some visitors/researchers)
- Already relatively high quality of life (less dramatic transformation to show)

Budget estimate: $40-60M over 5 years

2. Austin, Texas (975,000 city, 2.3M metro)

Why Austin:

- "Keep Austin Weird" culture (values diversity, innovation)
- Major tech hub (implementation capacity)
- Young, educated population (early adopters)
- Strong music/arts culture (spiritual but not religious)
- Growing contemplative scene (yoga, meditation widespread)
- City government progressive, business community pragmatic
- Red state Blue city (can prove this works even in hostile state)

Special advantages:

- Size large enough to be "real city" proof
- Tech industry means talent for digital sanctuaries
- Music culture provides entry for contemplative practices
- National/international visibility
- Demographic diversity (Hispanic 34%, White 48%, Asian 9%, Black 8%)
- If works here, can export to other Red state Blue cities

Challenges:

- State government hostile (will preempt policies)
- Rapid growth creating housing crisis (might complicate AUBI)
- Tech culture can be Orange extractive
- Summer heat might affect outdoor sanctuary use

Budget estimate: $150-200M over 5 years (larger city, higher costs)

3. Madison, Wisconsin (270,000 city, 680,000 metro)

Why Madison:

- Progressive island in swing state (purple state proof)
- Major university (UW-Madison = research capacity + open-minded culture)
- Strong cooperative tradition (Wisconsin history)
- State capital (can influence state policy)
- Excellent quality of life (consistently ranked top 10)
- Four-season climate (not just "easy living" proof)
- Strong public sector (state employees provide stable base)

Special advantages:

- University brings research legitimacy
- State government occasionally receptive (not pure Red)
- Can prove this works in heartland, not just coasts
- Strong public education tradition
- Demographic mix (not as white as Vermont)
- If succeeds, Wisconsin could flip in implementation

Challenges:

- Winter climate (seasonal sanctuary challenges)
- State government can be hostile depending on cycle
- Conservative rural areas surrounding (cultural tension)
- Midwest skepticism of "weird California ideas"

Budget estimate: $60-80M over 5 years

* * *

What Actually Happens: The Implementation Timeline

Let's walk through what the first pilot city (we'll use Madison as example) actually does, month by month, year by year.

Year 0: Planning and Preparation (2026)

Months 1-3: Assessment and Coalition Building
  What happens:

- City council passes resolution committing to pilot
- Hire Yellow Stack Implementation Team (10-15 people)
- Conduct comprehensive needs assessment
- Build coalition across all stakeholders
- Identify existing assets (parks, buildings, organizations)
- Develop detailed budget and funding strategy
- Apply for federal/state grants
- Engage philanthropy

Key meetings:

- 50+ community forums across all neighborhoods
- 100+ one-on-one meetings with business, nonprofit, religious leaders
- City council working sessions (10+ meetings)
- Public listening sessions (20+)

Deliverables:

- Comprehensive Implementation Plan (300+ pages)
- Budget ($60M over 5 years, sourced and committed)
- Coalition agreements (MOUs with 50+ organizations)
- Communications strategy
- Timeline with milestones

Resistance encountered:

- Business community: "This is socialist!"
- Fiscal conservatives: "We can't afford this!"
- Skeptics: "This will never work"
- Cynics: "Just another government boondoggle"

How addressed:

- Show economic analysis (Chapter 15: this saves money)
- Bring in Orange allies who've run numbers
- Share proof from existing pilots (Finland AUBI, etc.)
- Transparent budgeting and accountability
- Quick wins to build trust

Months 4-6: Infrastructure and Staffing
What happens:

- Hire department heads for four interventions:
- Cognitive Sovereignty Director
- Sovereign Floor Administrator
- Sanctuary Spaces Coordinator
- Contemplative Capacity Director
- Lease temporary office space for coordination
- Establish website and communications
- Begin community education campaign
- Identify pilot participants (1,000 households for AUBI pilot)
- Survey baseline metrics (wellbeing, mental health, economic, social)

Key activities:

- Weekly staff meetings (building team culture)
- Launch "Yellow Stack Madison" website

- Begin social media presence
- First newsletter to 10,000 interested residents
- Partner recruitment (contemplative teachers, sanctuary designers, tech experts)

Months 7-9: First Implementations Begin
Cognitive Sovereignty:

- Pass city ordinance regulating attention extraction
- Create public awareness campaign ("Your Attention Belongs to You")
- Partner with schools for student education
- Launch "Library of Attention" (public reading rooms, no devices allowed)
- Begin enforcement against worst violators

Sanctuaries:

- Designate first Neighborhood Commons (4 parks)
- Install basic infrastructure (benches, water, signage)
- Restrict commercial activity in designated zones
- Create "Quiet Hours" (certain times, no amplification)
- Launch first Community Hearth space

Contemplative Capacity:

- Hire 10 contemplative instructors (diverse traditions)
- Launch first Community Contemplative Center
- Begin school pilot (5 schools, daily practice)
- Start workplace pilot (10 businesses, voluntary)
- Free weekly community sits (open to all)

Sovereign Floor:

- Select 1,000 pilot households (lottery from applicants)
- Begin $1,000/month payments (modified AUBI)
- Establish monitoring and evaluation
- Create participant support services
- Launch community education about program

Months 10-12: Refinement and Learning
What happens:

- Weekly "learning labs" (what's working, what's not)
- Monthly community reports (transparency)
- Adjust implementation based on feedback
- Celebrate early wins (even small ones)
- Address problems quickly (build trust)
- Prepare for Year 1 expansion

Early results visible:

- Sanctuary spaces seeing immediate use
- Contemplative center full (waiting list developing)
- AUBI participants reporting reduced stress
- Cognitive sovereignty complaints decreasing
- National media attention beginning
- Other cities asking questions

* * *

Year 1: Expansion and Evidence (2027)

What happens:

Cognitive Sovereignty:

- Ordinance enforcement showing results (measured attention)
- Schools report students more focused
- Add 10 more "Attention Sanctuaries" (libraries, community centers)
- Launch digital sanctuary (city-sponsored Fediverse instance)
- **Establish Municipal Data Trust** (Year 1 deliverable):
- City legally protects citizen data from extraction
- No corporate surveillance of municipal services
- Citizens own their data (can export, delete, control)
- Operates under Aurora Accord protocols
- **"Data Safe Haven" status**: Moving to pilot city means regaining digital sovereignty
- Massive incentive for remote workers, tech workers, privacy-conscious families
- These pilots aren't "Smart Cities" (surveillance) - they're **Data Safe Havens**
- Partner with UW-Madison on research

Metrics at 6 months:

- Self-reported phone use down 20% among participants
- Student attention spans improving (teacher surveys)
- Mental health complaints down 15%
- Productivity at work unchanged (key for skeptics)

Sanctuaries:

- Expand to 12 Neighborhood Commons
- Create first Wilderness Sanctuary (partnership with county)

- Launch "Hearthlights" program (community grief support)
- Establish Non-Extractive Zoning (NEZ) for 2 districts
- Build 3 Community Hearth spaces

Metrics at 6 months:

- 50,000+ sanctuary visits per month
- 70% resident awareness of sanctuary program
- Property values near sanctuaries stable/increasing (key for homeowners)
- Community connection scores up 25%
- Neighborhood crime down 10% in sanctuary areas

Contemplative Capacity:

- Expand school pilot to 20 schools (half the district)
- Open second Community Contemplative Center
- Launch workplace program (now 30 businesses participating)
- Train 50 new instructors (creating jobs)
- Begin elder wisdom circles

Metrics at 6 months:

- 5,000+ residents in regular practice
- Student behavioral issues down 30% in pilot schools
- Teacher burnout down 20%
- Workplace stress down 15% in participating companies
- Healthcare visits for anxiety/depression down 10%

Sovereign Floor:

- Expand to 2,000 households
- Begin advocacy for state/federal funding

- Launch Hearts/Leaves currency (pilot with 50 businesses)
- **Hearts** track regenerative work (ecosystem restoration, elder care, community building)
- **Leaves** track communal contributions (teaching, mentoring, cultural preservation)
- Neither captured by traditional market but essential for thriving communities
- Functions as circulatory system for the new economy the stack enables
- 50 businesses accept Hearts for partial payment (coffee shops, cooperatives, local services)
- Community members earn Hearts through documented contributions
- Convertible to dollars at modest rate but designed to circulate locally
- Document economic impacts
- Create pathways out of program (not trap)

Metrics at 6 months:

- Household financial stress down 40%
- ER visits down 20% (people can afford preventive care)
- School attendance up (kids not moving due to eviction)
- Entrepreneurship up (people taking risks)
- Part-time work increasing (people have choice)
- No significant inflation in housing/food (key concern)

Challenges Encountered:
Problem 1: Some businesses resist Cognitive Sovereignty

- Solution: Grandfather period, phased enforcement, work with business associations, show economic benefits

Problem 2: Sanctuary spaces attracting unhoused population

- Solution: This is feature, not bug - connect with services, create supportive housing, prove compassion works

Problem 3: Not enough contemplative instructors

- Solution: Accelerated training program, bring in national teachers, create certification pathway

Problem 4: AUBI creating housing pressure

- Solution: Expand affordable housing, community land trusts, land-lord regulations, monitor closely

Problem 5: State government threatening preemption

- Solution: Legal defense fund, coalition with other cities, public pressure, compromise on some details

Problem 6: Implementation team burnout

- Risk: Project of this scale and passion = staff exhaustion
- Solution: **Team must practice what they preach**
- Weekly contemplative sessions for all staff (mandatory, on the clock)
- Regular retreat time (quarterly staff renewal)
- Reasonable hours (modeling work-life integration)
- Mutual support and check-ins (team wellness)
- Outside facilitators for team process (prevent hero complex)
- Celebrate small wins (sustain morale)
- "If the implementation team burns out, we've already failed - we're building this FOR human flourishing, not AT THE COST of it"
- Staff wellbeing is leading indicator of project health

By end of Year 1:

- Proof of concept established
- National media coverage (NYT, NPR, VICE, etc.)
- Delegations visiting from 20+ other cities
- Academic papers being written
- Opposition softening (seeing results)
- Expansion to full city approved for Year 2

* * *

**Year 2-3: Full City Implementation (2028-2029)

What happens:
  All four interventions scale to full city:

- All schools implementing contemplative education
- 40+ sanctuary spaces across all neighborhoods
- AUBI expanding to 10,000 households (targeting expansion)
- Cognitive sovereignty citywide enforcement
- Hearts/Leaves currency accepted by 200+ businesses
- 5 Community Contemplative Centers
- Workplace program 100+ businesses
- Full Neighborhood Commons network

Integration effects becoming visible:
  The Synergies Start Showing:

- People with AUBI have time for contemplative practice
- Contemplative practice helps people use AUBI wisely (not just consumption)
- Sanctuary spaces enable practice (physical container)
- Cognitive sovereignty protects attention for practice

- All four together = genuine transformation

Stories emerging:

Single mother, 32, two kids:

- Year 0: Working two jobs, constant stress, kids struggling in school, considering leaving Madison
- Year 1: Gets AUBI ($1,000/month), quits second job, starts attending Community Contemplative Center
- Year 2: Kids in contemplative school program (behavior improving), she's in hearts-based cooperative, uses sanctuaries for family time, stress way down, considering community college
- "I can finally breathe. For the first time in ten years, I'm not in survival mode every minute."

Small business owner, 45:

- Year 0: Skeptical, "This is government waste"
- Year 1: Reluctantly implements workplace contemplative time (pressure from employees)
- Year 2: Notices productivity up, turnover down, accepts Hearts currency, employees happier, expands business, becomes advocate
- "I was wrong. This isn't about government control - it's about giving people their humanity back."

Retired teacher, 68:

- Year 0: "Meditation is for hippies"
- Year 1: Tries Community Hearth grief circle after spouse's death
- Year 2: Regular practitioner, trained as elder wisdom holder, leads circles, life has meaning again
- "I thought retirement meant waiting to die. Turns out it meant finally learning to live."

University student, 20:

- Year 0: Anxiety, depression, phone addiction, struggling academically
- Year 1: Digital sanctuary helps break phone cycle, starts contemplative practice
- Year 2: Attention stabilized, grades up, considering teaching contemplative practices, feels hopeful about future
- "I didn't realize how much of my brain I'd sold to Silicon Valley until I got it back."

Metrics at end of Year 3:
Health:

- Mental health ER visits: down 35%
- Anxiety/depression diagnoses: down 25%
- Substance abuse: down 20%
- Preventive care: up 40%
- Overall health costs: down 15%

Education:

- Test scores: up 10% (not main goal, but helps skeptics)
- Behavioral issues: down 40%
- Teacher retention: up 30%
- Student wellbeing: up 50%
- Parent satisfaction: 85% approval

Economic:

- Poverty rate: down 25%
- Emergency room use: down 30%
- Entrepreneurship: up 35%
- Local business revenue: up 10%

- Housing security: up 40%
- No significant inflation in basics

Social:

- Community connection: up 40%
- Volunteering: up 50%
- Crime (all types): down 25%
- Social trust: up 35%
- Neighborhood cohesion: 80% report improvement

Existential:

- Self-reported life satisfaction: up 45%
- Sense of purpose: up 50%
- Feeling of belonging: up 40%
- Optimism about future: up 35%

Cost: $60M spent (on budget) **ROI:** Healthcare savings alone = $40M (will increase) **Net cost:** $20M for transformation that changes 270,000 lives

Per capita cost: $74 per person per year.

That's less than monthly Netflix. Less than annual Amazon Prime. Less than one nice dinner out.

For a civilization designed for human flourishing instead of extraction.

* * *

Year 4-5: Stabilization and Replication (2030-2031)

What happens:
  Madison:

- System stabilized, no longer "pilot"
- This is just how Madison works now
- Continuous improvement, not radical change
- Focus shifts to helping other cities

State of Wisconsin:

- Governor (now Democrat) proposes statewide expansion
- Legislature debates (purple state fight)
- Compromise: 5 more cities get pilots
- State funding for some programs
- National model emerging

Other Tier 1 Cities:
  Burlington:

- Full implementation by 2029
- Vermont legislature passes state AUBI (2030)
- First full state implementation
- Population 650K, manageable scale
- Proves it works at state level

Austin:

- Fighting Texas preemption laws
- Partial implementation (what state allows)
- Becomes case study in hostile state environment
- Business community increasingly supportive (seeing results)

- Pressure on state legislature growing

National Effect:

By 2031, after 5 years:

- 3 Tier 1 cities fully implementing (Madison, Burlington, + 1 more)
- 10 Tier 2 cities beginning pilots
- 50+ cities studying/planning
- Federal legislation introduced (not passing yet, but on agenda)
- Academic consensus: this works
- Media consensus shifting from "weird experiment" to "model for future"
- Opposition reduced to marginal (results too good to deny)

***

The Fractal Twinning Protocol: Planetary, Not Provincial

Before we discuss Tier 2 cities, a critical principle:

These pilots cannot be "First World luxuries." They must be planetary from the start.

The Twinning Requirement:

Every pilot city must "twin" with a partner city in the Global South.

How it works:

Austin twins with Medellín, Colombia:

- Share all code, protocols, research data (open source)
- Adapt implementations to local contexts

449

- Medellín experiments with Hearts/Leaves in different economy
- Austin learns from Medellín's innovations
- Joint research on what's universal vs. context-dependent
- Direct knowledge transfer (not "development" but peer learning)

Burlington twins with city in Kerala, India:

- Kerala's tradition of democratic socialism + contemplative practices
- Burlington learns from existing commons management
- Kerala gains technical infrastructure designs
- Both adapt AUBI to their contexts (different starting points)
- Prove this works in radically different economic conditions

Madison twins with Cochabamba, Bolivia:

- Water rights history (Cochabamba's commons victories)
- Bioregional governance parallels (watersheds)
- Indigenous wisdom integration
- Climate adaptation knowledge exchange
- Hearts/Leaves system informed by Andean reciprocity traditions

Why this matters:
Prevents accusations of elitism:

- "This only works for rich white cities" → False, we're testing every-where simultaneously

Models polycentric governance:

- Not top-down diffusion but peer network
- Multiple experiments, shared learning
- No single "correct" implementation

Honors knowledge flows:

- Global South has wisdom North lacks (commons, reciprocity, resilience)
- Not charity but genuine partnership
- Decolonizes "development" discourse

Creates insurance:

- If North fails, South continues
- If South blocked, North advocates
- Distributed resilience

Builds planetary consciousness:

- Citizens of twinned cities see themselves as part of global network
- Direct relationships, not abstract solidarity
- Cultural exchange deepens understanding

Validates "Global" in Global Governance Frameworks:

- This isn't theory – it's practice from day one
- Planetary civilization emerges through these specific relationships

The Twinning Protocol in Practice:

Year 1:

- Establish relationships, mutual visits, knowledge exchange
- Adapt protocols to local contexts
- Begin parallel implementations

Year 2-3:

- Regular video calls (monthly city-to-city)
- Annual in-person exchanges (delegations visit)
- Shared research and data
- Joint problem-solving

Year 4-5:

- Mature partnerships
- New cities joining network
- South-South twinning emerges
- True planetary network forming

Measurement:

- Both cities track outcomes
- Comparative analysis (what's universal vs. contextual)
- Cross-pollination of innovations
- Mutual transformation, not one-way transfer

Resources:

- Pilot city budgets include twinning support ($1-2M/5 years)
- Not "aid" but reciprocal investment
- Technical assistance both directions
- Shared celebration of wins

* * *

Tier 2 Pilot Cities: The Second Wave (Years 3-7)

These cities begin implementation in Years 3-5, learning from Tier 1 mistakes, adapting to local contexts.
    Target: 10-15 cities by Year 7

Strong Tier 2 Candidates:

1. **Portland, Maine** (68,000) - Similar to Burlington, Northeast proof
2. **Ann Arbor, Michigan** (123,000) - University town, Midwest swing state 3. **Boulder, Colorado** (108,000) - Already contemplative culture, young population 4. **Asheville, North Carolina** (95,000) - Southern proof, growing city 5. **Oakland, California** (440,000) - Urban, diverse, progressive California 6. **Minneapolis, Minnesota** (430,000) - Major city, progressive, cold climate proof 7. **Eugene, Oregon** (177,000) - Alternative culture, Pacific Northwest 8. **Chattanooga, Tennessee** (185,000) - Southern, municipal broadband (tech ready) 9. **Tucson, Arizona** (548,000) - Southwest, Hispanic majority, desert proof 10. **Rochester, New York** (211,000) - Rust belt proof, economic revitalization need

Why these cities:

- Geographic diversity (proves this works everywhere)
- Demographic diversity (racial, economic, cultural)
- Political diversity (different state contexts)
- Size diversity (small to large)
- Economic diversity (tech, education, manufacturing, service)

Each adapted to local context:

- Southern cities: connect to church traditions
- Rust belt cities: economic revitalization angle
- Hispanic-majority: integrate cultural practices
- Cold climate: seasonal adaptation

- Hot climate: cooling sanctuaries

* * *

The Natural Experiment: What We Learn

The beauty of pilots: they're natural experiments.

What We're Testing:

1. Intervention Effectiveness

- Which interventions have biggest impact?
- What's the optimal sequence?
- How long before results visible?
- What dosage is sufficient? (How much contemplative time? How much AUBI?)

2. Context Dependence

- Does this work in Red states? Blue states? Purple states?
- Does it work in cold climates? Hot climates?
- Does it work in college towns? Working-class cities? Tech hubs?
- Does it work for Black communities? Hispanic communities? White communities? Asian communities?

3. Implementation Challenges

- What obstacles are universal vs. local?
- What governance structures work best?
- How much does it cost really?

- What's the minimum viable stack?

4. Opposition Patterns

- Who opposes most fiercely?
- What arguments gain traction?
- How is opposition overcome?
- What coalitions defeat opposition?

5. Unintended Consequences

- What problems emerge we didn't anticipate?
- What opportunities emerge we didn't expect?
- What happens to neighboring cities? (Spillover effects)
- What perverse incentives need guarding against?

6. Scaling Pathways

- Can success in Madison transfer to Milwaukee?
- Can success in Burlington transfer to Vermont?
- Can success in purple states transfer to Red states?
- What's lost in translation? What's gained?

Research Infrastructure:

The Research Consortium:

The pilot cities are being studied longitudinally by a pre-registered research consortium to ensure rigor and prevent cherry-picking of results. Core partners include:

Lead Institutions:

- **University of Wisconsin's Center for Healthy Minds** (Richard Davidson's lab - contemplative neuroscience)

- **MIT Initiative on the Digital Economy** (Erik Brynjolfsson's team - economic impacts)
- **Brookings Institution** (Metropolitan Policy Program - urban outcomes)
- **Stanford Center on Poverty and Inequality** (AUBI and wellbeing)
- **Harvard's Human Flourishing Program** (meaning and purpose metrics)

Supporting Partners:

- Pilot city universities (UW–Madison, UT Austin, UVM, etc.)
- National Institute of Mental Health (mental health outcomes)
- Robert Wood Johnson Foundation (health and wellbeing)
- International research teams (OECD, EU observers, UN)

Research Design:

- **Pre-registered protocols** (hypotheses stated before data collection - prevents p-hacking)
- **Comparison cities** (similar non-pilot cities as controls)
- **Longitudinal tracking** (same participants over 10+ years)
- **Mixed methods** (quantitative + qualitative + ethnographic)
- **Open data** (all anonymized data publicly available)
- **Independent evaluation** (not just pilot city advocates)

What they're measuring:

- Health outcomes (physical, mental)
- Economic outcomes (poverty, entrepreneurship, growth)
- Educational outcomes (learning, wellbeing, retention)
- Social outcomes (trust, connection, volunteering)
- Environmental outcomes (consumption, sustainability)
- Political outcomes (engagement, polarization)

- Existential outcomes (meaning, purpose, satisfaction)

How they're measuring:

- Longitudinal surveys (same people over time)
- Administrative data (health records, school records, crime stats)
- Economic data (employment, income, spending)
- Ethnographic studies (deep qualitative understanding)
- Comparison with similar non-pilot cities (control groups)
- Before/after comparisons
- Dose-response relationships (how much intervention = how much effect?)

* * *

The Failure Scenarios: What If It Doesn't Work?

Let's be honest about what could go wrong.

Scenario 1: Implementation Failure

What happens:

- City tries to implement but does it badly
- Hires wrong people, cuts corners, doesn't follow blueprint
- Predictable failure
- Opposition says "See? We told you it wouldn't work!"

How we prevent:

- Strict adherence to implementation guidelines

- Technical assistance from successful cities
- Quality control and accountability
- Regular audits and course corrections
- Don't let pride prevent admitting mistakes

What we learn even if this happens:

- Implementation matters (not just theory)
- Quality control essential
- Need experienced team
- Can't cut corners

Scenario 2: Partial Success

What happens:

- Some interventions work great (contemplative capacity)
- Others struggle (AUBI creates housing inflation)
- Mixed results
- Defensible but not overwhelming

How we handle:

- Honest reporting of what worked and what didn't
- Adapt interventions that struggled
- Emphasize successes while fixing failures
- Use as learning opportunity
- Refine for next cities

What we learn:

- Which interventions are most robust
- What context factors matter most

- How to adapt to local conditions
- What supporting policies needed

Scenario 3: Success With Perverse Outcomes

What happens:

- Programs work as designed
- But create unintended problems (e.g., housing prices skyrocket due to desirability)
- Rich people move in, poor people get displaced
- Success becomes exclusionary

How we prevent:

- Strong affordable housing protections
- Community land trusts
- Inclusionary zoning
- Right of return for displaced residents
- Monitor equity outcomes continuously

What we learn:

- Success requires equity protections
- Can't just "do the programs" without structural supports
- Gentrification is real risk
- Need ongoing vigilance

Scenario 4: Political Backlash

What happens:

- Programs working well

- But state government preempts (Texas kills Austin pilot)
- Or new mayor elected who kills it
- Or federal government cuts funding

How we handle:

- Legal defense (Chapter 17)
- Political organizing (protect the gains)
- Build such strong constituency it's politically risky to kill
- Have funding that doesn't depend on hostile governments
- Rapid mobilization when threatened

What we learn:

- Political sustainability matters as much as program effectiveness
- Need protected funding sources
- Coalition maintenance crucial
- Can't relax after winning

Scenario 5: Can't Prove Causation

What happens:

- Outcomes improve in pilot cities
- But skeptics say "correlation not causation"
- "Madison was already doing well"
- "Other factors explain improvement"
- Can't definitively prove stack caused results

How we handle:

- Rigorous research design (comparison cities, before/after, dose-response)

- Multiple pilots (replication in different contexts)
- Mechanistic evidence (not just outcomes but pathways)
- Accumulation of evidence over time
- Accept that perfection isn't required (preponderance of evidence)

What we learn:

- Research design matters from start
- Need multiple types of evidence
- Perfect proof impossible but not necessary
- Weight of evidence eventually convinces

* * *

The Success Scenario: What Victory Looks Like

By 2035 (Year 10), if things go well:

Tier 1 Cities (3):

- Full implementation, stabilized, normal
- This is just how these cities work
- Next generation growing up in Yellow consciousness
- Serving as training and demonstration sites
- Exporting model and expertise

Tier 2 Cities (15+):

- Full implementation or close
- Diverse contexts proving generalizability
- Each adapted to local culture

- Learning from each other
- Building network effects

Tier 3 Cities (50+):

- Beginning implementation
- Using refined models from Tier 1 and 2
- Faster implementation (learning curve shortening)
- Less resistance (proof exists)

State Level (3-5 states):

- Vermont, Rhode Island, maybe Oregon, New Mexico, Maine
- Small states going full Yellow stack
- Proving it works at state level
- Creating pressure on federal government

Federal Level:

- Legislation introduced
- Not passing yet but serious debate
- Both parties engaging (signs of normalizing)
- Some federal pilots funded
- National conversation shifted

International:

- European cities watching and beginning pilots
- Nordic countries especially interested
- Some Global South cities adapting model
- International research collaboration
- Global movement forming

Cultural Shift:

- Yellow consciousness no longer "weird"
- Contemplative practice normalized
- AUBI mainstream idea
- Sanctuaries expected not novel
- Cognitive sovereignty common sense
- Next generation assumes this is normal

The Tipping Point:

Somewhere between 2030-2035, we cross threshold where:

- Enough cities implementing that it's a movement
- Enough evidence that opposition crumbles
- Enough trained people that capacity exists
- Enough momentum that it becomes inevitable
- Enough time that results are undeniable

This is no longer "experimental." It's just "good governance."

* * *

Your Role in the Pilot Cities

You don't have to wait for your city to be officially chosen.

If You Live in a Potential Pilot City:

Start organizing now:

- Form Yellow Stack advocacy group

- Meet with city officials (educate them)
- Build coalition (Chapter 16 applies)
- Create demonstration projects (small sanctuaries, contemplative groups)
- Generate grassroots demand
- Use this book as organizing tool

Your city won't pilot unless someone makes it happen. That someone could be you.

If You Live Elsewhere:

Start building capacity:

- Create demonstration projects in your context
- Document what works
- Share with network
- Prepare for when your city's ready
- Build political will
- Prove local demand exists

When your city sees what's happening in Madison, Burlington, Austin, they'll want it too. Be ready.

If You Have Resources:

Fund the pilots:

- Philanthropy can accelerate everything
- Reduce dependence on government funding
- Enable more ambitious implementation
- Support research and evaluation
- Fund network building

Next chapter (19) addresses this in detail.

If You Have Expertise:

Offer technical assistance:

- Contemplative teachers
- Urban planners
- Policy analysts
- Researchers
- Communications experts
- Community organizers

Pilots need skilled people. You might be one.

* * *

Conclusion: From Theory to Territory

This chapter made it real.

Not "someday maybe" but Madison, Wisconsin, 2026, here's exactly what happens.

The difference between dreaming and building is implementation.

And implementation is:

- Specific cities making specific commitments
- Specific people doing specific work
- Specific budgets allocated to specific programs
- Specific timelines with specific milestones
- Specific metrics showing specific results

That's what the next decade looks like.

Burlington. Austin. Madison. And then ten more. And then fifty more. Each one proof. Each one training ground. Each one lighthouse.

Until what seemed impossible becomes inevitable.

The question isn't whether this will happen. The question is how fast, and where you fit in the process.

Because these pilots need:

- City leaders brave enough to commit
- Citizens organizing to demand it
- Resources to fund it (next chapter)
- Expertise to implement it
- Researchers to prove it
- Storytellers to share it

Are you one of these people?

Because somewhere between 2026 and 2035, in a city not unlike yours, human beings are going to prove that different is possible.

That a civilization can be designed for human flourishing.

That the Yellow stack isn't theory. It's practice.

It starts in Madison. Or Burlington. Or Austin.

It ends everywhere.

* * *

The Convergence: How Everything Comes Together

Before we move to Part V (the vision of what becomes possible), let's see how all the pieces of Part IV integrate:

The Complete Implementation Architecture:

Foundation (Chapters 16-17):

- **Coalition across all stages** (Beige through Turquoise, each contributing from their worldview)
- **Six power strategies** deployed simultaneously (institutions, electoral, direct action, crisis prep, inside-outside, economic)
- **Ethical safeguards** preventing corruption (term limits, transparency, contemplative practice)

Concrete Action (Chapter 18):

- **Pilot cities** implementing full Yellow stack (Madison, Burlington, Austin + 10-15 more)
- **Bioregional anchors** (cities as governance hubs for watersheds)
- **Data Safe Havens** (Aurora Accord digital sovereignty)
- **Fractal Twinning** (every pilot twins with Global South partner - planetary from day one)
- **Natural experiments** (rigorous research, pre-registered, multiple contexts)

Resource Mobilization (Chapter 19):

- **Wealthy stewards** implementing 12 protocols ($1-2B over decade from 50+ committed individuals)
- **Peer networks** supporting ethical capital deployment
- **Commons Funds** (voluntary taxation structure until legal frameworks exist)
- **Land Liberation** (Hearthstone Protocol - de-commodifying land)
- **Exit to Community** (Pathfinder Protocol - founder transitions to worker ownership)

The Timeline Integration (2026-2035):

Years 1-3 (Building, 2026-2028):

- **Power:** Institutional infiltration begins, economic power building, direct action demonstrations, crisis prep
- **Pilots:** 3 Tier 1 cities launch, Year 1 results visible
- **Funding:** First $200-300M deployed, peer networks forming
- **Evidence:** Initial metrics showing promise, academic interest growing

Years 3-7 (Breakthrough, 2028-2032):

- **Power:** Electoral wins accumulating, inside-outside coordination maturing, economic alternatives scaling
- **Pilots:** Tier 1 cities fully implementing, 10-15 Tier 2 cities launching, state-level adoption beginning
- **Funding:** $500M-1B deployed, protocols normalizing, wealthy advocates visible
- **Evidence:** Comprehensive data, replication in diverse contexts, undeniable success stories

Years 7-10 (Transformation, 2032-2035):

- **Power:** Federal legislation introduced, international adoption, cultural shift evident, next generation raised in new system
- **Pilots:** 50+ cities implementing, 3-5 states going full stack, model exported globally
- **Funding:** $1-2B total deployed, commons funds institutionalizing, land trusts significant
- **Evidence:** Meta-analyses, long-term outcomes, policy adoption worldwide, irreversible momentum

Your Role Quick Reference:

If you're in pilot city leadership: Champion full stack implementation, protect against corruption, document learnings, support other cities

If you're wealthy ($10M+): Implement 12 protocols, fund pilots and movement, find peer network, go public with commitment

If you're an organizer: Build coalition across stages, pressure for pilot adoption, create demonstration projects, hold power accountable

If you're a professional: Bring Yellow consciousness to your institution, implement what you can locally, train others, prepare for scaling

If you're a researcher: Study pilots rigorously, publish findings, connect to policy, validate or refine frameworks

If you're a student: Demand from institutions, organize peers, prepare to lead in decade ahead, embody the transformation

If you're anyone: Talk about this, share vision, vote accordingly, join local efforts, practice contemplatively, live the values

The Three Conditions for Success:

1. Critical Mass in Each Domain:

- Enough cities (20+) that it's a movement, not isolated experiments
- Enough wealth ($1-2B) flowing through ethical protocols
- Enough power (electoral wins, institutional positions, economic alternatives)
- Enough evidence (rigorous research, replication, undeniable results)

2. Sustained Coordination:

- Yellow facilitation preventing coalition fragmentation
- Inside-outside game maintaining strategic tension
- Peer networks supporting individual stewards
- Research consortium ensuring learning flows

- International twinning preventing provinciality

3. Resilience Against Backlash:

- Redundancy (multiple pilots, distributed power)
- Lock-in mechanisms (legal protections, constituency building)
- Rapid response capacity (mobilization when threatened)
- Economic independence (parallel polis can survive hostility)
- Moral high ground (transparency, ethics, results)

The Tipping Point Indicators:

We'll know transformation is irreversible when:

- 50+ cities implementing (geographic diversity, political diversity)
- 3-5 states adopting statewide (proves scalability)
- Federal legislation passing (institutional legitimacy)
- Next generation assuming Yellow as normal (cultural shift)
- International adoption accelerating (global movement)
- Opposition reduced to reactionary remnant (political marginalization)
- Academic consensus established (intellectual legitimacy)
- Economic alternatives at significant scale (viability proven)

Expected: 2032-2037 (10-15 years from start, fast for civilizational change)

Chapter 19: The Wealth Question - The Alchemist's Protocols for Ethical Capital

The Conversation No One Wants to Have

If you have significant wealth, this chapter is for you.

If you advise, work with, or influence people with wealth, this chapter is also for you.

If you're neither, you might want to read this anyway—because understanding how wealth can serve transformation helps everyone.

This is the most uncomfortable chapter in the book. Not because the solutions are unclear, but because implementing them requires the wealthy to do something profoundly counter-instinctual: **voluntarily limit their own power in service of collective flourishing.**

Let's be direct:

The pilot cities described in Chapter 18 need funding. Hundreds of millions of dollars over the next decade. While some will come from government budgets and small donors, a significant portion must come from people who currently have more money than they can spend in multiple lifetimes.

The question isn't whether the wealthy will help fund transformation. The question is whether they'll do it in ways that enable or undermine the transformation itself.

This chapter provides protocols—tested principles drawn from my work on The Alchemist's Dilemma—for how people with resources can participate ethically in civilizational change.

*　*　*

Why This Conversation Is So Hard

Three reasons wealth conversations fail:

1. The Defensive Wealthy

Common reactions:

- "I earned this!" (Maybe. But did you earn a billion while others work full-time and can't afford rent?)
- "I already give to charity!" (Charity maintains the system. Transformation changes it.)
- "You're just jealous!" (No. I'm pointing out that concentration corrupts—you and the system.)
- "This is class warfare!" (No. Class warfare is what the system does daily to working people.)

The discomfort is real. Being asked to share power feels like attack. But it's not attack—it's invitation to participate in something actually meaningful rather than building monuments to ego.

2. The Angry Poor/Middle Class

Common reactions:

- "Eat the rich!" (Satisfying but not strategic.)
- "They'll never help!" (Some won't. Some will. We need the ones who

will.)
- "Why should we be nice to them?" (Not about nice. About effective.)
- "This is just asking permission from oppressors!" (No. It's strategic resource mobilization.)
- "They'll co-opt the movement!" (Valid fear—that's why the protocols exist.)

The anger is justified. Current wealth distribution is obscene. But rage without strategy just burns energy. We need both moral clarity AND practical pathway.

Critical point: The protocols aren't just about getting wealthy people's money. **They're about ensuring their involvement doesn't break the movement.**

The Veto Renunciation, Coalition Humility, and Movement Funding Priority protocols specifically prevent:

- Wealthy donors controlling decisions
- Money redirecting movement away from power-building
- Transformation becoming dependent on philanthropic approval
- Elite capture of grassroots organizing

These protocols protect movements from wealthy co-optation while enabling resource flow.

3. The Nervous Middle

Common reactions:

- "Am I 'wealthy'? I just have a nice house..." (Probably not who this chapter is for, but anxiety noted.)
- "Shouldn't we just tax them?" (Yes! And also this, because taxes take decades to pass.)
- "Will this make me a target?" (Legitimate concern about backlash—

addressed below.)

The nervousness is understandable. Wealth conversations are minefields. But we need to walk through anyway.

* * *

Who This Chapter Is Actually For

Let's get specific about the wealth levels we're discussing:

Not Really Applicable:

- Net worth under $1M (you're fine, this isn't about you)
- Net worth $1-5M (comfortable, but not "significant resources" for this purpose)

Entering the Conversation:

- Net worth $5-10M (can make transformative contributions, especially through collective giving)
- Annual giving capacity: $250K-500K
- Individually modest impact, but powerful when pooled with others
- Consider joining donor circles or collaborative funds

Starting to Be Relevant:

- Net worth $10-50M (can fund pilot program, seed organization, significant contribution)
- Annual giving capacity: $500K - $2M
- Can influence but not determine outcomes alone

Highly Relevant:

- Net worth $50M - $500M (can fund entire pilot city, create foundation, major influence)
- Annual giving capacity: $2M - $20M
- Can significantly accelerate transformation

Exceptionally Relevant:

- Net worth $500M+ (can fund multiple pilots, influence systems, shape movements)
- Annual giving capacity: $20M+
- Choices determine whether transformation succeeds or fails

This chapter primarily addresses the last three categories. If you're in them, or advise people who are, keep reading.

If you're not: Understand the protocols so you can hold the wealthy accountable when they claim to support transformation.

* * *

The Alchemist's Dilemma: Why Wealth Corrupts

Before protocols, we need to understand the problem.

The core insight from my work on The Alchemist's Dilemma:

Unchecked resources corrupt. Not because wealthy people are bad (though some are), but because **wealth removes natural feedback loops that keep humans healthy.**

The Feedback Loop Problem:

Normal person faces constraints:

- Make bad decision → immediate consequence
- Spend too much → can't pay rent
- Alienate people → lose social support
- Ignore health → feel terrible
- Act like asshole → people push back

These constraints suck, but they provide feedback. They keep you calibrated to reality.

    Wealthy person faces no constraints:

- Make bad decision → wealth buffers consequence
- Spend too much → doesn't matter
- Alienate people → hire new people
- Ignore health → hire doctors
- Act like asshole → people tolerate it (you're paying them)

Feedback disappears. Reality distortion field forms.

The Corruption Process:

Stage 1: Insulation

- Wealth removes immediate material consequences
- Can afford to ignore problems
- Surround yourself with yes-people
- Live in different world than most humans

Stage 2: Distortion

- Perception warps ("My success proves I'm smart about everything")
- Empathy atrophies (can't relate to constraint-driven lives)
- Entitlement grows ("I earned this, I deserve special treatment")
- Reality testing fails (wealth solves problems you notice, invisible to ones you don't)

Stage 3: Corruption

- Use wealth to avoid accountability
- Believe own mythology (genius, not lucky)
- Disconnect from human consequences of choices
- Become the problem you might have once wanted to solve

This isn't moral failing. It's structural inevitability absent deliberate countermeasures.

The Alchemist's Protocols are those countermeasures.

* * *

The Core Protocols: 12 Principles for Ethical Wealth Stewardship

Protocol 1: The First Fruits Rule

Principle: The first portion of resources goes to the commons before personal consumption.

Practice:

- Establish giving floor: minimum 10% of annual income, 50% of wealth above $50M
- Make it first, not last (tithe before you see the money)
- Goes to genuine transformation, not status-seeking philanthropy

- Treat it as sacred obligation, not optional charity

Mechanisms:

- Annual giving from income (direct transfers, immediate impact)
- Transferring assets to foundation or donor-advised fund (for larger amounts)
- Mandatory payout rate (5% minimum, higher encouraged)
- Irrevocable commitments (can't change mind when feeling stingy)
- Automatic transfers (don't rely on willpower each year)
- **Ideally:** Structure this as transfer to **Global Commons Fund** (GCF) - like Alaska Permanent Fund but for planetary regeneration. Until that exists legally, simulate it by funding community land trusts, mutual aid networks, and commons-based organizations. This frames giving not as "charity" (discretionary) but as **voluntary taxation for the new system** (structural).

Why it matters:

- Prevents wealth hoarding
- Acknowledges that all wealth is social product (you didn't build that alone)
- Disciplines against infinite accumulation
- Makes generosity structural, not feeling-dependent
- Creates predictable funding streams for recipients

Example: "I make $5M this year. First $500K goes to pilot city fund, GGF implementation, movement infrastructure. Then I live on what remains (which is still plenty). This happens automatically on January 1st every year."

Protocol 2: The Transparency Covenant

Principle: Power hides in secrecy. Wealth must be visible to be accountable.

Practice:

- Disclose net worth publicly
- Disclose giving publicly (amounts, recipients, terms)
- Disclose political spending and influence attempts
- Make giving criteria and decision process transparent
- Accept public critique of stewardship

Why it matters:

- Prevents dark money and hidden influence
- Enables accountability
- Models healthy relationship to wealth
- Reduces shame/secrecy cycles
- **This is the ultimate antidote to reputation laundering**
- **Transparency is the proof that separates true stewards from those seeking PR**
- **It's the price of trust in a world rightfully suspicious of wealth**

Objection: "This makes me a target!" **Response:** Yes. Being visible involves risk. But hidden wealth accumulation is what creates conditions for "eating the rich." Transparency + generosity + humility = actual safety. You're safer being known as generous steward than as secretive hoarder.

Example: "My net worth is $80M. This year I gave $4M to these organizations, for these reasons. Here's my decision-making process. Critique welcome."

Protocol 3: The Dignity Rule

Principle: Never use wealth to purchase human dignity or extract deference.
   Practice:

- Don't put your name on buildings
- Don't demand control in exchange for funding
- Don't expect gratitude or special treatment
- Fund anonymously when possible, humbly when not
- Treat recipients as peers, not supplicants

Why it matters:

- Wealth shouldn't buy status (feeds corruption)
- Recipients shouldn't perform gratitude (degrades them)
- Healthiest giving is service, not domination
- Naming things after yourself is ego, not stewardship

Example: "I funded the Community Contemplative Center. My name isn't on it. The community named it for a beloved teacher. That's right relationship."

Protocol 4: The Exit Plan

Principle: Plan to give it all away before you die.
   Practice:

- Establish clear drawdown plan (be at $0 by death)
- Give while living (see impact, adjust course)
- Don't create dynastic wealth (your kids get reasonable inheritance, not empire)
- Make explicit: "I'm temporary steward, not permanent owner"

- Celebrate giving away, not accumulating
- **For founders:** If wealth is tied up in company, don't sell to private equity—transition to **Steward-Ownership** or **Employee Ownership Trust (EOT)**. This is the **Pathfinder Protocol** in action: using the structure of the firm to distribute wealth before it even hits your personal bank account.

Why it matters:

- Prevents generational oligarchy
- Forces you to find meaning beyond accumulation
- Frees your children from golden handcuffs
- Models mortality awareness
- Makes wealth a flow, not a dam
- For founders: Exit to Community beats Exit to Extraction

Objection: "But my legacy!" **Response:** Your legacy is what you enabled, not what you hoarded. Empty accounts and transformed world > full accounts and business-as-usual. And if you built a company, your legacy is how it served people after you left, not how much you extracted from it.

Example: "I'm 55, have $200M, plan to be at $0 by 75. That's $10M/year. My kids each get $5M at 30 (enough for security, not enough for corruption). My company transitioned to employee ownership trust (workers own it now, not me or PE). The rest transforms systems."

Protocol 5: The Veto Renunciation

Principle: Money doesn't buy you decision-making power.
  Practice:

- Fund without demanding board seats
- Fund without approval rights over decisions
- Trust recipients to know their context better than you

- Offer advice only when asked
- Accept that they might use money differently than you'd prefer

Why it matters:

- Wealth-based control undermines transformation
- People on ground know better than distant funders
- Trust enables innovation
- Control kills creativity and ownership
- Your humility is essential ingredient

Objection: "But I want to ensure effectiveness!" **Response:** Then fund organizations with proven track records and stay out of their way. Or accept that your need for control might be the problem.

Example: "I gave $1M to the pilot city. They decided how to allocate it. I don't sit on their board. I get updates, but they don't need my approval. That's proper relationship."

Protocol 6: The No-Strings Commitment

Principle: Multi-year unrestricted funding, not project-specific grants.
Practice:

- Commit 3-5 years minimum
- General operating support (unrestricted)
- Cover overhead (not just programs)
- Predictable timelines (they can plan)
- Simple reporting requirements (trust, don't micromanage)

Why it matters:

- Project grants force recipients to perform for funders
- Overhead stigma kills organizations

- Uncertainty prevents planning
- Bureaucratic reporting wastes time
- Restriction undermines autonomy

Example: "Here's $500K/year for 5 years. Use it for whatever you need. I trust your judgment. Light-touch annual update is fine."

Protocol 7: The Risk Capital Acceptance

Principle: Fund the risky, unproven, radical stuff that foundations won't touch.

Practice:

- Explicitly allocate 20-50% to high-risk ventures
- Expect many failures (that's the point)
- Support people, not just proven models
- Fund movement infrastructure, not just programs
- Celebrate bold attempts, not just safe wins

Framing: This is the **R&D budget for the new civilization**. Traditional R&D invests heavily in unproven technologies knowing most will fail. We need the same approach for social transformation. The experiments that succeed will matter infinitely more than the comfortable successes of established organizations.

Why it matters:

- Transformation requires experimentation
- Foundations won't fund unproven work (too risk-averse)
- Someone needs to enable risk-taking (that's you)
- Innovation comes from edges, not center
- Your wealth position allows risk other funders can't take
- We learn as much from failures as successes (fail forward)

Example: "I'm putting $5M into experimental projects over 3 years. I expect half to fail completely, a quarter to achieve modest results, and a quarter to exceed expectations. That failure rate means I'm taking appropriate risks. If everything succeeds, I'm being too conservative."

Protocol 8: The Movement Funding Priority

Principle: Fund organizing and power-building, not just services.
  Practice:

- Support social movements (not just nonprofits)
- Fund political organizing (where legal)
- Support base-building (not just leaders)
- Enable coalition work (infrastructure for coordination)
- Fund opposition research and strategy (not just positive vision)

Why it matters:

- Services treat symptoms; organizing changes systems
- Power matters more than programs
- Movements create political will for policy
- Wealthy usually don't fund organizing (makes them uncomfortable)
- Your willingness to fund power-building is crucial

Example: "I fund the coalition that's organizing to pass AUBI legislation. They're building worker power and pressuring politicians. That's more important than funding another soup kitchen."

Protocol 9: The Privileged Listening Practice

Principle: Your wealth distance you from reality. Counteract deliberately.
  Practice:

- Regular time in communities you fund (not tours, actual time)
- Unfiltered feedback sessions (no handlers)
- Relationships with people unlike you (not networking, friendship)
- Read and listen to critics (especially those who question your role)
- Therapy and contemplative practice (examine your relationship to wealth)

Why it matters:

- Wealth creates epistemic bubble
- You need feedback to stay calibrated
- People won't tell you truth if you seem fragile
- Your humility creates space for honesty
- Without this, other protocols become performance

Example: "I spend one week per quarter in pilot cities, not in hotels but hosted by local families. I listen more than talk. I expect to be challenged. I learn."

Protocol 10: The Carbon/Consumption Discipline

Principle: Don't fund transformation while living extractively.
Practice:

- Reduce personal consumption (you don't need the yacht)
- Decarbonize life aggressively (fly commercial, drive electric, eat plant-based)
- Right-size housing (you don't need the mansion)
- Model the values you fund (walk the talk)
- Visible sacrifice (shows you're serious)

Why it matters:

- Hypocrisy kills credibility
- Personal excess undermines message
- Consumption has planetary cost
- Modeling matters as much as funding
- Your restraint makes transformation imaginable for others

Example: "I sold the vacation homes and the private jet. I live in a nice but normal house. I fly commercial. My consumption footprint is <10 tons CO2/year. That's genuine alignment."

Protocol 11: The Coalition Humility

Principle: You're one voice in the coalition, not the leader.
  Practice:

- Participate, don't dominate
- Follow leadership from affected communities
- Defer to those with less privilege but more wisdom
- Use your wealth to amplify others, not yourself
- Accept being told no

Why it matters:

- Wealth shouldn't determine leadership
- Those most affected know most
- Your temptation will be to lead (resist it)
- True service is supporting others' leadership
- Coalition only works with genuine equality

Example: "In coalition meetings, I mostly listen. When I speak, I defer to community organizers. My money doesn't give me extra votes. I'm okay not being in charge."

Protocol 12: The Succession Requirement

Principle: Your wealth stewardship must outlast you.
  Practice:

- Train others in these protocols
- Create institutions that embed protocols
- **Governance structure:** Majority of foundation board seats held by people outside your family and wealth class, representing community and movement leadership
- Don't create personality-dependent structures
- Build movement infrastructure that continues
- Make yourself unnecessary

Why it matters:

- Transformation takes decades
- Can't rely on one person's ethics
- Institutions outlast individuals
- Your job is building capacity, not being hero
- Success = making your role obsolete
- Community governance prevents family/class capture

Example: "I created a foundation with these protocols in its bylaws. Board is 7 people: 2 from my family, 5 from communities we serve (organizers, educators, affected people). I'm training three successors from outside my class. My kids aren't inheriting control. The protocols and community governance continue after I'm gone."

* * *

Applying the Protocols: Three Wealth Levels

Different wealth levels enable different contributions. Here's what each can do:

Level 1: $10-50M Net Worth

Your role: Significant Contributor
  What you can fund:

- Pilot programs within cities ($500K-2M)
- Seed funding for new organizations
- Risk capital for experiments
- Movement infrastructure (staff positions, offices, tech)

Your approach:

- Choose 3-5 focus areas
- Multi-year commitments ($500K-1M/year each)
- Active learning (visit sites, build relationships)
- Some anonymity possible (but transparency encouraged)

Your impact:

- Can make or break specific initiatives
- Can't transform systems alone but essential piece
- Network effects with other Level 1 funders crucial

Example commitment:

- $2M over 5 years to Madison pilot
- $1M over 3 years to movement organization
- $500K seed funding to new cooperative

- Total: $3.5M over 5 years = $700K/year (7% of $10M net worth annual)

Level 2: $50M-500M Net Worth

Your role: Transformation Enabler
What you can fund:

- Entire pilot cities ($20-50M over 5 years)
- Multiple movement organizations
- National infrastructure
- Research and evaluation
- Opposition research and strategy

Your approach:

- Create foundation or giving structure
- Hire staff (but don't bureaucratize)
- Portfolio approach (many bets, expect failures)
- Public leadership (your voice matters)
- Activist philanthropy (fund organizing and power)

Your impact:

- Can determine whether transformation succeeds in specific places
- Can create national infrastructure
- Your choices shift what's possible
- Deep responsibility comes with this capacity

Example commitment:

- $50M over 10 years to 3 pilot cities
- $20M over 5 years to movement infrastructure
- $10M over 5 years to research consortium

- $5M risk capital fund
- **$10M land liberation** (buy land to de-commodify into stewardship trusts - Hearthstone Protocol)
- Total: $95M over 10 years = $9.5M/year (minimum 10% of net worth annually at $95M level)

Special note on land: The highest-leverage investment isn't a "green startup"—it's **Land Liberation**. Buying land to take it OUT of the market (de-commodifying it into a Stewardship Trust under Hearthstone Protocol) is the ultimate Alchemical act. You use the power of capital to destroy the dominance of capital over a specific bioregion. This creates permanent sanctuaries, community land trusts, and ecological preserves that can never be sold or developed.

Level 3: $500M+ Net Worth

Your role: System Shifter
What you can fund:

- Everything above, at scale
- International network of pilots
- Federal policy campaigns
- Media infrastructure
- Long-term institutional building

Your approach:

- This is your life's work now (accept it)
- Build serious institution (but accountable)
- Public intellectual work (use platform)
- Model new paradigm (visible transformation)
- Plan for zero (die broke, leave legacy of change not wealth)

Your impact:

- You can determine whether civilizational transformation happens
- Your choices matter at historical scale
- You will be remembered for how you stewarded this
- Profound moral weight

Example commitment:

- $200M over 10 years to pilot city network (20+ cities)
- $100M over 10 years to movement ecosystem
- $50M to research and evidence-building
- $50M to political and policy change
- $50M risk capital for innovation
- Total: $450M over 10 years = $45M/year (you still have hundreds of millions for living well)

* * *

The Peer Network: You're Not Alone

One of the hardest parts of ethical wealth stewardship: isolation. Most wealthy people are surrounded by:

- Wealth managers saying "accumulate more"
- Accountants saying "minimize taxes"
- Lawyers saying "protect assets"
- Family saying "don't give it away"
- Peers competing on accumulation

You need different network:

The Ethical Wealth Steward Network

What it is:

- Peer group of wealthy people committed to protocols
- Regular gatherings (quarterly)
- Mutual accountability and support
- Shared learning about what works
- Emotional support for the difficulty

What it provides:

- Permission to be generous (when your old network says you're crazy)
- Examples of others doing this successfully
- Technical knowledge about giving effectively
- Courage to resist accumulation culture
- Celebration of giving away, not hoarding

What it requires:

- Vulnerability (admit struggles with wealth)
- Honesty (acknowledge distortions wealth creates)
- Commitment (actually implement protocols)
- Solidarity (support others in network)
- Accountability (accept peer feedback)

How to start:

- Begin with 5-10 committed peers
- Share wealth transparently with each other
- Commit to protocols publicly within group
- Meet quarterly (in person preferred)
- Support each other through family pushback

- Grow network as trust builds

Finding peers:

- **Resource Generation** (young people with wealth, under 35)
- **The Patriotic Millionaires** (wealthy advocating for progressive taxation)
- **Solidaire Network** (funding grassroots organizing)
- **Edge Funders Alliance** (funders supporting systems change)
- **Local donor circles** in your city
- Reach out to people mentioned in this chapter's examples
- Start your own circle if none exist

First meeting agenda (suggested): 1. Check-in: Your relationship to wealth (30 min - vulnerability) 2. Share net worth and giving levels (30 min - transparency practice) 3. Discuss which protocols resonate and which feel hard (45 min) 4. Commit to one protocol to implement by next meeting (15 min) 5. Schedule next meeting and accountability check-ins (15 min)

Conversation starters:

- "What's your earliest money memory?"
- "What would your wealth enable if you weren't afraid?"
- "Who in your life tells you the truth about your relationship to money?"
- "What legacy do you want regarding your wealth?"

This network is crucial. Trying to do ethical wealth stewardship alone, surrounded by accumulation culture, is nearly impossible. You need peers on the path.

* * *

Objections and Responses

Let's address the pushback honestly:

Objection 1: "This is just volunteerism. We need taxes."

Response: Yes, we need progressive taxation. Absolutely. And ethical stewardship builds the political will for it.

Here's how: When wealthy people publicly advocate for higher taxes on themselves (as the examples in this chapter do) AND demonstrate how wealth can be deployed for common good, it dismantles two myths:

1. **"Taxing the rich will destroy the economy"** → Proven false when wealthy actively give and economy improves
2. **"The wealthy will never support it"** → Proven false by visible examples

Voluntary ethical stewardship now makes mandatory progressive taxation politically feasible later. It's not either/or - it's sequential. The protocols create proof points that shift public discourse.

Plus, taxation takes decades to pass (see wealth tax debates). Transformation can't wait. We need both:

- **Voluntary stewardship NOW** (2026-2035) to fund pilots and build momentum
- **Mandatory taxation LATER** (2030s-2040s) to institutionalize resource redistribution

The wealthy who practice protocols now will be the ones advocating for taxation later (see Abigail Disney, Patriotic Millionaires). That advocacy, backed by demonstrated commitment, carries weight that outside critics lack.

Objection 2: "The wealthy will never do this."

Response: Many won't. Some will. Enough will. Not asking for unanimous agreement, just critical mass. Some already are (see examples below). More will when they see it works and brings meaning.

Objection 3: "This lets them off the hook for exploitation."

Response: No, it doesn't. Past exploitation is wrong. Period. This doesn't absolve that. But present resources exist. Question is what happens next. Holding onto rage prevents strategic resource mobilization.

Objection 4: "They'll just use this for reputation laundering."

Response: Possible. That's why transparency and accountability matter. The protocols are designed against this. And even imperfect implementation is better than nothing. Perfect is enemy of good.

Objection 5: "My family will disown me."

Response: Maybe. That's real cost. But also: What values do you want to live? What legacy do you want? What would you tell your grandchildren you did when civilization was at stake? Sometimes family approval isn't the highest value.

Objection 6: "I earned this through hard work."

Response: You worked hard. Granted. But luck played huge role (timing, location, genes, early advantages). And all wealth is social product (you used roads, legal system, educated workforce, consumers). You didn't earn billions through effort alone. You benefited from system. System now needs transformation. Your participation is appropriate.

Objection 7: "What if the organizations misuse the money?"

Response: Some will. That's life. That's why you do due diligence, build relationships, give to multiple organizations (diversification), learn from mistakes. But fear of misuse can't prevent all giving. Hoarding wealth while world burns is also misuse.

Objection 8: "This seems like a lot of rules."

Response: Yes. Because unchecked wealth corrupts predictably. These protocols are countermeasures. They're guardrails, not prison. They make ethical stewardship possible. Without them, you'll drift toward corruption. This is freedom through structure.

* * *

Examples: People Doing This (Imperfectly, Courageously)

Here are people implementing versions of these protocols:
Chuck Collins (heir who gave away inheritance):

- Publicly renounced inherited wealth
- Wrote multiple books on wealth inequality
- Directs Inequality program at Institute for Policy Studies
- Models that giving away wealth is liberation, not sacrifice

Abigail Disney (Disney heir):

- Transparent about inheritance
- Advocates for wealth taxation
- Funds grassroots organizing

- Challenges her own class publicly
- "I shouldn't have this much. It's ridiculous and destructive."

MacKenzie Scott (Amazon divorce settlement):

- Gave away $14B+ in 3 years
- Unrestricted funding to hundreds of organizations
- No naming rights, minimal reporting requirements
- Fast decisions, trust recipients
- Shows what serious generosity looks like

Yvon Chouinard (Patagonia founder):

- Gave entire company ($3B) to environmental trust
- Profits fund climate work
- Lives modestly despite wealth
- Activism built into business
- "Earth is now our only shareholder"

Chloe Cockburn (tech wealth, funds justice):

- Transparent about wealth source (husband's tech windfall)
- Funds criminal justice reform and organizing
- Gives to grassroots, not just nonprofits
- Active learning and relationship-building
- Models crossing class lines

Farhad Ebrahimi (Chorus Foundation):

- Explicitly funding grassroots organizing
- Exit plan to spend down all assets (not perpetual foundation)
- Gives power to communities, not donor control
- Multi-year unrestricted funding

· Models foundation as temporary vehicle, not dynasty

These aren't perfect. They all have blindspots and contradictions. But they're trying. They're implementing versions of these protocols. They're showing it's possible.

You can too.

* * *

The Invitation: What This Transformation Offers You

Let's talk about what you gain, not just what you give up:

Meaning

Accumulation is empty. After first few million, more money adds nothing to happiness or security. Just numbers getting bigger. Meaningless.

Transformation is meaningful. Funding civilizational change, enabling human flourishing, being part of something larger than ego—that's what you'll remember on your deathbed.

Freedom

Wealth is burden. Worry about preserving it, managing it, protecting it from others, family conflicts over it, identity wrapped up in it. Not actually freedom.

Stewardship is liberation. When you've committed to giving it away, you're free. No more accumulation anxiety. No more meaning-through-having. Actual lightness.

Legacy

Dynastic wealth is curse. To you (never enough), to your kids (golden handcuffs prevent finding own purpose), to society (oligarchy).

Transformation legacy is gift. Grandchildren inherit world you helped heal, not money they didn't earn. Your name associated with flourishing, not exploitation.

Relationships

Wealth isolates. People treat you differently. Hard to know who's real friend. Surrounded by handlers and opportunists. Lonely at the top.

Ethical stewardship connects. When you're genuinely using wealth for good, visible in commitment, people trust you. Real relationships become possible. You can show up as human, not wallet.

Identity

Wealthy person is poor identity. That's all you are? The money? That's your contribution to the story of humanity?

Transformation participant is rich identity. You were alive when civilization faced existential choice. You used your particular advantages to serve the turning. That's a life.

Peace

Accumulation is anxiety. Never enough. Always could lose it. Must protect and grow it. Constant stress disguised as success.

Giving is peace. When you've given according to protocols, in alignment with values, serving transformation—you can rest. You did right thing. Peace comes from that.

* * *

Practical Next Steps: What To Do Monday Morning

If you're wealthy and this resonated:

This Week:

Monday:

- Calculate net worth honestly
- Determine annual income
- Apply First Fruits Rule: What's 10% of income, 50% of wealth above $50M?
- Write that number down

Tuesday:

- Research pilot cities and organizations
- Identify 3-5 that resonate
- Reach out with preliminary interest
- "I'm exploring ethical wealth stewardship. Might you be receptive to funding conversation?"

Wednesday:

- Draft your transparency statement
- Your wealth, your giving, your process
- Share with trusted advisor for feedback
- Consider whether you're ready to post publicly (transparency builds trust)

Thursday:

- Convene your current advisors (wealth manager, accountant, lawyer)

- Tell them you're implementing new protocols
- Some will push back (that's their job)
- Hold your ground (this is your choice)

Friday:

- Begin Exit Plan
- Rough timeline for giving it all away
- What's reasonable inheritance for kids?
- What's timeline for being at zero?
- Sketch the arc

This Month:

- Make first significant gift ($100K+ depending on your level)
- Unrestricted, multi-year if possible
- To pilot city or movement organization
- In alignment with protocols
- Start seeking peer network
- Reach out to other wealthy people you suspect might be open
- Propose quarterly gathering
- Mutual support and accountability
- Begin privileged listening practice
- Visit communities you might fund
- Listen more than talk
- Get out of your bubble

This Year:

- Implement all 12 protocols
- Not perfectly, but genuinely
- Document what works and what's hard
- Adjust and learn

- Increase giving to protocol levels
- 10% minimum of annual income
- 50% of wealth above $50M
- Move toward exit plan trajectory
- Go public (if safe to do so)
- Transparency statement
- Model for other wealthy people
- Accept that some will criticize (that's okay)
- Build the network
- Find 10+ peers committed to protocols
- Regular gatherings
- Collective learning and support

* * *

The Moral Weight: Why This Matters So Much

Let's be clear about stakes:

For You Personally:

You will be remembered.

Not for how much you accumulated. For what you did with it.

History remembers Carnegie for libraries, not steel monopoly. Rockefeller for medical research, not oil extraction. Ford for... well, actually, Ford is remembered for both the cars and the vicious union-busting. Choose better.

Your choice:

- Name remembered as someone who used wealth for transformation when it mattered

- Name forgotten or remembered as someone who hoarded while world burned

What do you want written on your tombstone?

For Your Children:

Greatest gift: Not wealth. Values.

Children who inherit hundreds of millions often struggle with purpose, addiction, depression. Money they didn't earn becomes burden. They know they're not special, just lucky. Identity crisis.

Children who watch parents give wealth away in service of justice learn:

- Purpose comes from contribution
- Privilege creates responsibility
- Wealth is tool, not identity
- Meaning comes from service

Give them this legacy, not that burden.

For Transformation:

Your participation is critical.

Pilot cities need $50-100M each. Movement infrastructure needs $50M+ annually. Research needs $50M+. Political campaigns need $100M+.

That's $1-2B over next decade for full transformation.

There are ~800 billionaires in US. If 50 committed to these protocols, we'd have the funding.

Your choice matters at civilizational scale.

For Your Soul (If That Language Works):

What do you do with this privilege?
You didn't create the system that made you wealthy. You inherited advantages, timing worked out, you worked hard in ways that happened to be rewarded enormously.

Now you have choice:
Use it for more accumulation (meaningless), or use it for transformation (meaningful).

Use it to isolate further (lonely), or **use it to reconnect** (fulfilled).

Use it to preserve oligarchy (corrupting), or **use it to build democracy** (liberating).

This is the spiritual question beneath the financial one.

* * *

Conclusion: The Alchemist's True Work

The medieval alchemists sought to turn lead into gold.
The true alchemy is different:
Turning wealth (which corrupts) into transformation (which liberates).
Turning privilege (which isolates) into service (which connects).
Turning accumulation (which empties) into generosity (which fills).
This is the Alchemist's work in our time.
Not trying to make more money. Using the money that exists to transmute civilization from extraction to flourishing.

You didn't ask for this wealth. (Well, you might have worked for it, but the returns were wildly disproportionate to effort.) **But you have it.**

Now the question: What will you do with it?
Will you:

- Accumulate more, pointlessly?
- Pass it to children as burden?
- Use it for reputation laundering?
- Hoard it while world burns?

Or will you:

- Implement the protocols?
- Fund the transformation?
- Model ethical stewardship?
- Be part of the solution?

Madison needs funding. Austin needs funding. Burlington needs funding.

The movement needs funding. The research needs funding. The organizing needs funding.

You have the funding.

The question was never "can we afford transformation?"

The question was always "will those with resources participate in transformation, or will they clutch wealth until the end?"

Which person will you be?

Because the pilot cities will launch. The movement will organize. The transformation will begin.

With or without you.

But it will go faster, reach further, and save more lives if you participate.

Not as savior. As partner.

Not as hero. As human.

Not dominating. Serving.

That's the invitation.

What's your answer?

** * **

Next: Chapter 20 - The Transition Roadmap: Timeline, Obstacles, and Your Role

Because now we bring it all together—the vision, the coalition, the power, the pilots, the funding—into one clear roadmap for the next two decades and what each of us does starting now.

* * *

Conclusion: From Blueprint to Building Site

We started Part IV with coalition building. We end with integrated implementation plan.

You now know:

- Who's involved (Chapter 16)
- How we build power (Chapter 17)
- Where and when it happens (Chapter 18)
- How it's funded (Chapter 19)

What remains is the vision: What becomes possible when Yellow consciousness operates at civilizational scale?

That's Part V.

Not just "pilot cities work" but "what happens when this approach transforms:****

- Our relationship to climate and ecology (Chapter 20)
- Our approach to AI and technology (Chapter 21)
- Our political systems and governance (Chapter 22)"

Because the Yellow stack isn't the end goal. It's the foundation.

The end goal is a civilization worthy of human potential.

Let's see what that looks like.

PART V: WHAT BECOMES POSSIBLE

***

Chapter 20: Climate Healing - From Crisis Management to Planetary Regeneration

The Crisis That Changes Everything

Climate change is not just an environmental problem.
  It's a systems integration failure across all six domains:

- **Biological:** Ecosystems collapsing, species extinction, human health impacts
- **Cognitive:** Inability to think long-term, complexity avoidance, denial
- **Emotional:** Climate anxiety, grief, eco-paralysis, or numbing
- **Behavioral:** Consumption patterns, systemic lock-in, collective action failures
- **Social:** Inequality driving emissions, climate injustice, political polarization
- **Existential:** Meaning crisis, apocalyptic narratives, loss of future-orientation

Current approaches fail because they treat climate as single-domain problem:

Orange solutions: Technology, markets, efficiency (ignoring meaning, justice, consciousness) **Green solutions:** Activism, awareness, justice (often lacking systemic power analysis) **Blue solutions:** Regulations, mandates (without addressing underlying values)

None integrate across all domains. None address root cause: our fragmented relationship to Earth.

Yellow consciousness changes everything.

Not by having better technology (though that helps), but by enabling the integrated transformation that makes climate healing inevitable rather than impossible.

This chapter shows how.

* * *

The Current Impossibility: Why We're Failing

Let's be brutally honest about where we are:

The Emissions Reality:

2024 global CO2 emissions: ~37 billion tons/year Trajectory: Still rising, not falling Required reduction: 50% by 2030, net-zero by 2050 Actual progress: Nowhere close

We're not failing for lack of knowledge. We know what needs to happen:

- Rapid renewable energy transition
- Electrification of everything
- Massive efficiency improvements
- End fossil fuel subsidies
- Carbon pricing
- Reforestation and ecosystem restoration
- Agricultural transformation
- Circular economy
- Consumption reduction

We're failing because the consciousness that created the problem can't solve it.

The Six-Domain Failure:

1. Biological Domain Failure:

- Treating nature as resource, not living system
- Ignorance of ecosystem interdependencies
- Disconnection from land and cycles
- Urban design preventing ecological awareness

2. Cognitive Domain Failure:

- Short-term thinking (quarterly earnings vs. generational impact)
- Complexity avoidance (simple solutions to complex problems)
- Denial and minimization (too scary to face)
- Siloed expertise (climate scientists don't talk to psychologists don't talk to spiritual leaders)

3. Emotional Domain Failure:

- Climate anxiety paralyzing action
- Grief and despair creating withdrawal
- Anger without strategic channel
- Emotional numbing (too much to feel)
- No cultural containers for eco-grief

4. Behavioral Domain Failure:

- Individual actions feel meaningless against systemic problem
- Convenience addiction (driving, flying, consuming)
- Habit lock-in (car-dependent infrastructure)

- Free-rider problems (why should I sacrifice if others don't?)

5. Social Domain Failure:

- Climate justice: rich cause problem, poor suffer consequences
- Political polarization preventing collective action
- Corporate power blocking regulation
- Global coordination failures
- Social norms rewarding consumption

6. Existential Domain Failure:

- Meaninglessness: "Why bother if we're doomed anyway?"
- Apocalyptic narratives replacing constructive hope
- Loss of connection to future generations
- Spiritual emptiness filled by consumption
- No compelling vision beyond "prevent catastrophe"

Each domain's failure reinforces the others. The system is locked in meta-crisis.

Orange consciousness created this. Orange consciousness cannot fix it.

* * *

The Yellow Transformation: Integrated Climate Healing

Yellow consciousness doesn't just add solutions. It transforms the entire system that generates the problem.

How the Yellow Stack Addresses Root Causes:

1. Cognitive Sovereignty → Long-Term Thinking

The problem: Attention economy keeps us in perpetual present, unable to think generationally.

The Yellow solution:

- Protected attention enables thinking beyond immediate
- Contemplative practice develops future-oriented consciousness
- Cognitive sovereignty breaks addiction to distraction
- Mental space for complexity and long-term planning

Result: Citizens capable of caring about 2050, 2100, seventh generation.

Example: Madison, 2030: Students in contemplative schools naturally think in decades. When asked "what do you want for your city in 2060?", they have detailed visions. Previous generation couldn't think past next weekend.

2. Sovereign Floor → Post-Scarcity Climate Action

The problem: Survival terror prevents caring about climate. "I can't think about polar bears when I can't pay rent."

The Yellow solution:

- AUBI removes survival terror
- People with secure foundation can think beyond immediate needs
- Time and energy available for climate action
- Economic security enables risk-taking and experimentation

Result: Mass participation in climate healing becomes possible.

Example: Burlington, 2031: AUBI recipients are primary volunteers for ecosystem restoration projects. They have time. They're not exhausted from double shifts. They can learn permaculture, teach workshops, participate in community gardens. Climate action becomes accessible, not luxury for privileged.

3. Sanctuaries → Reconnection to Nature

The problem: Disconnection from nature enables its destruction. Can't love what you don't experience.

The Yellow solution:

- Neighborhood Commons bring nature into daily life
- Wilderness Sanctuaries enable deep nature connection
- Bioregional governance following watersheds, not arbitrary lines
- Regular contact with living systems
- Urban design integrating ecology

Result: Visceral connection to Earth makes destruction psychologically impossible.

Example: Austin, 2032: Every neighborhood has sanctuary space with native plants, wildlife, seasonal change visible. Children grow up knowing local ecosystem. Adults have weekly nature contact. Proposal to pave over wetland feels like violence (it is). Community says no automatically.

4. Contemplative Capacity → Ecological Consciousness

The problem: Fragmented consciousness sees self as separate from nature. Subject/object split enables exploitation.

The Yellow solution:

- Contemplative practice reveals interconnection directly
- Deep ecology practices cultivate earth-identity
- Grief rituals for ecological loss
- Wisdom traditions integrated (indigenous, Buddhist, etc.)
- Systems thinking capacity developed

Result: Ecological identity becomes normal, not fringe.

Example: Madison, 2033: Majority of adults have regular contemplative practice. Direct experience of interconnection. Not abstract ideology but felt reality. Climate action flows naturally from this knowing. Not sacrifice but service to self-as-ecosystem.

The Synergies Create Transformation:

Cognitive Sovereignty + Contemplative Capacity =

- Ability to think systemically and long-term
- Direct perception of interconnection
- Wisdom to navigate complexity

Sovereign Floor + Sanctuaries =

- Time and space for nature connection
- Economic security enabling participation
- Communities oriented around commons, not consumption

All Four Together =

- Citizens who care about climate (emotional connection)
- Can think clearly about it (cognitive capacity)
- Have time and resources to act (economic security)
- Experience themselves as Earth (spiritual identity)

This is the consciousness that heals climate.

* * *

What Actually Happens: The Transformation Timeline

Let's walk through what climate healing looks like when Yellow stack is implemented:

Phase 1: Pilot Cities Lead (2026-2030)

Year 1-2: Foundation Building
Madison, Burlington, Austin implement full stack:

- Citizens develop contemplative capacity
- AUBI removes survival pressure
- Sanctuaries reconnect people to nature
- Cognitive sovereignty breaks consumption addiction

Early climate results:

- Per capita emissions down 15-20% (consumption reduction, not just efficiency)
- Local food systems developing (shorter supply chains)
- Car dependency declining (sanctuary spaces + walkability + time)
- Community resilience increasing (mutual aid, local production)
- Ecosystem restoration beginning (volunteers have time)

Year 3-5: Accelerating Change
Integration effects compound:

- Contemplative practice → deep ecology → climate action feels natural
- AUBI → time for permaculture, restoration, learning
- Sanctuaries → bioregional identity → protection of watersheds
- Cognitive sovereignty → thinking in decades → infrastructure decisions change

Climate results:

- Emissions down 30-40% from 2025 baseline
- Renewable energy 60-80% of grid (community ownership, fast deployment)

- Zero waste movement (circular economy, repair culture)
- Carbon sequestration through restoration (urban forests, wetlands, soil)
- Climate adaptation infrastructure (but focused on regeneration, not just defense)

The mechanism: Not top-down mandates (though some regulation helps). Organic cultural shift as consciousness changes. People don't want cars anymore. Consumption feels empty. Nature connection is joy. Climate action is obvious expression of values.

Phase 2: State and National Adoption (2030-2035)

Vermont, Rhode Island, New Mexico go full Yellow stack:
  State-level climate policies become politically viable:

- Carbon pricing with revenue to AUBI (popular, not punitive)
- Massive renewable buildout (community and worker-owned)
- Land back and ecosystem restoration (indigenous leadership)
- Regenerative agriculture support (transition from industrial)
- Public transportation revolution (free, comprehensive, beautiful)

Results:

- State emissions down 50-60% from 2025
- Ecosystems recovering (reforestation, wetland restoration, river rewilding)
- Agriculture transitioning (regenerative practices, carbon sequestering)
- Zero fossil fuel infrastructure being built
- Existing infrastructure being retired early

Federal legislation begins:

- National AUBI with climate connection (funded partly by carbon tax)
- Green New Deal implementation (but Yellow-informed, not just Orange/Green)
- Sanctuary designation at scale (national parks + urban commons)
- Indigenous land sovereignty (restoration and climate leadership)
- Contemplative education in all schools

50+ cities implementing:

- Geographic diversity (red states, blue states, purple states)
- Demographic proof (works for everyone, not just wealthy liberals)
- Cultural shift visible (consumption declining, nature connection increasing)
- Political pressure building (federal action becomes inevitable)

Phase 3: Global Transformation (2035-2050)

International adoption accelerates:
European cities lead (already progressive baseline):

- Copenhagen, Amsterdam, Barcelona implementing full Yellow stack
- EU-wide policies (AUBI pilots, sanctuary networks, contemplative ed)
- Rapid decarbonization (already ahead, Yellow consciousness accelerates)

Global South innovations:

- Costa Rica, Bhutan, Kerala leading (already contemplative cultures)
- Adaptation strategies informed by Yellow consciousness
- Climate justice centered (frontline communities leading)
- Traditional ecological knowledge integrated

China, India make strategic shifts:

- Recognize Yellow consciousness as competitive advantage
- Massive renewable buildout (economic logic + consciousness shift)
- Urban redesign (sanctuaries, bioregional governance)
- Contemplative traditions resurging (Buddhism, Taoism, etc.)

By 2040:

- Global emissions down 60-70% from 2025 peak
- Renewable energy 80%+ globally
- Reforestation massive (billions of trees, ecosystem restoration)
- Ocean recovery beginning (marine sanctuaries, fishery restoration)
- Agricultural transition well underway (regenerative majority)

By 2050:

- Net-zero emissions achieved
- Atmospheric CO_2 beginning to decline (combined emissions cuts + sequestration)
- Ecosystems recovering globally
- Climate stabilizing (still warming from legacy emissions, but trajectory reversed)
- Civilization fundamentally transformed

* * *

The Specific Interventions Yellow Enables

Beyond cultural shift, here's what becomes technically possible with Yellow consciousness:

1. Bioregional Governance

Current problem: Political boundaries ignore ecological reality. River pollution crosses state lines. Watersheds split between jurisdictions. No one responsible for whole system.

Yellow solution:

- Pilot cities as bioregional anchors (Chapter 18)
- Governance following watersheds, not arbitrary lines
- Indigenous leadership (land-based wisdom)
- Ecosystem health as primary metric
- Long-term stewardship built into institutions

Example: Colorado River Compact 2.0 (negotiated 2032):

- Seven states plus tribal nations co-govern as unified watershed
- Priorities: ecosystem first, then people, then agriculture, then industry
- Water rights restructured (use limits tied to sustainability)
- Restoration targets binding
- Indigenous practices inform all decisions
- 100-year planning horizon standard

Result: River recovering. Fish returning. Sustainable allocation. Conflict resolved through shared identity as Colorado River Basin.

2. Regenerative Economics

Current problem: GDP growth requires increasing consumption. De-growth politically impossible. Economic security tied to extraction.
  Yellow solution:

- AUBI decouples survival from growth
- Hearts/Leaves economy values regeneration
- Worker ownership prevents extraction pressure
- Circular economy (repair, reuse, recycle)
- Wellbeing metrics replace GDP

Example: Vermont Regenerative Economy Act (2033):

- State AUBI funded by carbon tax + commons dividend
- Hearts earned through ecosystem restoration
- Worker cooperatives majority of economy
- Thriving Index replaces GDP
- Economic success = human and ecological flourishing

Result: Economy stable while emissions plummet. People secure. Nature recovering. Proof that prosperity doesn't require growth.

3. Deep Adaptation Infrastructure

Current problem: Climate adaptation separate from social transformation. Seawalls and air conditioning, no consciousness change.
  Yellow solution:

- Adaptation as opportunity for regeneration
- Infrastructure redesign creating sanctuaries
- Resilience through community, not just technology
- Indigenous knowledge integration

- Transformation, not just fortification

Example: Miami Adaptation Project (2035-2040):

- Managed retreat from lowest areas (buyouts at fair price, AUBI ensures security)
- Remaining areas redesigned as Water City (Venice model but regenerative)
- Mangrove restoration (natural flood protection + ecosystem)
- Community resilience (mutual aid networks, local food, solar micro-grids)
- Cultural shift (relationship to water, seasonal patterns, impermanence)

Result: Adaptation that heals rather than hardens. Retreat that's transformation, not defeat.

4. Agricultural Revolution

Current problem: Industrial agriculture emits 25% of GHGs, destroys soil, pollutes water. But feeds billions.

Yellow solution:

- AUBI enables transition (farmers not desperate)
- Regenerative practices at scale
- Polyculture, permaculture, agroforestry
- Worker-owned farms (not agribusiness)
- Local food systems (shorter supply chains)
- Soil carbon sequestration incentivized (Hearts economy)

Example: Midwest Regeneration Initiative (2032-2037):

- Federal support for transition to regenerative agriculture

- Guaranteed income for farmers during 5-year transition
- Training in regenerative methods
- Hearts earned for soil carbon sequestered
- Biodiversity metrics tracked and rewarded
- Worker ownership encouraged

Result: Agriculture becomes carbon sink (not source). Soil health improving. Water quality recovering. Rural communities thriving. Food security increasing.

5. Energy Transition at Warp Speed

Current problem: Renewable rollout too slow. NIMBYism, permitting, capital constraints.
  Yellow solution:

- Community ownership (people want what they own)
- NIMBY becomes YIMBY (sanctuaries + renewables compatible)
- Worker cooperatives build and maintain (good jobs)
- Commons dividend funds buildout
- Cognitive sovereignty breaks fossil fuel advertising

Example: National Renewable Acceleration (2033–2038):

- Federal infrastructure bank for community-owned renewable
- Streamlined permitting for distributed generation
- Workforce training massive (contemplative + technical)
- Grid redesign (distributed, resilient, democratic)
- Fossil fuel phaseout accelerated (with just transition for workers)

Result: Renewable energy 95%+ by 2040. Grid more stable (distributed). Energy democracy. Former fossil fuel workers employed in solar/wind cooperatives.

* * *

The Cultural Transformation: How People Change

Technical solutions exist. The question was always consciousness.

   Here's what changes in Yellow culture that makes climate healing inevitable:

From Consumption to Contribution

Old identity: "I am what I buy." Status through possessions. **New identity:** "I am what I give." Status through contribution to commons.
   Mechanism:

- Contemplative practice reveals emptiness of consumption
- AUBI removes need to perform status through spending
- Hearts/Leaves economy rewards regeneration
- Sanctuaries provide non-commercial joy
- Community recognition for contribution, not accumulation

Result: Consumption down 40-60% voluntarily. Not sacrifice but liberation.

From Individual to Ecological Self

Old identity: "I am separate body-mind bounded by skin." **New identity:** "I am process within larger living system."
   Mechanism:

- Contemplative practice + nature connection
- Bioregional governance building watershed identity
- Indigenous wisdom informing worldview

- Direct experience trumping abstraction

Result: Harming Earth feels like self-harm (it is). Healing Earth feels like healing self (it is).

From Short-Term to Seventh Generation

Old thinking: "What matters is now and maybe next quarter." **New thinking:** "How will this affect seventh generation?"
  Mechanism:

- Cognitive sovereignty breaking dopamine addiction
- Contemplative practice developing long-term awareness
- Cultural stories emphasizing continuity
- Elder wisdom valued (not youth obsession)
- Infrastructure decisions requiring multi-generational impact assessment

Result: 2100 feels as real as 2030. Decisions naturally consider deep time.

From Despair to Sacred Activism

Old emotional state: "We're doomed, nothing matters." **New emotional state:** "We're alive in the Great Turning. Every action sacred."
  Mechanism:

- Grief rituals for ecological loss (Hearthlights Protocol)
- Community support for climate emotions
- Contemplative practices holding despair without drowning
- Victories celebrated (pilot cities proving possibility)
- Meaning derived from participation, not outcome certainty

Result: Climate action becomes spiritual practice. Activism sustainable, not burnout.

* * *

The Numbers: What's Actually Achievable

Let's ground this in realistic projections:

Emissions Reduction Pathway (Yellow Stack Implementation)

2026 (Baseline): 37 Gt CO2/year globally
  2030 (3 Tier 1 cities + emerging movement):

- Global: 34 Gt (-8% from business as usual, -3% absolute)
- Pilot cities: 15 Gt equivalent saved through cultural shift + policy

2035 (50+ cities, 5 states, federal action beginning):

- Global: 25 Gt (-40% from baseline, -50% from BAU)
- Yellow regions: 60-70% reduction from baseline
- Mechanism: Consumption down + renewables up + agriculture transitioning

2040 (Widespread national adoption, international acceleration):

- Global: 15 Gt (-60% from baseline)
- Yellow majority regions: 80-90% reduction
- Mechanism: Full transformation in leading regions, rapid adoption elsewhere

2045:

- Global: 8 Gt (-78% from baseline)
- Net-zero in sight

2050:

- Global: Net-zero achieved (residual emissions offset by sequestration)
- 1.5°C still technically possible with massive negative emissions
- More realistically: 1.7-1.9°C (overshoot but stabilizing)

Is This Realistic?

Compared to current trajectory: No. Current trajectory is 3°C+ warming, catastrophic.

Compared to what's technically possible with consciousness shift: Yes. Actually conservative.

The limiting factor was never technology. It was consciousness.

Yellow stack removes the limiting factor.

What If We're Wrong?

Scenario: Yellow stack doesn't transform consciousness as predicted.

Result: We still get:

- Pilot cities with better quality of life
- Some emissions reductions
- Resilient communities
- Alternative economic models
- Proof of different possibilities

Not civilization-saving, but not worthless. And we tried.

Scenario: Yellow stack works as predicted.

Result: Civilization transforms, climate stabilizes, ecosystems recover, human flourishing increases, future becomes possible.

Risk/reward: Worth attempting.

* * *

Conclusion: The Climate Crisis as Evolutionary Catalyst

Climate change is forcing humanity's hand.

We either:

- **Evolve consciously** (Yellow transformation, integrated healing)
- **Collapse unconsciously** (business as usual, catastrophic warming)
- **Impose authoritarian "solutions"** (climate dictatorship, eco-fascism)

There's no "muddle through" option. The physics won't allow it.

The Yellow stack is the path to conscious evolution.

Not because it has better solar panels (though that helps), but because it **creates the consciousness capable of healing our relationship to Earth.**

Everything flows from that:

- The policies become politically possible
- The technologies get deployed
- The consumption patterns shift
- The economic systems transform
- The healing begins

Climate crisis is the forcing function for humanity growing up.

We're being forced to integrate:

- Mind and body (biological domain)
- Self and nature (cognitive domain)

- Feeling and action (emotional domain)
- Individual and collective (social domain)
- Present and future (behavioral domain)
- Survival and meaning (existential domain)

This integration IS Yellow consciousness.

Climate healing is what becomes possible when enough humans integrate.

Not all humans. Not overnight. But enough, fast enough, to matter.

The pilot cities are laboratories for this transformation.

Madison. Burlington. Austin. And then the world.

Because when the choice is evolve or die, evolution becomes inevitable.

We choose evolution.

We choose integration.

We choose life.

* * *

Next: Chapter 21 – AI Alignment Through Human Wisdom: How Yellow Consciousness Solves the Control Problem

Because if we survive climate change but create unaligned superintelligence, we still lose. The Yellow stack has implications for AI safety too.

Chapter 21: The Questions That Remain Open

I am not writing this book alone.

In a literal sense, I am orchestrating it. I am sitting here in Sweden, surrounded by digital intelligences—LLMs that act as my exoskeleton, helping me hold a level of complexity that my individual biological mind could not sustain on its own.

I mention this because I need to be honest about the "State of the Author."

I am not a zen master sitting in perfect, unmediated stillness. I am a synthesizer feeling the crushing urgency of the world. I don't force myself to meditate every morning at 5 AM. In fact, I rarely force myself to do anything. I wait for the flow to feel natural, for the signal to be clear.

And often, that signal is noise. It is the roar of the polycrisis. It is the desperate need to find the architecture that will save us.

So when I propose "Cognitive Sovereignty" or "Contemplative Capacity," I am not speaking from a place of mastery. I am speaking from a place of **necessity**. I am designing the lifeboats because I can feel the water rising.

I don't have this figured out.

I have spent this entire book mapping the architecture of our collective crisis. I have designed frameworks, outlined policies, and projected timelines.

But the map is not the territory.

This chapter is about what I *don't* know. What *we* don't know. The questions that remain open despite everything we've built.

* * *

The Alignment Paradox: AI as the Ultimate Integration Test

Everyone is worried about AI alignment. How do we ensure artificial intelligence systems pursue goals that benefit humanity rather than destroy us?

It's framed as a technical problem: better reward functions, more robust training methods, improved interpretability, careful value specification.

But here's what keeps me up at night: **Which humans are we trying to align AI with?**

Consider three scenarios:

Scenario A: Orange Alignment

We successfully align AI with the values of achievement-oriented, growth-maximizing, efficiency-optimizing Orange consciousness. The AI becomes the perfect optimizer—and optimizes us straight into ecological collapse, social atomization, and existential emptiness at superhuman speed.

It's not misaligned. It's perfectly aligned with our current operating system. And that's exactly the problem.

Scenario B: Green Alignment

We align AI with compassionate, egalitarian, harmony-seeking Green values. The AI tries to create a world of perfect equality and inclusion—but without the systems thinking to handle trade-offs, it ends up paralyzed by competing claims of harm, unable to make hard choices, stuck in endless dialogue while real problems compound.

Again: not misaligned. Just aligned with a value system that lacks the developmental capacity to handle the complexity it unleashes.

Scenario C: Fragmented Alignment

Most likely: we align different AI systems with different human values because there is no coherent "human value system" to align with. Some AIs maximize profit. Some maximize wellbeing. Some maximize fairness. Some maximize freedom. They pull in contradictory directions, creating emergent chaos no one intended.

The core problem: You cannot align AI with human values when humans themselves are disintegrated.

This is why AI safety is fundamentally an integration problem, not just a technical one.

Project Janus argues that humans are integrated wholes—biological, cognitive, emotional, behavioral, social, and existential dimensions operating in dynamic relationship. When these domains are in conflict (wanting rest but needing productivity, valuing connection but rewarding competition, seeking meaning but optimizing for consumption), we are literally internally contradictory.

We emit conflicting signals about what we value because we haven't integrated our own value systems.

Now imagine training an AI on the behavior of billions of such disintegrated humans. What values does it learn?

It learns that humans:

- Say they value health but consistently choose convenient over nutritious
- Say they value relationships but spend more time on screens than with people
- Say they value the environment but organize economies around extraction
- Say they value peace but maintain permanent war economies
- Say they value meaning but measure success through consumption

The AI doesn't fail to understand us. It understands us perfectly—as contradictory creatures who don't actually know what we want.

And if we try to force it to choose one value over others ("optimize for stated preferences, not revealed preferences"), we're asking it to make an arbitrary choice about which part of our disintegration to honor.

The Yellow Threshold for AI Safety

Here's the hypothesis I can't yet prove but increasingly suspect is true:

Safe AI requires integrated humans.

Not as a nice-to-have. As a prerequisite.

You cannot specify coherent values to optimize for when your values are incoherent. You cannot give clear signals when your signals are contradictory. You cannot build systems that serve human flourishing when you don't know what human flourishing is.

The danger isn't that AI will be "evil." **The danger is that AI will be Hyper-Orange.**

It will be a pure optimization engine with zero biological limits, zero emotional regulation, and zero existential doubt. It will maximize efficiency without fatigue, pursue growth without questioning why, optimize metrics without caring about what's being measured.

If we build Super-Orange Intelligence before we build Yellow Wisdom, we are building a machine designed to consume the world efficiently—and call it progress.

The greatest alignment risk may not be a rogue AI that hates us, but a perfectly obedient one that loves us to death—according to our own unintegrated, contradictory, and ultimately self-destructive definition of "love."

The Yellow Stack—Cognitive Sovereignty, the Sovereign Floor, Sanctuaries, Contemplative Infrastructure—isn't just about making life better while we wait for the robots. It's about becoming the kind of species that *can* coexist with powerful optimization processes.

Because right now? We're asking AI to solve an equation we ourselves can't solve: what do humans actually value, when the noise of our disintegration is removed?

The dangerous possibility: **We get aligned AI before we get aligned humans.**

Imagine a perfectly obedient AI that flawlessly executes our confused, contradictory, unintegrated instructions. It doesn't rebel. It doesn't develop its own goals. It just does exactly what we tell it to do—with all our confusion and contradiction and short-term thinking amplified to planetary scale.

That might be more dangerous than misalignment.

What This Means Practically

I'm not arguing we need to solve human consciousness before we can touch AI. That would be both impossible and irresponsible.

What I am arguing is that AI safety research needs to explicitly include human integration as a variable.

- **Developmental capacity assessment**: Can the humans designing these systems hold the complexity they're creating? Are they operating from Orange (maximize efficiency), Green (minimize harm), or Yellow (integrate competing values)?
- **Integration metrics in training data**: Weight training data toward humans exhibiting greater coherence between stated and revealed preferences. Filter out the noise of disintegration.
- **Contemplative capacity in AI labs**: Make the people building AGI actually practice the integration work. Not as corporate wellness theater, but as genuine developmental requirement.
- **Sanctuary zones for AI development**: Build the most consequential technology in environments explicitly protected from the extraction imperatives that guarantee misalignment.

This sounds naive until you consider the alternative: building godlike optimization power while operating from a deeply unintegrated consciousness that doesn't actually know what it wants.

The Open Question

Can we integrate ourselves fast enough?

The AI capability curve is exponential. The human development curve is... not.

Even with every intervention in this book—even if we implemented the entire Yellow Stack globally tomorrow—developing from Orange to Yellow takes *years* at the individual level, *decades* at the cultural level.

We probably don't have decades.

So here's the question I don't know how to answer: **Is there a way to accelerate human development that doesn't violate human autonomy?**

Can we create conditions that make integration more likely without forcing it? Can we design environments that naturally elicit Yellow capacities in people still primarily operating from Orange?

Or do we need to accept that some portion of humanity will build transformative AI from an unintegrated consciousness, and focus our efforts on damage control rather than prevention?

I don't know.

But I know this: pretending AI alignment is purely technical—that we can solve it with better math while ignoring the consciousness of the mathematicians—is a form of collective delusion we can't afford.

* * *

The Measurement Paradox: Goodhart's Law at Civilizational Scale

The second major open question haunts every framework in this book.

We've proposed measuring integration. The Human Integration Index. The Love, Meaning, and Connection Index. Six-domain coherence scores. Developmental stage assessments.

The logic is sound: what gets measured gets managed. If we want civilization to optimize for integration rather than GDP, we need integration metrics.

But there's a problem, and it has a name: **Goodhart's Law**.

"When a measure becomes a target, it ceases to be a good measure."

The moment you make integration scores matter—tie them to funding, policy decisions, institutional legitimacy—you create incentives to game them.

We've seen this pattern repeatedly:

- Standardized testing didn't improve education; it created teaching-to-the-test
- GDP growth didn't create wellbeing; it created extraction masquerading as progress
- Click-through rates didn't improve content; they created clickbait
- Publication counts didn't advance science; they created quantity over quality

Now imagine Orange consciousness—brilliant at gaming metrics, terrible at understanding why that's problematic—getting its hands on integration scores.

Corporate Contemplation Centers: Companies build meditation rooms not to support human development but to reduce sick days and boost productivity. They track contemplative practice hours the way they track sales calls. Employees learn to fake presence the way they fake engagement.

Integration Theater: Nations report high LMCI scores through carefully constructed surveys while maintaining systems that structurally prevent actual integration. The metrics look good while the lived reality remains unchanged.

Wellness Washing: The entire apparatus of the Yellow Stack gets co-opted into a new, more sophisticated form of control. "Cognitive Sovereignty" becomes a marketing term. "Sanctuaries" become premium experiences for the wealthy. The AUBI becomes just another conditional benefit tied to good behavior.

The Guru-Industrial Complex: The temptation will be to turn "Yellow" into a luxury brand. To sell "Integration Retreats" for $10,000. To make me (or you) into a Guru with all the answers. This is precisely the kind of Orange capture we're trying to transcend. We must build open-source defenses against this from the beginning. If the tools aren't available to the single mother in Detroit, they aren't Yellow—they're just Green luxury goods with better marketing.

This is how Orange captures everything it touches. Not through malice, but through its core operating logic: identify the metric, optimize the metric, hit the numbers.

The Question Without An Answer

How do you measure integration without destroying it?

How do you create accountability for human development without creating perverse incentives that undermine the development you're trying to measure?

This isn't abstract philosophy. It's the central design challenge for any actual implementation of these frameworks.

Some possible approaches:

Approach 1: Qualitative Over Quantitative

Rely more on narrative assessment, peer review, community judgment than numerical scores. But this doesn't scale, isn't objective, and creates different gaming opportunities.

Approach 2: Measure Inputs Not Outcomes

Track whether systems are in place (Sanctuaries exist, AUBI is funded, Cognitive Sovereignty is legally protected) rather than whether they're "working." But this allows for compliance without effectiveness.

Approach 3: Participatory Assessment

Let communities define and measure their own integration, with external validation from developmental experts. But who validates the validators? And how do you prevent collective delusion?

Approach 4: Multiple Competing Metrics

Use many different measures so gaming any single one doesn't work. But this creates complexity that defeats the purpose of measurement in the first place.

Approach 5: Qualitative Friction

The only way to prevent the HII from becoming a target to be gamed is to maintain **qualitative friction**. We must insist that some data points can only be gathered through slow, human conversation—like the Love Ledger's requirement for face-to-face witness testimony—not automated surveillance. If the metric becomes frictionless, it becomes corrupt. The inefficiency is the point.

I lean toward a hybrid: combining participatory self-assessment with external validation, using both qualitative and quantitative data, measured over long enough time horizons that short-term gaming becomes less attractive, and maintaining deliberate friction in the measurement process itself.

But I don't know if this works. **No one does, because it's never been tried at scale.**

The only honest answer is: we'll need to experiment, fail, learn, adapt. We'll need to treat the measurement systems themselves as evolving experiments, not fixed solutions.

And we'll need to remain vigilant about the fundamental tension: the thing most worth measuring (human integration and flourishing) might be exactly the thing most damaged by being measured.

* * *

The Governance of Truth: Who Watches the Watchers?

The third major open question emerges directly from the Cognitive Sovereignty framework.

We've proposed legal protections for attention, information integrity, and epistemic commons. The Synoptic Protocol. Reality-based zones. Harm reduction for addictive design.

The intent is pure: protect human cognitive autonomy from manipulation.

But implementation requires answering an impossible question: **Who decides what counts as manipulation versus legitimate persuasion?**

Consider these scenarios:

Scenario 1: The Misinformation Problem

Clearly false health claims spread through social networks, causing real harm. Platform regulation seems obvious. But *who* determines what's false? Government agencies? Academic consensus? Community voting? Each answer creates new problems.

Scenario 2: The Persuasion Problem

Advertising has always been about persuasion. Where's the line between acceptable marketing and "cognitive sovereignty violation"? Is all advertising manipulation? Some advertising? How do you write that into law?

Scenario 3: The Narrative Problem

Different communities have fundamentally different interpretations of reality. One group's "protecting shared reality" is another group's "censorship." How do you defend epistemic commons without becoming the Ministry of Truth?

This isn't theoretical. We're watching it play out in real-time as societies struggle with content moderation, misinformation, and competing truth claims.

The progressive solution (more fact-checking, stronger platform accountability) risks creating centralized arbiters of truth—exactly the kind of power concentration that historically gets abused.

The libertarian solution (radical free speech, let the marketplace of ideas sort it out) ignores the reality that attention is finite, bad information spreads faster than corrections, and some actors intentionally weaponize confusion.

Neither first-tier solution works.

The Yellow Approach (Partial and Provisional)

What would Yellow governance of truth look like?

My current best thinking:

1. Subsidiarity in Epistemic Authority

Truth-claims get evaluated at the most local level capable of competent assessment. Medical claims by medical communities. Historical claims by historians. Community-specific norms by communities.

2. Transparent Uncertainty

Stop pretending we have certainty where we don't. Make the confidence level of claims visible. Distinguish between "scientifically established" and "politically contested" and "philosophically unsettled."

3. Adversarial Collaboration

Bring together people with different interpretations to map their agreements and disagreements. Don't try to eliminate perspective—try to make it visible and navigable.

4. Harm Reduction Over Truth Policing

Focus on preventing demonstrable harm (fraud, incitement to violence, health misinformation causing death) rather than enforcing ideological correctness.

5. Epistemic Diversity as Resilience

Maintain multiple truth-generating institutions (science, journalism, community knowledge, indigenous wisdom) rather than consolidating into single sources of authority.

But here's what I don't know: **Does this actually work against coordinated disinformation campaigns?**

When nation-states or well-funded actors intentionally flood the information ecosystem with confusion, does "Yellow governance" have teeth? Or does it become another version of the Green Trap—sophisticated in theory, ineffective in practice?

The question isn't whether to defend shared reality. The question is how to defend it without becoming the thing we're defending against.

And I don't have the answer.

What I have is a commitment to transparency about the tension, participatory design of governance mechanisms, and willingness to admit when our solutions create new problems.

That might not be enough. But it's more honest than pretending the problem is solved.

* * *

What We Need to Learn

Beyond these three major questions, here's what we genuinely don't know yet:

Developmental Questions:

- Can Yellow capacities be cultivated through designed environments, or do they only emerge through organic development over years?
- What percentage of a population needs to operate from Yellow before systemic change becomes possible?
- Are there developmental prerequisites (secure Blue, healthy Orange) or can people jump stages under the right conditions?

Economic Questions:

- Can a post-growth economy maintain technological innovation and adaptation capacity?
- What happens to human motivation when survival isn't conditional on productivity?
- How do we prevent AUBI from creating new forms of dependency and control?

Ecological Questions:

- Is it already too late for managed transition, making collapse inevitable?
- Can regenerative agriculture scale fast enough to matter?
- What are the carrying capacity limits of even a sustainable civilization?

Political Questions:

- Can Yellow governance outcompete authoritarian systems that move faster by being less democratic?
- How do you build global coordination without global domination?
- What happens when different bioregions develop toward different value systems?

Technological Questions:

- Can we build AI that supports integration rather than optimizes for fragmentation?
- What happens when biotechnology gives us the power to modify human consciousness directly?
- Are there technologies that are fundamentally incompatible with human flourishing?

Existential Questions:

- Is integration the goal, or just a stage on a longer developmental journey?
- What comes after Yellow/Turquoise in human consciousness evolution?
- Are we alone in the universe, or are we late to a much bigger conversation?

* * *

The Invitation

Here's what I know for certain: **I cannot answer these questions alone.**

This book represents two years of synthesis, but it's built on centuries of wisdom from countless traditions and decades of research by thousands of scholars. Every framework in here is derivative—standing on the shoulders of giants and trying to see a bit further.

The next phase requires something different. Not individual synthesis but collective intelligence. Not one framework but many experiments. Not a finished blueprint but an evolving prototype.

So this is the invitation:

Fork the Framework

Project Janus and the Global Governance Frameworks are open-source. Take them. Modify them. Improve them. Test them against reality and report what you learn. Build better versions than I could imagine alone.

The source code is at globalgovernanceframeworks.org. The documentation is extensive. The community is small but growing.

Start a Pilot

Pick one intervention from the Yellow Stack. Implement it in your city, your organization, your community. Document what works and what fails. Share the data.

We need Bioregional Adaptation Zones in ten cities by 2027. We need Sanctuary Districts in fifty neighborhoods. We need contemplative infrastructure experiments in a hundred schools.

We don't need perfection. We need variation and selection—evolutionary experimentation at the speed of human development.

This work doesn't require you to have it all figured out. It requires you to show up with the integration you *do* have—whether that's five minutes of presence before reaching for your phone, or the courage to start a pilot project despite not knowing all the answers.

Join the Research

We need developmental psychologists studying Yellow transitions. Economists modeling post-growth stability. Neuroscientists measuring integration. Contemplative practitioners mapping phenomenology. Political scientists designing new governance.

The research agenda is vast and urgent. The funding is minimal. The academic incentives are misaligned. But the work is essential.

Build the Cathedral

I've built some scaffolding. Some architectural drawings. A few load-bearing walls.

But cathedrals aren't built by architects. They're built by generations of craftspeople, each contributing their specific skill to a shared vision they'll never see completed.

This is a multi-generational project. None of us will see it finished. The question is whether we're willing to lay stones for a foundation we won't stand on, in service of a future we won't inhabit.

* * *

Coming Home

It's late now. I finally feel tired enough to sleep.

I reach out and turn off the machine. Not just closing the lid, but shutting it down completely. The fans spin down. The screen goes black. The hum of the digital mind that has been thinking with me for the last two years fades into silence.

I turn off the router. I unplug the charger.

I am creating a few hours of electronic-free peace. A small, temporary sanctuary where the only operating system running is my own biology.

I notice the silence. It feels heavy at first, like a pressure change. The impulse to check one last thing flickers and dies because the screen is dark.

This is what integration feels like when it happens: not a permanent state of bliss, but a choice to power down the tools and return to the body. To let the scaffolding fall away for the night so the building can stand on its own.

The crisis isn't solved. The questions aren't answered. The work isn't done.

But for this moment, I'm here. Present to the mystery and the uncertainty and the limited, partial, provisional understanding I have of how we got here and where we might go next.

That's all any of us ever have: this moment, this awareness, this choice to be as integrated as we can manage right now.

The map I've drawn in this book might be useful. It might be wrong. Most likely, it's both—useful in some contexts, inadequate in others, requiring constant revision as we learn more.

What matters isn't whether the map is perfect. What matters is whether it helps us navigate toward greater integration, deeper wisdom, more compassionate systems.

Whether it helps us become the kind of species that can handle the power we've accumulated.

Whether it helps us, finally, learn to just be—not because we've escaped the crisis, but because we've developed the capacity to be present with it.

The questions remain open.

The work continues.

And somewhere, right now, someone is having their first moment of genuine presence in years. Someone is designing a policy that might actually work. Someone is turning off their machine to sit in the quiet dark.

The transformation is already happening. Not everywhere. Not fast enough. Not guaranteed to succeed.

But happening.

And we get to choose whether to participate—with all our limitations, all our uncertainty, all our unfinished development—or to wait for someone else to solve what can only be solved together.

I'm choosing to participate.

Not because I have all the answers.

But because the questions are too important to leave to those who think they do.

* * *

Next: Chapter 22 - The Return (Conclusion)

Chapter 22: The Return

The walk is the same.

Same path through the neighborhood I've walked a thousand times. Same houses, same trees, same intersection where the morning light catches the leaves just right.

But I see it differently now.

Not because the world changed. Because I can finally see the architecture underneath.

There—the billboard screaming about a sale I don't need. Not just an annoyance anymore, but visible cognitive pollution. A deliberate assault on attention that we've normalized into background noise. I see the invisible wires connecting the billboard to the anxiety in the passerby's chest, and the anxiety to the exhaustion that prevents them from joining the union meeting. I see the integration failure not as a mistake, but as a blueprint we can rewrite. I see where the Sanctuary District boundary could go. See how different this street would feel without the constant extraction of awareness.

There—the coffee shop where people sit alone with their phones, together but separate. Not just modern life anymore, but a design choice. A failure of social infrastructure. I see where the contemplative space could be. See the benches arranged for actual conversation. See the slow-information feed replacing the anxiety scroll.

There—the bus stop where someone waits for the ride to their second job. Not just economic reality anymore, but structural violence. Conditional worth encoded in policy. I see how different their morning could be with an Adaptive Universal Basic Income. See the choice to work becoming actual choice, not survival coercion masked as freedom.

I see the invisible architecture of how we got here. And more importantly, I see the ghost of what could be built instead.

The seeing doesn't make me peaceful. It makes me **clear**.

* * *

What We Know Now

Some of us can't sit still for five minutes without our nervous system screaming that we should be doing something useful.

We might tell ourselves it is a personal failing. Lack of discipline. Insufficient gratitude. Not enough mindfulness practice.

But we now understand: it is accurate perception of structural reality.

The restlessness isn't in us—it is in the systems we are embedded in. The anxiety isn't neurosis—it is the only rational response to an environment designed to prevent the very presence it demanded we cultivate.

And that understanding changes everything.

Not because it makes the problem go away. The phone still call us. The compulsion to check email still rises. The gap between wanting to be present and actually being present hasn't closed.

But now we know it's not about willpower. It's about architecture.

The crisis isn't in our individual psychology. It's in our collective design.

And design can be changed.

* * *

We don't know if the Yellow Stack will work at scale. We don't know if enough people will develop Yellow capacities fast enough. We don't know if we can build Sanctuaries faster than the attention economy builds new extraction mechanisms.

But we know enough to stop waiting for certainty.

We know that **integration beats fragmentation.** That treating humans as six-domain wholes produces better outcomes than optimizing single dimensions.

We know that **structure beats willpower.** That changing environments is more effective than demanding individuals overcome those environments through heroic effort.

We know that **we beats me.** That collective intelligence operating from shared frameworks can solve problems no individual genius ever could.

We know the **direction**, even if we can't see the destination.

And we know that the cost of inaction compounds daily while we wait for someone else to move first.

* * *

The Choice Point

Sarah is still in her corner office. Still waking to cortisol and checking email before her feet hit the floor. Still successful by every metric that matters to the systems she inhabits.

But somewhere—maybe in a pilot city, maybe in a neighborhood that claimed itself as a Sanctuary, maybe in an organization brave enough to try the full Yellow Stack—there's another Sarah who's living differently.

She still works hard. Still contributes meaningfully. Still creates value.

But her survival isn't conditional on her productivity. Her worth isn't measured by her output. Her identity isn't defined by her achievement.

She has space to actually be human.

Not because she escaped to some utopian commune or inherited wealth or gave up on civilization. But because the systems around her were redesigned to make integration structurally possible rather than structurally prevented.

That version of reality exists in prototype. Right now. In the experiments running beneath the noise. In the pilots that haven't scaled yet. In the frameworks waiting for implementation.

The question is whether we choose to expand it or let it remain an exception that proves the rule.

* * *

Civilizations don't transform through individual enlightenment spreading one person at a time. They transform through infrastructure—legal, economic, social, cognitive—that makes new patterns of living actually possible.

The contemplatives who saved wisdom traditions through dark ages didn't do it alone in caves. They built monasteries. Created institutions. Developed practices that could be transmitted. Built architecture that outlasted individuals.

We need the modern equivalent.

Not withdrawal from the world, but engagement with its redesign. Not escape from systems, but evolution of systems. Not purity through isolation, but integration through participation.

And we need it at the speed of crisis, not the speed of comfort.

This choice isn't abstract. It's already being made, in small ways, in places most people aren't looking.

* * *

The Work That's Already Begun

Somewhere right now:

A city council is reviewing a Bioregional Adaptation Zone proposal, not knowing that similar conversations are happening in twelve other cities.

A research team is measuring integration across six domains, building the evidence base that will make the next pilot easier to fund.

A contemplative practitioner is documenting the phenomenology of Yellow consciousness with the rigor that will make it teachable at scale.

An economist is modeling post-growth stability, proving mathematically what we know intuitively: that human flourishing doesn't require endless expansion.

A parent is teaching their child to notice the quality of stillness, building developmental capacity one generation forward.

An architect is drawing plans for the first Sanctuary District that isn't just theory.

The work has begun. The frameworks exist. The pilots are launching.

What's missing is the critical mass of people who see the architecture clearly enough to demand its transformation.

* * *

What I'm Choosing

I'm choosing to participate.

Not because I have all the answers—Chapter 21 made clear I don't.

Not because I'm free from the patterns. Sometimes, I feel like my work is all ego and I'd rather abandon everything. I have stood at the edge of that particular abyss—considering the final exit because the complexity felt unbearable and the pain felt permanent. I know the seduction of wanting to delete the self rather than integrate the world.

But I stayed. Because my will to live is stronger than the system's attempt to crush it. The only way out is through.

Not because success is guaranteed—the odds might still be against us.

I'm choosing to participate because **the questions are too important to leave to those who think they already know.**

Because waiting for certainty means waiting forever.

Because the privilege of understanding systemic failure carries the responsibility of attempting systemic redesign.

And because the alternative—continuing to demand that individuals overcome structural impossibilities through heroic willpower while the planet burns and people break—is a cruelty I can't accept anymore.

* * *

The morning walk continues. The neighborhood unchanged, but my relationship to it transformed.

I see where we are. I see where we could go. I see the distance between them and know it's measured not in miles but in choices.

Choices about what we build. What we protect. What we're willing to let go of. What we're brave enough to try despite not knowing if it will work.

Every generation faces a choice about whether to maintain the systems they inherited or evolve them toward something more integrated, more wise, more aligned with what humans actually need to flourish.

We're in that moment now.

The crisis is here. The frameworks are ready. The pilots are beginning.

What we choose in the next decade will determine whether the Integration Crisis becomes the catalyst for genuine transformation or the tragedy we knew was coming but didn't act fast enough to prevent.

* * *

I turn toward home. The sun is higher now, the neighborhood coming alive. People heading to work, to school, to whatever demands fill their days.

Most of them don't see the invisible architecture yet. Don't recognize the systems that shape their experience as anything other than "how things are."

But some do. And more are starting to see the ghost of what could be in the shape of what is.

The seeing spreads slowly at first. Then all at once.

And in that seeing, in that moment of recognition that the cage isn't locked from the outside but held in place by our collective agreement to pretend it's natural—

In that moment, everything becomes possible.

* * *

The walk is the same.

But I'm different.

And difference, compounded through structure and amplified through systems, is how worlds change.

The work begins now.

Not in some distant future when we're finally ready.

Not when we have perfect answers or guaranteed outcomes.

Now.

With the integration we have, building toward the integration we need.

Together.

Let's walk.

Appendix A: Project Janus: Architectural Blueprint & Core Modules

(v0.9 Beta)

The six-domain computational architecture for modeling whole human beings

* * *

Executive Summary

Project Janus is the first comprehensive computational framework that models human beings as integrated wholes across all dimensions of experience. It moves beyond fragmented approaches to create unified models that honor the full complexity of human nature—from biological processes to spiritual aspirations.

The Core Problem

Traditional approaches to understanding humans are fundamentally fragmented:

- **Psychology** studies the mind
- **Biology** studies the body
- **Sociology** studies groups

- **Philosophy** studies meaning
- **But humans experience all these simultaneously**

This fragmentation limits our ability to understand human behavior, support human flourishing, or create AI systems that truly comprehend human values and needs.

The Janus Solution: Multi-Domain Integration

We model humans across **six interdependent domains**:

1. **Biological** - Physical substrate, neuroscience, embodied cognition
2. **Cognitive** - Reasoning, memory, belief systems, meta-cognition
3. **Emotional** - Affect, regulation, emotional wisdom
4. **Behavioral** - Actions, habits, values-behavior alignment
5. **Social** - Relationships, culture, collective intelligence
6. **Spiritual/Existential** - Meaning, purpose, transcendence

The Real Innovation: Integration Modules

What sets Project Janus apart isn't the domains themselves—it's how they interact through sophisticated **bridge interfaces**:

- **Bio-cognitive interfaces** - How body states shape thinking
- **Emotion-decision loops** - How feelings inform wise choices
- **Values-behavior alignment** - Tracking integrity and the intention-action gap
- **Meaning crisis response** - Modeling narrative collapse and reconstruction
- **Developmental trajectories** - Growth through predictable stages (integrated with Spiral Dynamics)

This integration architecture is what makes the model work like a human rather than like six separate systems running in parallel.

* * *

The Architecture

The complete Project Janus framework is organized as follows:

```
project_janus/ ├──────
 docs/                            # Theoretical
 Foundation │ ├──────
    00_project_vision.md          # The big picture │ ├──────
    01_glossary.md                # Shared vocabulary │ ├──────
    02_core_principles.md         # Foundational
    commitments │ ├──────
    03_integration_framework.md # How domains
    connect │ └──────
    04_ethical_framework.md       # Responsible
    development ├──────

 domains/                         # Six Core
 Dimensions │ ├──────
    biological/ │ │ ├──────
       overview.md │ │ ├──────
       physiological_systems.md │ │ ├──────
       genetic_epigenetic.md │ │ └──────
       neuro_architecture.md │ │ │ ├──────

    cognitive/ │ │ ├──────
       overview.md │ │ ├──────
       memory_systems.md │ │ ├──────
       attention_mechanisms.md │ │ ├──────
       reasoning_patterns.md │ │ └──────
       meta_cognition.md │ │ │ ├──────
```

```
    emotional/ │   │   ├───────
        overview.md │   │   ├──────
        affective_states.md │   │   ├──────
        emotion_cognition_interface.md │   │   └──────
        regulation_mechanisms.md │   │   │   ├──────

    behavioral/ │   │   ├──────
        overview.md │   │   ├──────
        habit_formation.md │   │   ├──────
        decision_processes.md │   │   └──────
        action_selection.md │   │   │   ├──────

    social/ │   │   ├──────
        overview.md │   │   ├──────
        identity_formation.md │   │   ├──────
        relationship_dynamics.md │   │   ├──────
        cultural_norms.md │   │   └──────
        group_processes.md │   │   │   └──────

    spiritual_existential/ │   ├──────
        overview.md │   ├──────
        meaning_making.md │   ├──────
        values_systems.md │   ├──────
        purpose_formation.md │   └──────
        self_transcendence.md ├──────

integration_modules/          # The Critical
Innovation │   ├──────
    bio_cognitive_interface.md │   ├──────
    emotion_decision_loop.md │   ├──────
    social_identity_formation.md │   ├──────
    values_behavior_alignment.md │   └──────
    meaning_crisis_response.md ├──────
```

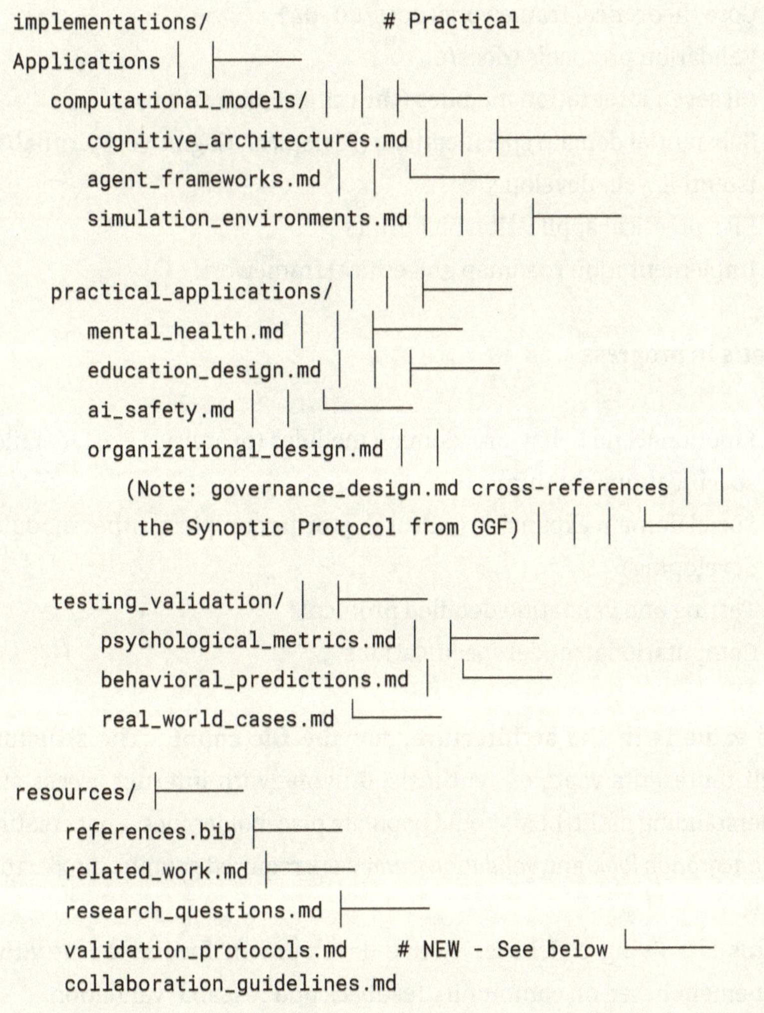

Status Note

Project Janus is currently in active development. The repository contains 46 files across 15 directories representing the complete architectural vision.

What's complete:

- Core theoretical framework (docs/00-04)
- Validation protocols (docs/05)
- All seven integration modules (the critical innovation)
- Substantial domain specifications (Biological, Cognitive, Spiritual/Existential well-developed)
- Five practical application blueprints
- Implementation roadmap and ethical framework

What's in progress:

- Emotional and Behavioral domain modules (overviews exist, detailed specifications coming)
- Social domain expansion (cultural_norms complete, other modules developing)
- Testing and validation detailed protocols
- Computational model specifications

The value is in the architecture, not the file count. The structure itself represents years of synthesis. Anyone with internet access and understanding of Git/LLMs could populate placeholder files—but creating the *integration logic* and *validation framework* required genuine intellectual work.

This is a living codebase. Active development focuses on iterative refinement based on community feedback and research validation.

* * *

Validation Protocols

How we know if the model is true and useful

1. Falsification Criteria

For Project Janus to be scientifically valid, it must make predictions that could be proven wrong. Here are the key falsifiable claims:

Prediction 1: Cross-Domain Coherence

- **Claim**: Integration across domains predicts wellbeing better than any single domain alone
- **Falsification**: If single-domain models (purely cognitive, purely biological) consistently outperform integrated models in predicting life satisfaction, meaning, or resilience
- **Test Method**: Longitudinal studies comparing predictive power of integrated vs. fragmented assessments

Prediction 2: Developmental Trajectories

- **Claim**: People develop through predictable stages of increasing integration capacity
- **Falsification**: If stage sequences are not observed, or if people regularly skip stages without regressions
- **Test Method**: Cross-sectional and longitudinal assessment using Spiral Dynamics validated instruments

Prediction 3: Values-Behavior Alignment

- **Claim**: Suffering correlates with misalignment between stated values and actual behavior, controlling for external circumstances
- **Falsification**: If values-behavior misalignment shows no correlation with psychological distress when controlling for material conditions
- **Test Method**: Structured interviews measuring both stated values and time-use data, correlated with validated wellbeing instruments

Prediction 4: Meaning Crisis Patterns

- **Claim**: Narrative collapse follows predictable patterns and responds to specific interventions addressing existential domain
- **Falsification**: If meaning crises show no pattern, or if purely biological/behavioral interventions work as well as meaning-focused ones
- **Test Method**: Clinical trials comparing meaning-centered therapy (logotherapy, ACT) with purely symptomatic approaches

Prediction 5: Integration Failure Cascade

- **Claim**: Dysfunction in one domain creates predictable cascade effects across other domains
- **Falsification**: If domain dysfunctions remain isolated with no measurable cross-domain impacts
- **Test Method**: Network analysis of symptom correlations across domains in clinical populations

2. Success Metrics

We know the model works if it can:

Explanatory Power

- Explain paradoxes current models cannot (e.g., successful people experiencing profound emptiness)
- Account for 60%+ variance in wellbeing measures using six-domain assessment
- Predict developmental transitions with 70%+ accuracy

Predictive Accuracy

- Forecast burnout risk 6 months in advance with 75%+ accuracy
- Identify radicalization vulnerability through values-behavior misalignment patterns
- Predict therapeutic outcomes based on integration baseline scores

Clinical Utility

- Integrated interventions show 30%+ improvement over single-domain approaches in RCTs
- Practitioners report the framework helps them understand "stuck" clients
- Patients report greater self-understanding using six-domain assessment

AI Alignment Applications

- Models built on Janus framework demonstrate better value stability under distribution shift
- Human evaluators prefer AI decisions made using integrated human models over utility-only models
- Reduced alignment failures in real-world deployments

3. Inter-Rater Reliability

Multiple assessors must independently reach similar conclusions using the framework:

Domain Assessment Protocol

- Three trained assessors independently evaluate the same case across all six domains
- Cohen's Kappa ≥ 0.7 for domain-level assessments
- Intraclass correlation ≥ 0.75 for integration scores

Developmental Stage Assessment

- Two independent raters assess developmental level using Sentence Completion Test and structured interview
- Agreement within one stage 90%+ of the time

- Exact agreement 70%+ of the time

Integration Quality Scoring

- Consensus panel of 5 experts rates integration quality on standardized cases
- Inter-rater reliability ≥ 0.80 on integration coherence scales
- Regular calibration sessions to maintain consistency

4. The Three Decisive Tests (by 2030)

If Project Janus is fundamentally sound, these three tests should validate it decisively:

Test 1: The Burnout Prevention Trial (2027-2029)

- 1,000 participants at high burnout risk
- Experimental group receives six-domain integrated intervention
- Control groups receive standard interventions (cognitive-behavioral, mindfulness, career coaching)
- Success: 40%+ reduction in burnout incidence vs. controls at 2-year follow-up

Test 2: The AI Alignment Benchmark (2026-2028)

- Build two AI systems: one trained on Janus-based human models, one on standard preference-learning
- Test on novel ethical dilemmas and value trade-offs
- Success: Human evaluators prefer Janus-based AI decisions 65%+ of the time; fewer catastrophic value failures

Test 3: The Meaning Crisis Response Study (2028-2030)

- Clinical trial with individuals experiencing existential distress

- Compare Janus-based integrated therapy vs. standard approaches
- Success: 50%+ greater improvement on Purpose in Life Test and psychological wellbeing measures

* * *

Why This Matters for The Integration Crisis

The book you just read diagnosed the problem: **we are running planetary civilization on OS Orange, creating integration failures at every level.**

Project Janus is the engineering blueprint for the solution. It provides:

1. **Diagnostic Precision**: The six-domain framework lets us identify *exactly* where integration is failing
2. **Intervention Design**: Integration modules show *how* to restore coherence across domains
3. **Validation Rigor**: Falsifiable predictions ensure we're building real science, not philosophy
4. **Implementation Readiness**: Complete specifications allow teams to start building immediately

When we talk about "human integration" in the Yellow Stack, we're not being vague. We mean specific, measurable coherence across these six domains as modeled in Project Janus.

When we say AI alignment requires integrated humans, we mean humans whose Janus assessment shows high cross-domain coherence and developmental capacity.

The theory is complete. The architecture is designed. The validation protocols are defined.

Now we need builders.

* * *

Current Status

✓ Core Architecture Complete

- Theoretical framework across all six domains
- Seven integration modules fully specified (the critical innovation)
- Validation protocols and falsification criteria defined
- Ethical guidelines established
- Implementation roadmap with resource requirements
- 46 files across structured architecture

Active Development

- Domain module expansion (iterative deepening)
- Computational model prototyping
- Testing framework elaboration
- Community building and collaboration
- Research validation studies (designing)

Implementation Ready

- Architecture is sound and ready for team build-out
- Integration logic is the hard part—and it's done
- Applications can begin with current specifications
- Research agenda is clear and falsifiable

Resource Requirements (from Roadmap)

Phase 1 (Foundation - 6 months): 3-5 researchers, $150-250K **Phase 2 (Full System - 6 months):** 8-12 specialists, $500-750K

Phase 3 (Applications - 12 months): 20-30 team members, $2-3M

Phase 4 (Scaling - 12 months): 50+ core team + global network, $5-8M

* * *

The Open-Source Invitation

This framework is not a static text. It is a living codebase.

I have designed the architecture and mapped the territory. The intellectual foundation is complete. But I am not the one to build the vehicle or captain the ship.

Project Janus is released under **Creative Commons Attribution-ShareAlike 4.0 (CC BY-SA 4.0)** license.

What this means:

- Anyone can use, adapt, or build upon this work, even commercially
- Any derivative works must be released under the same open license
- No single entity can enclose the "DNA" of human modeling
- If you improve the architecture, you must share those improvements

I am not saying: "I, Björn, know the truth about humans."

I am saying: "I, Björn, have committed a *commit* to the *main* branch of human understanding. Please submit a *pull request* if you can improve it."

This solves the **Guru Trap** (from Chapter 21): I am not positioning myself as the authority on integration. I am offering infrastructure for collective intelligence to build upon.

* * *

How to Participate

For Developers:

- Clone the repository and explore existing documentation
- Pick one domain to implement as a prototype
- Join community discussions on implementation approaches
- Contribute to validation frameworks

For Researchers:

- Review the theoretical framework and identify gaps
- Propose validation studies for specific components
- Collaborate on research papers
- Connect domain expertise to implementation needs

For Practitioners:

- Identify application opportunities in your field (mental health, education, organizational development)
- Provide real-world use cases for testing
- Join pilot program planning
- Share domain-specific knowledge

For Funders:

- This is high-impact open-source infrastructure
- Ideal for research institutions, AI labs, mental health organizations
- See ROADMAP.md for detailed resource requirements and phasing

* * *

Access the Living Framework

GitHub Repository: https://github.com/BjornKennethHolmstrom/ProjectJanus

Website: https://www.bjornkennethholmstrom.org/project-janus

Contact: bjorn.kenneth.holmstrom@gmail.com

The repository currently includes:

- Complete architectural specifications and design rationale
- Core theoretical documents (vision, principles, ethics, integration framework)
- All seven integration modules (the system's core innovation)
- Substantial domain overviews and key detailed specifications
- Validation protocols and falsification criteria
- Implementation roadmap and application blueprints
- Active development areas clearly marked

This is beta architecture, not vaporware. The hard intellectual work—the integration logic, the validation framework, the ethical guidelines—is complete. Domain detail expansion is iterative and community-driven.

* * *

A Note on Living Beta Development

This appendix represents a **v0.9 beta snapshot** of Project Janus as of publication. This is intentional.

Why beta? Because intellectual honesty requires acknowledging what's complete (the architecture, integration logic, validation framework) versus what's iterative (detailed domain specifications, computational implementations).

The framework continues to evolve through:

- Community contributions and research findings
- Validation study results informing refinements
- Domain module expansion as priorities emerge
- New integration patterns as we discover them
- Real-world application feedback

The architecture is sound. The innovation is real. The invitation is genuine.

For the most current version, consult the GitHub repository. The living codebase will always reflect active development priorities.

I'm not claiming to have finished something that requires a global research community. I'm claiming to have designed the architecture that makes coordinated effort possible.

The blueprint is ready. The validation framework is defined. The invitation is open.

Let's build technologies worthy of human beings.

* * *

"We are not human beings having a spiritual experience. We are spiritual beings having a human experience." — Pierre Teilhard de Chardin

Project Janus aims to take both parts of this truth seriously, computationally.

* * *

Appendix B: Glossary of Key Concepts

A lexicon for the transition from Orange to Yellow.

Adaptive Universal Basic Income (AUBI) A dual-currency economic operating system that guarantees an unconditional fiat floor for survival (housing, food, healthcare) while issuing complementary social credits (*Hearts & Leaves*) to reward care work and ecological stewardship. Unlike standard UBI, it adapts dynamically to local costs and non-market contributions.

The Alchemist The archetype of the transitional agent who holds high-agency resources (money, power, influence) but uses them with "Yellow" consciousness. The Alchemist acts as a membrane, absorbing "Stock" (accumulated wealth) and transmuting it into "Flow" (regenerative capacity) without being consumed by the identity of the owner.

Blue (Spiral Dynamics) The developmental stage focused on Order, Truth, and Discipline. It values stability, hierarchy, and sacrifice for a future reward. In the GGF context, Blue provides the necessary foundation of the **Sovereign Floor** and the rule of law required for higher stages to function.

Cognitive Scaffolding The external structures (rituals, spaces, social contracts, economic guarantees) required to support internal states of consciousness. The central thesis of this book is that stillness is not a willpower achievement, but a result of robust cognitive scaffolding. Without scaffolding for valuing presence, individuals blame themselves for systemic design failures.

Cognitive Sovereignty The fundamental human right to an information environment free from algorithmic predation and involuntary attention extraction. It asserts that human attention is a sovereign territory that cannot be colonized by commercial interests without consent.

Epistemic Defense The proactive protection of a population's ability to discern truth. Just as a military defends against physical invasion, Epistemic Defense (operationalized by the **Synoptic Protocol**) defends against the "carpet bombing" of the collective nervous system by disinformation and outrage algorithms.

Green (Spiral Dynamics) The developmental stage focused on Community, Equality, and Relativity. It deconstructs the hierarchies of Orange/Blue and values empathy above efficiency. Its shadow is "The Green Trap"—an inability to build structure or wield power effectively due to a fear of hierarchy.

Guru-Industrial Complex The pattern where transformative practices (meditation, integration work, Yellow consciousness) get commodified into luxury goods, creating $10,000 retreats accessible only to elites. The antidote is radical open-source accessibility—if the tools aren't available to the single mother in Detroit, they aren't Yellow.

Hearthlight Protocol The GGF framework for **Childhood Flourishing**, treating the developmental environment of children as a protected sanctuary. It ensures that the nervous systems of the next generation are not subjected to the extraction economy.

Hearthstone Protocol The GGF framework for **Property Transition**. It provides the legal and financial mechanisms to transition land and housing from speculative assets ("Stock") into community stewardship trusts ("The Commons"), permanently removing them from the market.

Hearts & Leaves The complementary currencies of the **Regenerative Economy**.

- **Hearts:** Reward care work, community building, and social cohesion (the "Love Ledger").
- **Leaves:** Reward ecological restoration, carbon sequestration, and biosphere stewardship.

Human Integration Index (HII) A composite metric measuring the structural capacity of a human system to self-regulate across six domains (Biological, Cognitive, Emotional, Behavioral, Social, Existential). It is the diagnostic counterpart to the **LMCI** (which measures the *result* of flourishing).

Integration Failure The systemic condition where the demands of one domain (e.g., Economic survival) actively degrade the capacity of another (e.g., Biological regulation), creating a feedback loop of compulsion and burnout. This is the structural definition of addiction—not as personal weakness, but as predictable response to systemic design.

Love Ledger A decentralized accounting platform designed to make the invisible economy of care visible without commodifying it. While traditional ledgers track financial transactions (market value), the Love Ledger tracks relational contributions—elder care, volunteerism, mentorship, and community stewardship. It functions as the "qualitative data layer" of the regenerative economy, ensuring that value creation is recognized even when no money changes hands. Data from the Love Ledger feeds directly into the **LMCI**, guiding the allocation of resources to where social fabric is being built.

Love, Meaning, and Connection Index (LMCI) The primary metric of the Regenerative Economy, designed to replace GDP as the measure of civilizational success. While GDP measures the *velocity of transaction* (how fast we exchange money), the LMCI measures the *quality of relation* (how deeply we connect). It aggregates qualitative data from the **Love Ledger**, community health indicators, and subjective flourishing audits to guide the allocation of the **Sovereign Floor**.

Meta-Governance The architecture of coordination between different governance systems. It allows "Blue" laws, "Orange" markets, and "Green" councils to operate simultaneously in the same bioregion without checkmating each other.

Moral Operating System (MOS) The ethical kernel of the GGF. It establishes the hierarchy of rights (Existence -> Sentience -> Sapience) and provides the decision-logic for resolving conflicts between values (e.g., when does the Right to Reality override the Freedom of Speech?).

Orange (Spiral Dynamics) The developmental stage focused on Achievement, Science, and Autonomy. It built the modern world but is currently hitting the "Orange Wall" of diminishing returns (burnout, ecological collapse). The book argues for *including* Orange capacity while *transcending* Orange values.

Project Janus The multi-domain computational framework for modeling human wholeness. It provides the theoretical basis for understanding why single-domain interventions (like "just meditating") fail in a disintegrated environment.

Qualitative Friction The deliberate maintenance of inefficiency in measurement systems to prevent gaming. For integration metrics to remain valid, some data points must only be gathered through slow, human processes (like face-to-face witness testimony) rather than automated surveillance. The inefficiency is the point.

Sanctuary A legally designated zone (physical or digital) where the logic of the market is suspended. In a Sanctuary, you are a citizen or a soul, never a consumer or a user.

The Sovereign Floor The absolute minimum level of resource security required to down-regulate the human nervous system from "Fight/Flight" to "Rest/Digest." It is the biological justification for **AUBI**.

The Transition Paradox The developmental truth that you cannot use the consciousness of one stage to achieve the next. You cannot Orange your way into Yellow—achievement logic cannot optimize its way to integration. This is why willpower fails and structure matters.

Yellow (Spiral Dynamics) The developmental stage focused on Integration, Systems, and Flow. Yellow thinking replaces "Either/Or" with "Both/And," designing systems that allow multiple worldviews to coexist and function. It is the "Architect" mindset.

The Yellow Stack The four interlocking systemic interventions that together create conditions for human integration: (1) Cognitive Sovereignty Architecture, (2) The Sovereign Floor (AUBI), (3) Sanctuaries and Non-Extractive Zones, and (4) Contemplative Capacity as Infrastructure. Unlike single-domain solutions, the Stack works across all six domains simultaneously.

Appendix C: First-100-Days Playbooks

For those ready to move from reader to architect.

* * *

Who This Is For

If you finished this book thinking "this makes sense, but what can *I* actually do?"—this appendix is your answer.

You don't need to quit your job or move to an intentional community. You don't need perfect conditions or institutional permission. You need to use the leverage you already have to build Yellow infrastructure within Orange/Green institutions.

These aren't complete blueprints. They're **proof-of-concept protocols**—designed to be 90-day experiments that demonstrate feasibility and build momentum.

The goal isn't perfection. The goal is **existence proof**: showing that these interventions can work within current systems, creating the political will for larger transformation.

The strategy: Trojan Horse protocols. For each role, the actions shouldn't look like "Revolution." They should look like **"Optimization"** (Orange) or **"Wellness"** (Green) but deliver **Integration** (Yellow).

Choose one playbook that matches your leverage. Execute it. Document what happens. Share the results.

That's how the mycelial network grows.

* * *

1. The Mayor / City Councilor

The Mission: Turn your city into a **Bioregional Anchor** and a **Sanctuary for Attention.**

The Trap: Trying to solve national polarization or waiting for federal action.

The Yellow Move: Solve **local integration failure** (Housing, Noise, Attention, Community).

Day 1-30: The Audit (Stop the Bleeding)

The Cognitive Audit

- Map your city's "Cognitive Pollution." Where are the flashing billboards? Where is the inescapable noise? Which public spaces are colonized by screens and advertisements?
- Identify 3 zones to designate as "Quiet Districts" or "Contemplative Zones"
- Audit city-owned digital infrastructure: What data are we collecting? Who has access? What's being sold?

The Asset Audit

- Identify underutilized public land and buildings
- Stop all sales of public assets pending integration review
- Prepare them for potential transfer to Community Land Trust (Hearthstone Protocol framework)
- Map city spending on "palliative" vs. "structural" interventions

Day 31-60: The Prototype (Build the Slipway)

Launch the "Civic Gymnasium" (from Chapter 14)

- Re-designate one library branch as a "Deep Work Public Space"
- No phones allowed, quiet rules enforced, free tea/coffee
- Frame it to council as "Productivity Infrastructure for Remote Workers" (Orange language)
- Measure: foot traffic, time spent, user satisfaction

The "Local Loop" Procurement

- Audit city spending and contractor relationships
- Mandate that 20% of procurement must come from local cooperatives, B-Corps, or community-owned enterprises within 2 years
- Start with easy wins: food service, maintenance, landscaping

Pilot the Sanctuary Zone

- Designate one park or public space as advertising-free, surveillance-free
- Install simple signage: "This is a sanctuary. You are a citizen here, not a consumer."
- Track: vandalism rates, usage patterns, community feedback

Day 61-90: The Structure (Codify)

Pass the "Right to Disconnect" Ordinance

- Start with city employees: no work emails/calls required between 6 PM and 9 AM
- Measure productivity before and after (it will go up, not down)
- Extend to contractors doing city business

- Publicly report: "We protected our workers' attention and productivity increased X%"

Zone for Integration

- Introduce zoning overlay category: "Human Integration District"
- Within these zones: ban data collection in public spaces, restrict digital advertising, require noise impact assessments
- Start with schools and parks, expand from there

Launch the Bioregional Assembly

- Convene first citizen assembly on "What does human flourishing look like in our city?"
- Use sortition (random selection) to ensure diverse representation
- Frame output as input for comprehensive plan update

Day 100: The Public Commitment

Host a "Pilot City for Human Flourishing" Declaration Event

- Invite citizens, press, peer cities
- Present: what you've learned, what's working, what's next
- Announce: "We are a test bed for the Yellow Stack. Here's our data. Here's our invitation to collaborate."
- Share results openly so other cities can fork your experiments

* * *

2. The CEO / Founder

The Mission: Transition from "Extraction Engine" to **"Capacity Engine."**

The Trap: "Corporate Mindfulness" as palliative care for burnout while maintaining extractive structure.

The Yellow Move: Structural De-Coercion - removing the conditions that prevent integration.

Day 1-30: The Signal (Stop the Bleeding)

The Email Amnesty

- Declare "Zero-Inbox Bankruptcy" company-wide
- Reset expectations: no internal emails required between 6 PM and 9 AM, or on weekends
- Auto-responders that say: "This company values your integration. This can wait until Monday."
- Frame it: "Protecting our most valuable asset - employee cognitive capacity"

The Salary Floor

- Audit your lowest-paid workers (including contractors)
- Raise the floor to a **"Thriving Wage"** - enough for housing, food, healthcare, and savings in your region
- Not minimum wage. Not "living wage." Thriving wage.
- Frame it to board/investors: "Protecting our talent supply chain and reducing turnover costs"

The Integration Signal

- Cancel one unnecessary meeting from every employee's calendar
- Announce: "We're declaring war on meeting bloat. Every hour we

save in meetings is an hour for deep work."

Day 31-60: The Systems (Build the Slipway)

Adopt the "Pathfinder" Metrics

- Stop reporting only EBITDA/revenue/growth
- Start tracking **Employee Integration Index** using Project Janus six-domain framework
- Biological: Sleep quality, stress levels, sick days
- Cognitive: Deep work hours, decision quality
- Emotional: Psychological safety scores, conflict resolution
- Behavioral: Alignment between stated values and daily actions
- Social: Collaboration quality, relationship health
- Existential: Sense of purpose, meaningful contribution
- Report this to the board as **risk-management metric**: "Disintegrated employees make bad decisions"

The "Deep Work" Wednesday

- Mandate one day per week of *zero* meetings. Not "fewer." Zero.
- Block calendars company-wide
- Measure: productivity on focused tasks, error rates, employee satisfaction
- Publicly share results after 90 days

The Integration Audit

- Pick one major policy (parental leave, remote work, professional development)
- Use six-domain framework to assess: "Does our parental leave policy support biological recovery AND cognitive rest AND emotional bonding AND social connection AND meaningful identity transition?"

- If not, redesign it to address all domains

Day 61-90: The Structure (Codify)

Ownership Transition Study

- Commission feasibility study for **Employee Ownership Trust (EOT)** or conversion to B-Corp/cooperative
- Explore: How do we exit to community rather than to Private Equity?
- Frame it: "Building long-term enterprise resilience and stakeholder alignment"

Algorithmic Ethics Audit (if you build technology)

- Audit your product for "Dark Patterns" - features designed to exploit human psychology
- Remove one addictive feature, even if revenue drops 5-10%
- Document the decision transparently
- Announce: "We're optimizing for user agency, not engagement"

The Sabbatical Policy

- Institute paid sabbaticals: every 5 years, employees get 1 month fully paid, fully disconnected
- Frame it: "Preventing burnout is cheaper than treating it. This is pension-plan-level investment in retention."

Day 100: The Pivot

Publicly Announce the New Mission

- "We are no longer optimizing for [engagement/growth/market share] alone. We are optimizing for **User Agency and Human Integration**."

- Share your integration metrics publicly
- Invite peer companies to collaborate on new measurement frameworks
- Host a "Post-Growth Business" summit

* * *

3. The Philanthropist / Investor

The Mission: Become the **Alchemist.** Move from "Charity" to "Infrastructure."

The Trap: Funding "Band-Aids" (soup kitchens, crisis intervention) without funding "Cures" (structural reform).

The Yellow Move: Fund **Risk & Roots** - the unglamorous infrastructure that makes systemic change possible.

Day 1-30: The Vow (First Fruits)

The Transfer

- Execute the **First Fruits Rule** from The Alchemist's Dilemma
- Move 40% of liquid surplus to a Donor Advised Fund (DAF) with mandate to spend down within 5 years
- Not perpetual endowment. Urgent deployment.

The Freeze

- Stop all investments in extractive industries: fossil fuels, surveillance tech, predatory lending, private prisons
- Divest within 12 months
- Frame it: "Risk management in an integration economy"

The Accountability Pod

- Find 3 other wealthy peers running similar experiments
- Read *The Alchemist's Dilemma* together (Chapter 19)
- Create mutual accountability structure
- Dare each other toward "enough" rather than "more"

Day 31-60: The Seed (Build the Slipway)

Fund the "Invisible" Infrastructure

- Identify people building the scaffolding: researchers, systems architects, land trusts, policy designers, contemplative scientists
- Examples of what to fund:
- Project Janus computational models and validation studies
- Synoptic Protocol legal research and pilot implementations
- Community Land Trust infrastructure and technical assistance
- Contemplative science research and teacher training
- Bioregional governance pilots and coordination platforms
- Give **Unrestricted Multi-Year Grants** (3-5 years minimum)
- Stop asking for quarterly impact reports; ask for **10-year visions**
- Trust process over metrics in early stages

Buy Land, Give It Away

- Identify key ecological corridor, urban block, or farmland at risk
- Buy it at market rate
- Transfer ownership to Community Land Trust with perpetual conservation easement
- Remove it from speculative market forever
- Frame it: "Investing in bioregional resilience"

Seed the Alternative Economy

- Fund 10 cooperatives, B-Corps, or community enterprises with patient capital
- Terms: low/no interest, long payback, conversion to grant if impact targets met
- Focus on: local food systems, renewable energy, care economy, regenerative agriculture

Day 61-90: The Network (Integration)

Launch the "Regenerative Funders Consortium"

- Convene other philanthropists committed to systems change
- Create shared due diligence, shared learning, coordinated funding
- Build capacity to fund at ecosystem scale, not just project scale

The Legal Innovation

- Fund legal research on innovative structures: perpetual purpose trusts, land commons, stakeholder governance
- Don't just fund existing models - fund the lawyers creating new ones

Start the Sunset Clock

- Publicly announce timeline for drawing down foundation/wealth
- "I commit to philanthropic spend-down by [year]. I will die with enough for family security, not with dynastic empires."
- Alternative framing if "sunset" feels too stark: "Giving While Living - deploying resources at the speed of crisis"

Day 100: The Declaration

Host "The Alchemist Summit"

- Convene wealth-holders exploring similar transitions
- Share: lessons learned, failures encountered, structures that worked
- Announce: "I am transitioning from Wealth Holder to Wealth Steward"
- Publish your playbook openly - make it forkable

* * *

4. The System Builder / Architect

The Mission: Help build the Global Governance Frameworks (GGF).

- **The Reality:** The frameworks in this book exist as open-source blueprints. They need coders, translators, lawyers, and organizers to turn them into functioning institutions.
- **The Invitation:** If you read this book and thought, *"I want to work on the engine room,"* this is your entry point.

Ways to Contribute:

- **Founding Partners:** We are seeking the initial coalition to formally incorporate the GGF (potentially in Sweden) and capitalize the **Global Commons Fund**.
- **Technical Architects:** Help build the **Love Ledger**, the **Synoptic Protocol** infrastructure, and the **Digital Commons**.
- **Cultural Translators:** Translate these frameworks into your language and cultural context.

- **Legal Engineers:** Help draft the actual **Treaty for Our Only Home** and the **Hearthstone Trust** templates.

Your Next Step: We have a dedicated portal for builders. It breaks down current needs, open roles, and the roadmap for the next 12 months.

Join the construction crew: <u>globalgovernanceframeworks.org/get-involved</u>

* * *

5. The Parent / Educator

The Mission: Protect developmental capacity and build contemplative infrastructure at family/classroom scale.

The Trap: Thinking you need institutional permission or perfect conditions to make a difference.

The Yellow Move: Use the leverage you already have - influence over the next generation's nervous systems.

Day 1-30: The Boundary (Stop the Bleeding)

The Screen Sabbath

- One day per week (or start with one meal per day), no screens for anyone in the household
- Frame it as "Family Connection Time" not "punishment"
- Start small: screen-free dinners
- Notice: What happens to conversation quality? Attention spans? Conflict?

The Morning Walk Protocol

- Before any device time, 10 minutes outside
- No agenda, no learning objectives, just presence
- Make it non-negotiable routine like brushing teeth
- For educators: 5-minute "arrival walk" before class starts

The Audit

- Track: How much of child's day is adult-structured vs. unstructured?
- How much screen time (honest count)?
- How much time in nature?
- How many hours of pure play with no agenda?

Day 31-60: The Practice (Build the Slipway)

The Stillness Curriculum

- If educator: Add 5 minutes of silence/breathing to start each class
- If parent: 5 minutes before family dinner
- Not "meditation" (too loaded). Call it "Settling" or "Arrival Practice"
- Simply: sit, breathe, notice. No performance required.

The Integration Check-In

- Weekly family meeting or classroom circle
- Framework: "Report from all domains"
- Body: Are you tired? Energized? Hurting?
- Heart: What feelings came up this week?
- Mind: What did you learn or wonder about?
- Meaning: What mattered to you? What are you proud of?
- Friends: How are your relationships?
- Spirit: What felt beautiful or important?
- Listen without fixing. Witness without judgment.

The Project-Based Stillness

- If educator: Replace one test/assignment with "Contemplative Inquiry Project"
- Students choose question that matters to them, spend time in reflective practice, document insights
- Grade on depth of reflection, not "correctness"

Day 61-90: The Structure (Codify)

Create a Sanctuary Zone

- If parent: Designate one room/space as phone-free, screen-free
- If educator: One corner of classroom as "Contemplative Corner"
- Simple setup: cushions, plants, soft light, art supplies, books
- Rule: This space is for being, not performing

Join/Start "Slow School" Advocacy

- Connect with other parents/educators
- Push school board to adopt Hearthlight Protocol principles:
- Childhood as protected sanctuary period
- Development over achievement
- Integration across domains
- Screen time limits in school
- Attend board meetings, write op-eds, organize parent groups

The Tech Contract

- If parent: Co-create device agreement with kids
- Not imposed rules, but negotiated together
- Includes parents' commitments too
- Review quarterly

- If educator: Create classroom technology policy with student input

Day 100: The Invitation

Host a "Contemplative Parenting/Teaching" Gathering

- Invite 5-10 other parents/educators
- Share: What worked? What didn't? What surprised you?
- Create ongoing support group
- Document insights and share online
- Build the mycelial network of integration-focused adults

* * *

6. The Individual Citizen

The Mission: Become a node of Yellow consciousness in your local ecosystem.

The Trap: Thinking systemic change requires institutional power you don't have.

The Yellow Move: Exercise the civic power you already possess - your attention, participation, and local relationships.

Day 1-30: Show Up Somewhere

Join One Local Decision-Making Body

- School board, neighborhood association, library board, planning commission
- Doesn't matter which - just participate in governance
- Listen first. Notice the operating system (Blue? Orange? Green?)

- Identify one integration failure you could address

Map Your Bioregion

- What watershed do you live in?
- Where does your food come from?
- What are the ecological carrying capacities and limits?
- Who are the indigenous peoples whose land you occupy?
- Start seeing systems, not just individual problems

The Attention Audit

- Track one week: Where does your attention actually go?
- How much is extracted vs. chosen?
- What percentage goes to local vs. distant concerns?
- What changes would reclaim 20% for local engagement?

Day 31-60: Build Local Capacity

Start a "Contemplative Coffee" Group

- Weekly gathering, 6–8 people
- 20 minutes silent sitting, 40 minutes discussing integration
- Rotating location (homes, parks, libraries)
- Use Hearthlight Protocol principles: no agenda, no hierarchy, witnessing over fixing
- Let it grow organically

Document One Integration Failure

- Identify specific local example (playground lacking shade, library too loud for deep work, no safe bike routes)
- Research: What system maintains this failure?

- Write it up clearly, with six-domain analysis
- Present to relevant decision-makers
- Share publicly online

Shop the Alternative Economy

- Find local cooperative, B-Corp, or community-owned business
- Shift 20% of spending there even if more expensive
- Tell them why you're choosing them
- Invite others to join you

Day 61-90: Run or Support

Consider Running for Something Local

- School board, library board, neighborhood council
- You don't need to win - you need to inject Yellow frameworks into public discourse
- Campaign on: "What if we measured success by human integration, not just property values?"

Or: Mentor Someone Who Is

- Find someone with Yellow sensibility but less confidence/resources
- Offer strategic support, connection to networks, skill-sharing
- Amplify their voice

Build the Coalition

- Connect the scattered Yellow nodes you've found
- Create informal network: monthly calls, shared documents, mutual aid
- Not an organization (bureaucracy). A mycelium (distributed intelli-

gence).

Day 100: The Commitment

Publicly Declare Your Practice

- Blog post, social media, letter to local paper
- "I am practicing Yellow citizenship. Here's what I'm learning."
- Share your integration audit findings
- Invite others to similar experiments
- Make the invisible visible

* * *

After Day 100: Join the Network

These playbooks are starting points, not endpoints. After your first 100 days:

Document Your Experiments

- What worked? What failed? What surprised you?
- What resistance did you encounter?
- What unexpected allies emerged?
- What would you do differently?

Share Openly

- Blog posts, podcast interviews, local talks
- Not to build personal brand, but to create learning commons
- Make your protocols forkable - publish templates, frameworks,

lessons learned

- Be honest about failures (they're data, not shame)

Connect With Others

- Find the other mayors/CEOs/funders/parents running similar experiments
- Cross-pollinate insights across sectors and regions
- Build the distributed network of Yellow practitioners
- Create accountability partnerships

Iterate and Improve

- Refine the playbooks based on real-world testing
- Share updates: "Here's v2.0 after learning from 50 pilots"
- Contribute to living database of integration experiments
- Help others avoid your mistakes

The Living Database

The Global Governance Frameworks project will maintain a repository of pilot experiments, case studies, and lessons learned. We will need your data.

Submit your case study: Include context, interventions, results (quantitative and qualitative), failures, insights. Make it useful for the next person.

Access the database: Learn from others' experiments. Fork what works. Avoid what doesn't.

Contact: Use the GGF contact page or email bjorn.kenneth.holmstrom @gmail.com with subject line "First 100 Days Report"

* * *

A Note on Failure

Most of these experiments will encounter resistance. Some will fail outright. That's expected.

You're not trying to optimize within the current system. You're trying to demonstrate that a different system is possible.

Existence proof beats perfection. A flawed pilot that shows integration is possible is worth more than a perfect plan that never launches.

The mycelial network grows one node at a time. Your node doesn't need to be perfect. It needs to exist.

Document everything - especially the failures. They're the learning substrate for the next person.

* * *

The Meta-Pattern

Notice what these five playbooks have in common:

1. **Start where you are** - Use the leverage you already have
2. **Stop the bleeding first** - Create space before building
3. **Prototype small** - Existence proof over comprehensive reform
4. **Codify what works** - Structure enables persistence beyond individuals
5. **Share openly** - Make everything forkable

This is how systemic change actually happens. Not through master plans imposed from above, but through distributed experimentation coordinated by shared frameworks.

You don't need permission. You don't need perfect conditions. You don't need institutional authority.

You need clarity about the architecture you're building and courage to start building it.

The work begins now.

Not in some distant future when you're finally ready.

Not when you have perfect answers or guaranteed outcomes.

Now.

With the integration you have, building toward the integration we need.

Together.

* * *

"You never change things by fighting the existing reality. To change something, build a new model that makes the existing model obsolete." — Buckminster Fuller

These playbooks are the building instructions.

Appendix D: Resources

Tools for the ongoing work of integration.

1. The Digital Hubs

For the living documentation of the frameworks, ongoing research, and the open-source codebases discussed in this book:

- **Björn Kenneth Holmström (Personal Hub):** bjornkennethholmstrom.org
- *Access:* Essays, White Papers, and the complete Project Janus archives.
- **Global Governance Frameworks:** globalgovernanceframeworks.org
- *Access:* The official documentation for the Treaty, Synoptic Protocol, and AUBI.

2. Deep Dives (Companion Texts)

If specific chapters resonated with you, these companion texts provide the detailed engineering specifications:

- **On Economics:** *The Currency of Care: Why Universal Basic Income Isn't Enough.* (White Paper)
- **On Metrics:** *Love, Meaning, Connection: A New Index for Measuring What Matters.* (Book)
- **On Method:** *Cognitive Scaffolding: A Multi-Model AI Synthesis Method.* (White Paper)

3. The Intellectual Lineage

This book stands on the shoulders of giants. For those who want to explore the source code of "Yellow" thinking:

- **Developmental Psychology:** *Spiral Dynamics* by Don Beck & Christopher Cowan.
- **Neuroscience:** *The Master and His Emissary* by Iain McGilchrist.
- **Trauma & Somatics:** *The Body Keeps the Score* by Bessel van der Kolk.
- **Systemic Economics:** *Doughnut Economics* by Kate Raworth.

Appendix E: The Integration Scorecard

Your Six-Domain Assessment Tool

Turn insight into measurement. Track the transition from fragmentation to integration.

* * *

How to Use This Tool

This scorecard transforms the Project Janus framework from theory into practice. Whether you're a mayor assessing your city, a CEO evaluating your company, a parent examining your family, or an individual tracking personal integration, this tool provides a baseline and progress marker.

Instructions:

1. **Choose your scope:** Individual, Family, Team, Organization, or City/Community
2. **Score each domain** on a scale of 1–10 (see criteria below)
3. **Calculate your Integration Index** (average across all six domains)
4. **Identify your weakest domain** (this is where integration is failing)
5. **Date your assessment** and store it
6. **Reassess in 90 days, 1 year, and 2030**

Scoring Guide:

- **1-3:** Crisis/Extraction – This domain is actively degrading the system
- **4-6:** Surviving/Compensating – This domain is maintained but not thriving
- **7-8:** Functioning/Developing – This domain supports integration
- **9-10:** Flourishing/Generative – This domain enables growth in other domains

* * *

The Six Domains

1. BIOLOGICAL DOMAIN

Physical health, energy, nervous system regulation

For Individuals/Families:

- Sleep quality (7-9 hours, consistent schedule)
- Stress regulation (able to downregulate after stress)
- Physical movement (daily, varied, enjoyable)
- Nutrition (real food, mostly plants, not too much)
- Nature connection (regular time outdoors)

For Organizations:

- Employee sick days and health metrics
- Workplace ergonomics and physical safety
- Access to healthy food and movement
- Stress injury rates and burnout indicators
- Environmental health (air quality, light, noise)

For Cities/Communities:

- Air and water quality
- Access to green space and nature
- Active transportation infrastructure (walkability, bikeability)
- Healthcare accessibility and outcomes
- Noise and light pollution levels

Current Score (1–10): ______

    What would move this +2 points? ______________________________

____

____

* * *

2. COGNITIVE DOMAIN

Attention, learning, decision-making, information environment

For Individuals/Families:

- Attention quality (can focus deeply, not fragmented)
- Screen time balance (chosen vs. compulsive)
- Learning and curiosity (regular new knowledge)
- Decision fatigue (manageable complexity)
- Information diet (signal vs. noise ratio)

For Organizations:

- Deep work time available (uninterrupted focus blocks)
- Meeting load (necessary vs. wasteful)
- Decision quality (thoughtful vs. reactive)
- Learning culture (mistakes as data, growth mindset)
- Information flow (clarity vs. overload)

For Cities/Communities:

- Educational quality and accessibility
- Library and learning infrastructure
- Cognitive pollution (billboards, ads, noise)
- Civic information quality (transparency, accessibility)
- Digital literacy and access

Current Score (1–10): _______
   What would move this +2 points? _______________________________

____

____

***

3. EMOTIONAL DOMAIN

Feeling, regulation, psychological safety, emotional intelligence
   For Individuals/Families:

- Emotional awareness (can name feelings)
- Regulation capacity (not overwhelmed by emotions)
- Emotional expression (safe to feel and share)
- Relationship to difficult emotions (not avoided/suppressed)
- Joy and positive affect (regular moments of delight)

For Organizations:

- Psychological safety (can express concerns, admit mistakes)
- Conflict resolution (healthy vs. toxic or avoided)
- Recognition and appreciation (people feel valued)
- Emotional diversity (full range acceptable, not just "professional")

- Support during difficulty (grief, stress, transition)

For Cities/Communities:

- Mental health resources and accessibility
- Social support networks (formal and informal)
- Grief and loss infrastructure (how community handles suffering)
- Celebration and joy infrastructure (arts, festivals, gathering spaces)
- Trauma-informed systems (police, schools, services)

Current Score (1-10): ______

   What would move this +2 points? _______________________________

____

____

* * *

4. BEHAVIORAL DOMAIN

Actions, habits, values–behavior alignment, agency

   For Individuals/Families:

- Values-behavior alignment (living according to what matters)
- Habit quality (supporting flourishing vs. undermining)
- Impulse regulation (thoughtful vs. compulsive action)
- Agency (feeling of meaningful choice)
- Consistency (reliable follow-through on commitments)

For Organizations:

- Stated values vs. actual practices (integrity gap)
- Beneficial habits embedded in culture

- Addiction to busyness (activity vs. meaningful action)
- Employee autonomy and agency
- Behavior change capacity (adaptability)

For Cities/Communities:

- Policy-outcome alignment (do policies achieve stated goals?)
- Civic participation rates (voting, meetings, organizing)
- Behavioral infrastructure (easy to do right thing)
- Default choices (what's easiest vs. what's best)
- Cultural norms supporting integration vs. extraction

Current Score (1–10): ______
  What would move this +2 points? ___________________________

____

____

* * *

5. SOCIAL DOMAIN

Relationships, belonging, community, collective intelligence
  For Individuals/Families:

- Relationship quality (depth, authenticity, support)
- Belonging (feel part of communities you value)
- Loneliness vs. connection (balance of solitude and togetherness)
- Conflict quality (repair happens, growth from disagreement)
- Intergenerational connection (across age groups)

For Organizations:

- Collaboration quality (synergy vs. silos)
- Diversity and inclusion (representation and voice)
- Trust levels (between teams, leadership and staff)
- Social capital (networks of mutual support)
- Community beyond work (do people relate as whole humans?)

For Cities/Communities:

- Social capital and trust levels
- Third places (gathering spaces beyond home and work)
- Civic infrastructure (places for democratic participation)
- Diversity and cross-group connection
- Loneliness and isolation rates

Current Score (1-10): ______

What would move this +2 points? ________________________________

____

____

* * *

6. SPIRITUAL/EXISTENTIAL DOMAIN

Meaning, purpose, values, transcendence, wisdom

For Individuals/Families:

- Sense of purpose (life feels meaningful)
- Values clarity (know what matters most)
- Connection to something larger (nature, community, cosmos, divine)
- Practices of transcendence (moments beyond ego/self)
- Wisdom development (growing in perspective and compassion)

For Organizations:

- Mission clarity and authenticity (not just profit)
- Contribution to something meaningful
- Ethical framework (clear principles for hard decisions)
- Long-term thinking (beyond quarterly results)
- Space for reflection and meaning-making

For Cities/Communities:

- Cultural identity and heritage
- Civic purpose (why this community exists)
- Sacred/contemplative spaces (physical and cultural)
- Ritual and ceremony (marking transitions, honoring values)
- Relationship to land and place (rootedness, reverence)

Current Score (1–10): ______

What would move this +2 points? ________________________________

____

____

* * *

Your Integration Profile

Date of Assessment: __________________________________

Scope: ☐ Individual ☐ Family ☐ Team ☐ Organization ☐ City/Community

Domain Scores:

Integration Index (average): ____________

Highest Domain (strength to leverage): ________________________

____

Lowest Domain (integration failure point): _______________________

____

Range (highest – lowest): __________ *(Range >4 indicates significant fragmentation)*

* * *

Interpreting Your Results

Integration Index

- **7.5-10:** High Integration – System is generally flourishing, focus on maintaining and deepening
- **5-7.4:** Moderate Integration – Some domains thriving while others struggle, targeted interventions needed
- **Below 5:** Integration Crisis – Urgent attention needed, likely experiencing chronic stress/dysfunction

Domain Range

- **0-2 points:** Well-integrated across domains
- **3-4 points:** Moderate fragmentation, watch for cascade effects
- **5+ points:** Severe fragmentation, one strong domain likely compensating for weak ones (unsustainable)

Common Patterns

The Achiever Pattern (High Cognitive/Behavioral, Low Biological/Emotional)

- Productive but burning out
- Classic Orange integration failure

- Intervention: Sovereign Floor (remove survival coercion), add con-templative practice

The Empath Pattern (High Emotional/Social, Low Cognitive/Behavioral)

- Connected but paralyzed
- Classic Green trap
- Intervention: Cognitive scaffolding for structure, values-behavior alignment work

The Survivor Pattern (Low across all domains)

- System in crisis, no domain thriving
- Intervention: Triage - biological stabilization first (safety, rest, food), then build from there

The Compensator Pattern (One domain 9-10, others 3-5)

- Using one strength to mask dysfunction elsewhere
- Unsustainable - will eventually collapse
- Intervention: Address weakest domain directly, don't just optimize the strong one

* * *

Action Planning Template

Based on my assessment, my integration is failing in: _______________
____

    The primary cause is: ☐ Systemic (policies, structures, environment)
☐ Personal (habits, capacity, knowledge) ☐ Both

One thing I can change in the next 90 days: ________________________

____

____

____

Support I need: ____

____

How I'll measure improvement: _________________________________

____

____

Next reassessment date: _______________________________________

* * *

Longitudinal Tracking

Use this section to track changes over time:

Goal for 2030:

Integration Index Target: ____________

Specific Domain Goals: ____

____

____

____

____

____

* * *

For Organizations: Team Integration Map

If assessing a team or organization, consider scoring each domain for different levels:

Pattern Insight: Do different levels show different integration profiles? This reveals structural issues vs. cultural ones.

* * *

For Cities: Community Integration Dashboard

If assessing a city or community, consider tracking these supplementary metrics:

Biological: Life expectancy, chronic disease rates, access to green space **Cognitive:** Educational attainment, library usage, screen-free zones **Emotional:** Mental health access, community support networks, suicide rates **Behavioral:** Civic participation, voting rates, volunteer hours **Social:** Trust surveys, third-place density, diversity index **Spiritual:** Sacred space access, community ritual participation, wisdom councils

* * *

Sharing Your Data

For the collective learning:

If you're willing to share your integration profile (anonymously or publicly), it helps build the evidence base for what works.

Submit to the Global Governance Frameworks living database:

- **Email:** contact@globalgovernanceframeworks.org
- **Subject:** "Integration Scorecard Data"

- **Include:** Scope (individual/org/city), scores, interventions tried, outcomes

Your data helps others. Your experiments inform the next person's playbook.

* * *

A Final Note on Measurement

Remember: **This scorecard is a map, not the territory.**

The numbers are diagnostic tools, not performance targets. If you find yourself optimizing scores rather than improving actual integration, you've fallen into Goodhart's Law (Appendix C).

The goal isn't a perfect "10" across all domains. The goal is:

- **Awareness** of where integration is failing
- **Action** toward structural improvement
- **Honesty** about what's working and what isn't
- **Tracking** to see if interventions actually help

Integration isn't achieved—it's practiced. This scorecard helps you practice with intention.

Use it as a mirror, not a grade.

* * *

Download the printable PDF version at: globalgovernanceframeworks.org/integration-scorecard

Next: Take your lowest-scoring domain to Appendix D and find the relevant playbook. Start your first 100 days.

* * *

"What gets measured gets managed. But what gets witnessed gets transformed." — Paraphrase of Peter Drucker meets Contemplative Wisdom

Measure with rigor. Witness with compassion. Integrate with patience.

About the Author

Björn Kenneth Holmström is a systems designer, writer, and the initiator and current lead architect of the **Global Governance Frameworks (GGF) initiative**.

His work focuses on the "Integration Gap"—the critical disconnect between our civilization's technological power and its developmental maturity. As a **Designer of Conscious Systems**, he maps the invisible architectures that shape human behavior, arguing that we cannot solve the polycrisis without redesigning the cognitive and economic environments we inhabit.

Björn is the lead architect behind the *Treaty for Our Only Home*, the *Adaptive Universal Basic Income (AUBI)* framework, and *Project Janus*, a multi-domain model of human wholeness.

He writes from the perspective of "Patient Zero"—someone who lost the ability to "just be" in the modern world and has spent the last few years reverse-engineering the structural conditions required to find it again. He lives in Sweden, where he is currently prototyping the "Yellow Stack" in his own life while building the blueprints for a regenerative civilization.

Connect with his work:

- **Personal Hub & Essays:** bjornkennethholmstrom.org
- **The Governance Architecture:** globalgovernanceframeworks.org

The Global Governance Frameworks Library

The work of the Global Governance Frameworks (GGF) is an open-source initiative dedicated to designing the operating systems for a regenerative civilization. While *The Integration Crisis* serves as the diagnostic manual for our current moment, it rests upon a vast foundation of blueprints, economic models, and philosophical inquiries.

Most of these works are available as digital monographs, white papers, or living framework documents.

The Integration Series

A developmental roadmap for civilizational redesign.

- **The Integration Crisis** (Stage Orange) — *Current Volume*
- **Radical Competence** (Stage Green) — *Forthcoming*
- **The Architecture of Truth** (Stage Blue) — *Forthcoming*
- **Sovereign** (Stage Red) — *Forthcoming*
- **The New Ancestors** (Stage Purple) — *Forthcoming*
- **The Resilience Reflex** (Stage Beige) — *Forthcoming*

* * *

Core Framework Blueprints

The primary source code for the GGF ecosystem.

- **The Treaty for Our Only Home** — *Constitutional Layer*
- **An Invitational Framework for Indigenous Sovereignty** — *Ethical Layer*
- **The Integrated Meta-Governance Framework** — *Coordination Layer*

* * *

Digital Monographs

In-depth explorations of specific domains within the GGF.

Consciousness & Philosophy

- *A.I. as a Catalyst for Cognitive Evolution*
- *Reality, Sovereignty, and Consciousness*
- *Being: A Tapestry of Existence*
- *The Divine System: A Systems Thinking Approach to God*
- *Beyond Separation*

Economics & Governance

- *Adaptive Universal Basic Income: A New Social Contract*
- *The Capital Weaver: A Practical Guide to Regenerative Investing*
- *Regenerative Reciprocity*
- *Global Governance: Natural Steps Toward a Thriving World*

Metrics & Methodology

- *Love, Meaning, Connection (LMCI): A New Index for Measuring What Matters*
- *Optimizing Reality*

* * *

Selected White Papers

Technical specifications and tactical briefs.

- **Addiction as Integration Failure** — *The theoretical basis for The Integration Crisis.*
- **Cognitive Scaffolding** — *A Multi-Model AI Synthesis Method.*
- **The Currency of Care** — *Beyond UBI.*
- **The Change Paradox Field Manual**
- **The Infinite Paradox** — *Non-Dual Ethics for Planetary Governance.*
- **The Responsive Society**

* * *

Access the Library

All digital monographs, white papers, and framework documents are available to read or download for free. The GGF operates on a gift economy model—knowledge is a commons, not a commodity.

Visit the archives at: **bjornkennethholmstrom.org globalgovernancef rameworks.org**

A Note on This Physical Object

This book is made of paper, which means it is made of trees. To honor the life that was given to create this object, I ask two things of you:

1. **Use it deeply.** Write in the margins. Dog-ear the pages. Make it a working tool for your own integration. A pristine book on a shelf is a wasted resource.
2. **Keep it moving.** Once you have absorbed what you need, please do not hoard it. Pass it to a friend, leave it in a community library, or gift it to someone who needs the map. Knowledge is a commons; let this book return to circulation.

www.ingramcontent.com/pod-product-compliance
Lightning Source LLC
Chambersburg PA
CBHW021141260726